THE LIFE OF JOHNNY REB

A JOHNNY REB

Thomas Taylor, Private, Company K, 8th Louisiana Regiment. He served under Stonewall Jackson, was wounded at Sharpsburg and taken prisoner.

The Life of
JOHNNY REB

The Common Soldier of
the Confederacy

BELL IRVIN WILEY

LOUISIANA STATE UNIVERSITY PRESS
BATON ROUGE AND LONDON

ISBN 0-8071-0477-9 (cloth)
ISBN 0-8071-0475-2 (paper)
Library of Congress Catalog Card Number 71-162618
Copyright © (renewed 1970), 1971, 1978 by Bell I. Wiley
Manufactured in the United States of America
Reissued by Louisiana State University Press in 1978
by special arrangement with the author

To
M. F.

"Then call us Rebels, if you will,
We glory in the name,
For bending under unjust laws,
And swearing faith to an unjust cause,
We count as greater shame."
—Richmond *Daily Dispatch*, May 12, 1862

CONTENTS

LIST OF ILLUSTRATIONS

INTRODUCTION

DURING the thirty-five years that have elapsed since the first publication of *The Life of Johnny Reb* I have continued to read, for pleasure and information, letters and diaries of the common soldiers of the Confederacy. This additional reading, which aggregates several thousand letters and scores of diaries, has enriched my knowledge of the men who wore the gray, but it has not changed in any substantial way the impressions that I published in 1943 and which are summed up at the conclusion of the final chapter.

What I have read since 1943 has enhanced considerably my admiration of the common soldiers and the sturdy yeomanry to which most of them belonged. This is not to state that such folk were without blemish, for this class has its sprinkling of rogues, villains, croakers, and cowards. But in the great crisis of the 1860s, the "lowly" people gave a better account of themselves than did the more privileged members of Southern society. They quarreled less than those who were rated their superiors; they were more cooperative with each other and with their leaders than were the ruling caste whose rampant individualism was a major factor in Southern defeat. They bore their hardship, which exceeded that of any other group, North or South, with less complaint than the bigwigs, partly because they were more habituated to deprivation, suffering, and sorrow.

Generally speaking they were not the drab, improvident, depraved, ignoramuses depicted in *Tobacco Road* and other fictional works. Many of them were deeply religious; most of those who had families repeatedly manifested concern for the education of their children; the overwhelming majority were generous in their impulses, wholesome in their reactions, and stalwart in their adversity.

Those who acquitted themselves most admirably of all were the wives left at home to maintain themselves and their children while their menfolk marched and fought for Southern independence. Lacking the luxury of slaves and the help of adult white males, they plowed the fields, harvested the crops, cut the firewood, made the clothing, nursed the sick, and buried their dead. Some had a sufficient reserve of stamina and character to enable them to write cheering letters to their soldier-husbands. A Virginia woman took time out from an arduous labor of sustaining herself and several children to address her spouse in November 1864: "donte be

11

uneasy about us. We will try and take care of [our]selves the best we can. I donte mind what I have to do [just] so you can get back safe." She was of the same mold as the Georgia mother who, while struggling to hold on to a small farm which creditors were threatening to foreclose, wrote in response to her husband's apology for his inability to send her money: "John dont disfurnish yourself on our account and dont be oneasy about us. We will git along somehow." Little wonder that her husband stayed at his post until the end, accepted defeat with equanimity, and that he and his family survived the ordeal of Reconstruction to become worthy and respected citizens of a new South and a united nation.

BELL I. WILEY

Emory University
1 July 1978

PREFACE

The common soldier of the Confederacy has for a long time borne the title of Johnny Reb. The name seems to have originated from the practice of Yankees who called out, "Hello, Johnny" or "Howdy, Reb" to opponents across the picket line. Gray-clads liked the sobriquet, and accustomed as they were to appropriation of Federal food, clothing and guns, they saw no reason to spurn a catchy name because it was used first by their opponents. So they adopted the term in both its separate and combined forms. Descendants might be irked by the connotation of rebellion, but not the original Johnny. He not only considered himself a rebel but he gloried in the name.

Only a few years after Appomattox one of Lee's veterans remarked that future historians "would hardly stop to tell how the hungry private fried his bacon, baked his biscuit, smoked his pipe" and performed the various other details of camp life. This Reb's prophecy has been fulfilled to an impressive but regrettable extent. For in the flood of history and near-history published during the past half-century, the doings of common soldiers have usually served as a hazily sketched backdrop for dramas featuring campaigns and leaders. The present work is an attempt to give the man of the ranks, who after all was the army, something of his rightful measure of consideration.

Since the writer's dominant aim has been to present soldier life as it really was, and not as a thing of tradition, he has based his narrative chiefly on primary sources. The most extensively used records were wartime letters and diaries. These interesting and fascinatingly human documents were found by the thousands in public depositories and in private possession. The most vivid and the most significant information was frequently obtained from the barely decipherable missives of rustic privates.

Mary Frances Wiley, my wife, contributed so vitally to the research and writing as to deserve a co-author's rating, and it is only her firm refusal that prevents this recognition. In gathering material for this study we were impressed anew with the efficiency and courtesy of Southern archivists and librarians, and to them we owe a heavy debt of gratitude. Fellow historians and their wives who entertained and assisted us all along the route of research added greatly to our well-being and enjoyment. Laymen far and wide, and in such numbers as to preclude individual mention, generously gave us untrammeled access to family papers. Professor J. G. de Roulhac Hamilton of the University of North Carolina and Mr. W. B. Phillips of the University of North Carolina Press read the manuscript and made helpful suggestions. Richard D. Steuart, editor of the Baltimore News-Post, read chapter XV and from a wealth of knowledge acquired as an arms collector set me right on a number of statements about Confederate guns.

The writer makes grateful acknowledgment for financial assistance received from the Julius Rosenwald Fund and the Social Science Research Council. Without these subsidies the research for this book would not have been possible.

BELL IRVIN WILEY

University, Mississippi.
5 January, 1943

CHAPTER I

OFF TO THE WAR

THE man who was to be Johnny Reb was "rarin' for a fight" in the spring of 1861. "So impatient did I become for starting," wrote a young enthusiast from Arkansas, "that I felt like ten thousand pins were pricking me in every part of the body, and started off a week in advance of my brothers." [1]

Countless other men throughout the South showed a similar eagerness to be off to the war. They were urged on by many different motives. Some were incited to arms by a deep-seated hatred of the North which had been accumulating from the time of their earliest recollections. Antipathy aroused by Northern opposition to admitting Missouri as a slave state had been increased by recurrent threats to levy a "tribute" on the agricultural South in the form of a high protective tariff; further aggravation had come from the attempt of Northern congressmen to bar Southerners from the fruits of the Mexican War by closing western territory to slavery. And in the fifties the Negro question came to be the highest provocation of all.

Most Southerners were convinced that Northerners were utterly unreasonable in their attitude toward the "peculiar institution," and in support of this opinion they advanced these charges: The Yankees refused to live up to the Federal law requiring the return of fugitive slaves; they closed their eyes to the beneficent aspects of slavery; they made heroes of such fantasies as Uncle Tom, and chose to look upon Christian slaveholders as Simon Legrees; they tolerated monsters like William Lloyd Garrison; they contributed money and support to John Brown, whose avowed purpose was the wholesale murder of Southern women and children, and when he was legally executed for his crimes they crowned his vile head with martyrdom. Yankees, moreover, were considered a race of hypocrites: While they were vilifying Southerners for enslaving blacks, they were keeping millions of white factory workers in a condition far worse than slavery; while denouncing Southern wickedness, they were advocating free love and all sorts of radical isms. All in all, Yankee society was a godless and grasping thing.

15

So long as Northern Democrats worked with Southerners to hold the more radical elements in check, there was hope that the South might secure something like her just due under the Union. But in the late fifties there was wide defection among Northern Democrats on the slavery issue, and a rise to political power of the Republican Party, made up of elements deemed hostile to Southern institutions. At the head of this new party was Abraham Lincoln, a man regarded by many Southerners as the epitome of unreason and vulgarity. The election of Lincoln to the presidency seemed to spell the doom of Southern security under the Union: States' rights would be trampled under foot; tariff rates would increase beyond endurance; slavery would be restricted to the narrowest limits that fanatical abolitionists could impose, or done away with altogether. Non-slaveholding whites of the South were told by their favorite editors and politicians that emancipation would be followed by measures to enforce social equality of the races, and the specter of their women being jostled on the street by "big black niggers" was too fearful for contemplation.

There were of course many moderates in the South, including some of the most influential planters, who wanted to give the Lincoln government a trial, even after South Carolina seceded. Not that they doubted the right of secession. The question was rather one of expediency. But Fort Sumter and Lincoln's call for volunteers took the ground from under these middle-of-the-roaders. The issue now was whether to fight with or against secessionists, and this left no choice for most Southerners.

Hatred for the North received a tremendous boost from the prevailing agitation in favor of secession. The fire-eating element, made up largely of country editors, preachers, lawyers, and politicians-on-the-make, was the most vocal and eloquent. Recrimination and name-calling in private conversation, in public meeting, in editorial columns, from professor's desk and country pulpit, produced a tide of emotion in the early months of 1861 that reached all sections and all classes. Its effect is illustrated by the fulmination of an overseer on a plantation forty miles below New Orleans. On June 13, 1861, he wrote in his journal:

"This day is set a part By presedent Jefferson Davis for fasting & praying owing to the Deplorable condishion ower Southern country is In My Prayer Sincerely to God is that Every Black Republican in the Hole combined whorl Either man woman o chile that is opposed to

negro slavery as it existed in the Souther confederacy shal be trubled
with pestilents & calamitys of all Kinds & Dragout the Balance of there
existence in misray & Degradation with scarsely food & rayment enughf
to keep sole & Body togeather and O God I pray the to Direct a bullet
or a bayonet to pirce the Hart of every northern soldier that invades
southern Soile & after the Body has Rendered up its Traterish Sole
gave it a trators reward a Birth In the Lake of Fires & Brimstone my
honest convicksion is that Every man wome & chile that has gave aide
to the abolishionist are fit Subjects for Hell I all so ask the to aide the
Sothern Confedercy in maintaining Ower rites & establishing the confederate Government Believing in this case the prares from the wicked
will prevailith much Amen." [2]

Whether or not the scribbler of this entry went to war is not
known, but the spirit that provoked his hostile utterance contributed
greatly to the wave of volunteering which swept over the South during
the first year of conflict.

It would be misleading, however, to give the impression that all who
took up arms in 1861 were moved by hatred of Yankees, or that all
who expressed hostility felt any considerable depth of antipathy. Later
events proved the contrary. The dominant urge of many volunteers
was the desire for adventure. War, with its offering of travel to far
places, of intimate association with large numbers of other men, of the
glory and excitement of battle, was an alluring prospect to farmers who
in peace spent long lonely hours between plow handles, to mechanics
who worked day in and day out at cluttered benches, to storekeepers
who through endless months measured jeans cloth or weighed sowbelly,
to teachers who labored year after year with indifferent success to drill
the rudiments of knowledge into unwilling heads, and to sons of
planters who dallied with the classics in halls of learning.

Long before Virginia seceded restless boys at the state university
and at Washington College raised the Confederate flag on their respective campuses.[3] At the University of Mississippi a company was
recruited on the campus, and the faculty advanced the date of examinations so that students could be off to the war.[4] The Centenary
College faculty assembled on October 7, 1861, for the purpose of opening the fall session, but "there being no college students and few
preparatory students," the dispensers of learning had to go home.
Opposite the minutes of this futile session in the faculty record book
the secretary splashed in bold script diagonally across the page this

entry: *"Students have all gone to war. College suspended: and God help the right."* [5]

The University of Alabama continued to operate, but with reduced enrollment and increased emphasis on military training. That this compromise by no means alleviated the eagerness of young men for the battlefield, however, is indicated by the letter of a student to his father early in 1862:

"I have delayed answering your letter in order that I might reflect on its contents. I have done so and come to the conclusion that if I do not participate in this war it will be the source of the deepest regret and disappointment in life. Like a bird of evil omen it will follow me and mar all my undertakings. . . . I believe I know the value of an education . . . but the time has come when even this can be neglected. . . . Shall I sit ignobly here and suffer [others] to fight my battles for me. . . . I rejoice that there is scarcely one of our name in all the South but who are engaged in some capacity in this glorious cause; and, moreover, I hope and pray you will not allow it to be said that there was even one, capable of bearing arms, not on the list of his country's defenders." [6]

There was also a large group of those who volunteered not from any great enthusiasm, but simply because enlistment was the prevailing vogue. Scions of leading families rode about the country organizing companies for their command, thus adding the weight of social position to that of patriotism. Community belles offered their smiles and praise to men who joined the ranks of "our brave soldiers," but turned with the coolest disdain from those who were reluctant to come forward in defense of Southern womanhood. In some communities young men who hesitated to volunteer received packages containing petticoats, or were seized by boisterous mobs and thrown into ponds.[7] Thousands of persons indifferent to enlistment, and many who were downright opposed to it, were swept into the ranks in 1861 by the force of articulate popular pressure.

Henry M. Stanley, famous after the war as the searcher for Livingstone in Africa, is a case in point. Of English birth and only recently established in this country, he was temporarily living in Arkansas at the outbreak of war. He volunteered simply to follow the example of his acquaintances, and to avoid social ostracism. After fighting bravely at Shiloh he was captured. When offered release from prison in return for Federal service, he joined the Yankees and fought for some time against his erstwhile comrades. And he evidently suffered no qualms of conscience for his turncoating.[8]

Men so indifferent as Stanley, however, formed only a small minority of the Confederate volunteers. And even those, once they had "joined up," shared in most cases the prevailing desire to come to blows with the Yankees, and that quickly. Almost everyone seemed to think that the war would be decided by a battle or two in Virginia or Kentucky; it was necessary, therefore, to get to the fight with dispatch or run the risk of not making it at all.

But most of these recruits were to endure a long siege of waiting before they thrilled to the excitement of conflict. Filling up the companies took time—and there was an interval, sometimes long and sometimes short, before they could be mustered in by the Confederate Government. Sometimes there was an intermediate step of being accepted into state service.

In the meantime the companies had been looking for arms, clothing and other equipment. State and Confederate authorities soon exhausted their supplies, and volunteer units had to scramble for themselves. But during the high tide of patriotism of 1861 there was no lack of will and effort to provide all necessities.

Women volunteered to make uniforms, and even bullets. Wealthy men gave money for the complete equipment of entire companies. Society leaders raised funds by putting on fairs and amateur plays. Blacksmiths repaired ancient muskets and contrived deadly looking knives and sabers from farm implements and scrap steel. Local leatherworkers fashioned saddles, harness and bridles. But all this caused a delay that was hard to bear.

Meanwhile the recruits were learning how to drill. In some instances militia units already in existence furnished a nucleus for the volunteer groups, and in these outfits the exercises were apt to be well done. But in other cases the initial efforts were exceedingly awkward—and this maladroitness often persisted unduly because of the lackadaisical attitude of the men, and because of the inefficiency and ignorance of self-appointed officers. But on the whole, thanks largely to the popularity of military education among the upper classes, the volunteers made fair progress in acquiring the rudiments of drill.

At some convenient stage in their organization companies and regiments elected officers. This was a privilege jealously cherished by the volunteers, and much ado was made of its exercise. In many cases the office of captain was more or less automatically voted to the person who had been most active in raising the company; to some extent this was true also in the choice of colonels. Rivalry was generally keen enough to produce considerable electioneering. A Georgia private encamped in North Carolina expressed his view of these high-pressure methods:

"Our election has not yet come off, and to one who like myself is not a candidate it is a time replete with feelings of disgust and contempt. The candidates of course are interested and busy. I could start out here now and eat myself dead on 'election cake,' be hugged into a perfect 'sqush' by most particular, eternal, disinterested, affectionate friends. A man is perfectly bewildered by the intensity of the affection that is lavished upon him. I never dreamed before that I was half as popular, fine looking, and talented as I found out I am during the past few days." [9]

As might be expected, such elections often resulted in ill feeling. Candidates disgruntled by defeat sought transfers or discharges. Privates who backed losers sometimes expressed their disappointment in emphatic terms, as is evidenced by a Mississippian's statement that the " 'Madison Guards' rebelled and disbanded on account of the election of regimental officers," and "the 'Brown Rebels' were put in their place." [10] Elections were repeated at the expiration of the original term for which the unit was pledged to serve.

The names of some of the volunteer companies reflected their patriotism and the terror which they sought to inspire. The following are characteristic:

Tallapoosa Thrashers; Baker Fire Eaters; Southern Avengers; Amite Defenders; Butler's Revengers; Bartow Yankee Killers; Chickasaw Desperadoes; Dixie Heroes; Clayton Yellow Jackets; Hornet's Nest Riflemen; Lexington Wild Cats; Green Rough and Readys; Raccoon Roughs; Barbour Yankee Hunters; Southern Rejectors of Old Abe; Cherokee Lincoln Killers; Yankee Terrors; and South Florida Bull Dogs.

A few titles had an occupational flavor, as for instance Coosa Farmers, Cumberland Plough Boys, and Cow Hunters. Chivalry was not forgotten in such captions as Ladies' Guards, Pocahontas Rescues, and Ladies' Dragoons. An Alabama cavalry group called itself the Burr Tailed Regiment, and a mounted aggregation from Tennessee had the title of Bell's Babies. [11]

As the time ripened for Johnny Reb to take his departure for the seat of war, he was a part of a ceremony that was staged with such flourish as to thrill the hearts of the homefolk if not his own. This was the flag presentation—and files of newspapers for 1861 indicate that the exercises were almost identical throughout the length and breadth of Dixie. Speeches of presentation and response were as stereotyped and platitudinous as the high-school valedictories of later years.

A battle flag was considered indispensable to organization. So when a company or battalion was being formed, some woman, frequently one having or hoping to have a heart interest in one of the volunteers, began the making of a banner. In due time the work was completed, the speeches memorized, and a time appointed for the presentation. This might be at a dress parade, a banquet, a religious assembly, or a mass meeting called especially for the ceremony. After being duly assembled the volunteers listened to the flowery tribute of some beauteous, behooped patriot, kept eyes fixed as an officer stepped up to receive the banner, and then gave respectful hearing to the grandiloquent response of their captain.

Among the innumerable companies that received flags from fair hands in 1861 were the DeSoto Rifles of Louisiana. A reporter of the New Orleans *Daily Crescent* recorded the presentation ceremony which took place in late April, 1861. Miss Idelea Collens offered the colors with "appropriate remarks," including the following:

"Receive then, from your mothers and sisters, from those whose affections greet you, these colors woven by our feeble but reliant hands; and when this bright flag shall float before you on the battlefield, let it not only inspire you with the brave and patriotic ambition of a soldier aspiring to his own and his country's honor and glory, but also may it be a sign that cherished ones appeal to you to save them from a fanatical and heartless foe." [12]

The color-sergeant, who advanced with his corporals to receive the flag, rose to the occasion with an impressive response:

"Ladies, with high-beating hearts and pulses throbbing with emotion, we receive from your hands this beautiful flag, the proud emblem of our young republic. . . . To those who may return from the field of battle bearing this flag in triumph, though perhaps tattered and torn, this incident will always prove a cheering recollection and to him whose fate it may be to die a soldier's death, this moment brought before his fading view will recall your kind and sympathetic words, he will . . . bless you as his spirit takes its aerial flight. . . . May the God of battles look down upon us as we register a soldier's vow that no stain shall ever be found upon thy sacred folds, save the blood of those who attack thee or those who fall in thy defence. Comrades you have heard the pledge, may it ever guide and guard you on the tented field . . . or in the smoke, glare, and din of battle, amidst carnage and death, there let its bright folds inspire you with new strength, nerve your arms and steel your hearts to deeds of strength and valor." [13]

Even more flowery were the remarks of a Georgia captain who in response to the presentation of a banner to the Mercer Guards by a Miss Collier in May 1861 said: "Those tri-colors are emblematical of your rosy lips, fair cheeks, and your blue eyes; in future when we look up at those glorious stars which borrow a lustre from your bright eye, and whose radiance will guide us to victory and fame, we will fondly remember the loved ones at home." [14]

Occasionally a presentation ceremony would be marred by a flaw in the proceedings. When some ladies of Fayetteville, North Carolina, presented a flag which they had made to the Forty-third North Carolina Regiment, not one of them could be found who was willing to make the speech. As a consequence, they invited a local male who enjoyed some reputation for eloquence to speak on their behalf. The proxy must have been a bit nervous, for before the ceremony he imbibed too heavily of liquor. As he rose to perform his part of the program his unsteadiness was obvious. He managed to get through with his speech in a halting manner, but then as if utterly oblivious of that which had gone before, he said most of it a second time. After this he sat down and cried. It is not hard to imagine the mortification of the women and the amusement of the soldiers. [15]

Speechmaking over, the hour finally came when Johnny Reb was to take leave of his home community. Let New Orleans furnish the setting for the departure, and let the troops be the Battalion of Washington Artillery. Members of this organization are men of wealth and high standing in the community. The time is late May, 1861. Soldiers of the battalion are gathered at the depot waiting to board the train. They have listened to a patriotic and admonitory sermon by the Reverend B. M. Palmer. A large company of relatives and friends is present to bid them farewell and to load them down with parting gifts.

Writing a few years after Appomattox, one of them recalled: "That certainly is the only time we can remember when citizens walked along the lines offering their pocketbooks to men whom they did not know; that fair women bestowed their floral offerings and kisses ungrudgingly and with equal favor among all classes of friends and suitors; when the distinctions of society, wealth, and station were forgotten, and each departing soldier was equally honored as a hero." [16]

The day is an exceedingly hot one, the discomfort increased by the surging crowds, and two soldiers die from sunstroke before the train is boarded. At length the partings are finished, and the three hundred men composing the battalion begin the long and uncertain train ride to Virginia.

As the coaches roll along the men partake generously of the delicacies with which they have been loaded. Some achieve merriment after long pulls at their heavily charged flasks. But fatigue eventually triumphs, and the volunteers settle into such fitful slumber as circumstances will allow.

The next morning the train stops near a stream of running water. The volunteers pile out to relieve their thirst and to bathe, taking combs, soap, towels, and other articles that a year hence will be regarded as luxuries and excess baggage. When travel is resumed packs of cards appear, and for many poker becomes the order of the day.

At almost every station crowds wave, and shout godspeed. At Iuka, Mississippi, the battalion gets out for a reception and feast. (Early in the war companies of soldiers traveling in the South could get a free meal in any city or town by giving prior notice of their arrival.) At Huntsville, Alabama, there is another stop for a reception and a brief round of dancing. At various intermediate stations bolder and more agile members of the group take advantage of the slowing down of the coaches to jump off and steal, with such ease as hardly to incur guilt, kisses from pretty lassies who adorn the right of way.

Eventually they reach Richmond, and as they march down the streets of the capital city to patriotic tunes played by a brass band brought from Louisiana, their resplendent uniforms—made, allegedly, by New Orleans' best tailors at a cost of $20,000—their lustrous array of sabers, and their other fine accouterments afford a spectacle that dazzles the eyes of Richmond's citizens. Little wonder that President Davis remarks, when the battalion reports to him, that no organization ever presented a braver appearance. And that their valor was not limited to their appearance was shortly to be proved by the baptism of fire at Manassas and to be vouchsafed by a record of distinction unmarred during four years of conflict.[17]

Other organizations of volunteers had experiences similar to the Washington Artillery, but few moved to the seat of war in such luxurious state. Captain B. F. Benton's company, recruited in the environs of San Augustine, Texas, had to make the first stages of their journey to Richmond on foot. After a flag ceremony they left San Augustine on September 12, 1861. The first day they marched two miles, camped, and "proceeded to prepare Super which was rather an Awkard thing for new beginners." [18] The second day they marched three miles. At the beginning of the third day they were drawn up in line of battle to hear a patriotic address by a veteran of the Texas and Mexican Wars. When this function ended, they "Set out on the line of March in Earnest for Richmond, Va., with Collors flying, Fife and drum Sounding the never to be forgot Tune The Girl I Left behind Me." [19] The subsequent march of 120 miles to Alexandria produced sore feet and other discomforts, but the volunteers joked and bantered all along the way. At Alexandria they boarded a ferryboat—the captain was too impatient to wait for a steamboat—and proceeded jauntily down the Red River. The troops amused themselves en route by shooting alligators which were sighted frequently along the banks of the stream. Presently they were transferred to a steamboat which took them to New Orleans, whence they boarded a train for Richmond, arriving there in early October.[20]

Another Texas company, a cavalry outfit called the W. P. Lane Rangers, moved in the opposite direction from most of the volunteers. Their course was westward for service on the frontier. On April 19, 1861, they assembled at Marshall for the election of officers. This took up most of the day, and by night many of the "Rangers" and the citizens as well were considerably affected by the tippling that had accompanied the day's festivities. But the Reverend Mr. Dunlap proceeded to preach a farewell sermon, according to schedule. The next day, after being lauded and feasted, they set off toward Austin.

Like most troops departing for service in 1861, they were overloaded with equipment. W. W. Heartsill, one of these Rangers, who in the seventies printed his reminiscences at odd times on his own hand press, gave the following enumeration of his "cargo": "Myself, saddle, bridle, saddle-blanket, curry comb, horse brush, coffee pot, tin cup, 20 lbs. ham, 200 biscuit, 5 lbs. ground coffee, 5 lbs. sugar, one large pound cake presented to me by Mrs. C. E. Talley, 6 shirts, 6 prs. socks, 3 prs. drawers, 2 prs. pants, 2 jackets, 1 pr. heavy mud boots, one Colt's revolver, one small dirk, four blankets, sixty feet of rope with a twelve inch iron pin attached . . . and divers and sundry little mementoes from friends." And he added that he was no exception in the matter of equipment.[21] Little wonder that the Rangers began to shed accouterments in the early stages of their march!

A bugler tooted occasionally to keep the troopers on the right road, a precaution all the more necessary because of saloons visited along the route, and the barrel of beer that was sent to them by the citizens of Marshall. At Springfield they were greeted with the firing of anvils. Their arrival at the Texas capital was celebrated with a banquet tendered by the Austin Light Infantry. In San Antonio the Rangers went on a big spree, only four out of a total of about one hundred and two showing up at camp in the evening. Before they left San Antonio for Camp Woods, 200 miles to the west, they were sworn into Confederate service and equipped with uniform arms.[22]

Going to war in 1861, whether to west Texas, northern Virginia, western Kentucky, the seaboard of the Carolinas, or the Gulf coast of Florida and Alabama, was a rollicking experience for the men of the South. Their ardor could not be repressed by the speeches that invariably accompanied the gift of articles ranging from flags to frying pans, and to "a wagon load of bandages to be worn next to the skin in case of the fatigue and sickness to which all young men are exposed upon setting out to and encountering the roughness and exposure of military life." [23] After all, the speeches might soon be forgotten and useless gifts could be discarded when train or boat had placed a polite interval between donor and receiver. Along the way there were pretty girls to be kissed, and Unionists like "old Brownlow" and Andy Johnson to be hissed, or perhaps shot, if they would but show themselves.[24]

For many volunteers the train ride itself was a novel experience. When they rode in boxcars, the occupants often used the butts of their guns to knock holes in the sides for ventilation and sight-seeing, and as they rode along yelling and singing, with their heads sticking out of the openings, they reminded onlookers of chickens in a poultry wagon. The practice of climbing atop the coaches, though forbidden by officers, resulted in the injury and death of a regrettably large number. Doubtless the liquor which flowed so freely among war-bound troops contributed in some part to the general recklessness and unsteadiness.[25] But the prospect of exciting times made tolerable all the discomfort and risk of the journey.

Youngsters left behind found their lot almost unbearable. Sadly and enviously they bade more fortunate friends adieu. When J. E. Hall, en route from Montgomery to Virginia in May 1861, passed through Auburn, Alabama, a number of schoolmates whom he had recently abandoned for the allurements of army life boarded his train. "They were all so glad to see me," he wrote his sister, "I thought they would kill me. I could not shake their hands fast enough. . . . When the cars started Henry Harris and some others . . . said they couldn't leave me and went on to Opelika with me and there got off, all but H. Harris. He said he still must go farther and went to West Point [Georgia] with me." [26]

An Alabama recruit, after getting settled in camp near Memphis, wrote home about the awesome sights in the "citty" and urged his brother to come on up and bring a shotgun with him.[27] To this and countless other country boys, the travel following upon enlistment opened up a wonderful new world. And great was the awe inspired by the novelty of their experiences.

The reaction of J. B. Lance, a Tar Heel rustic who in 1861 joined the Twenty-fifth North Carolina Regiment, was probably quite typical. He left his native Buncombe County, in the North Carolina mountains, for Charleston and Beaufort on the South Carolina coast. Not long after his arrival he wrote his father back in North Carolina:

"Father I have Saw a rite Smart of the world Sence I left home But I have not Saw any place like Buncomb and henderson yet." [28]

Johnny Reb joined the army to fight, and he was not disposed to tolerate any interference with this purpose. The experience of a company of Mississippians who got only within earshot of the first battle at Manassas illustrates this temper. Four days after the battle, W. G. Evans, a sergeant of the company, wrote to his sister in Aberdeen:

"Sunday a scene was enacted here long to be remembered. . . . Our Company, much to our regret, were not participants in the action. . . . A railroad collision on Saturday evening detained us. The conductor was court martialed and shot, charged with bribery by court and intentionally producing the collision so as to prevent reenforcements. . . . We first heard the cannonading when about 18 miles distant. Imagine our impatience on a freight train going only 6 miles to the hour." [29]

But these volunteers, like most of the others, were to discover that much preparation must come between the "joining up" and the shooting. Drilling three or four times a day was serious and unromantic business, the more so when these exercises were done under the scorching rays of the summer sun. Chopping down trees lost little of its odium by being dignified with the name of "policing." [30] Marching to new locations, preparing food, washing clothes, fighting lice and cleaning camp were duties that bore little resemblance to Johnny Reb's conception of soldiering. But of all camp and field duties standing guard was rated the most noxious and the most senseless. Why walk up and down a beat, or keep on the alert with gun in hand when there wasn't a Yankee in two hundred miles? Officers must lie awake nights thinking up meaningless duties for privates!

At first the volunteers were inclined to regard routine tasks jauntily—and at times this attitude was encouraged by the attitude of officers, who realized as well as the men that they held their positions in virtue of the good will of their charges. Under these circumstances it is not surprising that soldiers of '61 frequently left camp without the formality of a pass, went to sleep when assigned to guard post, omitted drill when the ground was wet, and balked at the performance of other non-fighting duties.[31]

Orderly Sergeant A. L. P. Vairin, of the Second Regiment of Mississippi Volunteers, throws significant light on the frame of mind of the man who was destined to bear the brunt of the Confederacy's cause on scores of battlefields, by a note in his diary, dated May 1, 1861: "Made my first detail . . . for guard duty to which most men objected because they said they did not enlist to do guard duty but to fight the Yankies—all fun and frolic." [32]

But this attitude could not persist. Under the supervision of "old-timers" like Joseph Johnston, Robert E. Lee, Braxton Bragg, and Thomas Jackson, complaisant officers were gradually weeded out and West Point ideas of discipline were adopted in the Southern armies. Before the campaigns of 1862 Johnny Reb was for the most part a changed man. He had shed most of his surplus equipment, and, of much greater importance, he had abandoned the idea that military life was "all fun and frolic."

In short, the volunteer had become a soldier.

CHAPTER II

THE BAPTISM OF FIRE

SOLDIERS of all times have been eager for their first trial at arms, but Confederate volunteers who rushed so impetuously to war in 1861 seem to have been exceptionally zealous to come to blows with the enemy. Most of them had to wait until 1862 for this to be realized, but in the meantime they never ceased longing.

"Often at the still hour of midnight," wrote one who was stationed near a border stream during the war's first winter, "I wish the next day will be the 'cross over,' and we will meet the 'grand army' on fair ground." [1]

The accidental firing of a shot or two on the picket line would cause a precipitate, unordered lining up for battle of men still in process of dressing. Even those who had been confined to their cots for days with sickness would join the rush to arms; and when a messenger would announce another false alarm, all would go back to their tents "looking as downcast as if they had lost a purse laden with gold." [2]

When finally the day of battle arrived and the order to advance was given, so great was the urge to meet the foe that it was almost impossible for officers to prevent troops in the rear from marching through lines in front.[3] But before the ordeal of fire was begun, a halt was called to permit officers of artillery to complete disposition of their units, and to give opportunity for full contact of supporting ranks. These adjustments required perhaps an hour or two.

What are the thoughts and feelings of these Rebs who stand on the threshold of their first battle? Fear? Yes, of a sort. Most of them have in months past expressed contempt for Yankees and made positive statements as to the licking which they would administer at first opportunity to the "vandals" who dared to invade the South. Now that the zero hour has come, will they be able to match word with deed? Can they stand up under the actuality of combat—the sharp whistle of Minié balls, the hideous screeching of shells, the thunderous roar of cannon? Or will they, seized by an uncontrollable panic, play the quaking coward? Anxiety over ability "to stand the gaff" probably

28

was greater in initial conflicts than was concern for life and limb. "I may run," wrote a Reb in anticipation of his first fight, "but if I do I wish that some of our own men would shoot me down." [4]

Some who were philosophically inclined pondered over the fact that now for the first time in their lives they were going to attempt to destroy their fellow beings. A few abhorred the folly and wickedness of the impending destruction. Many thought fondly of homefolk—wives, sweethearts, parents, children, sisters, brothers—and hoped earnestly to be spared to them through the approaching conflict. Christians gave themselves to spiritual meditation and silent prayer; sinners, in some instances, sought emergency benefits of Providence by temporary renouncement of their evil ways.

The dominant sensation, however, was that of extreme nervousness; this rather than fear. Some sought to conceal or escape their keyed-up condition by joking or by casual conversation, but with little success. Perspiration dotted the brow, a dull emptiness seized the stomach, and breathing became difficult. The craving for movement, for action, was so great as to seem intolerable.[5]

What a tremendous relief, then, when finally came the order to charge or to fire. After the first volley or so the initial tension would abate to a remarkable degree, and some who had been the most nervous were now surprised to find themselves able to load and to discharge their weapons with what seemed complete indifference to the pandemonium raging about them.

The metamorphosis was well described by one who was at First Manassas. "With your first shot you become a new man," he said. "Personal safety is your least concern. Fear has no existence in your bosom. Hesitation gives way to an uncontrollable desire to rush into the thickest of the fight. The dead and dying around you, if they receive a passing thought, only serve to stimulate you to revenge. You become cool and deliberate, and watch the effect of bullets, the showers of bursting shells, the passage of cannon balls as they rake their murderous channels through your ranks . . . with a feeling so callous . . . that your soul seems dead to every sympathizing and selfish thought." [6]

Attitudes and impressions brought out by the baptism of fire varied considerably with different individuals. Not all felt their tension supplanted by a sense of calm and indifference. Some skulked and ran, though these constituted a decided minority. Others were keenly sensi-

tive to the injury and death of friends. A few continued to think of
home and loved ones throughout the fight.

"This was my first battle," wrote S. G. Pryor to his wife after an engagement in the fall of 1861. "It was a pretty severe anniciation [ini-
tiation] the test was severe but thank god I had the nerve to stand
it. . . . Time rolls off very fast in time of battle when wee had been
in . . . 3½ hours it appeared to me that it hadent been two . . . I
have been told that at such a time that men did not care for anything
but it is different with me I thought of more things in a short space
of time than ever I did before a man to go out with the expectation of
being shot every minute he has but a short time to think a heap in the
thought of you and those dear little ones hurt me worse than anything
else." [7]

The calm which new soldiers professed to experience was to a great
extent an illusion. They were cool only in comparison with the excessive
agitation which they felt before the battle. Unconscious excitement
lingered throughout the fight, manifesting itself in such phenomena as
savage yelling, throwing away of canteens, haversacks and bayonets,
and improper use of guns. More than one Reb forgot to bite off the
end of the paper that encased bullet and powder before he placed the
charge in his musket. As a result the spark did not set off the powder
when the trigger was pulled. But Johnny, with utter unwareness of the
failure of his piece to fire, continued to ram in charge upon charge,
with intermittent though quite futile aiming and trigger pulling, until
the barrel refused to receive further ammunition.[8]

Many Rebs who were able to load and discharge their guns properly were singularly ineffective in their first fights when it came to
drawing a bead on the Yankees. One who was lying in a fence corner
during an early skirmish, taking careful aim at every fire, had to shoot
about five times before he attracted sufficient notice to provoke a
reply.[9]

Granted that a considerable amount of wild shooting is inevitable in
any battle, evidence points strongly to the conclusion that marksmanship at Manassas, Shiloh and other fights involving for the most part inexperienced soldiers was notoriously bad. "I recollect their first volley,"
wrote George Baylor of a Virginia regiment at Bull Run, "and how
unfavorably it affected me. It was apparently made with guns raised
at an angle of forty-five degrees, and I was fully assured that their
bullets would not hit the Yankees, unless they were nearer heaven
than they were generally located by our people." [10]

CONFEDERATE WORKS IN FRONT OF ATLANTA

Photograph from Barnard's Photographic Views of Sherman's Campaign.

CONFEDERATE WORKS IN FRONT OF ATLANTA

Photograph from Barnard's Photographic Views of Sherman's Campaign.

Such ineffectiveness was not wholly without benefit, however, as the excitement and disorganization attendant upon early battles sometimes resulted in troops firing upon their comrades. During the Peninsula campaign of 1862, a Mississippi regiment, mistaking two Georgia regiments for Yankees, fired upon them. The Georgians, naturally assuming that their assailants were enemies, returned the fire immediately without waiting for a command. The only damage done by the Georgians, according to the report of one of them, was the killing of their own major's horse! [11]

A general characteristic of Rebs fighting their first battles was the informality with which they conducted themselves on the field. When Private A. N. Erskine became tired in a charge at Gaines's Mill he "halted in an apple orchard to blow," while his regiment went on over a hill. At First Manassas troops suffering from hunger and thirst "would stop in the middle of the fight and pick blackberries, loading, firing, and eating by turns." In this conflict also "most of the Southerners would rush forward, aim and discharge their pieces, and then retire behind trees and bushes and there reload, and again advance."

First Manassas, like Shiloh, had more the character of a conglomeration of small engagements, featuring individual combat, than of a single co-ordinated enterprise. It was almost exceptional for a man to find himself at the day's end with his own regiment. Not infrequently a soldier fought with several different outfits in the course of twelve hours of battle, taking time off at intervals for rest and sustenance. An officer who commanded a company at Bull Run turned, after leading a valorous charge at twilight, to thank his men for their gallant day's work; the group receiving his compliment was "composed of three of his own men, two 'Tiger Rifles,' a Washington artilleryman, three dismounted cavalry of the 'Legion,' a doctor, a quartermaster's clerk, and the Rev. Chaplain!" [12]

Soldiers participating in their first engagements frequently had curious and humorous experiences. A South Carolina sharpshooter was annoyed to hear the Reb in his immediate front cry out to the cannon balls flying overhead, "Howl, ye dogs of war." [13] Another Reb, seeing the large balls ricocheting across a wheat field, remarked that they were hopping along like rabbits.[14] Private W. A. Fletcher reported the most surprising experience of all. "I with a number of others," he said, "were sufferers from camp diarrhea, as it was called, and up to that time we had found no cure—so, entering the battle, I had quite a great fear that something disgraceful might happen and it was somewhat uppermost in my mind; but to my surprise the excitement or something else, had effected a cure. I inquired of some of the others and they reported a cure." [15]

In the wake of his baptism of fire Johnny Reb experienced a deep and persistent depression. His complete exhaustion, coupled with the incessant groaning and piteous wailing of the wounded, pierced his unhardened soul to the quick. The sight of dead bodies, many of them mutilated beyond recognition, overwhelmed him with horror and made the thought of continuing war utterly repulsive. His sensitiveness to the scene of carnage was often so great as to keep him from smiling or even talking for several days, and to make his nights fearful with recurrent nightmares of the ghastliness of combat.[16]

For most of the participants this introduction to the horror of war was by far the most terrible experience of their lives. They naturally were anxious to communicate their doings and impressions to those who meant most to them. So, as soon after the battle as possible, they "took pen in hand" to address wives, parents and sweethearts. For some the experience of letter writing was almost as novel as that of fighting. And the letters that went out from camp on the day after a battle gave vivid expression to the sharpness of reaction to the baptism of fire.

After the battle of Gaines's Mill, June 27, 1862, a Texan wrote to his wife:

"Yesterday evening we (the Texas Brigade) was in one of the hardest fought battles ever known . . . I dont think the Regt (4th Tex) could muster this morning over 150 or 200 men & there were 530 yesterday went into the engagement. . . . I got some of the men from the 5th Regt to go and look up our wounded. . . . I never had a clear conception of the horrors of war untill that night and the [next] morning. On going round on that battlefield with a candle searching for my friends I could hear on all sides the dreadful groans of the wounded and their heart piercing cries for water and assistance. Friends and foes all togather. . . . Oh the awful scene witnessed on the battle field. May I never see any more such in life. . . . I am satisfied not to make another such charge. For I hope dear Ann that this big battle will have some influence in terminating this war. I assure you I am heartily sick of soldiering." [17]

A like reaction was expressed by a Georgian:

"I felt quite small in that fight the other day when the musket balls and cannon balls was flying around me as thick as hail and by best friends falling on both sides dead and mortally wounded Oh Dear it is impossible for me to express my feelings when the fight was over & I saw what was done the tears came then free oh that I never could behold such a sight again to think of it among civilized people killing one another like beasts one would think that the supreme ruler would put a stop to it but wee sinned as a nation and must suffer in the fleash as well as spiritually those things wee cant account for." [18]

Thomas Warrick, who was evidently a member of that underprivileged group of Southerners known for lack of more accurate designation as "poor white," laboriously recounted to his Alabama wife his impressions of the Battle of Murfreesboro:

"Martha . . . I can inform you that I have Seen the Monkey Show at last and I dont Waunt to see it no more I am satsfide with Ware Martha I Cant tell you how many ded men I did see . . . thay ware piled up one one another all over the Battel feel the Battel was a Six days Battel and I was in all off it . . . I did not go all over the Battel feeld I Jest was one one Winge of the Battel feeld But I can tell you that there Was a meney a ded man where I was men Was shot Evey fashinton that you mite Call for Som had there hedes shot of and som ther armes and leges Won was sot in too in the midel I can tell you that I am tirde of Ware I am satsfide if the Ballence is that is one thing Shore I dont waunt to see that site no more I can inform you that West Brown was shot one the head he Was sent off to the horspitel . . . he was not herte very Bad he was struck with a pease of a Bum" [19]

Another Alabamian, his handwriting barely decipherable and his spelling marked by an unusual degree of originality, expressed a strikingly similar disillusionment following his introduction to the fighting at Chickamauga:

"We have had avery hard fite a bout ten miles from Chat ta nooga on Chick a mog ga creak in gor ga . . . i com out safe but it is all i can say i have all ways crave to fite a lit [tle] gust to no what it is to go in to a bat tle but i got the chance to tri my hand at last anough to sad isfi me i never wan to go in to an nother fite any more sister i wan to come home worse than i eaver did be fore but when times gits better i will tri to come home thare has ben agrate meney soldiers runing a way late ly but i dont want to go that way if i can get home any other way." [20]

An unidentified soldier who participated in the Shiloh fight utilized a sheet of stationery that he picked up near an abandoned Federal tent to tell his wife of that engagement:

"April 17 April the 17 run Yank or die Yankey paper
    Yankey paper Corinth Miss April 17
Dear Wife: i take the opitunity to rite you a few lines to let you now i am well at this time and i hope these few lines may come to hand and find you enjoying the same blesson. . . . we was in a battle on the 6 and 7 day of April we got one cild two woned the captin was woned slitly in the arm i come out saft i was . . . sceard at first i tell you it is not . . . [what it] was cract up to be i was glad to git out of it shore as you bonn i was not in the regiment i was in the tenth miss regt i saw plenty of yankeys out ther i thout every minet was the las the ball whisle around me worse than ever bees was when they swarm but i am saft yet this it some them paper i got in there camps i got a par shoes i . . . [got an] over coat it is caintuckey geans and a larg nife five pound two foot in the blaid well i could a got eney thing i wanted if i coulda toated it." [21]

The reaction of these five soldiers is typical: sensitiveness to blood-shed, revulsion from carnage, and a yearning to be done with the horror of war. But with the passing of time, for the most part spent in active campaigning, the specter of the first conflict lost its sharpness of horror. The second and third battles were faced with greater composure and were followed by less acute reaction. Soldiers who nervously dodged screaming missiles at Shiloh cheered each other onward at Perry-ville, rendering superfluous the forward command of officers, disdaining with a few exceptions to seek any sort of shelter. "The men stood right straight up on the open field," wrote one who was in the Perryville fight, "loaded and fired, charged and fell back as deliberately as if on drill." [22] This is perhaps an overstatement of the case, but there can be no doubt of the hardening influence of continued experience under fire.

By the time of the Atlanta campaign it was not uncommon to see a Reb walking around in a hail of bullets with the apparent unconcern of a man taking a relaxing stroll in the cool of the day; and during the siege of Petersburg a veteran whose bacon frying was disturbed by a Minié which scattered his fire took no further notice of the interruption than to pull the coals back together and remark: "Plague take them fellows! I 'spect they'll spile my grease yet before they stop their foolishness." [23]

A certain amount of philosophizing contributed to the soldier's increasing indifference to danger. He consoled himself by the time-worn maxim that comparatively few die in battle, and the conviction that he would be among the lucky majority who were destined to survive. "If killed in battle," wrote J. E. Hall during the Wilderness campaign, "what more glorious death would you wish me die?" His next statement, however, belied his aspiration to immediate immortal renown: "But I do not expect to be killed," he said. "All men that go into fights are not killed. Why should I not be one to escape." [24] Another fatalistic philosophy of comfort heard frequently as the long roll sounded was, "When a fellow's time comes, down he goes. Every bullet has its billet." [25]

Not only did the seasoning of experience bring steadiness under fire, but it also inured the men to scenes of suffering and bloodshed. Soldiers were mystified by the hardening process which they underwent. "I saw the body [of a man killed the previous day] this morning," wrote Private Henry Graves, "and a horrible sight it was. Such sights do not affect me as they once did. I can not describe the change nor do I know when it took place, yet I know that there is a change for I look on the carcass of a man now with pretty much such feeling as I would do were it a horse or hog." [26]

Many troops were as appalled by their growing insensitiveness to human suffering and death, as they were surprised by their increasing indifference to danger. John T. Sibley wrote from Vicksburg in March 1863 that he was expecting a fight soon but the time of its coming gave him no concern whatever. Recently, he said, a shell had taken away the arm of a man standing near him, but no one seemed to manifest the slightest fear, though the bombardment continued with unabated fury. "I am astonished at my own indifference," he added, "as I never pretended to be brave; it distresses me at times when I am cool and capable of reflection to think how indifferent we become in the hour of battle when our fellow men fall around us by scores. . . . My God what kind of a people will we be?" [27]

Countless others who experienced a similar change were too thoroughly hardened to give the ultimate consequences a thought.

CHAPTER III

BESETTING SINS

SOLDIER life is notoriously conducive to degeneration of some standards of morality. This has been true since organized warfare came into being. To those of us whose own kinfolk were wearers of the gray the thought comes easily and pleasantly that the Confederate Army offers a striking exception to the rule. But this conception is as mistaken as it is pleasant. Granting an impressive susceptibility to religious impulse, as witness periodic outbreaks of great revivals among the fighting men, objective study of soldiers' letters and diaries makes inescapable the conclusion that all the evils usually associated with barrack and camp life flourished in the Confederate Army.

The Old South was orthodox, Calvinist, evangelical. It took the Bible with great literalness, rigidly ranked an infringement of any one of the Ten Commandments as sin, and spread the designation over borderline cases. The mores might often be in opposition to the religious conceptions, but there was no confusion in the conceptions.

The most pervasive of the "sins" which beset Johnny Reb was gambling. General Lee issued an order in November of 1862 in which he announced that he was "pained to learn that the vice of gambling exists, and is becoming common in this army." [1] If Lee was just then discovering this propensity of his troops he was far behind time, for that evil had flourished in the Army of Northern Virginia, as elsewhere, long before he assumed command. Soldiers from Louisiana, Tennessee, Mississippi, Texas, and other sections of the South gambled extensively as they rode to war in 1861, and when they landed in Richmond they found innumerable games of chance already in progress among their Virginia comrades. In spite of the prohibitions of Lee and his fellow generals, and in disregard of the warnings of chaplains, the vice gained as the war went on. In February 1864 a soldier wrote: "A young man cannot guard himself too closely in camp . . . where to be considered an accomplished gentleman it is necessary to be a scientific and successful gambler." [2]

Pious soldiers in all Southern armies were appalled at the prevalence

36

of gambling. G. W. Roberts of Mississippi was one of the many who chafed at his enforced association with the evil. But his messmates, who were evidently chronic gamblers, gave him little heed. "I have ask them to quit playing cards in our tent or about our tent," he wrote. "It does not become any man to entrude upon me like they do. If they wish to play cards let them Build a house off to themselves then they could play to their own satisfaction." Roberts resolved to deal patiently with the sinners and prayed God for grace to win them from their evil ways. But his efforts were unsuccessful. Gambling continued to flourish under his tent roof, provoking finally the observation, "There is men in this encampment that does not care for anyone." [3]

Another Mississippian, apprehensive of the effects on a younger brother, unburdened himself in a letter of advice. "I hope that after you join the army you will not forget the virtuous resolutions that have directed you so far in life," he wrote in December 1863. "The temptations that will beset you will be very great. . . . of all the evil practices that abound in Camp, gambling is the most pernicious and fraught with the most direful consequences." [4]

The commonest form of gambling was card playing—poker, twenty-one, euchre and keno. Cards—some of them decorated with likenesses of Jefferson Davis and of high-ranking generals—were stocked by sutlers, but as the war progressed they became increasingly difficult to procure.[5] In some instances new decks were obtained from Yankee prisoners, and from the haversacks of the dead, both Rebel and Federal. But in 1864 and 1865 cards dealt around Confederate campfires generally were as ragged and battleworn as the uniforms of the players.

Faro and chuck-a-luck, banking games played respectively with cards and with dice, were also common devices for gambling. There was a notorious gamblers' den near Fredericksburg known as "Devil's Half-Acre," where soldiers ran chuck-a-luck boards for weeks during the winter of 1862-1863, and this despite repeated efforts of officers to break up the nuisance. "Crap shooting," while not without its devotees, was not nearly so popular among Rebs as among their grandchildren.

Raffling, in some form or other, was also popular. "You never heard of so much gambling as is carried on here," wrote a soldier from Yorktown in December 1861; "raffling of any and everything—watches, gold pins, coats, and blankets. You can hear on every side someone saying, 'Do you want to take a chance for a watch?' or something else." A year later one of Bragg's command wrote from Murfreesboro: "There is a panfel [painful] spell of Rafalin here at this time But I dont take no hand in non of it Some makes money at it But some Dus Loose all That they have got." But this soldier admitted having had his fling at the evil, with what he seemed to regard as great cost. "I lost one half of a Dollar," he said, "and that Broke me from sucking Eggs that is one thing s[h]ore." [6]

In cavalry outfits the laying of wagers on horse races had a considerable vogue. Stakes in some of these affairs reached proportions that would have made the fifty-cent raffling loser dizzy. Wrote A. E. Rentfrow from Fort Chadbourne, Texas, in 1862:

"I have bin Horse racesing since I left home. I have Lost one hundred dollars an have got arace to be run on Saturday next I have got dick [his horse] bet on the race and if I loose him I will loose aheap more on the day of the race. I am going to win or loose something." [7]

The racing of horses for bets, even while on duty, became so notorious in the Texas Frontier Regiment that Colonel McCord was constrained to issue the following order on June 17, 1863:

"All officers belonging to the Texas Frontier Regiment . . . are hereby required to prohibit gaiming by horse racing . . . whenever the same in any company or detachment shall become a nuisance to the service. If any member of the Regiment should so far lose sight of the interest and reputation of the service as to be caught horse racing or gaiming while on duty . . . the same shall be punished by court martial or otherwise." [8]

Lacking race horses, cards, dice, or other facilities, chance-loving Rebs would readily find a way to diminish or increase their holdings. Those quartered along rivers sometimes fitted tiny boats with paper sails and raced them for wagers. Even the vermin that infested the camp were pitted against each other in trials of speed. The louse races were staged on pieces of canvas or on other small objects. One soldier, who boasted a champion speedster, insisted on having each of the competitors placed on a plate, the winner being the louse that first vacated its dish. After this promoter had won a great deal of his comrades' money, it was found that the consistent success of his louse was due to his heating the plate before each contest.

Even more remarkable than these races were the louse fights. The omnipresence of the pests and their ever-readiness to attack Rebs probably suggested setting them against each other for stakes. A canteen side, having a circle marked off with charcoal, made a convenient arena. Contestants placed in the circle would, soldiers claimed, go at each other savagely, until one—and sometimes both—was *hors de combat*. "It was nothing unusual," according to a veteran, "to see a dozen groups of men so engaged, eagerly witnessing one of these encounters." [9]

Stakes of gambling contests were adapted to the circumstances of the gamesters. Money was, of course, the most desirable prize, but cash was notoriously scarce among Confederates. Consequently cards were drawn and dice were cast for a great variety of items such as pocket knives, jewelry, clothing and even rations. A Louisiana veteran recalled a card game late in the war in which the stake was a stolen chicken.[10]

Several factors influenced the amount of gambling. Payday always provided a powerful fillip. Many gambled then who at other times were not attracted by dice or cards. If the paymaster's tent happened to be a mile or so from camp, some would lose six months' wages before they got back to their quarters.[11] Long periods of inactivity, as while men were in winter quarters, also led to gaming as a relief from the intolerable boredom. Holidays, particularly Christmas, were usually marked by an increase of the sport. Among factors tending to diminish gambling were religious activities of officers and chaplains. The great revival movements among troops were always accompanied by an abatement of betting in all its forms. An officer of respected piety such as Stonewall Jackson might by influence and example prevent to some degree open and flagrant gambling, but there were indications that Jackson's chief accomplishment in this connection was driving the betting under cover.[12] Issuance of general orders prohibiting gambling was extremely ineffective. In fact, during flush periods all deterrents failed and gamblers waxed bold.

"Yesterday was Sunday," wrote Ruffin Thomson right after a visit of the paymaster, "and I sat at my fire and saw the preachers holding forth about thirty steps off, and between them and me were two games of poker, where each one was trying to fill his pockets at the expense of his neighbor. Chuck-a-luck and faro banks are running night and day, with eager and excited crowds standing around with their hands full of money. Open gambling has been prohibited, but that amounts to nothing." [13]

The immediate prospect of battle brought fear of death and the punishment of an angry God to the hearts of many gamblers. The result was a temporary renunciation of the instruments of sin. The road to the battlefield was commonly littered with playing cards and dice. For a brief season during and after the battle cards would be as conspicuously missing as Bibles were everywhere to be seen.[14] But there was one gambler who went into a conflict without throwing away a deck of cards that he was carrying loose in his pocket. During the battle a bullet struck this pocket, was deflected by the cards, and so the soldier's life was saved. By strange coincidence a comrade next in line, who was carrying a Bible, had his pocket struck also. The Bible failed to turn the bullet and this man was killed instantly.[15] Such an incident must have confused sinners and driven religious expositors to that portion of the sacred word which reads: "How unsearchable are his judgments, and his ways past finding out." [16]

An evil hardly less prevalent than gambling in the Confederate Army was excessive drinking. This showed itself early in the war, and during the long period of inactivity that followed First Manassas it increased. According to a chaplain, "Drunkenness became so common as to scarcely excite remark, and many who were temperate . . . at home fell into the delusion that drinking was excusable, if not necessary, in the army." [17]

Commanding generals were appalled at the prevalence of the vice. In December 1861 Braxton Bragg issued an order prohibiting the sale of liquor within five miles of Pensacola. His accompanying statement throws significant light on the deleterious effects of tippling: "The evils resulting from the sale of intoxicating liquors in Pensacola have become intolerable. More than half the labor of the courts-martial result from it—demoralization, disease, and death often prove it. . . . Our only military executions have been caused by it. We have lost more valuable lives at the hands of whiskey sellers than by the balls of our enemies." [18]

Impressed by General Bragg's action on the Gulf, the War Department issued a general order early in 1862 entreating commanders of all grades to suppress drunkenness by every means in their power. "It is the cause of nearly every evil from which we suffer," the order stated; "the largest portion of our sickness and mortality results from it; our guard houses are filled by it." [19]

Some improvements doubtless resulted from the policy adopted at that time by Richmond authorities of keeping encampments away from cities as much as possible, but even so, drunkenness continued to an alarming extent throughout the war. Prohibitive orders were issued periodically from the capital and from headquarters of the various armies, but these lost their effectiveness in many instances because of the poor example of lieutenants, captains, colonels and even generals. A Southern editor charged that "a large number of the officers of our Southern Army are both profane and hard drinkers, where they are not drunkards." [20]

In spite of a decided decline in the distilling of spirits after 1862, soldiers continued to obtain and to consume alcoholic beverages in amazing quantities. Sources and methods of procuring them were devious. Troops who were stationed near cities—and it was impossible entirely to avoid establishing camps in urban localities—were always able, by sundry stratagems, to get to town in large numbers. Here those who had the price and who were not too critical as to quality were able, almost without exception, to obtain liquor in sufficient doses to make them gloriously tight—and Rebs were as accustomed to the term as are we—or to furnish swift oblivion. Newspapers of Richmond, New Orleans and other urban centers testify repeatedly and convincingly to the fact that drunken soldiers were a common sight on the streets.

Complained the Richmond *Examiner* of June 9, 1862: "Whiskey —the sale of this popular but vitiating and deleterious beverage is lamentably on the increase in the alleys and purlieus of Richmond. Upwards of a dozen drunken soldiers were knocked down in the streets and robbed Saturday night." Earlier in the year this paper had observed: "One has to go into the streets of the city [at night] and see hundreds of good looking young men wearing the uniform of their country's service, embruted by liquor, converted into bar room vagabonds." [21]

When cities were not within reach, some Rebs were able to satisfy their thirst by visits to the country. And in many cases whiskey was obtainable in camp. Sutlers and camp followers sold it on the sly; soldiers representing bootleggers, or dispensing on their own account stocks sent by homefolk, sold it by the drink or by the bottle; and peddlers from city or countryside sold it under the guise of legitimate wares.[22]

A correspondent wrote from camp near Dalton, Georgia:

"A stranger would be smitten with the great number of mysterious men seen walking around with canteens by their sides and tin thimbles in their hands retailing pestilence at the rate of two dollars a jigger." [23]

During periods of unusual exposure to dampness, or of excessive hardship, whiskey was included in the regular ration issued to soldiers. The amount was small but by bargaining with teetotaler comrades some were able to accumulate sufficient rations to make them merry if not dead drunk.

"A soldier will get whiskey at any risk—if anywhere in the neighborhood," wrote a lieutenant who was having trouble with his men on this score.[24] One group of Rebs noticing a pile of liquor barrels in front of a store put on a "circus" to detract the shopkeeper's attention; after the performers passed on the merchant discovered to his amazement that a full barrel had been replaced by an empty one.

And the ruses devised for "flanking" the officers were ingenious. These same soldiers took to camp a barrel of whiskey, which they had secured by some other trick, and buried it above a spring to which they were accustomed to go for water. They were thus, to the utter dismay of their officers, enabled to keep themselves continually in a state of buoyancy.[25]

Members of a Mississippi company smuggled a half-gallon of liquor into camp in a hollowed-out watermelon, cached it beneath the floor of their tent, and tapped it with a long straw. When one of them wanted a drink he lay flat on the floor and sucked the straw. His comrades stood by to cut him off after his Adam's apple registered his ration of two swallows.[26]

But the most daring stratagem of all was attributed to an Irishman of the Second Tennessee Volunteers. The colonel of this outfit while walking through camp one day saw Pat elevate his gun and take a long pull at the muzzle. He called out:

"Pat, what have you got in your gun?"

Came back the answer, "Colonel, I was looking in the barrel of my gun to see whether she was clean."

And after the unwary officer walked on the Irishman completed draining his gun barrel of the whiskey thus smuggled in from a near-by town.[27]

Naturally some of the contraband liquor was vile. The frequently used epithet "mean" was a gross understatement for some of the bootleg concoctions described by the Richmond *Enquirer* in an article headed "The Whiskey Erysipelas." According to this account, the scarcity of spirits in Virginia in 1863 produced "as arrant a race of rogues as ever breathed. They doctor whiskey. They make whiskey out of apple brandy, and French brandy out of whiskey, all sorts of brandies and wines out of ingenious concoctions of all three. The whiskey— that is to say the most of it—is not composed of but about thirty per cent of genuine alcohol, and the rest is made up with water, vitriol, and coloring matter. An old and mellow taste is secured by adding the raw flesh of wild game, or young veal, or lamb . . . [and] soaking for three or four weeks." [28] Little wonder that Rebs referred to contraband liquor as "bust-head," "pop-skull," "old red eye," "spill skull," and "rifle knock-knee."

Certainly these and other bootleg products obtained by soldiers were not lacking in potency. Violent and strange were the doings of some who applied themselves too long to the bottle. Hotels in Savannah, Georgia, and Grand Junction, Tennessee, were torn up by rioting inebriates; officers were attacked or insulted on numerous occasions by drunken privates; and one berserk Reb was moved to damn "the whole Southern Confederacy." Private John Brown of the Seventh South Carolina Cavalry rode up to a civilian's house and asked for a refilling of his whiskey bottle; when refused he drew his pistol, spurred his horse, and rode on into the house. John Anderson of the Texas Rangers went to town one day to have some teeth pulled; in the afternoon he returned minus his molars but full of liquor. As he approached the camp he began to shoot his pistol and to yell with such energy that the captain, thinking he was being attacked in force by hostile Indians, called out his men and rode full tilt to meet the enemy. During the Battle of Leesburg a Confederate staff officer was so befuddled by whiskey that he mistook a group of Yankees for Southerners, rode up to them and ordered them to charge a group of gray-clads whom he thought to be Federals. The men receiving the order, thinking that the aide was one of their own officers, obeyed, and in the resulting attack quite a number of them were killed. [29]

Another evil of far-reaching proportions among Confederate soldiers was that of theft and destruction of private property. One of the earliest examples of this was the stealing of rails for campfires by volunteers and their servants. As time went on the practice spread, and in the spring of 1862 it had become so prevalent that President Davis was constrained to take notice of it, as the following note from the Secretary of War to General Joseph E. Johnston indicates: "I am instructed by the President," wrote Randolph, "to call your attention to the habit in which many of the regiments have fallen of burning the fences near their encampments and bivouacs, and I must request that you will issue orders requiring . . . Army Regulations to be executed.

. . . Unless the destruction of fences can be arrested it will materially lessen the crop . . . and impair the power of the Government to subsist the Army." [30] General orders enjoining the practice were issued by Johnston and by commanders óf other armies from time to time, but with little result. By the spring of 1865 a rail fence in an area occupied for any considerable length of time by a Rebel army was rarely to be seen.

The theft of hogs and poultry was another form of plundering which showed up early in the war. And this evil, like rail burning, increased as the conflict went on. This was due in part to the diminishing quantity and quality of army rations. A hog that made the mistake of wandering near a camp at any time during the war had small chance of survival. Soldiers of all units of the army enjoyed a story, always applied to one of their particular outfit for the sake of realism, illustrating the weakness of Rebs for stray pigs. Details varied somewhat, but the gist of the incident was this:

One day a soldier came to camp with a bulky object concealed under his coat. On being asked by an officer what he was carrying, he immediately responded, "It's a pig."

When the officer inquired if he was aware of rules against such practices as shooting hogs, he responded, "Yes, sir, I know it's against the rules, but I killed the pig in self-defense."

"How was that?" asked the officer.

"Well," responded the culprit, "I was coming up to camp when I heard something roaring, and looking that way, I saw a pig coming out of a hole in the ground, and just before it got to me, I fired, and the pig was killed."

Whereupon, as the story goes, the officer smilingly appropriated the meat for his own use.[31]

A great many soldiers undoubtedly accepted the tenet that the country for which they were fighting owed them sustenance, and when meat was not forthcoming from regular sources they saw little if any wrong in taking it from the noncombatants. This point of view is suggested by one Reb's statement to his brother that "the Government tries to feed us Texains on Poor Beef, but there is too Dam many hogs here for that, these Arkansaw hoosiers ask from 25 to 30 cents a pound for there pork, but the Boys generally get it a little cheaper than that I reckon you understand how they get it." [32]

Another Texan expressed pride in his ability to get food by informal means. "We dont get much to eat here," he wrote. "Sometimes we

. . . get it by the slide of hand and that is not very hard for me to do, for I can steel the buttons of[f] an old negroes coat when he is wide awake so you can see that I can get along pretty well for [a] new beginner but I think David Lane can beat me at it and pretty bad." [33]

Gardens, orchards and watermelon fields were often visited by Confederate soldiers in search of additions to their rations. Smokehouses and beehives were likewise plundered. "I now have some idea of the devastating effects of an army marching through a Country," wrote a Reb to his wife June 2, 1862, from a camp near Baldwyn, Mississippi; "our Soldiers act outrageously, not with standing the strict orders and their sure execution in reference to the destruction of private property. Our soldiers have not left a fat hog, chicken, Turkey, goose, duck, or eggs or onions behind." [34]

Theft and plunder were most common in areas where nearness of the Yankees or prospect of attack had caused withdrawal of part of the civilian populace or a reduction of policing. Thus an exposed section of Virginia was robbed to such an extent in the autumn of 1861 as to elicit a stinging rebuke to offending soldiers by General Magruder. Columbia, Tennessee, witnessed a siege of pillaging of both public and private property the day following Federal evacuation in November 1864. The vicinity of Tupelo, Mississippi, experienced such a wave of depredation at the hands of soldiers of the Army of Tennessee in January 1865 that Hood talked of issuing an order for the summary shooting of soldiers who were found killing livestock.[35]

The cavalry seems to have been more addicted to the evil of pillaging than the infantry. This was probably due to the greater mobility of this branch of the service; contact with the commissariat was hard to maintain when on roving missions, and there was greater opportunity of stealing with impunity. Commissary officers in the field were authorized to impress necessary commodities under certain conditions. This encouraged plunder-bent privates and subalterns to pose as duly qualified officers with manufactured orders, for the purpose of making illegal appropriations for their own use.

The outfits that were the most notorious for theft and destruction were those more or less independently operating units known as partisan rangers or independent scouts. A great many of these companies, raised under state or Confederate authorization—and holding a status so uncertain as to be a continual source of argument among commanders of armies, the War Department and state governors—operated in areas near Federal lines. They undoubtedly attracted more than their share of undesirable characters, and the detached, irresponsible nature of their service subjected them to especial temptation to plunder. Complaints of villainies suffered at their hands poured into Richmond from western Virginia, eastern Tennessee, Missouri, Kentucky, North Carolina, Mississippi and western Louisiana.

While it is true that much of the pillaging attributed to cavalrymen was done by unauthorized groups of guerrillas posing as soldiers, it must be admitted in the light of abundant and reliable evidence that accredited scouts and partisan rangers were guilty of plenty of plundering. In 1863 Secretary of War Seddon expressed the conviction that the policy of authorizing such outfits had proved to be a mistake, and that their license and irregularities had frequently "excited more odium and done more damage with friends than enemies." Governor Z. B. Vance, though frequently given to overstatement when corresponding with Richmond authorities, expressed an opinion widely held among civilians and soldiers alike when he wrote Seddon in December 1863:

"If God Almighty had yet in store another plague worse than all others which he intended to have let loose on the Egyptians in case Pharaoh still hardened his heart, I am sure it must have been a regiment or so of half-armed, half-disciplined Confederate Cavalry." [36]

Both infantry and cavalry were guilty to a regrettable extent of robbing fellow soldiers of clothing, knives, watches, blankets and other personal belongings. "They steal for practice," complained one Reb of his comrades. Another gave his opinion that "the men in this Regiment are the most scientific stealers I ever saw, they can steal anything and hardly ever be found out." A third said that "petty stealing has . . . developed into a perfect epidemic in our brigade." A South Carolinian boldly stated in 1863 that a soldier had to steal to live, and that he thought no more of taking another Reb's cup, spoon, or plate than he did of shooting a Yankee.[37]

Perhaps the form of pilfering that ranked lowest in Rebel esteem was that of plundering dead comrades, but there were some who were mean enough not only to take their money and watches, but also the clothing from their bodies.[38] Ransacking of deceased Federals was regarded with less disapproval and was therefore woefully common, though a distinction was made by some between dead and dying Yanks. Jim Randall was observed after a fight sitting near a Union officer. When asked what he was doing he replied: "Am waiting for this fellow to die, so I can get his watch and ring." But just at this moment another Reb of less delicate conscience came up and took the articles, much to Randall's chagrin and disappointment.[39] However, instances of despoiling dead Yankee soldiers are less frequently reported than of robbing live Southern civilians.

The number of pillagers in the Confederate Army was always large. And despite repeated interdictions by Lee, Bragg, Longstreet, Polk and other commanding generals, remonstrances of Richmond authorities, and the meting out of severe punishments by courts-martial and other military tribunals, plunder and theft increased with the declining fortunes of the Confederacy. So great were the proportions attained by the evil that soldiers wrote home that a visitation of Rebels was hardly less disastrous than that of Yankees. A Georgian thus sized up the situation for his wife:

"I have but little or no fears that the Yanks will ever git down to whare you are, but I think that you will be pesterde by our own soldiers . . . strowling about . . . and stealing your chickens, etc. I had almost as leave have the Yanks around my hous as our own men, except they will not insult ladies." [40]

Descendants of Confederate soldiers have derived great satisfaction from the conduct of the men in gray during their invasion of Pennsylvania in 1863. The order of General Lee requiring strict respect for private property is frequently offered as evidence in proof of their exemplary behavior. But observations made during the campaign by some of the soldiers themselves indicate considerable discrepancy between Lee's pronouncement and the troops' obedience.

A private wrote his homefolk of sharing in the destruction of a wheat field that was ready for harvesting, and of taunting the protesting owners with reminders of similar havoc wrought by Federals who invaded the South.[41]

A surgeon noted in his diary while at Chambersburg that "hogs, sheep, and Poultries stand a poor chance about here for their lives," and added significantly, "We are living on the 'fat of the land'." [42]

A Virginia captain wrote to his wife:

"We . . . today marched into Pennsylvania. . . . The men . . . made many threats of vengeance before coming here. . . . We are sitting by a fine rail fire. It seems to do the men good to burn Yankee rails as they have not left a fence in our part of the country. . . . In spite of orders, they step out at night and help themselves to milk, butter, poultry, and vegetables." [43]

Another Virginia officer told his family that Southern soldiers "took everything" from farms along the line of march to Harrisburg. "They even stripped their houses," he said, "though it was against orders. . . . I was made sorry at times for some who looked so inosent and so much alarmed." [44]

It would be misleading to infer from these testimonials that the Gettysburg campaign was nearly so destructive as Sherman's march through Georgia; but it is equally erroneous to assume that Confederates who plundered comrades and fellow citizens were transformed into gentlemen by crossing the Mason and Dixon Line.

Another besetting sin of Confederate soldiers was swearing. Many Rebs who successfully withstood other camp influences fell victim to the practice of "cussing." Private Adrian Carruth of Mississippi affords a good instance of a soldier whose one slip from consistent and triumphant righteousness was the utterance of an occasional oath. With great seriousness he addressed his sister on the subject of his patent weakness. "I think if we could have Brother Stovall here," he wrote in August 1863, "we could get up a considerable meeting—and I am sure one was never needed more than at this place and time. You can have no conception of the wickedness that is carried on here in the Army by Swearing and gambling, the latter of which I am as clear as the new born babe. I have never bet a cent on any thing since I entered the service, but must confess . . . with Shamefacedness that I am guilty to some extent of the former, though it is quite seldom that I make use of profane language; and think every day of my life that I will quit it." [45]

Private Carruth, who was religiously inclined, placed himself with a small group when he said that his use of profanity was rare. Those who swore frequently constituted a much larger class. "You have no idea how demoralizing camp life is," wrote a Mississippi Reb to his wife. "Oaths, blasphemies, imprecations, obscenity, are hourly heard ringing in your ears until your mind is almost filled with them." [46]

Certainly there was no lack of provocation to swearing. Long marches, rain, mud, putrid beef, weevil-infested beans, inefficient commissaries, shoddy clothing, strutting subalterns, body lice, and objectionable comrades caused no end of irritation, not to mention the greater provocation of Yanks who flanked instead of fighting, who made

war on wives and children, and who stooped to such meanness as
throwing elongated shells called "lamp posts" in Rebel bivouacs at
Shiloh to disturb sleep after the Yanks had been driven off the field.[47]

The case of Robert M. Gill affords a particularly interesting example. When Gill went to the war he was inclined toward religious
skepticism, hence his propensity for swearing gave him no great bother.
But his wife, a devout woman concerned about the welfare of her
husband's soul, urged him continually in her letters to curb his wickedness and to become a Christian. And Gill, impressed by her entreaty
and by the uncertainty of a soldier's life, tried diligently to make
amends. He finally was able to reduce his evil ways to the one offense
of swearing; and he could prevail over this sin except when he was
engaged in active combat. In the pitch and excitement of battle all his
previously made resolutions were reduced to emptiness, and irrepressible
oaths poured forth from his lips. Afterward he would write contritely
to his wife and renew his pledges; but these would not survive the
next fight.[48]

There were some Rebs who held their cussing within fairly decent
bounds; a few even substituted such niceties as "dad burn," "doggone,"
and "I'll be dad shame"; but these constituted an insignificant minority.

Irate or drunken Johnnies occasionally made the sad mistake of
swearing at officers on duty. In such instances they were haled before
a court-martial. In the trial that followed the exact phrasing of offensive utterances was made a part of the court records. Search of these
records gives convincing evidence that the stock of profane language
which Johnny Reb could call to his command was not a whit inferior
in robustness and variety to that in use today.

Two specific instances will suffice for illustration. A general court-
martial sitting at Savannah, Georgia, found Private George Bedell of
the Columbus Artillery guilty of calling his commanding officer "a
damned son of a bitch, a damned tyrant, a damned puppy, a damned
rascal," and of "using other disrespectful and contemptuous language."
And another court sentenced Private Spencer Carlton of the Joe
Thompson Artillery to a ball-and-chain assignment for saying to his
captain: "I want to go home; my furlough has been signed, and you
must let me go; but by God! I intend to go tonight if I have to wade
up to my neck in mud, blood, or sh-t." [49]

Allied to the sin of profanity was indulgence in obscene expression
and anecdote, and there are indications that this had a wide prev-

alency in Southern armies. A Mississippian whose background was conducive to broadmindedness remarked shortly after he entered the army, "I had no idea of the filth and vulgarity of men in camp until I tried this little experiment." [50] Another Mississippian expressed even greater revulsion at the licentiousness that he encountered. "You have no idea," he wrote his wife, "how I loath a soldier's life. The more I see of it, the more I hate . . . the low flung camp jest, the disgusting, nauseating obscenity universally indulged in by soldiers." On another occasion he said, "I abhor [such society] from my inmost soul—one unceasing tide of blasphemy & wickedness, coarseness and obscenity. . . . Is it possible that God will bless a people as wicked as our soldiers? I fear not." [51]

Allowance should be made for this soldier's maladaptation to army life and for his extreme religiousness, but even so, there was much support for his observations. In more than one instance Rebs who were advised of intended visits of their wives in camp wrote regretfully, but with obvious alarm, advising that they had better not come on account of the coarse and vulgar language to which they would unavoidably be exposed. [52]

Sabbath-breaking was an evil which caused no end of grief to chaplains and others who were interested in the religious well-being of the soldiers. Confederate generals encouraged Sabbath observance as much as possible by ordering cessation on Sundays of drill and all other military activities that could be suspended without danger to Confederate arms; but the conditions of camp life were such as to discourage respect of the fourth commandment. Fatigue from marching, boredom and general indifference to things spiritual caused many soldiers to spend the holiday not in Bible reading or attendance upon religious exercises, but rather lolling about, gambling, washing clothes, and playing games.

"If you were to ride up just now," wrote a soldier to his wife in 1862, "You would think it was anything else but the 'holy Sabbath day' here. In the company next to us . . . is a fellow playing the fiddle . . . in an old field near by are several boys playing ball & by looking around doubtless I could find several playing cards." [53] This letter was written from Arkansas on a Sunday of October 1862, but it might have come from almost any camp during any period of the Confederacy.

The evil of illicit sexual indulgence, though admittedly common to every large army that history has known, is scantily treated in Confederate records. The difficulty of obtaining information on this point is attributable to several factors. One is the veil of reticence which enshrouded the whole subject of sex in generations past—though strange is the inconsistency of a society which utterly barred mention of sex in polite conversation, and yet permitted column-length advertisements of venereal remedies on front pages of the daily paper, as well as elaboration in police columns of obscene details of bawdy-house raids. Admitting the inconsistency, there can be no doubt of the effectiveness of the taboo enforced by delicacy—so effective, indeed, that a soldier could not address his wife on the prescribed subject except with the most obvious embarrassment, as witness the following:

"We have a good spring of water and the health of our Regt. is good except some disease that I feel a delicacy in spelling them out to you as you are a female person but however I reckon you cant blush at little things these times. It is the POCKS and CLAP. The cases of this complaint is numerous, especially among the officers, and by the by Co. A has got one officer toillin with the pock and one private with the clap. I now drop the subject as I have no interest [idea] it will interest you to be reading about that." [54]

Another reason for scarcity of material on this point is the touchiness of the war generation and its immediate descendants as to the reputation of Confederate soldiers. The author has questioned several veterans about the irregularities of their comrades, but with meager results; one octogenarian, obviously nettled at the inquiry, testily responded, "Confederate soldiers were too much gentlemen to stoop to such things."

The jealous regard for the good name of comrades and of kinsmen has no doubt led to many instances of suppression of letters and other items that treat of soldier incontinence. But the present generation of descendants is more inclined toward the viewpoint that Johnny Reb can be presented in his various aspects, the bad as well as the good, and still be appreciated. Those who take this attitude have been of great help to historians by turning over to them uncensored diaries and correspondence with the privilege of unrestricted use. From occasional references in letters and journals of the soldiers, from court-martial proceedings, from scattered regimental sick lists, and from police reports in newspapers chronicling arrest of disorderly prostitutes and their uniformed guests, a general picture of the seamiest side of army life may be drawn.

There were some instances of prostitution on military premises.

Early in the war the presence of women in camp was not unusual, and that some of these were of the unsavory sort is indicated by a communication that Israel Gibbons, a soldier-reporter serving with Albert Sidney Johnston's army, sent to his paper at New Orleans in the winter of 1861. "It is really curious to observe how well and how strictly the three classes of women in camp keep aloof from each other," he wrote. "The wives and daughters of Colonels, Captains and other officers constitute the first class. The rough cooks and washers who have their husbands along . . . form the second class. The third and last class is happily the smallest; here and there a female of elegant appearance and unexceptionable manners; truly wife-like in their tented seclusion, but lacking that great and only voucher of respectability for females in camp—the marriage tie." [55]

As the war progressed, increasing hardship and roughness eliminated the great majority of respectable women, and tightening discipline got rid of most of the undesirables. Even the domestics associated with the army declined in number. It is not unlikely that an order requiring that "company laundresses who do not actually wash for the men must be discharged," was inspired by affinity of bad women for Rebel camps.[56]

Some lewd women probably continued to make occasional visits to winter encampments throughout the war, the excuse for their coming being the theatricals presented by soldiers. In March 1863 a group of Rebs quartered near Fredericksburg staged an all-male burlesque which featured the complete disrobing of one of the principals. In the audience there were a goodly number of civilians, including some women; of these, one of the soldiers remarked, "they ware dresses [but there is about them] not much of the Lady." [57]

In rare instances virtueless women were able to hoodwink officers and maintain their camp connections. The Richmond Enquirer of October 31, 1864, reported an incredible example. "Two females of questionable morality, answering to the names of Mary and Mollie Bell, alias Tom Parker and Bob Morgan, arrived in this city on Friday night by the Central train in charge of a guard," wrote the reporter. "They were dressed in Confederate uniforms, and were sent to this city from Southwestern Virginia, where they have been in service during the past two years." The charge against them was "aiding in the demoralization of General Early's veterans." They were committed to a military prison, but it is doubtful if persons possessed of such boldness and ingenuity remained long in close confinement.[58]

But for the most part Rebs were forced to go beyond the limits of camp to find prostitutes, though these hovered as near the army as circumstances would permit. Petersburg, because of its location near the seat of hostilities, was a haven for shady females throughout the war, and some of the young soldiers who patronized them communicated their experiences to boon companions in other localities.

Most of these letters are unprintable, but an excerpt from one of them affords an idea of their general import. "John, about 2 weeks ago there was a woman come from petersburg," wrote a young Tar Heel in the fall of 1863, "and stoped about 200 yards from our camp several of the boys went up and had lots of fun with her. It was about drill time and one of the boys missed drill and they put him on double duty." Others told of the fees charged by Petersburg prostitutes, and of their contamination with venereal diseases.[59]

During the Chattanooga and Atlanta campaigns Dalton, Georgia, was a favorite resort for prostitutes. In the spring of 1864 a staff officer of the Army of Tennessee wrote to the post commander at Dalton:

"Complaints are daily made to me of the number of lewd women in this town, and on the outskirts of the army. They are said to be impregnating this whole command, and the Commissariat has been frequently robbed, with a view of supporting these disreputable characters."

The vice situation became so serious that General Johnston issued an order to have the town and the surrounding country searched, so that all women who were not able to give proof of respectability and the means of an honest livelihood could be sent to points beyond the reach of soldiers. He ordered further that women who returned after being sent off should be confined in the guardhouse on bread and water. Stringent measures were invoked to guarantee faithful compliance with these instructions by provost marshals and train officials. But in view of previous failures of generals commanding this army to cope with prostitution it is doubtful if these restrictive regulations met with any considerable success.[60]

Mobile, New Orleans and other large towns all over the South were bad enough, but Richmond, being the center of government and the focal point of large-scale military activity, became the true mecca of prostitutes. Frequenting saloons, hotels, restaurants, bawdy houses, and walking late in the day on the city's popular promenades, they made known their unsavory characters to troops on leave. One madam had the temerity to open a lewd establishment immediately across the street from a soldier hospital run by the Young Men's Christian Association. Thereafter the manager had occasion to complain to the provost marshal that the recovery of the patients was being deterred by the doings of the prostitutes, who appeared at windows in semi-undress and made gestures calculated to lure convalescents to chambers of vice, and whose efforts were not devoid of success.[61]

A few weeks before the Seven Days' campaign a newspaper reported a large influx of prostitutes of both sexes into the capital, and remarked that "they have been disporting themselves extensively on the sidewalks, and in hacks and open carriages . . . [indulging in] smirks and smiles, winks, and . . . remarks not of a choice kind in a loud voice." [62]

Press comments then and throughout the war indicate that female solicitors had a large patronage among Confederate soldiers. Mayor Mayo, in commenting on this evil in the autumn of 1864, said: "Never was a place more changed than Richmond. Go on the Capital Square any afternoon, and you may see these women promenading up and down the shady walks jostling respectable ladies into the gutters." He observed that during public soirées prostitutes arrayed in flashy finery had been seen leaning upon the arms of Confederate officers.[63]

Previously the growth of vice had so alarmed one lover of decency that in a letter to the papers he advocated horsewhipping the abandoned women. The Enquirer's comment was that nymphs du monde were as invariable and necessary a concomitant of large armies as the vultures and buzzards, and a protest was therefore made against the flogging proposal.[64]

But prostitution was by no means restricted to towns and cities. When large bodies of soldiers camped for a considerable time in a rural area, the vice flourished there as well. Sergeant A. L. P. Vairin entered in his diary on December 27, 1862, near Weldon, North Carolina, the statement that "this section of the country seems to abound in very bad women." [65] Private Orville C. Bumpass wrote to his wife from the piny section of northern Alabama, "The state of the morals is quite as low as the soil, almost all the women are given to whoredom & the ugliest, sallowfaced, shaggy headed, bare footed dirty wretches you ever saw." [66] Concerning a brief sojourn in southwestern Texas a soldier observed, "Some of the boys broke themselves . . . dissipating, running after women &c. I did not however expend a cent in that way." [67]

Captain Thomas J. Key, stationed near the Georgia-Tennessee line, confided to his diary January 2, 1864, that "the war appears to have demoralized everybody," that the girls thereabout were said "to smoke, chew tobacco, and drink whiskey" and that "almost half of the women in the vicinity of the army, married and unmarried, are lost to all virtue." [68]

A few months before, Major W. J. Mims had written to his wife from a camp in eastern Tennessee that two pickets had been lured from their posts of duty by the "arts of designing women" and shot. After the comment, "I hardly think a Union woman could be invested with such personal charms as to woo me successfully for a moment from the post of duty to the treacherous embrace," he makes the following observation as to the general state of morals in this vicinity: "I will state as a matter of history that female virtue if it ever existed in this Country seems now almost a perfect wreck. Prostitutes are thickly crowded through mountain & valley, in hamlet & city." "I suppose," he adds, "[that] the influence of the armies has largely contributed to this state of things, as soldiers do not seem to feel the same restraints away from home, which at home regulated their intercourse with the gentler sex." [69]

The unhappy aftermath of visiting bawdy houses was the outbreak in camp of venereal diseases. The medical data is too sparse to permit any accurate estimate of the prevalence of syphilis and gonorrhea in the Confederate Army. But scattered sick reports in the National Archives for sundry regiments of the Army of Northern Virginia, covering mainly the period from July 1861 to March 1862, afford significant information as to venereal tendencies during the first part of the war. [70]

These reports give only the number of new cases coming to the attention of regimental surgeons each month. In July 1861, 12 regiments representing 5 states and having a mean strength of 11,452 men reported 204 new cases of gonorrhea and 44 new cases of syphilis. The next month 29 regiments from 7 states with a mean strength of 27,042 had 152 additions to the gonorrhea list and 102 new syphilitic patients. In September the figures were: 38 regiments, 33,284 mean strength, 148 new cases of gonorrhea, and 70 of syphilis. In December, 43 regiments from 7 states with 34,865 mean strength had 36 new cases of gonorrhea and 40 of syphilis. In March 1862, 28 regiments from 7 states, 19,942 mean strength, reported 14 new cases of gonorrhea and

10 of syphilis. From April to September there is a hiatus in the reports, and after December they cease altogether. But in one fall month of 1862, 8 regiments from 2 states, with 6,253 mean strength, had 36 new cases of gonorrhea and 10 of syphilis.

These figures became yet more significant when given in terms of 1,000 of mean strength. In July 1861 there were for each 1,000 men, 17.8 new cases of gonorrhea and 3.8 of syphilis; in August, the figures were 5.6 and 3.8 respectively; in September, 4.4 and 2.1; in December, 1.03 and 2.1; in March 1862, .7 and .45; and in a fall month of 1862, 5.7 and 1.6.

It is readily apparent that venereal infection gradually declined from a high rate in July 1861 to a negligible figure in the spring of the following year, and that in the fall of 1862 it was on the increase. Keeping in mind the thinness of data for the summer of 1861 and the fall of 1862, some explanation of this fluctuation may be offered. The large number of new cases appearing in July 1861 may be attributed in part to the concentration in Richmond and vicinity in June and July of large bodies of troops recently arrived from the deep South. Poor discipline, excessive drinking, the festivity incident to going to war, and the lure of a strange city teeming with prostitutes, combined to send large numbers of volunteers to Richmond bawdy houses.

William R. Barksdale, recently arrived in the capital city with a group of Mississippians, wrote on June 11, 1861, that there was a great deal of sickness in his regiment, and that measles and improper sexual indulgence accounted for most of the cases.[71] Regimental sick reports show that the Tenth Alabama Regiment, which arrived in Richmond in the early summer of 1861 and remained there for some time before joining Joseph E. Johnston, had in July (with a mean strength of 1,063 men), 62 new cases of gonorrhea and 6 of syphilis. Other regiments had similar experiences. The Eighteenth Mississippi (mean strength— 975) had 25 new cases of gonorrhea in July, and in August the Sixteenth Mississippi (mean strength—972) reported 32 new cases of gonorrhea and 11 of syphilis. The Eighth South Carolina (mean strength—828) in the same month reported 25 new cases of gonorrhea.

The decline in the rate of infection in the autumn and fall must have been due to the tightening of discipline and to the fact that active campaigning took the bulk of the army away from Richmond. Close confinement in winter quarters from December to March probably accounted for the further decline during these months. No data are available for the summer of 1862, but the increased outbreaks in the

fall bear striking relation to the assignment of some of the North
Carolina regiments to provost duty in Petersburg—a town that was
notorious as a resort for camp followers. The Fifty-fifth Tar Heel
Regiment, for instance, was transferred from Kinston to Petersburg on
October 1, 1862, and remained on guard duty in the latter city throughout the month; and regimental sick reports from that month list, for
a mean strength of 420 men, 13 new cases of gonorrhea. The Forty-
seventh North Carolina (mean strength—838), likewise engaged, had
for the same month 10 new cases of gonorrhea.

A dark picture of the bad effect of city vice districts on army morals
and health is presented by an article in the Richmond *Examiner* of
December 1862: "If the Mayor of Richmond lacks any incentive to
stimulate . . . breaking up the resorts of ill-fame in the city, let him
visit the military hospitals, where sick and disabled soldiers are received
for treatment, and look upon the human forms lying there, wrecked
upon the treacherous shoals of vice and passion which encounters the
soldier at the corner of every street, lane, and alley of the city." The
correspondent proceeds to quote a lieutenant of artillery stationed near
Richmond to the effect that out of a company of forty-five men, thirteen were in the hospital for venereal diseases. "In this way," concludes
the writer, "more than by wind and weather—more than by natural
causes—is the army depleted, and the efficiency of its soldiers weak-
ened." [72]

The author of this article let his zeal for reform lead him into an
overstatement of his case. It is very easy for anyone in discussing evil
to fall into the same error. Hence it is necessary in this survey of the
sins of Johnny Reb to guard against the impression of a too great
prevalency of the vices considered. For every regiment that had a
score of new venereal cases breaking out in any given month, there
were several that had none; and regiments having only three or four
new cases were far more numerous than those having as many as ten.
The majority of Confederate soldiers—probably the overwhelming
majority—could in reference to fornication say with Private Bumpass,
"Uncomtaminated I left home & so I expect to return," and this at
war's end.[73] Likewise a decided majority probably were innocent of
plunder and theft. Larger numbers certainly took to gambling and
swearing, but even so a substantial portion was guiltless of all of these
offenses.

With these basic postulates in mind, it may be admitted that the
category of evils which the Reverend Mr. Ransom designated as "sins

of the camp viz. Sabbath breaking Drunkenness, Stealing, Cardplaying & Profanity" [74] flourished among Confederate soldiers from the beginning, and that with brief interruptions occasioned by religious revivals they increased with the passing of time until they affected such great numbers as to support a soldier's advice to his wife: "dont never come here as long as you can ceep away for you will smell hell here." [75]

CHAPTER IV

IN WINTER QUARTERS

THE chief campaigns of the war were fought in the northern part of the Confederate States. The winters of Virginia, North Carolina, Tennessee, Kentucky, Arkansas, and the northern half of Georgia, Alabama and Mississippi are surprisingly cold and marked by heavy rains and occasional snows. The commanders of neither side were particularly anxious to carry out large-scale movements under such circumstances. Consequently, when the rigors of winter besieged military encampments the prevailing practice was to lay aside offensive weapons and to go into a state of semi-desuetude, known politely as winter quarters.

The move to winter encampments generally took place in late November or early December, but sometimes active fighting kept on much longer. The Fredericksburg campaign of 1862 did not end till mid-December; the bloody battle of Murfreesboro was fought two weeks later, and Hood's Tennessee expedition of 1864-1865 kept troops on the move until January. In such cases the soldiers were known to dub their tardily constructed shelters as "spring quarters." [1] The time for ending hibernation was also variable, but it normally occurred in March or April.

When cold weather set in, the commanding general of an army would try to select—so far as the disposition of the enemy allowed—a good place for his troops to spend the winter. There must be plenty of wood and water, adequate drainage, and the necessary facilities for transportation. In 1864 General Lee tried to get wood in advance for his troops about Richmond, but failed because planters were reluctant to lend the services of their slaves. Likewise a plan of General Joseph E. Johnston to have barracks constructed before the coming of winter in 1861 was defeated by delays and misunderstanding.[2]

Such shelters as were built to keep out the blasts of winter were generally constructed by the soldiers themselves. Some officers compelled their men to erect wooden houses, while others left the whole matter to the discretion and ingenuity of the privates.

The prevailing type of shelter was a small hut made of logs, chinked and daubed after the fashion of a pioneer cabin. These houses were thrown up with speed and zest, particularly when officers promised a gallon of whiskey to the Rebs who first completed their shelter. Each project was shared by a group of from four to ten men, usually those composing a mess. First the builders went into a wood or thicket with axes—rarely did they have saws—and chopped down the necessary trees. These were trimmed and cut to the proper length and snaked back to camp. Men in the artillery and cavalry used horses for pulling the logs, but the less fortunate infantrymen had to drag them in with their own muscles.[3] With the logs assembled each group selected a site for its cabin and began the heavy and tedious work of notching and laying the logs. When the walls were about eight feet high, some sort of roof had to be devised. If a frow and a maul could be obtained, and there was sufficient energy left for splitting large timbers, a substantial covering of boards would be put on. But more often a tent cloth would be used. The outside construction was completed with the building of a chimney.[4]

Once the roof was on, openings for doors and windows could be cut at leisure. The laying of a floor could be dispensed with—but there were a surprising number of Rebs who insisted not only on having wood beneath their feet but many conveniences that were not strictly necessary. Some put up partitions so as to have separate rooms for cooking and other purposes. A few built double or triple-decker sleeping bunks. Others added a comic touch by scrawling across their cabin fronts such appellations as "Growlers," "Howlers," "Pilgrims," "Buzzard Roost," "Sans Souci," and "No. 4 Carondolet." [5]

Seats were mostly made of boxes—begged from the commissary or the quartermaster, or sent with provisions from home—logs, ammunition chests and kegs. Tables were rigged up from pieces of board laid across upright barrels or sections of sawed logs. Slight modifications of these contrivances might be optimistically referred to as chairs and desks. The more skilled and fastidious of the soldiers were able to devise furnishings of considerable comfort if not of impressive appearance, an example being the curved-back seats made of flour barrels.[6] Kitchen utensils and tableware varied to an extent beyond description.

But regardless of their appearance and equipment, when the huts were completed they became the pride of their occupants. "We have finished our house," wrote a Texan to his mother from Virginia in January 1862. "It is made [of] pickets chinked and dubbed with a tent fly for a roof. We have the best fire place and chimney in the company. The fire place is made of brick to above the Jam and from there up mud and sticks. Our house is about 12 feet square . . . our guns are in racks on the walls; our utensils consist of one skillet a stew kettle a bread pan a frying pan & a large kettle Our china ware is, half dozen plates and the same number of forks & spoons (silver of course) our cups are of tin, 4 quart cups and two pint cups. Just above the fire place you will see something which we call a mantle piece and is made by making two holes one in each side of the fire place putting pegs in them and putting plank on them. . . . There are only four of us in this house."

In a letter written five weeks later he said that the return of two messmates from the hospital necessitated the building of a larger cabin; but that "we sold our old house to some of the boys for ten dollars." [7]

A Georgian whose quarters were considerably less pretentious than these was no less boastful. "I hate to leave 'my chimney,'" he wrote his "Dear Molley" from Fredericksburg, early in March, 1863. "You would be surprised to know how comfortable aplace I have to live in a white hous and good fire place and a box, chunk, or the ground which are all used for seats." [8]

There was one drawback to all this comfort. When the call came periodically to take a turn on the picket line, the contrast was so great as to make the duty almost intolerable. But as one Reb observed, "You have to go or march to the guardhouse," and "the latter is no good place to be in now as a fellow has no fire and of course freezes nearly every day during confinement." [9]

Occasionally the threat of a Yankee foray or the whim of some officer would compel a shift of encampments in the dead of winter. Then loud were the lamentations of those who dwelt in huts, and longing the glances cast back toward the cabins as the line of march to unprotected expanses was begun.

Doubtless the uncertainty of tenure contributed to the failure of many soldiers to build any huts at all. Most of those who reneged, however, contrived some other mode of combating the weather.

Much ingenuity was shown in adapting tents for the purpose. A common device was to build a wall of plank, brick, or stone about the sides of the tent, and to erect a fireplace at the end opposite the door. Many of the men, however, from laziness or lack of materials did without the wall and simply provided heating facilities. "The Tensas

Cavalry," wrote Theodore Mandeville, "are in Winter quarters, which means fireplaces to their tents." [10]

Probably the most industrious of the tent dwellers were a group of Louisianians who wintered near Columbus, Kentucky, in 1861-1862. These soldiers dug cellars under their tents and covered them over with boards. The canvas-enclosed upper story was used as a sleeping room, while cooking and eating were done "deep in the earth beneath." [11]

Instead of building chimneys and fireplaces for their tents, some of the soldiers attempted to solve the heating problem by making underground furnaces. This scheme, however, proved less successful than building fires in large perforated kettles suspended from the tent poles.[12] A final remnant of the shiftless or hardy followed the line of least resistance and shivered away the winter months without making any attempt to heat their quarters at all.

There were never enough tents to go round in the Confederate Army, and a considerable number of Rebs, without building materials or canvas, either had to improvise some other form of protection or to suffer intolerably from cold. This led to various forms of "digging in." Soldiers encamped near Columbus, Kentucky, during the first winter of the war devised shelters which they called "gopher holes." Some of these were prepared on an elaborate scale. First a large open-top room was dug in the side of a ravine; then fires were built to dry and harden the sides and bottom. Logs were next laid across the top and covered with a foot or more of earth. At the inner end a big fireplace was dug out, and along the outer, three-tier bunks were constructed. When a mess table and other furnishings were added, the occupants considered themselves quite snug and cozy.[13]

During the last winter of the war soldiers about Richmond spent a great deal of time in dugouts called "bombproofs." Wood was unobtainable, and the chill and dampness of these structures, the restricted space, the rats and the foul air, made them utterly noxious for any long abode. They were consequently abandoned, whenever possible, for small shelters of board or canvas along the edge of the trenches.[14] Of this type of shelter O. T. Hanks said:

"Some build a small pen about Twelve inches high. Cover it over on top with Small split pine poles put leaves & pine straw on them Spread a Blanket over & that is the bed It is now Roofed with Small Tent Cloth Captured from the Enemy . . . We now have a real Snug little Nest for two Fellows." [15]

Troops who lived in huts and in heated tents were fairly comfortable except in very cold weather. At first the respite from drill and marching, the inactivity of the Yankees, and plenty of time for lounging and sleeping brought to the campaign-weary Rebs a delightful sense of coziness. Haircuts and shaves, combs, brushes, mirrors, towels, soap, shoeshines, a "biled" shirt now and then and the privilege of puttering about in a homelike cabin added to the soldiers' satisfaction in their new way of life.[16]

But as weeks lengthened into months most Rebs tired of the inactivity and confinement. Small mannerisms that had once seemed amusing now provoked irritation, jokes and stories no longer entertained, and conversation became dull. Discipline, once accepted as a matter of course, now began to irk and offend. Officers who were followed gladly on the battlefield now became the subject of gossip and criticism. Resentments deepened, tempers quickened, quarreling and fighting increased.

Some relief was found in reading and the other recreations of camp life. Prayer meetings and preaching claimed the interest of those who were religiously inclined, and on several occasions these grew into revivals that played havoc in the ranks of the sinners. A long-continued cold spell sometimes made skating possible—but skates were hard to get, and the sport put a heavy strain on Confederate shoe leather. Sledding was also popular, even when the sleds were makeshift affairs. The building of snow men—snow effigies, as one Reb called them—was also popular from time to time.[17]

But of strictly winter sports snowballing was by far the most pervasive and the most hilarious. Day after day, from the first arrival of a few inches of snow in November or December until the melting of the last particles by the spring sun, soldiers were wont to pelt each other unmercifully with tightly packed snowballs. Even officers were not spared. "I knew that I would have to be snow balled at some time," wrote Colonel C. Irvine Walker from Dalton, Georgia, in 1864, "for the men did not let off any one in the brigade except Gen'l M. So I thought it would be best to go down and take part in the fight and be snow balled. . . . The men made however a regular Pandean frolic of it. All distinctions were levelled and the higher an officer the more snow balling he received." With evident satisfaction the Colonel observed the salutary consequences of his good sportsmanship: "After that I did not have a snow ball thrown at me."[18]

Small-scale and impromptu hurling fests gave way on occasion to affairs planned and executed after the fashion of a bona-fide trial-at-arms. As if unable to satisfy his martial urges by fighting Yankees with guns and sabers in regular season, Johnny Reb now armed himself with snowballs, formed regiments and brigades from his own ranks, dubbed opposing comrades "the enemy," raised a yell, and charged with a realism that quickened the pulse of participants and spectators. And when the contest had been pushed to the victory of one side or the other, there was a further similarity to actual combat in the black eyes, skinned heads, sprained ankles and sometimes more serious wounds of the combatants, as some of them, with more zeal than sportsmanship, would load their pellets with cores of rock or lead. "Prisoners of war" were also brought in for parole or exchange.

And these affairs had their heroes just like scraps with Yankees. T. B. Hampton wrote from Dalton, Georgia, March 24, 1864:

"We had a Great Battle yesterday between the 63rd and 54th Va. Regt. It lasted some 2 or 3 hours. I never saw such a snow balling before some times one would drive the other & then in return the other would charge and drive them. I did not Intend to engage in it but the 54th was like to drive us all out of camp & I let in made a charge & drove them out Kept them out until we quit the Officers of the 54th invited me over after the fight was over to drink with them complimenting me for Bravery they saw I wounded more men than nearly all the rest of the Regt last night I was visited by some of them & complimented at a very high Rate they seemed to think as the Indian thought about Washington that they could not hit me though I was the nearest to them I enjoyed the sport fine but it made me horse [hoarse] on account of our great charges and cheering." [19]

The pandemonium and excitement that characterized large-scale snowball engagements is vividly indicated by a letter of a Georgia private who witnessed several combats in Virginia during the second winter of the war:

"Some times the hole brigade formes, and it looks like the sky and the hole elements was made of snow and a hole had broke right through the middle and it is no rare thing to see a Cpt or a Col with his hat nocked off and covered in snow Gen Longstreet and his agitant took regs the other day and had a fight with snow balls but the Gen charged him and took them prisners." [20]

The diary entry of Lieutenant T. Otis Baker for March 22, 1864,

A TAR HEEL'S SKETCH OF REBEL WINTER QUARTERS

Note the three types of shelter: (1) A tent with chimney; (2) a "barricaded tent—i.e. walls of logs; (3) a log hut. (From John Steele Henderson Papers, University of North Carolina. Henderson belonged to the 10th North Carolina Regiment.)

LOUSE RACE

This drawing was made by Private Harry St. John Dixon in his diary (manuscript, University of North Carolina); it accompanied the entry for June 20, 1864. Dixon served with the 28th Mississippi Cavalry.

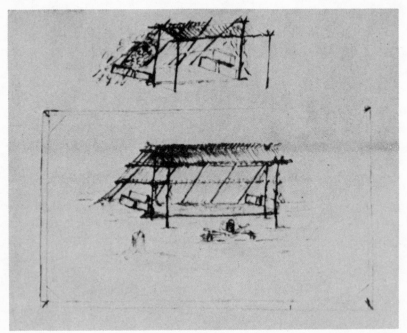

TEMPORARY WINTER QUARTERS, AS SKETCHED BY A SOLDIER

The shed roof consisted of pine limbs. Boxes, in which supplies had been sent from home, were stacked at each end to act as walls. (From George W. F. Harper Papers, University of North Carolina.)

was devoted largely to the account of a snow battle in which the fighting was so realistic and so martial that his account reads like an official report of a genuine encounter with the Yankees:

"About the latter hour 9 A. M. two lines of battle were formed by the 10 & 44 Regts which charged the . . . [camp] of the 41st Miss. On the route [they] were reinforced by a few recruits from the 7th & 9th Miss. The result of the battle was the dispersion of the 41 who for a short time fought stubbornly, the capture of their Colonel and several other officers and the occupation of their Regimental Parade. When we began to retire our adversaries rallied and being joined by our faithless allies of the 7th & 9th they made an attack upon our rear. Three times a halt was made and the attacks repulsed. After crossing the road and the brook which separate the camps of the enemy from our own we made a determined stand. Many unsuccessful attempts were made by the foe to pass the bridge and to cross the stream lower down. Discouraged by their repeated failures they finally withdrew altogether. In the afternoon they again advanced upon our camp in three columns, having previously made an insolent demand for the unconditional surrender of the army of the East, as we were called, allowing us but ten minutes in which to decide. The demand being refused a hot attack was made and after an engagement of a half or three quarters of an hour terminated in their repulse. Their losses were their commdr in chief, their three corps commanders, besides several other officers of rank, and two or three stands of colors." [21]

The roughness and zeal of these battles were amazing. A soldier diarist told of an affair between Louisianians and Georgians in which the combatants, after rallying every man in camp, both black and white, advanced to the edge of a stream and let loose volley after volley of snowballs and ice. The Louisianians eventually prevailed, though not without heavy casualties. According to the diarist, who participated on the side of the Louisianians, "Capt C H Slocomb lost two front teeth—Lieut Challeron a blackeye—Among the Privates of the 5th Co was 5 bloody noses a Blackeye—all of them more or less bruised among the captured property is the flag of the Ga Regiment 8 or 10 caps and Hats 1 frying pan and 4 or 5 pones of corn bread." [22] Another soldier reported that two men were killed in snow fights near Dalton, Georgia.[23]

Occasionally visitors from neighboring towns and countryside witnessed the encounters. The presence of ladies on the side lines in one instance proved a decisive factor in the tide of battle. "We all commenced snow balling," wrote a participant of this engagement, "our battalion & the 3rd Ga. Regt against the 48th and 22nd Ga. Regts. . . . Gen Wright, his wife and daughters & other young ladies came to see the fight. We got whiped but the ladies were the cause the boys all stoped to look at them and the other side fought so our party kept giving back until the others got the general and the girls prisners." [24] That a group of hard-bitten campaigners should be so overpowered by the presence of feminine onlookers that they let victory slip out of their hands is delightfully revealing of Johnny Reb's chivalry.

Another means of abating the tedium of winter quarters was to visit the city, if one were near at hand, or call on the country folk who lived near camp. A Reb who spent the winter of 1864-1865 near Richmond wrote that "we spend the winter pleasantly here. Sometimes we are granted a pass to visit the Citty. If not we run the Blockade, visit the Theaters maybe get on a big Whope [whoopee?] & Paint the thing red." He added that with good luck such a spree might be enjoyed with impunity.[25]

Ordinarily, common soldiers had little opportunity to meet civilians. But camp-weary Rebs usually knew how to make the most of such chances as came their way; and there were some who showed remarkable ingenuity at securing invitations to private homes without prior introduction, especially when there was likelihood of finding there either food or females. Among these was one Charles Moore of Louisiana. Moore was on exceptionally good terms with the officers of his company; he ingratiated himself not only by helping out with clerical work, for which he seems to have had a flair, but also by giving occasional singing and drinking parties in his tent. His standing certainly was not injured by the custom of taking a lieutenant or captain along with him on social excursions through the countryside. Because, perhaps, of that same charm and talent which endeared him to his superiors, he always had large groups of feminine acquaintances in the vicinity of winter quarters. And the frequency of his calls upon the ladies was nothing short of amazing. Excerpts from his diary for a twelve-day period in December 1861 throw interesting light on his social achievements:

"Dec. 18, 1861, Groves's Wharf, Va. Went out Riding with Miss Lettie on Horse Back
Dec. 19, 1861 After dinner Lieut Adams and Miss Lettie went out Riding also Miss Willie and myself

Dec. 21, 1861 Went to Williamsburg on Business . . .
Dec. 22, 1861 Slept at Pussie's [a feminine acquaintance in or near Williamsburg] last night.
Dec. 25, 1861 Went to a party with the Girls on Board the Steamer Curtis Peck. . . .
Dec. 29, 1861 Took a walk over to Jones Farm with Dr. Sowers Company Surgeon. Introduced the Miss Gambols." [26]

The next winter Moore's penchant for visiting and partying was indulged even more frequently. Sometimes he and a few comrades would visit two or three homes on the same day, singing, dancing, and eating with the girls at each place, and it was not unusual for festivities to extend beyond midnight.[27] He lost a leg as the result of a wound at Gettysburg, but his journal contains no word of complaint. As soon as he was able to hobble about he began a social campaign against Richmond, but we have no information as to his success.

Few indeed were the soldiers who had the respite from winter quarters enjoyed by Moore. Snow fights, reading and cards all offered their hours of diversion, but as the days grew longer and warmer, troops grew increasingly weary of their inactivity and seclusion. When the call came for abandonment of cabins and renewal of active campaigning, the response was, with few exceptions, genuinely enthusiastic. Amid the flurried hubbub of decampment Johnny Reb eased the straps binding the blanket roll to his back, shouldered his musket, fell in line, and set his course in the direction of the Yankees.

CHAPTER V

HEROES AND COWARDS

WHILE it may be granted that there were significant changes in the reactions of soldiers as they became accustomed to combat, the fact remains that the experiences and behavior of those taking part in Confederate battles followed the same general pattern. These more or less common characteristics must be described in some detail.

When an encounter with the Yankees was expected certain preliminaries were necessary. One of these was the issue of extra provisions, accompanied by the order to "cook up" from three to five days' rations, so that time would not have to be taken for the preparation of food during the anticipated action. This judicious measure generally fell short of its object because of Johnny Reb's own characteristics: he was always hungry, he had a definite prejudice against baggage, and he was the soul of improvidence. Sometimes the whole of the extra ration would be consumed as it was cooked, and rarely did any part of it last for the full period intended. About the same time that food was dispensed the general in command would address his men for the purpose of firing their spirit and inspiring them to deeds of valor. Soldiers en route to Shiloh, for example, were thus charged by Albert Sidney Johnston:

"I have put you in motion to offer battle to the invaders of your country. With the resolution and disciplined valor becoming men fighting, as you are, for all worth living or dying for, you can but march to a decisive victory over the agrarian mercenaries sent to subjugate and despoil you of your liberties, property, and honor. Remember the precious stake involved; remember the dependence of your mothers, your wives, your sisters, and your children on the result; remember the fair, broad, abounding land, the happy homes, and the ties that would be desolated by your defeat.

"The eyes and the hopes of eight millions of people rest upon you. You are expected to show yourselves worthy of your race and lineage; worthy of the women of the South, whose noble devotion in this war has never been exceeded in any time. With such incentives to brave

68

deeds and with the trust that God is with us, your general will lead you confidently to the combat, assured of success."[1]

Presently each man would be given a supply of ammunition. This was delayed as long as possible, so that the powder would not become dampened through carelessness of the men. If Confederates held the initiative, the issue of ammunition would take place the night before the attack; but if the Rebs were on the defensive, without any definite knowledge of the time of assault, the issue of cartridges had to take place at an earlier stage. The customary allotment to each fighter was from forty to sixty rounds, a round being a ball and enough powder for a single shot.[2]

Prior to their issue lead and powder for each load had, for convenience, been wrapped in a piece of paper with the bullet at one end, the powder behind it, and the other end closed with a twist or a plug to hold the powder in place. This improvised cartridge was cylindrical in shape, somewhat resembling a section of crayon. When Johnny Reb loaded his gun—usually a muzzle loader—he bit off the twisted end so that the powder would be exploded by the spark when the trigger was pulled, dropped the cartridge in the muzzle, rammed in a piece of wadding and waited for the opportunity to draw bead on a Yankee. Surplus rounds were kept in a cartridge box—a leather or metal container that hung from the belt—or in a haversack, or in trouser pockets.

Knapsacks and other baggage not actually needed on the field were supposed to be left in the rear with the quartermaster, but officers always had trouble preventing their men from throwing aside their equipment at random. After Bull Run and Shiloh most soldiers did not have to be cautioned about their canteens, as the acute suffering from thirst experienced in those engagements was a sufficient reminder to carry well-filled water tins into subsequent fights.

The day of battle finally comes. The men are roused from sleep at a very early hour, perhaps two or three o'clock. The well-known call to arms is an extended beat of the snare drum known as the "long roll." After the lines are drawn up officers inspect equipment, giving particular attention to ammunition, to see that all is in readiness.

Then a few words of advice and instruction: Do not shoot until you are within effective musket range of the enemy; fire deliberately, taking care to aim low, and thus avoid the overshooting to which you have been so markedly susceptible in previous battles. If you merely wound a man so much the better, as injured men have to be taken from the field by sound ones; single out a particular adversary for your fire, after the example of your sharpshooting forefathers at Bunker Hill and New Orleans. When possible pick off the enemy's officers, particularly the mounted ones, and his artillery horses. Under all conditions hold your ranks; avoid the natural but costly inclination to huddle together under heavy fire. When ordered to charge, do so at once and move forward rapidly; you are much less apt to be killed while going steadily forward than if you hesitate or retreat; but in case you have to fall back, do so gradually and in order; more men are killed during disorganzied retreat than at any other time; if your objective is a battery, do not be terrorized—artillery is never as deadly as it seems; a rapid forward movement reduces the battery's effectiveness and hastens the end of its power to destroy. Do not pause or turn aside to plunder the dead or to pick up spoils; battles have been lost by indulgence in this temptation. Do not heed the calls for assistance of wounded comrades or stop to take them to the rear; details have been made to care for casualties, and the best way of protecting your wounded friends is to drive the enemy from the field. Straggling under any guise will be severely punished. Cowards will be shot. Do your duty in a manner that becomes the heroic example your regiment has already set on earlier fields of combat.[3]

Orders to march are now given, and to the waving of colors and the stirring rhythm of fife and drum the regiments proceed to their appointed place in the line of battle. As the dawn mist clears away, a scene of intense activity is revealed on all sides. Surgeons are preparing their kits; litter bearers and ambulances are ominously waiting.[4] Arrived at their place in line, the men wait for what seem interminable hours while other units are brought into position. There is some talk while they wait, though less than earlier in the war. Comrades quietly renew mutual pledges to seek out those who are missing at the battle's end—for help if they are wounded and for protection of belongings and notification of homefolk if they are dead. A few men read their testaments, some mutter soft prayers—a devout captain is observed standing with Bible in hand reading aloud to his Mississippians, but this scene is unusual.[5] Here and there a soldier bites off a chew of tobacco and joins a host of comrades whose jaws are already working. Very rarely an officer or a private sneaks a swig of "How Come You So" to bolster his spirit for the ordeal ahead.[6] Everywhere suspense bears down with crushing force, but is indicated largely by silence.

Presently the rattle of musketry is heard in front. Skirmishers must have made contact with enemy pickets. All are alert. A signal gun is fired and the artillery joins in with accumulating fury. At last the command—"Forward!"—and an overpowering urge to make contact with the enemy. Soon lines of blue are discernible. Comrades begin to fall in increasing numbers. Now the shout, lost perhaps in the din of battle—"Charge!"—accompanied by a forward wave of officer's saber and the line leaps forward with the famous "Rebel yell."

This yell itself is an interesting thing. It was heard at First Manassas and was repeated in hundreds of charges throughout the war. It came to be as much a part of a Rebel's fighting equipment as his musket. Once, indeed, more so. Toward the end of an engagement near Richmond in May 1864, General Early rode up to a group of soldiers and said, "Well, men, we must charge them once more and then we'll be through." The response came back, "General, we are all out of ammunition." Early's ready retort was, "Damn it, holler them across." And, according to the narrator, the order was literally executed.[7]

The Confederate yell is hard to describe. An attempt to reproduce it was made a few years ago when Confederate veterans re-enacted battle scenes in Virginia. But this, by the very nature of things, was an inadequate representation. Old voices were too weak and incentive too feeble to create again the true battle cry. As it flourished on the field of combat, the Rebel yell was an unpremeditated, unrestrained and utterly informal "hollering." It had in it a mixture of fright, pent-up nervousness, exultation, hatred and a pinch of pure deviltry. Yelling in attack was not peculiar to Confederates, for Yanks went at Rebels more than once with "furious" shouts on their lips.[8] But the battle cry of Southerners was admittedly different. General "Jube" Early, who well understood the spirit of his soldiers, made a comparison of Federal and Confederate shouting as a sort of aside to his official report of the battle of Fredericksburg. "Lawton's Brigade, without hesitating, at once dashed upon the enemy," he said, "with the cheering peculiar to the Confederate soldier, and which is never mistaken for the studied hurrahs of the Yankees, and drove the column opposed to it down the hill." Though obviously invidious, the general's observation is not wholly inaccurate.[9]

The primary function of the rousing yell was the relief of the shouter. As one Reb observed after a fight in 1864, "I always said if I ever went into a charge, I wouldn't holler! But the very first time I fired off my gun I hollered as loud as I could, and I hollered every breath till we stopped." [10] At first there was no intention of inspiring terror in the enemy, but the practice soon attained such a reputation as a demoralizing agent that men were encouraged by their officers to shout as they assaulted Yankee positions. In the battle of Lovejoy's Station, for instance, Colonel Clark cried out to his Mississippians, "Fire and charge with a yell." [11] Yankees may not have been scared by this Rebel throat-splitting, but they were enough impressed to set down in their official reports that the enemy advanced "yelling like fiends," or other words to the same effect.[12]

Naturally a thing of such informal character as the Rebel yell varied considerably with the time and circumstance. Mississippians had a note quite different from that of Virginians. Rebs attacking Negro troops injected so much hatred into their cry as to modify its tonal qualities. A most interesting variant was that of the trans-Mississippi Indians organized by the Confederacy. Colonel Tandy Walker, commander of the Second Indian Brigade, reporting an action of his troops in Arkansas, said that when the Federals retreated Private Dickson Wallace was the first man to reach their artillery, "and mounting astride one of the guns gave a whoop, which was followed by such a succession of whoops from his comrades as made the woods reverberate for miles around." [13]

But those Rebs who are now charging at the Yankees know that yelling is only a small part of their business. Yankee lines loom larger as the boys in gray surge forward. Now there is a pause for aiming, and the roar of countless muskets, but the individual soldier is hardly conscious of the noise or the kick of his weapon. Rarely does he have time to consider the effectiveness of his shot. He knows that scores of Yankees are falling, and his comrades as well, but he cannot attend to details of slaughter on either side. He drops to his knee, fumblingly bites off and inserts a cartridge, rams it home with a quick thrust of the rod, then rises and dashes forward with his fellows. On they go, these charging Rebs, feeling now that exaltation which comes after the fight gets under way. "There is something grand about it—it is magnificent," said Robert Gill of his experience under fire near Atlanta. "I feel elated as borne along with the tide of battle." [14]

Presently there is an obvious slowing down of the advance, as resistance increases and attacking ranks become thin. Artillery fire comes in such force as to shatter good-sized trees, and men are actually killed by falling limbs.[15] The lines of gray seem literally to bend beneath the weight of canister and grape, and yelling soldiers lean forward while walking as if pushing against the force of a wind.[16] Slaughter becomes so terrible that ditches run with blood.[17] The deafening noise is likened by one Reb to "a large cane brake on fire and a thunder storm with repeated loud thunder claps." The flight of shells (called "lamp posts" and "wash kettles" according to their size and shape) reminds Robert Gill of "frying on a large scale only a little more so"; and Maurice Simons thinks of a partridge flying by, "only we would suppose that the little bird had grown to the size of an Eagle." [18] Some of the men, unable to confront this holocaust, seek the protection of rocks, trees and gullies. Others of stronger nerve close the gaps and push onward.

The overwhelming urge to get quickly to the source of danger brings an end to loading and shooting. With one last spurt the charging troops throw themselves among their adversaries, gouging with bayonets, swinging with clubbed muskets, or even striking with rocks, fence rails and sticks.[19] Presently one side or the other gives way, and the charge is over.

But not the battle. Before the day's fighting is completed there will be several charges, each followed by lulls for reorganization. And perhaps the conflict, as at Gettysburg, will extend to a second and third day, each characterized by repetitions of attack over various portions of the field; or perhaps the main action, as at Fredericksburg, will be defensive, staving off repeated Federal assaults.

Moving to the charge, though by far the most dramatic part of the fighting, actually made up only a small portion of a soldier's experience in battle. There were hours of lying on the ground or of standing in line, perhaps under the heat of a broiling sun, while troops on other parts of the field carried out the tasks assigned them. Then there was endless shifting, to bolster a weak spot here, to cut off an enemy salient there, or to replenish ammunition. These and many other activities, coupled with repeated advances on enemy positions, took a heavy toll of the soldier's strength.

As the day wore on he was increasingly conscious of exhaustion. Though accustomed before the war to long hours of labor on the farm or extended jaunts in pursuit of game, he found fighting the hardest work he had ever done. Fatigue was sharpened by the fact that rest and food had been scarce during the days before the battle. By midafternoon his strength was often so depleted that he could hardly load and fire his gun, if indeed he was able to stand at all.[20] Those who fought at Shiloh may have joined in the postwar criticism of Beauregard for not pushing the battle as Sunday's sun sank in the west, but officers' reports made soon after the fight show that most of the men were so exhausted that further aggression was impossible.[21]

Increasing with the combatant's fatigue came intolerable thirst. Sweating in the grime and dust, he had emptied his canteen early in the day, hoping to refill it from some stream. But rarely was there any such chance. If he were lucky enough to reach a pond he was apt to find it so choked with the dead and wounded as to be unfit for use. But even so, that soldier considered himself lucky who could sweep aside the gory scum and quench his thirst by greedy draughts of the muddy water underneath.[22]

If the battle happened to be in winter, as at Murfreesboro, Fredericksburg, or Nashville, the suffering from thirst was not so intense. But the exposure to cold was hardly less severe. Discomfort was increased by damp weather, scarcity of clothing, and the inability to make fires. At Murfreesboro, for instance, soldiers lay in line of battle for nearly a week under a cold rain without fire.[23]

When the combat extended over several days, as was frequently the case, hunger was added to other discomforts. At Gettysburg Washington Artillerymen became so famished that a captain sent a detail to gather food from the haversacks of Federal dead.[24] Many other hungry soldiers were not so fortunate as to have this opportunity.

The coming of night usually brought a rest from fighting, but not from suffering. The disorganization which characterized Confederate battles often separated the soldier from his regiment.[25] The command of duty, plus a desire to know the lot of his friends, would cause him, tired to the point of prostration though he was, to set out on a tedious search for his fellows. When he found the scattered remnants of his company he would probably discover that some messmate, committed to his care by mutual pledge before the battle, was missing. Then he must make a round of the battlefield and the emergency hospitals, inquiring patiently, calling out the name of his friend, and scanning by candlelight the ghastly faces of dead and wounded. The quest might end in happy discovery, but more likely it would prove futile. At last the weary soldier would fall down on the ground. And in spite of the piteous cries of the wounded he would sink at once into heavy slumber.

The morrow of a battle, whether its duration was for one or several days, was in some respects more trying than the conflict itself. Scenes encountered in the burial of the dead were strange and appalling: there a dead Yankee lying on his back "with a biscuit in his hand and with one mouthful bitten off and that mouthful still between his teeth";

here "the top of a man's Skull Hanging by the Hair to a Limb some 8 or 9 feet from the ground"; yonder another "man Siting behind a large oak tree his head . . . shot off"; to the right a small, whining dog curled up in the arms of a dead Yankee, refusing to be coaxed from its erstwhile master; to the left a lifeless Reb sprawled across the body of a well-dressed Federal, the gray-clad's hand in the Northerner's pocket— a gruesome warning to those who are tempted to plunder during battle; farther on, the field is strewn with nude figures blackened and mutilated by a fire that swept across the dry foliage in the wake of the fight.[26] One of the burying party working in Federal-traversed territory is shocked to find that before his arrival "the hogs got a holt of some of the Yankey dead." [27] In any direction one chances to gaze lie heaps of disfigured bodies; to a rural-bred Georgian the scene following Fredericksburg suggested "an immense hog pen and them all killed." [28]

After a prolonged summer encounter the task was unusually repulsive. Wrote a soldier who helped in the burial of the Gettysburg dead:

"The sights and smells that assailed us were simply indescribable— corpses swollen to twice their original size, some of them actually burst asunder with the pressure of foul gases and vapors. . . . The odors were nauseating and so deadly that in a short time we all sickened and were lying with our mouths close to the ground, most of us vomiting profusely." [29]

While some were burying the dead, others were walking about picking up spoils. Trinkets of all sorts, such as Yankee letters, diaries, photographs, and pocket knives are much in demand as souvenirs to be sent home to relatives. "I am going to send you a trophie that come off the battle field at Gettysburg," wrote a Reb to his sister. "I got three pictures out of a dead Yankees knapsack and I am going to send you one. . . . The pictures are wraped up in a letter from the person whose image they are. . . . She signed her name A. D. Spears and she lived in Main somewhere, but I could not make out where she lived." [30] Occasionally Rebs laughed over the sentimental contents of such letters. Some soldiers profited financially from their plundering of battlefields. Following the Franklin engagement of December 1864 George Athey wrote:

"I got agood knapsack fuol of tricks whitch I sold $4.5 dolars worth out of it and cepe as mutch as I wanted." [31]

Articles essential to personal comfort were eagerly gathered up. After the Seven Days' Battles a Reb wrote exultantly:

"We have had a glorious victory with its rich Booty A many one of our boys now have a pair of Briches a nice Rubber cloth & a pair of Blankets also a pair or more of Small Tent Cloths." [32]

The avidity with which an impoverished Confederate might pounce upon the riches left in the wake of Federal defeat, as well as the unhappy consequence of overenthusiasm, is evidenced by an entry in a Tennessean's diary following the battle of Seven Pines:

"I awoke quite early yesterday morning, and everything seemed very quiet, I went over the field seeing what I could see. Here were Sutlers' tents, filled with luxuries, oranges, lemons, oysters, pineapples, sardines, in fact, almost everything that I could think of. My first business was to eat just as much as I possibly could, and that was no small amount, for I had been living on hard tack several days. I then picked out a lot of stationery, paper, envelopes, ink, pens and enough to fill one haversack, then I found a lot of puff bosomed linen shirts, and laid in a half dozen together with some white gloves and other little extras enough to fill another haversack. Then I filled another with nuts and candies and still another with cheese. With this load, I wandered around picking up some canteens to carry back to the boys. Then adding to my load such articles as a sword, an overcoat, etc. . . . I quickened my pace and before I had gone twenty steps, the Yankees opened fire . . . and the balls whistled around me in a perfect shower. I had about two hundred yards to go before reaching my regiment, and by the time I reached it, I had thrown away all my plunder." [33]

If the battle ended in defeat, falling back might be so hurried as to leave the dead and wounded in Federal hands. This, added to the increased hardships of retreat and the disappointment of being whipped, caused the soldier's cup to overflow with bitterness.

But whether victorious or not, Johnny Reb began within a remarkably short time to recall and to enjoy the interesting and humorous detail of the combat. Campfire groups must have delighted in teasing Private Joseph Adams about losing his pants when a shell exploded near him at Murfreesboro; and there was doubtless plenty of laughter when M. D. Martin told how a shell cut off his two well-stocked haversacks and scattered hardtack so promiscuously that "several of the boys were struck by the biscuits, and more than one thought he was wounded." [34]

James Mabley could always get a good laugh with his story of the
Reb at Chancellorsville who while in the act of drawing a bead on a
Yank was distracted by a wild turkey lighting in a tree before him; the
Federal was immediately forgotten, and in an instant the crack of this
Reb's gun brought the turkey to the ground.[35]

The men of Gilmor's Battalion never tired of asking their colonel
after a valley engagement of 1864 "if spades are trumps"; for during this
fight a ball went all the way through an unopened deck of cards that
he was carrying in his inside coat pocket, stopping only at the last card,
the ace of spades.[36]

Almost everyone could tell of a "close shave" when a bullet hit a
knapsack, perforated a hat, or spent itself by passing through a bush
immediately in front, to fall harmlessly to the ground in plain view.
One soldier marveled at hearing through the din of battle the cry of
John Childress as he fell: "I am killed, tell Ma and Pa goodbye for
me." [37]

Then someone may have mentioned the tragic case of Jud and Cary
Smith, Yale-educated brothers from Mississippi. While in the act of
lying down under fire, the younger, Cary, putting his hand under his
coat found his inner garments covered with blood; and with only the
exclamation "What does this mean?" he died. Jud was so overwhelmed
with grief that he spent the entire night muttering affectionate words
over his brother's corpse. He passed the next day and night in uncon-
solable solitude. The third day was that of Malvern Hill, and when
the first charge took place Jud kept on going after his comrades fell
back under the murderous fire, and he was never seen or heard of again.
After the father learned of the fate of his two sons he joined Price's
army as a private soldier; when his regiment charged at Iuka, he followed the example set by Jud at Malvern Hill, and he likewise was
never heard of again.[38]

But there was not much lingering on tragic notes. It was more pleasant to talk of how Jeb Stuart at Second Manassas beguiled the Yankees
into exaggerated ideas of Rebel strength by having his men drag brush
along the roads to stir up huge clouds of dust; or of how the Yankee
General Banks was duped into abandoning several strong positions during his Red River campaign by such Confederate ruses as sending
drummers out to beat calls, lighting superfluous campfires, blowing bugles,
and "rolling empty wagons over fence rails"; or of how George Cagle,
while lying on a ridge at Chickamauga, kept at work four or five muskets
gathered from incapacitated comrades, and as Yankee bullets whistled

overhead he simulated the activity of an artillery unit, giving such commands as "attention Cagle's Battery, make ready, load, take aim, fire";
of how Sergeant Nabors scared nervous Yankee prisoners who asked him
at Atlanta if he were going to kill them by replying, "That's our calcula-
tion; we came out for that purpose." [39]

By no means was all of the fighting in the open field. Warring in
trenches—Johnny Reb usually called them "ditches"—made its appearance in the spring of 1862 on the Virginia peninsula where Magruder's
army was entrenched for a month. At Vicksburg, where Pemberton's
troops were under siege for forty-seven days, soldiers spent most of the
time in earthworks along the line, or in caves to the rear. During the
Atlanta campaign Rebs of the Army of Tennessee saw considerable
trench warfare. But by far the longest stretch of this sort of campaigning was done by Lee's troops, who spent the greater part of the war's
last year in the ditches around Petersburg.

Occasionally the routine of trench fighting was broken by an assault of one army or the other, but the time was mostly spent in desultory exchanges of artillery and musket fire. The Federals, being the
besiegers and having vastly superior resources, did the larger part of the
firing. So unlimited, indeed, were their supplies of ammunition that
they could make the countryside reverberate with repeated discharges
of their heavy cannon.[40]

The defenders of Vicksburg were subjected to heavier fire than
any other trench fighters in the war. Back of them lay the Mississippi,
dotted with gunboats, and before them were the troops of Grant and
Sherman well equipped with artillery. The besieged were deficient in
both guns and ammunition. Hemmed in thus by superior forces and
equipment, conscious of their inability to give effective retaliation, living on ever dwindling rations, suffering from a shortage of drinking
water, and cut off largely from their friends, they were subjected day
after day and night after night to a cannonading that was so severe at
times as to make heads ache from the concussion.[41] One of the defenders wrote in his diary at the midpoint of siege:

"The fighting is now carried on quite systematically . . . in the
morning there seems to be time allowed for breakfast, when all at once
the work of destruction is renewed. There is about an hour at noon &
about the same at sunset, taking these three intervals out the work goes
on just as regularly as . . . on a well regulated farm & the noise is not
unlike the clearing up of new ground when much heavy timber is cut
down! Add to that the nailing on of shingles by several men & one has

a pretty good idea of the noise. It might be supposed that a score of villages had sprung up all round him & that the inhabitants were vieing with each other to see who could be the most industrious." [42]

The caves dug in the hillside were poor protection against the heavy shells that came screeching through the air with varying notes of terror. If one lifted his head ever so little above the earthworks, the crack of a sharpshooter's rifle, followed instantly by a dull thud, would announce the doom of another Reb. A man who was slightly wounded in the trenches stood in considerable danger of being more seriously injured, if not killed outright, as he traversed the open space between battle line and hospital. Life under such conditions became a torturing ordeal, and the situation was not helped by jesting speculation as to the prospective comforts of Johnson's Island, Camp Chase and Camp Douglas.[43]

In the trenches before Atlanta and Petersburg existence was not so perilous nor so gloomy as at Vicksburg. Common to all, however, was the intolerable heat of the summer sun. Some men sought alleviation by building little brush arbors along the trenches. The sultriness of the ditches became so unbearable at night that some of the men resorted to sleeping on the edge—and when the Federal batteries opened they would simply roll over to safety. But immunity from danger in the Atlanta and Petersburg trenches was only comparative. The killing and wounding of men by Federal sharpshooting and artillery fire were of such common occurrence as hardly to elicit notice save by the company to which the casualty belonged.[44]

The number of killed and wounded would have been much greater but for the skill of the men in side-stepping arched shots. "The mortars are thrown up a great height," wrote an Alabamian from Petersburg, "and fall down in the trenches like throwing a ball over a house—we have become very perfect in dodging them and unless they are thrown too thick I think I can always escape them at least at night." He added that the dugouts which they contrived at intervals along the trenches and which they were wont to call bombproofs were not impervious at all to mortar shells, and that "we always prefer to be out in the ditches— where by using strategy and skill we get out of their way." [45] So confident did the troops become of their ability to escape these lobbed shots of the Yankees that they would keep up a derisive yelling throughout a bombardment.[46]

During periods of truce ladies from Petersburg made several visits to the lines, walking down the ditches in their cumbersome hoop skirts to see how bombproofs were made, climbing upon the parapets to get a look at the Yankees, giggling and oh-ing at the strange sights confronting them. Both Federals and Rebs enjoyed these interludes in crinoline but some of the latter could not refrain from mischievously expressing the wish that the Yanks would throw a few shells over to see if the fair visitors would shake with terror or raise the Rebel yell.[47]

But these tantalizing glimpses of Petersburg belles afforded only brief respite from the terrible filth, the smothering heat of summer and the cold of winter, the rain and mud of all seasons, the restricted movement and the countless other deprivations that made trench warfare the most unpleasant aspect of Confederate soldierhood. Open fighting with all its dangers was immeasurably preferable to such existence as this.

But what of valor and of cowardice on the field of battle? There were numerous manifestations of both, though many more of the former than of the latter. Deeds of Rebel bravery, individual and collective, were of such common occurrence as to be quite beyond all estimation. A few definite instances will serve as examples of the glory that lighted up the fields of Manassas, of Shiloh, of Antietam, of Gettysburg, of Spottsylvania—and of countless others.

At Shiloh Private Samuel Evans refused to go to the rear when a ball passed through both cheeks, "but remained and fought for a considerable length of time, cheering on the men and loading and shooting as fast as he could." An officer who saw his men reduced from twenty-eight to twelve as he led them into the ravaging fire at Seven Pines cried out as he fell pierced through the heart, "Boys, I am killed, but you press on." [48] Private Ike Stone was severely wounded at the beginning of the Murfreesboro fight, but he paused only to bind up his injuries, and when his captain was incapacitated Stone took charge of the company and led it valorously through the battle, this despite a second wound. In the thick of this same fight Sergeant Joe Thompson was overwhelmed with the impulse to take a prisoner; leaping ahead of his comrades he overtook the retreating Federal column, seized a Yank and started to the rear with him; but this man having been shot down in his grasp, Thompson ran back to the still-retreating lines, seized a second Federal and brought him away safely. When Private Mattix's left arm was so seriously injured that he could no longer fire his musket, he went to his commanding officer and said, "Colonel, I am too badly

wounded to use my gun but can carry the flag; may I?" Before this three
standard-bearers had been shot down in succession, but when the requested permission was given him, Mattix seized the staff, stepped
boldly in front of the regiment, and carried the colors throughout the
remainder of the contest.[49]

In his official report of Second Manassas Major J. D. Waddell,
commanding Toombs' Georgians, said that he "carried into the fight
over 100 men who were barefoot, many of whom left bloody foot-prints
among the thorns and briars through which they rushed, with Spartan
courage and really jubilant impetuosity, upon the serried ranks of the
foe." Colonel E. C. Cook of the Thirty-second Tennessee Infantry
reported after Chickamauga that one of his men, J. W. Ellis, who had
marched for six weeks without shoes, "went thus into battle and kept
up with his company at all times till wounded." [50]

At Chickamauga Private Mayfield was wounded in the thigh by a
Minié ball and at the same time dazed by a shell. Litter bearers picked
him up and were carrying him to the rear when he recovered from the
shock and sprang to the ground with the remark, "This will not do for
me," and rushed back to continue the fight. In this same engagement
Private McCann fought gallantly until his ammunition was exhausted;
then he picked up cartridge boxes of the dead and wounded and coolly
distributed ammunition among his comrades. When the colonel com-
mended his heroic conduct McCann asked that his bravery be cited in
the official report of the battle. Shortly afterward he received a mortal
wound and as he was borne dying to the rear, he turned smiling to his
colonel and reminded him of the promise of honorable mention.[51]

Of all the brave those who were entrusted with the colors had the
most consistent record. Almost every official report of regimental commanders mentions the courageous action of standard-bearers. To keep
the flag flying was a matter of inestimable pride, and its loss to the
enemy was an incalculable disgrace. Consequently men vied with each
other for the honor of holding the cherished emblem aloft in the thickest of the fight.[52] The Federals, knowing the close association of morale
and colors, and being easily able to single out standard-bearers because
of their conspicuousness, were wont to concentrate an unusually heavy
fire upon them. Literally thousands of those who aspired to the honor
of carrying and guarding the flags paid for the privilege with their lives.

"In my two color companies," reported Colonel Jenkins of the
Palmetto Sharpshooters after Seven Pines, "out of 80 men who entered 40 were killed and wounded, and out of 11 in the color guard, 10

were shot down, and my colors pierced by nine balls passed through four hands without touching the ground." At Antietam the First Texas Infantry lost eight standard-bearers in succession, and at Gettysburg, the Twenty-sixth North Carolina lost fourteen.[53] At Antietam also, the flag of the Tenth Georgia—which regiment lost fifty-seven per cent of its men and officers in this one engagement—received forty-six shots. The standard of Lyle's Regiment was torn to tatters at Corinth, and color-bearer Sloan when last seen by his comrades was "going over the breast works waving a piece over his head and shouting for the Southern Confederacy." [54]

Color Sergeant Rice of the Twenty-eighth Tennessee Infantry, downed by a bullet at Murfreesboro, still clung to the flag, holding it aloft as he crawled on his knees until a second shot brought death and delivered him of his trust. On another part of this bloody field Color Sergeant Cameron advanced too far ahead of his comrades and was captured. He tore the flag from its staff, concealed it on his person, carried it to prison with him, escaped, and brought it back to be unfurled anew above its proud followers.[55]

Murfreesboro likewise afforded the setting for perhaps the most extraordinary of all color-bearer feats. While this contest raged at its greatest fury the opposing lines came very near each other in that portion of the field occupied by the Nineteenth Texas Cavalry (dismounted). A Yankee standard carrier stood immediately to the front of the Texas Color Sergeant, A. Sims, waving his flag and urging the blue column forward. Sergeant Sims, construing this as something of a personal insult, rushed forward, planted his own flag staff firmly on the ground with one hand and made a lunge for that of his exhorting adversary with the other. At the moment of contact, both color-bearers, Yankee and Rebel, "fell in the agonies of death waving their banners above their heads until their last expiring moments." The Texas standard was rescued, but not until one who rushed forward to retrieve it had also been shot down.[56]

Confederate authorities sought to stimulate the men by offering medals and badges to those who were cited by officers. Unable to supply these emblems, Congress passed an act in October 1862 providing for the publication of a Roll of Honor after each battle which should include the names of those who had best displayed their courage and devotion. Such lists were read at dress parades, published in newspapers and filed in the adjutant general's office. As a further inducement commissions were offered to those who should distinguish themselves, and special inscriptions were placed on flags of those regiments that captured artillery or gave other proof of unusual achievement. [57] But the most effective incentive was probably that of personal and family pride. This was strikingly evidenced by the remark of a Georgian to his brother after Franklin: "I am proud to say that there was no one between me and the Yankees when I was wounded." [58]

Cowardice under fire, being a less gratifying subject than heroism, has not received much attention from those who have written or talked of the Confederate Army. Of the various sources of information on this obscure point the most fertile are the official reports of battles by commanders of units ranging from regiments to armies. But the most numerous of these reports—those submitted by regimental commanders—are characterized by a reluctance to admit wholesale cowardice because of possible reflections on the conduct of the commanders themselves. This reluctance sometimes resulted in misrepresentation of the rankest sort, as in the following case: After the attack on Battery Wagner, Morris Island, South Carolina, July 18, 1863, Colonel Charles W. Knight, commanding the Thirty-first North Carolina Regiment, said in closing his report, "It is useless to mention any officer or man, when all were acting coolly and bravely." In the body of his report he mentioned being repulsed, but there is absolutely no suggestion of bad conduct on the part of the regiment. But when Knight's superior, General William B. Taliaferro, reported the battle, he said: "The Thirty-first North Carolina could not be induced to occupy their position, and ingloriously deserted the ramparts. . . . I feel it my duty to mention . . . [their] disgraceful conduct." [59]

In the reports of higher ranking officers, who could admit bad conduct of portions of their commands with more impunity than colonels, and in the wartime letters and diaries of the common soldiers, much testimony on the subject may be found. This evidence shows clearly that Confederate soldiers were by no means immune to panic and cowardice.

At First Manassas a few Rebs fled into the woods when shells began to fly. There was disgraceful conduct at the beginning of McClellan's peninsula campaign, when General D. H. Hill wrote that "several thousand soldiers . . . have fled to Richmond under pretext of sickness. They have even thrown away their arms that their flight might not be impeded." At Seven Pines there were a few regiments that "disgracefully left the battle field with their colors." General W. H. C. Whiting in reporting the battle of Gaines's Mill said: "Men were leaving the field in every direction and in great disorder . . . men were skulking from the front in a shameful manner; the woods on our left and rear were full of troops in safe cover from which they never stirred." At Malvern Hill, General Jubal Early encountered "a large number of men retreating from the battle-field," saw "a very deep ditch filled with skulkers," and found a "wood filled with a large number of men retreating in confusion." [60]

Men ran, skulked and straggled by the hundreds at Shiloh. A Tennessee regiment took fright during an advance, ran back on supporting lines crying, "Retreat! Retreat!" and caused great confusion; but they were rallied and set in motion toward the Federal position; again they were overcome with fear, and this time they rushed back so precipitately that they ran over and trampled in the mud the color-bearer of the regiment behind them. A Texas regiment behaved in the some manner; placed in line of battle it began firing, but before the guns had all been discharged, "it broke and fled disgracefully from the field." An officer who attempted to bring back the fugitives and threatened to report them as "a pack of cowards" was told that "they did not care a damn" what they were called, they would not follow him. When General W. J. Hardee tried to rally another demoralized regiment he was fired on by its members. Some of the straggling for which Shiloh was notorious was due to circumstances that exonerate those involved, but there can be no doubt that a large part of those who found various pretexts for leaving the firing line were playing the coward. Said Colonel O. F. Strahl in his official report: "On Monday morning we . . . had a great number of stragglers attached to us. The stragglers demonstrated very clearly this morning that they had strayed from their own regiments because they did not want to fight. My men fought gallantly until the stragglers ran and left them and began firing from the rear over their heads. They were then compelled to fall to the rear. I rallied them several times and . . . finally left out the stragglers." General Beauregard clinched this evidence in his official report: "Some officers, non-commissioned officers, and men abandoned their colors early in the first day to pillage the captured encampments; others retired shamefully from the field on both days while the thunder of cannon and the roar and rattle of musketry told them that their brothers were being slaughtered by the fresh legions of the enemy." [61]

General Bushrod Johnson reported that at Murfreesboro troops on his right became demoralized and "men of different regiments, brigades, divisions, were scattered all over the fields," and that he was almost run over, so precipitate was their flight. Captain Felix Robertson said that he had never seen troops so completely broken as those demoralized at Murfreesboro. "They seemed actuated only by a desire for safety," he added. "I saw the colors of many regiments pass, and though repeated calls were made for men of the different regiments, no attention was paid to them." [62]

At Chancellorsville and Gettysburg the conduct of the soldiers seems to have been exceptionally good. This may have been due in some part to vigorous efforts of General Lee and of the War Department early in 1863 to tighten up the discipline of the Army of Northern Virginia. The fighting before Vicksburg was marred by shameful conduct in the action of May 16, 1863, of which General Pemberton said: "We lost a large amount of artillery. The army was much demoralized; many regiments behaved badly," and Colonel Edward Goodwin reported of a small number of troops immediately in front of him:

"At this time our friends gave way and came rushing to the rear panic-stricken. . . . I brought my regiment to the charge bayonets, but even this could not check them in their flight. The colors of three regiments passed through. . . . We collared them, begged them, and abused them in vain." [63]

The wholesale panic which seized Confederate troops at Missionary Ridge was as notorious as it was mystifying. A soldier who took part in the battle wrote in his diary, "In a few minutes the whole left gave way and a regular run commenced." After a retreat of several hundred yards, this Reb's battalion rallied momentarily, "but it was in such a confused mass that we made but a feeble resistance, when all broke again in a perfect stampede." His conviction was that the troops acted disgracefully, that they "did not half fight." [64]

General Bragg in his official report of the fight said that "a panic which I had never before witnessed seemed to have seized upon officers and men, and each seemed to be struggling for his personal safety, regardless of his duty or his character." He added that "no satisfactory excuse can possibly be given for the shameful conduct of the troops on our left in allowing their line to be penetrated. The position was one which ought to have been held by a line of skirmishers against any assaulting column, and wherever resistance was made the enemy fled in disorder after suffering heavy loss. Those who reached the ridge did so in a condition of exhaustion from the great physical exertion in climbing, which rendered them powerless, and the slightest effort would have destroyed them." What stronger indictment could there be of any soldiery by its general-in-command! [65]

But the woeful tale is not ended. In connection with Early's campaign of 1864 in the Shenandoah Valley occurred some of the most disgraceful running of Confederate history. After an engagement near Winchester on July 23, General Stephen Ramseur wrote his wife:

"My men behaved shamefully— They ran from the enemy. . . . The entire command stampeded. I tried in vain to rally them & even after the Yankees were checked by a few men I posted behind a stone wall, they continued to run all the way to the breastworks at Winchester—& many of them threw away their guns & ran on to Newtown 6 miles beyond. They acted cowardly and I told them so." [66]

On September 19, 1864, during another hard fight near Winchester, a panic of unprecedented proportions struck the ranks of Early's army. Regiment after regiment broke and fled back toward the town. General Bryan Grimes, appalled by the demoralization and fearful that his brigade would succumb to it, threatened "to blow the brains out of the first man who left ranks," and then moved over to confront the fugitives, waving his sword and giving many a Reb the full weight of its flashing blade.[67] But fleeing regiments, increasing now in number, could not be stopped. They poured into the town, out the valley pike, and some continued their disordered course for miles beyond. "The Ladies of Winchester came into the streets and beged them crying bitterly to make a stand for their sakes if not for their own honor," wrote a captain who witnessed the rout; but "the cowards did not have the shame to make a pretense of halting." [68]

A month later at Cedar Creek, plunder combined with cowardice to inflict upon Early's veterans one of the most shameful defeats of the war. In the morning, by brilliant action, the Confederates pounced upon the Federals and drove them from their camps. As the Southern lines advanced large numbers of soldiers and officers turned aside, against positive orders, and began to ransack the rich stores abandoned by the foe. While the victors were absorbed in pillage, the Federals rallied, and in the afternoon they counterattacked. The disorganized Confederates broke first on the left, and then all along the line. Efforts of division commanders and of others who attempted to stay the tide of panic was to no avail, and the field was utterly abandoned.

"It was the hardest day's work I ever engaged in," Grimes said, "trying to rally the men. Took over flags at different times, begging, commanding, entreating the men to rally—would ride up and down the lines, beseeching them by all they held sacred and dear, to stop and fight, but without any success. I don't mean my Brigade only, but all." [69]

Price's Missouri expedition of 1864 was marked by an instance of large-scale panic. When the Federals attacked the Confederate rear on October 25, near Carthage, Missouri, demoralization set it. As Price rode rapidly to the point of danger he "met the divisions of Major-Generals Fagan and Marmaduke retreating in utter and indescribable confusion, many of them having thrown away their arms. They were deaf to all entreaties or commands, and in vain were all efforts to rally them." [70]

While the Atlanta campaign seems to have been remarkably free of demoralization under fire, there were at least two instances involving a considerable number of men. In a skirmish on June 9, 1864, a Texas cavalry unit that had a distinguished record in battle broke upon slight contact with the Federal cavalry, and fled in a manner described as disorderly and shameful by General Ross. Later, in the Battle of Jonesboro, August 31, 1864, an advancing brigade of Confederates halted without orders when it came to the Federal picket line, the men seeking shelter behind piles of rails. They seemed "possessed of some great horror of charging breastworks," reported Colonel Bushrod Jones, "which no power of persuasion or example could dispel." [71]

The last instance of large-scale panic during the war was at Nashville, December 16, 1864. On this occasion the division of General Bate, when assaulted about four o'clock in the afternoon by the Federals, began to fall back in great confusion and disorder. In a few moments the entire Confederate line was broken, and masses of troops fled down the pike toward Franklin. All efforts to rally the troops proved fruitless. General Bate in his official report leaves the impression that the rout, due to extenuating circumstances, cast little if any reproach upon his men. But General Hood, in chief command, was evidently of contrary opinion, as he says that Confederate loss in killed and wounded was small, implying that withdrawal took place without much resistance. He says further that the break came so suddenly that artillery guns could not be brought away.[72] Captain Thomas J. Key says in his diary that "General Bate's division . . . shamefully broke and fled before the Yankees were within 200 yards of them," and that there "then ensued one of the most disgraceful routs" that it had ever been his misfortune to witness.[73]

There were innumerable cases of individual cowardice under fire. When men are assembled in such large numbers, especially when many of them are forced into service, a certain proportion are inevitably worthless as fighters. Some of those who fled wanted earnestly to act bravely, but they had not the power to endure fire unflinchingly. This type is well exemplified by the Reb who covered his face with his hat during the battle of Fredericksburg, and who later, when told that his turn at the rifle pits was imminent, "made a proposition that he would go out from camp and strip" and let his comrades "get switches and whip him as much as they wanted" if they would obtain his release from the impending proximity to Federal fire.[74] A similar case was encountered by Colonel C. Irvine Walker. A man had been reported for cowardly behavior on the field. Walker called him to task and told him that he would be watched closely during the next engagement. When the time came the colonel went over to check his performance as the regiment advanced. "I found him in his place," reported Walker, "his rifle on his shoulder, and holding up in front of him a frying pan." The man was so scared that he sought this meager protection, yet he moved forward with his company and was killed.[75]

Another case of infamy converted to valor was cited by Colonel William Stiles, of the Sixtieth Georgia Infantry. During a charge this officer saw a robust Reb drop out of line and crouch behind a tree; the colonel slipped up and gave him a resounding whack across the back with the flat of his sword, and shouted, "Up there, you coward!"

The skulker, thinking evidently that he was the mortal victim of a Yankee shot, "clasped his hands, and keeled over backwards, devoutly ejaculating, 'Lord, receive my spirit!'"

After momentary bafflement, Stiles kicked the prostrate soldier violently in the ribs, exclaiming simultaneously, "Get up, sir! The Lord wouldn't receive the spirit of such an infernal coward."

The man sprang up with the joyful exclamation, "Ain't I killed? The Lord be praised," grabbed his musket, rejoined his comrades, and henceforth conducted himself with courage.[76]

Other officers had less success. Men who had no shoes were often excused from fighting, and a good many soldiers took advantage of this rule by throwing away their shoes on the eve of conflict. Others left the field under pretext of helping the wounded to the rear, and this in spite of strict orders against removal of casualties by anyone except those specifically detailed for the purpose. Still others feigned sickness or injury. A favorite ruse was to leave one's own regiment during the confusion of battle, and then to evade duty by a pretense of endless and futile searching for the outfit intentionally abandoned.[77]

Infuriated officers would curse these shirkers, beat them with swords and even threaten them with shooting, and on occasion carry out their threats on the spot. Commanders would place file-closers in the rear with instructions to arrest, and in some instances to shoot down, those who refused to do their duty.[78] Courts-martial sentenced great numbers to hard and disgraceful punishments. Private soldiers covered spineless comrades with scorn and ridicule.[79] But these measures were only partially effective.

There can be no doubt that the trying conditions under which Confederate soldiers fought contributed to the bad performance of some on the field of battle. Men often went into combat hungry and remained long under fire with little or nothing to eat. Sometimes, as at Antietam and Gettysburg, they fought after exhausting marches. Many of those who participated in the routs at Chattanooga and at Nashville were without shoes. Often the Confederate artillery protection was inadequate. The superior number of the Federals made Rebel flanks unduly vulnerable, and flank sensitiveness was the cause of more than one panic. Casualties among line officers were unusually heavy, and replacement with capable men was increasingly difficult after 1863.

When all of these factors are considered, it is rather remarkable that defection under fire was not more frequent than it actually was. Those soldiers who played the coward, even granting that the offenders totaled well up in the thousands, were a very small proportion of the Confederate Army. Taken on the whole of his record under fire, the Confederate private was a soldier of such mettle as to claim a high place among the world's fighting men. It may be doubted that anyone else deserves to outrank him.

CHAPTER VI

BAD BEEF AND CORN BREAD

"NEXT to the Yankeys Comes Rations which most interest a Soldier," wrote Private Jerome Yates from Virginia in January 1864.[1] He erred only in the emphasis. His statement should have been, "Next to rations comes the Yankees," for food was undoubtedly the first concern of Johnny Reb.

During the early part of the war, Confederate authorities optimistically appropriated as their standard for Southern soldiers the official ration prescribed for armies of the United States.[2] And for a while the volunteers in some camps fared bountifully.

"We have better meat hear than you have in St. James," wrote Fred Taber to his sister in September 1861; "we have Ice Water & Coffee three times a day." [3] Several months later a Louisianian stationed in Kentucky boasted of loaf bread from a "Confederate bakery," and "fresh beef all the time"; he concluded with the most obvious satisfaction that he was "in clover." [4]

But this abundance was short-lived, except in camps that were close to food-producing areas. As early as July 1861 many of the troops began to feel the pinch of diminishing rations. A week after First Manassas Beauregard wrote Davis not to send any more men to the Virginia front as "Some regiments are nearly starving." [5] In August Joseph E. Johnston was asking for more bacon, and several weeks later Commissary General Northrop was bemoaning a shortage of sugar.[6] In mid-September one of Johnston's soldiers (who was generally notable for his patience) revealed a continued shortage of food by jotting in his diary on one day that he "flanked" his dinner, on another that he whittled for his supper, and on a third that he had "a Scrummy breakfast." [7] There was apparently an improvement in the quantity of rations before Virginia troops went into winter quarters, but an investigating committee of Congress reported an inadequate supply of vegetables, milk, and molasses in January 1862.[8]

Soldiers of Albert Sidney Johnston's army wintering near Columbus, Kentucky, fared even worse than their Virginia comrades. Lard was issued occasionally as a substitute for bacon; beef was so tough that a Louisiana colonel threatened to requisition a lot of files to prepare the teeth of his men for mastication; and so many shanks and necks were included in the issue that this officer begged the meat contractor "for God's sake not to start throwing in the hoofs and horns." Live-stock attached to the camps were said to be so famished that they were chewing away at wagon beds, bridle reins, halters and stumps; one mule was even charged with attempting to devour a horse's tail.[9]

In the spring of 1862 Confederate authorities were forced by dwindling stores to declare a general reduction of the ration authorized at the war's beginning.[10] Generals Lee and Beauregard ordered parts of this ration to be increased, but both were called to task by the War Department; and instead of an increase, there were further curtail-ments.[11] In January 1863 Commissary General Northrop decreed a reduction of the meat issue, and on the eve of the Chancellorsville campaign Lee informed Seddon that for some time his army had been subsisting on a daily ration of eighteen ounces of flour, four ounces of bacon, and occasional supplies of rice, sugar or molasses.[12] Troops in the West fared somewhat better, but in the autumn of 1863 Northrop ordered a diminution of the bacon issue to one-third of a pound.[13] The year 1864 brought a further decrease of the flour or meal ration to one pound.[14]

Specifications made up in Richmond indicate little except general trends—for there was generally a wide discrepancy between the rations authorized and the issues received by soldiers in the field. Four months before Lee's surrender Northrop admitted that "for over two years he had found it impossible to provide the ration set up by army regula-tions, and that the issue had been gradually declining." [15] For a real picture of the deprivations experienced, it is necessary to turn to the reports of generals in the field and the immediate testimony of com-mon soldiers.

These indicate that hunger was greater and more frequent during periods of active campaigning than in times of comparative quiet. The first large-scale suffering seems to have occurred in connection with the Fort Donelson incident, where, according to General Buckner, men received no regular issue of rations for several days, and the situation was made worse by the want of cooking facilities.[16]

But the destitution at Donelson was neither so great nor so pro-longed as that experienced in the spring campaign in Virginia. Deep mud and poor organization combined to cut off large bodies of Rebs falling back before McClellan. For several weeks rations were scant, being restricted largely to flour and salt meat. The rear guard of this action, composed mainly of D. H. Hill's division, subsisted for three days on dry corn, issued in the shuck and shelled and parched by the men.

"I came nearer starving than I ever did before," wrote one soldier after the long march from Yorktown to Richmond; and another testified:

"I have never conceived of such trials as we have passed through. We were for days together without a morsel of food, excepting occasionally a meal of parched corn. . . . The army was kept on the march day & night and the roads were in some places waist deep in mud. . . . Many of the men became exhausted and some were actually stuck in the mud & had to be pulled out. . . . The men on the march ran through the gardens . . . devouring every particle of vegetables like the army worm leaving nothing at all standing. Whenever a cow or hog were found it was shot down & soon despatched." [17]

During the Seven Days' fighting, as in many other actions where the enemy was forced to retreat, Rebs were able to alleviate their hunger somewhat from Yankee spoils. Even so, many claimed they could get only hard crackers and fat meat, but under the circumstances this seemed as good as chicken pie at any other time.[18]

The Shiloh campaign, especially the falling back after the fight, was accompanied by considerable hardship, but suffering was not nearly so great as that experienced later in 1862 when Bragg moved into Kentucky and when Lee ventured into Maryland. In each of the latter cases, rapid movement, particularly in retreat, made it difficult to maintain a flow of supplies to men on the march. Cooking was so hindered as to be almost impossible. Had it not been for the cornfields and orchards dotting the country traversed by Lee, the suffering of his men would have been much greater.

The day after the awful carnage of Antietam, a Reb wrote to his wife:

"We have got some verry good apples all through this country. . . . I have had plenty of them sense we left Richmond infact we have lived some days on raw baked and rosted apples some times on green corn and some times nothing." [19]

Four days later another participant noted in his diary:

"Our army is . . . almost starved out. Our rations has been Beef and flour since we left Richmond [August 22] and not more than half enough of that many times we had Green Corn and apples issued to us and were glad to get that." [20]

And after the army got back to Culpepper, Virginia, a Tar Heel remarked to his parents: "People says that a man borned of woman and enlisted in Jacksons army is of a few days and short rations and i think it is nearly the same way with Longstreets." [21]

During Bragg's withdrawal from Kentucky an artilleryman wrote:

"Our company drew a young yearling today the first beef we have had for many weeks. We ate it raw, without salt or bread." [22]

The colonel of a South Carolina regiment sharing in this retreat recalled later that he "frequently saw the hungry Confederate gather up the dirt and corn where a horse had been fed, so that when he reached his bivouac he could wash out the dirt and gather the few grains of corn to satisfy in part at least the cravings of hunger. Hard, dry, parched corn . . . was for many days the sole diet for all." [23]

The scantiness of food at Perryville and Antietam was repeated to a large extent in connection with the Chancellorsville-Gettysburg campaign, and the Bragg-Longstreet operations in Tennessee of the fall and winter following. But the nadir of Rebel deprivation was probably reached by soldiers under siege at Vicksburg and Port Hudson. At the beginning of the forty-seven-day period of encompassment Pemberton's army was subsisting on one-third of the meat ration and two-thirds of the meal issue prescribed at Richmond. Field peas were ground and mixed with meal, and later in the siege soldiers were introduced to a copper-colored, elastic sort of concoction made entirely of pulverized peas but optimistically referred to by subsistence officers as bread. Ground rice was also used as a substitute for meal. Eventually, though not until the last days of siege, bread of all sorts was dropped from the ration. Wheat flour was largely reserved for the sick, though after the near-exhaustion of meal, about the middle of June, four-ounce portions were distributed to all for a while. To supplement the dwindling ration half-grown peaches, unripe blackberries, cane roots, tree buds, and even grass and weeds were simmered in a little water and used for food. By June 28 troops were receiving only "one small biscuit and one or two mouthfuls of bacon per day." [24]

Then came mule meat! It is possible that some of the hungry men had previously partaken of the flesh of dogs, of horses and of mules, but if so they had acted on their own responsibility. It was not until July 3 that the butchering of mules was officially ordered. The following is a copy of the historic document issued to brigade commissaries by Pemberton's chief of subsistence:

OFFICE, CHF OF SUBS
Vicksburg, July 3, 1863

MAJOR:

The issue of meat tomorrow will be one half (½) pound of mule to the ration. Please report to me at once the amt you require for your Command so that I may have it prepared

Respectfully
GEO. S. GILLESPIE
Maj. & C. S. [25]

Major Simons, commissary officer of Moore's Brigade, indicated that his requirement was 5,106 pounds, and this amount was issued to him on July 4. Apparently on this, the day of capitulation, and possibly in some portions of the army on the night before, soldiers at Vicksburg ate the first and only bona-fide mule issued to them by Confederate subsistence officers. Rations were drawn on July 5 from Grant's commissariat, and with what zest and envy did famished Rebs attack the abundance of Yankee larders! The five-day portion issued by the Federal officers "appeared to be as much as we have for some time drawn for a month supply," observed Major Simons.[26]

How did the mule meat taste? Soldiers who tried it said it wasn't bad. "The flesh," according to one, "seemed of coarser grain, but more tender than that of the ox, and had a decidedly 'horsey' flavor." Yet he deemed it "sweet" under the circumstances. Another said that it was tolerable, but he did not relish it like the beef pie that he was accustomed to eat.[27] Major Simons must have thought it passable as he ate it for two meals on the day of surrender. His only remark was "a new way to celebrate the fourth of July or rather a new dish!" [28]

The Confederate garrison at Port Hudson, several miles below Vicksburg, did not surrender until July 9. The deprivation experienced there seems to have been greater than that suffered at Vicksburg. One of the besieged stated in his diary that he and his comrades ate "all the beef—all the mules—all the Dogs—and all the Rats" that could be obtained prior to the capitulation.[29]

Soldiers taking part in the Georgia campaigns of 1864 fared better than usual from the standpoint of meat, bread, and rice. The same cannot be said of sugar, as is shown by the entry of March 4 in a Louisianian's diary:

"Drew twelve gobers pease [goober peas, i. e., peanuts] . . . today as ra[t]ions in lieu of four days rations of sugar." [30]

Here, as elsewhere, there was a chronic deficiency of vegetables. Irish potatoes and dry peas were issued now and then, but never in ample quantities. Greens and other fresh vegetables were dispensed on rare occasions by subsistence officers, but as one Reb observed, "when they have to be divided among so many they amount to little." [31] Scurvy and emaciation naturally followed. "Our old Ration of Corn Bread and meat . . . has very nearly worn [me] out," wrote one of Johnston's veterans to his wife in August; he added that his weight had fallen during the summer from 162 to 137 pounds.[32]

In the Shenandoah Valley movements of 1864, General Early's men also were subjected to great deprivation as a result of their rapid shifts of position and the previous ravaging of the country which they traversed. General Bryan Grimes testified that on one march his command had not a particle of bread for forty-eight hours, and very little meat; and that occasionally when General Rodes or Early passed the line, the cry was "bread, bread, bread." [33] A lieutenant wrote that some troops had to eat bacon raw and without bread, and that combined effects of heat, dust, exhaustion and hunger caused a few men to drop dead in the ranks.[34]

Soldiers of the trans-Mississippi Department were, with few exceptions, better fed than those east of the river. From 1862 on there were complaints of the poor quality of beef issued, but rarely of the quantity of meat and meal. Until the latter part of 1862 supplies of these two staples were generally ample.[35]

Late in 1864 great suffering accompanied General Hood's disastrous movement into Tennessee. During the October march from Palmetto, Georgia, to Tuscumbia, Alabama, a private remarked that he and his associates subsisted for three days on parched corn; and Colonel Ellison Capers of the Twenty-fourth South Carolina Infantry reported that in late November his command proceeded northward through rain and mud for two days sustained only by an issue of three biscuits a day to each man.[36]

The final campaigns in the East were marked by the most acute suffering for food. In January 1865 the temporary breakdown of the Piedmont Railroad forced Lee to make a personal appeal to the people of Virginia to supply food for his army. In February he wrote Seddon that his command had been without meat for three days.[87]

The retreat to Appomattox in April, with its failure of supply trains and general demoralization, brought still greater misery. Concerning the period of final operations, a soldier wrote:

"Two days fasting, marching, and fighting was not uncommon; . . . no rations were issued to Cutshaw's battalion of artillery for one entire week, and the men subsisted on the corn intended for the battery horses, raw bacon captured from the enemy, and the water of springs, creeks, and rivers." [38]

And an erstwhile member of Jackson's staff stated, "Once I took some corn from my horse, beat it between stones and tried to swallow it." He, like comrades reduced to similar straits, doubtless found that "chewing the corn was hard work" and that it "made the jaws ache and the gums so sore as to cause almost unendurable pain." [39]

The continually dwindling ration of soldiers from early months of the war till the closing campaigns of 1865 was all the more tragic in view of the fruitfulness of Confederate fields. Rebel armies were in no sense famished because of failure of food production. By voluntary action, by public pressure and by state legislation cotton acreage was sharply curtailed during the war, and much of the land thus diverted was given to the growth of cereals, peas, potatoes and other foodstuffs. Everywhere in the South, except in sections drained by invading or occupying armies and infertile areas peopled largely by less privileged whites, Negro workers grew bountiful crops in every year of the war. Production, with the possible exception of meat, was always more than ample for both civilians and soldiers. The failure, then, was not one of production but of distribution.[40]

Several factors contributed to poor distribution. There was doubtless some corruption on the part of lesser commissary officials, but this was of far less importance than inefficiency.[41] The subsistence department was the worst administered of all Confederate bureaus. L. B. Northrop, the head of this division, was a veritable "sour-puss" who, by his obstinate devotion to red tape, antagonized every general in the field, and who apparently took greater satisfaction in consistency than in delivering food to the army.[42]

A RABBIT IN A CONFEDERATE CAMP

Rabbits were stalked in wood or meadow and killed with rocks and clubs, or hemmed in and caught by hand. Drawing by W. L. Sheppard, one of Lee's soldiers, from *Battles and Leaders of the Civil War.*

Photo by U. S. Army Signal Corps

GROUP OF CONFEDERATE PRISONERS

(No date, no place)

Another cause of scarcity in the midst of plenty, particularly of meat, was the dearth of salt and of other preservatives. This unhappy condition caused the loss or waste of untold quantities of precious provisions.

But far and away the most serious difficulty was the inadequacy of transportation facilities. The Confederacy's railroad system was never equal to war needs, and after 1862 it began to deteriorate rapidly from inability to replace worn-out rails and rolling stock. From 1863 till the war's end, while armies were struggling along on half-rations, immense quantities of foodstuffs assembled by commissary agents and collectors of the government's tax-in-kind simply rotted at the depots.[43]

Another explanation of deficiency is found in Confederate finance. Commissary officers complained repeatedly of lack of funds. And they had difficulty procuring supplies with the money that was available, because the constant depreciation of Rebel currency made producers hold their crops as long as possible in order to take advantage of ever soaring prices. Then, after resort to impressment of supplies, farmers were reluctant to take provisions to market, lest they be pounced upon en route by ubiquitous government agents.

A further hindrance was the shortage of sacks, kegs, boxes, cans and barrels for the packing of fruits, vegetables, sugar and meat.

Finally, the cutting in two of the Confederacy by Yankee operations along the Mississippi in 1863 did incalculable damage by reducing to a mere trickle the flow of meat, sugar, molasses and other essentials produced west of the river.

Because the government could not deliver to him the abundance produced by his homefolk, Johnny Reb fought the Yankees for four years on rations composed mainly of cornbread and beef. There were, to be sure, admixtures now and then of field peas—which humble plant General Lee was said to have called the Confederacy's best friend —of flour, pork, potatoes, rice, molasses, coffee, sugar and fresh vegetables, though it was for the last that the soldiers always suffered most. But meal and meat were the staple fare. A Texas Reb summed up the food situation with fair accuracy for all when he said of his own experience: "Well Lizer, I will let you know what I livon . . . beef & bread bread an beef upper crust under crust an crum Som Sugar & molasses when that is said all is said." [44]

Since cornbread was the most constant item in the diet, Rebs naturally became exceedingly tired of it—especially since the meal was generally coarse and unsifted. A Mississippian wrote his sister in 1863,

"I want Pa to be certain and buy wheat enough to do us plentifully—for if the war closes and I get to come home I never intend to chew any more cornbread." A Louisianian was even more pointed: "If any person offers me cornbread after this war comes to a close," he observed just before Lee's surrender, "I shall probably tell him to—go to hell!" [45]

Unfortunately for Johnny Reb, his rations were poor in quality as well as short in quantity. Flour bread was called everything from "leather" to "ginned cotton." But it was upon beef that the heaviest denunciation fell. In more generous moments, a Reb would refer to his meat simply as "mule." But under provocation he could rise to heights of derogatory eloquence.

"Take it as it comes hare skin and dust and it is so rank that it can hardly be eat," was the appraisal of a Georgian whose language was undoubtedly restrained by ministerial inclinations.[46] "[Our] poor Buck and Grind Stone bread would kill the Devil," mused a Texan.[47] "The beef is so poor it is Sticky and Blue," commented another Reb; "if a quarter was thrown against the wall it would stick." [48] An Alabamian declared that the cows which supplied the meat for his outfit were so emaciated that "it takes two hands to hold up one beef to shoot it." [49] And a Mississippian expressed the conviction that "buzzards would not eat it at any season of the year." [50] With full allowance for the exaggeration of wrath, this beef must have been pretty bad.

Sometimes dissatisfaction with rations went beyond mere grumbling. When a group of Texans received an issue of spoiled beef from their regimental commissary, they took it to brigade headquarters and presented it to the major of subsistence with their compliments; in two instances troops refused to draw their meat ration because of its poor quality.[51] After being deprived of beef for a few days, some Rebs camping near Fredericksburg made a night raid upon the commissary for what they termed a "special requisition," and another meat-hungry outfit of even greater temerity visited the stock pen attached to the headquarters of General Rodes and made off with the milch cow reserved for that officer and his wife.[52]

Several companies of Louisiana troops were provoked to open mutiny by what they construed as a "huge swindle" to deprive them of supplies. According to the report of an observer of this affair, "The sutlers' establishments were the first reached, and were speedily gutted, while the butcher and quartermaster saved themselves by running off." [53]

That more frequent and serious mutinies were not incited by the

food situation is a tribute to the adaptability and forbearance of the
Confederate soldier.

Johnny Reb's hunger was often forestalled by his own efforts and
devices. During the first two years of war food was frequently sent from
home. With transportation getting worse this practice declined after
the summer of 1863, but even in 1864 the railroads continued to deliver such a quantity of home packages to the army as to reflect on
the judgment of shipping officials, who should have given precedence
to more vitally needed military stores.

In some cases express companies offered free transportation to
provisions for soldiers. An Alabamian serving in Lee's army wrote from
Petersburg, October 25, 1864:

"Sister i want you to send me a box of proveshens . . . some potatoes and meat and butter and some honey if yo have got it if yo have
not got the honey send me some surrup send me some pepper too yo
nead not to fear to express them for the ex agence [express agency]
. . . has takend mo[r]e responseibility on they sellf they have in shord
[insured] all frate that belongs to soldiers in the armmy or boxes to go
threw saft they will ship them first if they dont ship eney thing els." [54]

An immense amount of food from home was carried by personal
agents, with or without railroad assistance, depending on distance and
other factors. In this multitude of neighborhood-army commuters,
were troops on furlough, domestic servants, relatives and friends. Soldier relief societies furnished considerable assistance in storing and
delivering commodities. Letters written during the war indicate that
boxes of foodstuff went from homefolk in Alabama to Tennessee in
1862 and 1863, to Georgia during the Atlanta campaign, and to Virginia during the last year of the war; from western Virginia to Georgia
in 1864, and to Johnston's army in North Carolina in March 1865; and
from Texas to Arkansas from 1862 to the war's end. Transmission
over shorter distances was frequent throughout the conflict.

Foods in greatest demand were vegetables and sweets, and these
seem to have constituted the great bulk of packages sent from home.
But there was often an inclusion of delicacies not obtainable from
other sources. Fried chicken was received with surprising frequency by
troops serving around Richmond early in the war, and in one instance
300 live fowls were shipped from Mecklenburg County, Virginia, to
soldiers stationed at Jamestown.[55]

Private John Crittenden proposed to send his brother a lot of ammunition in exchange for a mess of squirrels. He also asked his wife to send along a bottle of tomato catsup and a jar of green-pepper pickles.[56]

Private T. B. Hampton was immensely pleased with the "little notions" sent by his wife, including apple butter, sausages, and chestnuts. "The Butter and Honey was also devoured," he said, "with as much ferocity as a wolf would devour a sheep." He requested that on the next occasion she add "more of the buck wheat Bread," or send "a small bunch of flower." [57] But the simpler request of Private George W. Athey for "alofe of lite bread and abig potatoe" was doubtless more typical of the majority of Rebs.[58]

A considerable proportion of the packages sent by rail was lost in transit, and many articles delivered by both express companies and private individuals were in bad shape when they arrived. In acknowledging receipt of supplies soldiers mentioned shattered jars, broken eggs, rancid butter and "strong" meat, and sometimes when a box of provisions escaped all hazards to reach camp in good condition it was spoiled by lying on the shelf until a period of active campaigning was finished.[59]

But after all is said about provisions from home, the fact remains that these items supplemented government issues only to a slight extent. A more productive expedient was the purchase of supplies in camp or its environs from peddlers and producers.

Sutlers made their appearance early in the war. A Mississippian wintering at Manassas observed in December 1861 that "the sutlers kept a great many luxuries which we could buy at reasonable prices." [60] This statement does not correspond with the reputation generally held by camp vendors. A newspaperman attached to Joseph E. Johnston's command said, in 1861, that sutlers made profits of several hundred per cent on their transactions.[61] Excessive charges for ginger cakes, half-moon pies, dried fruit and other stock items was a source of chronic irritation to officers, and sometimes soldiers became so infuriated that they ran the Shylocks out of camp—minus their provisions.[62] But despite their increasing unpopularity, sutlers continued to flock about Rebel camps at payday, and to take a lion's share of wages, until late in the war when paymasters virtually ceased to function.[63]

The most reasonable source from which troops might purchase foodstuffs, and the one patronized most frequently, was the producer himself. Sometimes farmers came to camp with their provisions, and on other occasions soldiers sought out the countrymen. If Rebs had no money, they might trade in kind from their army rations; for instance, some men on picket duty in Tennessee exchanged three pounds of sugar for two gallons of buttermilk.[64] The character of the purchase was determined largely by the soldier's financial state on the one hand and the producer's stock on the other.

To prevent exorbitant charges, General Bragg resorted to the expedient, in 1863, of permitting Rebs to take without payment the produce of citizens who placed excessive prices on items brought to camp.[65] In another instance he forbade soldiers buying anything from civilians near Chattanooga because of the suspicion that Union sympathizers had poisoned the pie offered for sale.[66] In portions of the country long occupied by troops, exhaustion of supplies often made impossible any purchase from civilian sources.

The most successful subsister on the citizenry encountered by this writer was a private in Bragg's army named L. G. Hutton. On the Kentucky campaign of 1862, he bought along the way almost every conceivable item of food, including milk, butter, chickens, eggs, flour, molasses, cider, whortleberries, strawberries, peaches, apples, watermelons, meat and lightbread. Repeatedly he used the excuse of flux or colic, frequently vouched for by surgeon's certificate, either to go ahead of the columns or to lag behind. His alleged ailments also enabled him to unload his accouterments on the wagon or upon some sympathizing and perhaps conniving friend. Utilizing fully the advantage of his comparative freedom, and in utter disregard of the alleged frailty of his digestive system, he surfeited himself on the abundance of Kentucky and Tennessee flocks, fields and orchards. Often he dined at the tables of farm people for a fee of twenty-five or fifty cents, or for nothing. On one occasion, at least, he took some flour to a citizen's house and had it baked into bread. He was apparently unhampered by lack of funds.[67]

But few soldiers were as well equipped financially as Hutton. And where money was lacking other means must be found for supplementing government rations. Troops stationed along streams frequently procured fish by setting out hooks, by seining, and by "grabbling." [68] Rabbits, squirrels, possums and other small game were run down, stalked, or shot. Birds of various sorts were trapped or knocked from their roosts at night with sticks. An Alabamian boasted of a sparrow pie prepared by his mess in 1863.[69]

Soldiers in seacoast areas found variety in oysters and crabs, and a group of Georgians serving in Florida treated themselves to the meat of an alligator. "He tasted a good deal like catfish," according to one who sat in on the feast.[70] Even greater relish was professed by a Texan who helped consume a roasted armadillo. "I . . . found it to be very fine," he wrote his sister, "far superior to any possum meat I ever eat." He added that he and his friends had eaten a number of these little animals, which they referred to as "iron clad possum." [71]

The getting of food by any means other than purchase was known as "foraging." Included under this polite designation were activities as various as the gathering of nuts, berries and pawpaws, the plucking of fruit and vegetables from abandoned orchards and gardens, the solicitation of milk, eggs and other edibles at farmhouse doors—accompanied sometimes by woeful recitations of the sickness of comrades—and clandestine forays on stock pens and chicken roosts. Whether of the innocent or the blamable sort, foraging was a widely used and effective means of replenishing scant larders.

Of all possible ways of getting extra food capture from the Yankees was the most satisfying. During the battle of Shiloh avid rustics from Rebel ranks were wont to lag behind on captured camp sites, spread out blankets marked with Federal symbols, load them with spoils and strike out southward. In the wake of Seven Pines famished gray-clad troops had a field day among the delicacies left by the retreating Yankees. Even richer returns were enjoyed by soldiers who raided Federal depots at the command of Jackson and Stuart. At Gettysburg and elsewhere, the kits of slain enemies were rifled for hardtack and bacon. Men operating with Forrest had to learn to grab a bite on the run when they were riding in hostile country. A youngster participating in a thrust toward Nashville in the fall of 1864 wrote:

"We were now permitted to get something to eat. I ran into a store, got hold of a tin wash pan, drew it full of molasses, got a box of 'good Yankee' crackers, sat down on the ground in a vacant lot, dipped the crackers into the molasses, and ate the best fasting meal I ever had. I had [had] only two crackers since Wednesday and this was Saturday." [72]

Of all the goods obtained from Federals none was more appreciated than coffee. This became scarce in the early months of the war, and at the beginning of 1862 it disappeared from government issues to parts of the army. When notice came in January 1862 to the Washington Light Infantry that coffee rations would have to be suspended, German members of that organization arranged a pageant deemed appropriate for the observance of such a calamity. At night they filed into camp in a torchlight procession, "1st an illumination on one side a coffee pot pierced with an arrow, words 'no more grounds for complaint'. Other side—coffee mill—words 'the last grind'. Pall bearers followed, then priest—companies bearing lights. They marched through the camp, halted; a sort of funeral ceremony was performed, preaching, and singing, in German, and bonfire made and the last grounds burnt." [73]

In July 1862 a Texan suffering from chronic headache bemoaned: "How much I miss the good coffee I used to get at home. I would cheerfully pay one dollar for as much like it as I could drink. . . . We got some ground coffee from the Yanks in the Seven Days fight," he added, but since then, the only way to get it was "to pay two dollars and a half a pound." [74]

Like the folk at home, Johnny Reb concocted all sorts of substitutes for the precious coffee. An amber fluid was optimistically brewed from parched peanuts, potatoes, peas, dried apples, corn, or rye. "Tea" was made of corn bran, ginger and herbs of various sorts. Sassafras tea was drunk in large quantities by privates and generals alike.

Once foodstuff was procured, the problem of cooking had to be considered. And this, in view of the circumstances of army life, was no easy matter. Some of the more fortunate Rebs had Negro cooks, but for the most part, food consumed by privates was prepared by the soldiers themselves. Early in the war military authorities attempted to establish bakeries for each brigade, where bread enough for everybody would be cooked under the supervision of details trained for the purpose. This policy could not be carried out on a large scale, however, because of the difficulties of active campaigning. During periods of siege, as at Vicksburg and Petersburg, cooking was done en masse, and the food carried to men in the trenches. But the general practice was preparation of rations by individuals or small groups.

The most immediate worry of the soldier cook was a shortage of utensils. Rarely did an outfit have anything like enough kettles, pans and skillets. Typical was the plight of a regiment whose colonel complained to his superiors in the fall of 1863:

"I have not a single vessel to cook one morsel of bread my cooking has to be done as we can beg the citizens to do it. . . . For God and the country's sake, make your fair-promising but never-complying quartermaster send me skillets, ovens, pots or anything that will bake bread or fry meat. . . . Send me skillets 225 in number. I cannot fight any more until I get something to cook in." [75]

But Rebs elsewhere, if not in this case, were becoming hardened to a scarcity of utensils. "The boys have made frying pans out of plates and picked up vessels until they ask Bragg no odds," wrote a soldier whose regiment had been deprived of its original equipment by the active campaigning of Chickamauga.[76]

To make up for such deficiencies, the troops contrived various expedients. Skillets, plates and corn graters were made from halves of captured canteens. Hollow stumps and wood pestles were used to convert corn into grits for dodger pones.[77]

The practice of broiling beef over the fire on sharpened sticks was so universally followed as to become standard. Bacon was often cooked the same way, though the necessity of conserving grease for shortening made the use of skillets preferable.

Bread was mixed and kneaded in turtle shells and pumpkin rinds, on oil cloth, shirt-tails, boards, stumps, chips of wood, or any other surface that was available. One Negro cook when given a barrel of flour to prepare under duress knocked off the head, poured in river water and other ingredients as needed, and thus converted the entire contents into dough with rare dispatch.[78] A prevalent mode of cooking flour bread was by wrapping the dough about a ramrod and turning it over the fire until brown. Both cornbread and wheat bread were cooked on a board or some other flat surface, placed in a slanting position near the fire; or the batter might be wrapped in a shuck and buried in hot ashes.

Corn on the cob was likewise roasted in the original husk. Potatoes, sweet and Irish, were baked in their jackets beneath heaps of glowing embers. Given time and a lucky forage, Johnny Reb might indulge in a treat of barbecued lamb, pig, turkey, or beef quarter, prepared with critical finesse over a pit of lazy coals. But empty stomachs and over-active salivary glands protested against such a slow process.

Shortage of utensils and ingredients combined to produce some astonishing dishes. The most frequently mentioned was a concoction known as cush—dubbed "slosh" by one of its less admiring partakers. This dish was born of the greater convenience of cooking small portions of meat together instead of separately; but let a soldier give the recipe: "We take some bacon & fry the grease out, then we cut some cold beef in small pieces & put it in the grease, then pour in water and stew it like hash. Then we crumble corn bread or biscuit in it [some soldiers made mush or paste of flour or meal and added one or both of these at this point instead of crumbs] and stew it again till all the water is out then we have . . . real Confederate cush." He added that he and his comrades on Missionary Ridge considered the preparation to be quite a luxury.[79]

Another combination dish was made of Irish potatoes and green apples, boiled together, mashed, and seasoned with salt, pepper, onions, or garlic.

A third mixture grew out of an emergency retreat from Nashville in late 1864: Soldiers having flour, side meat, Irish potatoes and a stew pot, but nothing in which to bake bread, "boiled some meat and potatoes together until about done, when some one suggested that we have what they called at his home 'drap dumplins,' which was to make batter for flap jacks, and while potatoes and meat were boiling to drop in a spoonful of batter at a time, and we eventually stirred the whole together, ate supper that night, and next morning for breakfast in cutting it out of the camp kettle, we got meat, bread, and potatoes all in the same slice." [80]

During the early days of the war Johnny Reb was a notoriously bad cook. Newspapers attributed a considerable portion of the prevalent sickness to improper preparation of food by volunteers. An investigating committee of Congress reported in January 1862 that while rations were sound and wholesome, "the cooking particularly the bread, rendered it unsuitable for either sick or healthy men." [81]

But with experience the preparation improved, and in late 1862 a Reb was boasting to his wife that "I will be able to learn you something in the art of cooking by the time I get home." [82] Not only did soldiers become adept at preparing staple items of diet, but some also developed proficiency at concocting such specialties as huckleberry pie, plum preserves, molasses custard, grape pie, yeast rolls, roast turkey, and baked 'possum "chained with potatoes."

Taking the good with the bad, Confederate fare could hardly have been relished except by men whose appetites were unduly sharpened by hunger and whose digestive systems were hardened from abuse. And bread made of flour mixed with muddy water, without soda and lard, or army crackers soaked to softness and then fried in bacon grease, or stew made from beef so poor that ribs would come apart when the hide was removed, "strong" from age, and deficient in salt—these must have tried even the war-inured stomachs of Rebs.[83]

Scarcity of tableware came to be universal after a year or two of fighting. For example, a member of an officers' mess in Johnston's army wrote from Georgia in February 1864:

"We have no utensils to eat with. We have but one knife, i.e. case knife, in our mess and no plate nor fork nor spoon." [84]

Sticks, splinters and pocketknives had to suffice for eating implements. And in numberless cases, Rebs sopped molasses from tin cups, or even from hats, and transferred greasy bacon or "cush" from skillet to mouth with no better means than their scrawny fingers. A slab of solid fat pork laid on a piece of hardtack "was passable or luscious as the time was long or short since the last meal." [85]

During the early months of the war a degree of order was maintained in some camps in the serving of meals, and in one formality was carried to an extreme. This was at Camp Beauregard in Louisiana where, according to testimony of a volunteer, "we are marched to our meals in company, stand behind our respective chairs until the command is given 'take seats,' after which a certain time is allowed for eating, when we are commanded to 'rise' and are marched back in regular convict style. We are not allowed to speak to the waiter at all but must ask the orderly who sits at the head of the table for whatever we want." [86] Such punctiliousness was exceptional even at the time, and after the spring of 1862 it must have been without parallel save in a few military academies.

The general rule was for Rebs to prepare and consume their food in messes of from four to eight men, with each taking his turn at cooking, cleaning the skillet belonging to the group or borrowed from another, going after rations, and performing other duties incident to the preparation and serving of food. Messes were usually composed of men who were drawn together by ties of kinship or congeniality. As would be expected, such groups were beset occasionally with drones who shirked duties, avoided contribution of their proportionate share to the mess fund, and consumed more than their share of the food. And woe to that soldier who was not present in full force when the meal was attacked! A Georgian who took time out to read a letter brought to him at lunchtime wrote later to his wife:

"Yours of the 29th was received to day Jest as I commenst eating dinner we had chicken pie made out of bacon and of corse I could not eat enny more untel I read your letter and by the time I got through it was all eat up so I lost my dinnor." [87]

Informality was the prevailing vogue. Uncertainty of food issues led to the practice for a time in Lee's army of the commissary blowing a horn or beating a pan when supplies sufficient to merit distribution came to hand.[88] Food was eaten, not according to a set schedule, but rather when availability, appetite and other circumstances dictated.

"Som times I Git a nuff and Som times I don't," wrote an Alabamian in 1863 from Bragg's army. "We dont have no Regeler way out here of Eatting we Eat just when we git Hungerey." [89]

Occasionally the Yankees would interfere with culinary activities. In one instance during the Atlanta campaign Federal artillery opened on a group of Rebs as they were cooking their noon meal. One of the number was sent to a point of observation to call the shots so that the cooks could lie down after each salvo until the shells passed over.[90]

More than one meal was interrupted by the sounding of the long roll, and hungry men, snatching up hot remnants, fell into line cursing Yankees for their lack of consideration.

When he first went to war Johnny Reb was wont to grumble much about the many bad features of his fare: scantiness, poor quality, lack of variety and slovenly preparation. Toward the end he complained little of anything save quantity. His years of deprivation brought him to the point of view expressed by a Mississippian in the last year of conflict. "If I ever get home to live in peace," he said, "I am going to have plenty to eat that is good and nice." He added that he and his comrades swore that in future cotton would give way to food crops. "I think carriages horses &c nice house & going in style an[d] all [are] good things," he concluded, "but having plenty of good things to eat . . . is . . . worth all the rest." [91] And a Texan sorely tried by the failure of Bragg's commissariat during the Chattanooga campaign said that if he ever got back to his father's house he intended "to take a hundred biscuit and two large hams call it three days rations, then go down on Goat Island and eat it all at ONE MEAL." [92]

CHAPTER VII

FROM FINERY TO TATTERS

THE Confederate private envisioned by Richmond authorities in 1861 was a nattily dressed person.

His coat was a long double-breasted tunic of cadet gray, fronted with two rows of buttons and trimmed at the edges and at collar and cuffs with colors designating the branch of service—infantry in blue, cavalry yellow and artillery red; the collar was the stand-up type, very much like that worn by soldiers of recent times. For fatigue purposes a double-breasted light-gray blouse with turn-down collar might be worn instead of the tunic.

Trousers were of sky blue, cut loose in the leg and of sufficient length to spread well over the shoe.

Overcoats, or "great coats" as they were sometimes called, were of gray flannel, double-breasted and fitted with capes; for the infantry, capes were short, extending only to the elbows, while those of the cavalry extended the full length of the arm.

The headpiece was a cap modeled after the style of the French kepi; the crown was of cloth, colored to designate the branch of the wearer's service. Havelocks, of white duck for summer and of oil cloth for winter, were prescribed.

The cravat was of black leather. Boots were of the Jefferson type. Shirts, socks, and drawers completed the official regalia, but no requirements were published as to the color or material of these lowly items.[1]

These specifications were published in *Army Regulations* year after year without change, and when the *Official Records of the Union and Confederate Armies* were compiled long after the war ended, a section was included which set forth in rich color the uniforms thus prescribed.[2]

But there was considerable difference between the clothing designated and that actually worn by the soldiers. This discrepancy came first from the inability of the Confederate Government to provide uniforms for the men who were called to arms. Captains who wrote in to Montgomery to inquire about equipment for companies in process of organization were informed that "the volunteers shall furnish their own clothes." [3] The reason was obvious: Jeff Davis and company had none in stock, nor were any to be forthcoming until contracts with Southern manufacturers should bear fruit, or purchasing operations in Europe could be completed; and this was to require a long time.

In the meantime volunteer companies did the best they could. Some received issues of clothing from state authorities, though these were faced with problems of supply very much like those of the central government.

A procedure widely followed during the early months of the war was for captains to take funds appropriated by local authorities or donated by philanthropists—who sometimes were the captains themselves—or contributed by the recruits, to purchase cloth from whatever source it might be obtained, and to have the uniforms made up by local tailors or seamstresses. In many cases the volunteers arranged individually for the fabrication of their outfits.

Women of the South responded nobly to the difficulties by organizing sewing clubs and knitting societies. As a general rule the aid rendered by the volunteer seamstresses was both timely and valuable, though there were numerous instances where coats, pants and socks turned out by the ladies indicated considerably more zeal than skill. [4]

The inevitable result of these devious sources and methods of supply was a miscellany that made mockery of the Richmond regulations. This is not to imply that the regalia worn by early volunteers were of poor quality. On the contrary many of the companies were resplendently clothed. Captain Alexander Duncan of the Georgia Hussars, a regiment hailing from Savannah, boasted that $25,000 was spent for that organization's initial outfit. [5]

In not a few instances, regiments went into Confederate service garbed in the flashy suits which they had worn for parade purposes as militia organizations. The Orleans Guard Battalion of New Orleans arrived at Shiloh while the battle was in progress, and went into the thick of the fight wearing blue dress uniforms. Fellow Rebels mistook the newcomers for Yankees and began to shoot at them. When the Guards realized the cause of their plight, they hastily turned their coats inside out so as to present a whitish color instead of blue; and thus they went through the battle. [6]

But blue was just one of many colors worn by soldiers of '61 and '62. The Emerald Guards of Mobile went to Virginia attired in dark green, a color adopted in honor of old Ireland, the land from which most of the members came.[7] Captain Patterson's company of East Tennesseans dressed themselves in suits of yellow to give meaning to their previously adopted designation of "Yellow Jackets." [8] The Granville Rifles of North Carolina sported uniforms featuring black pants and flaming red flannel shirts that must have made easy targets for Yankees considerably removed.[9] Some of the Maryland companies who espoused the cause of the Confederacy were clothed in uniforms of blue and orange.

But most resplendently attired of all were the Louisiana Zouaves, whose trousers were of scarlet cloth, cut in such fashion as to suggest the term "bloomers" to derisive comrades, belted at the waist with large blue sashes and bound at the ankles with gaiters of white; jackets were heavily adorned with varicolored lace; shirts were of blue, cut low to reveal sunburnt throats and hirsute chests; headpieces consisted of fezzes, perched at angles indicating the jauntiness of the wearers.[10]

These flashy regalia contrasted markedly with other types observed in the streets of Richmond in the summer of 1861. Here might be seen a rugged Texan mounted on a high-pommel saddle, attired in homespun gray, peering disinterestedly from beneath the expansive brim of a western hat; there a native of the southern Appalachian area, ambling along in bearskin blouse, nondescript trousers and rawhide leggings. Occasionally one might encounter "the dirty gray and tarnished silver of the muddy-complexioned Carolinian; the dingy butternut of the lank, muscular Georgian, with its green trimming and full skirts; and the Alabamians from the coast nearly all in blue of a cleaner hue and neater cut." [11]

As the war went into the second and third years clothing became simpler and less diverse. Contributing to this change was the increasing ability of the quartermaster general to meet requisitions made upon the government for uniforms. By the end of 1862 Caleb Huse's purchasing operations had yielded substantial returns in trousers and cloth for coats. Contracts with domestic manufacturers were also beginning, after heartbreaking delays, to achieve a partial degree of fulfillment. In recognition of these developments Congress, on October 8, 1862, passed an act which modified the prior policy of allowing cash payments of fifty dollars a year to soldiers who clothed themselves, and announced the intention of the government to provide the uniform prescribed by regulations. The following schedule of allowances, based

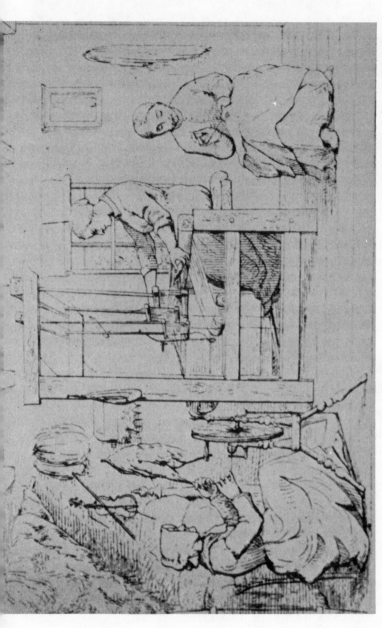

SOUTHERN WOMEN MAKING CLOTHES FOR THE SOLDIERS

From a wartime etching by Dr. A. J. Volck of Baltimore, Maryland. Volck made more than a score of etchings of Northern and Southern subjects in 1861-1863. He was eventually captured by Federals and imprisoned at Fort McHenry. Only a few copies of his etchings were ever run off. The plates were then sent to England where they were injured beyond use.

Courtesy Maud Morrow Brown, University of Mississippi

SOLDIER IN HOMESPUN SHIRT

William Decatur Howell in the homespun shirt his mother made him to go to war in. He was a Mississippian and served as private in Forrest's Cavalry.

upon that used in the United States Army prior to the war, was published for the guidance of captains and quartermasters:

	1st year	2nd year	3rd year	Price
Caps, complete	2	1	1	2.00
Cover	1	1	1	.38
Jackets	2	1	1	12.00
Trousers	3	2	2	9.00
Shirts	3	3	3	3.00
Drawers	3	2	2	3.00
Shoes	4	4	4	6.00
Socks	4	4	4	1.00
Leather stock	1			.25
Great coat	1			25.00
Stable frock (mounted men)	1	1	1	2.00
Fatigue overalls (engineers, ordnance) ..	1		1	3.00
Blanket	1			7.50 [12]

Company officers were required to keep a record of clothing dispensed—two general issues a year were contemplated, one of winter uniforms in the fall, and the other of summer outfits in the spring—and soldiers who did not draw the full amount allowed were to be credited on the pay roll with the value of articles due them; on the other hand, those who overdrew their allowances were to be charged in like manner with items received in excess of the quantity authorized.[13]

Notwithstanding the intention expressed by the act of October 8, 1862, the clothing issued by government quartermasters deviated considerably from Army Regulations. Blue trousers, for instance, seem to have been the rare exception rather than the rule. Certainly the impression derived from soldier correspondence is that gray was the standard color for trousers as well as coats, and this impression is corroborated by wartime uniforms on display in various Confederate museums. But the cadet gray of 1861 and 1862 gradually gave way, as the blockade drove the South to an increasing dependence on her own resources, to a yellowish brown resulting from the use of dye made of copperas and walnut hulls. This peculiar tint was dubbed butternut, and so wide was its use for uniforms that Confederate soldiers were rather generally referred to by both Yanks and Southerners as "butternuts." [14]

In a few instances at least, undyed outfits were issued by the government. The Second Texas Regiment was the recipient of such an issue a few days before leaving Corinth for Shiloh. When the men beheld the whitish-looking garments exclamations of the most unorthodox character went up on every hand such as "Well, I'll be damn'!" "Don't them things beat hell?" "Do the generals expect us to be killed and want us to wear our shrouds?" After the battle a Federal prisoner was said to have inquired: "Who were them hell cats that went into battle dressed in their graveclothes?" [15]

Boots soon proved ill adapted to hard marching and were replaced by more practicable and serviceable brogans. Short-waisted, single-breasted jackets took the place of coats so pervasively as to fasten irrevocably on Rebs the name "gray jackets."

Caps and havelocks prescribed by regulations may have been issued in considerable numbers, but hats were the prevailing vogue. Soft hats were preferred not only because they were more comfortable, but also because they gave greater protection from sun and rain; and at night they made "capital pillows." [16] Shapes varied from high-crowned "bee-gums" to low-topped bowlers, but the medium-brimmed slouch was by far the most popular. Not infrequently a Reb of modish bent pinned up the brim on one side of his hat and stuck in a feather.

The "Tiger Rifles" of New Orleans yielded even more to the decorative urge. Every man of the company in 1861 painted a picture or a motto on the band of his hat. Typical slogans were: "Lincoln's Life or a Tiger's Death," "Tiger by Nature," "Tiger during the War," "Tiger on the Leap," "Tiger—Try Me," "Tiger in Search of a Black Republican," "Tiger Bound for the Happy Land," and "Tiger in Search of Abe." [17]

It is doubtful if cravats were dispensed in any considerable numbers. Certainly they were not popular among seasoned soldiers. The attitude toward such nonessentials as ties is typified by a statement made by an Alabamian in a letter to his brother. "I . . . receive . . . the bundle you sent me," he wrote, and "can put everything to advantage except the cravat—If I was to put it on the Boys would laugh at me." [18]

Rebs who drew clothes from the government complained frequently of misfits. Trousers and sleeves were too long or too short, and coats were cut on too skimpy a scale. "We all look like a set of school boys," wrote a Louisianian after an issue of clothes early in the war.[19] Sometimes the ill-fitting garments were sent home to be remodeled by wives or mothers. In other instances, soldiers traded about among their fellows until passable sizes were procured.[20]

The intention implied by the Confederate Government in the law of October 8, 1862, of supplying the major portion of clothing for the army was destined to fall far short of fulfillment. The tightening of the blockade and the shortage of specie prevented the importation after 1863 of large quantities from Europe. The failure of importation was offset to a considerable extent by increased production of Southern factories. But the output of many of these establishments was gobbled up by state authorities, who insisted on outfitting their own soldiers and collecting commutation from the central government.

This would have been well enough if the supplies procured by each of the states beyond the needs of her own troops had been made available to Richmond authorities. But overzealous governors like Vance of North Carolina insisted on holding on to huge surpluses against the possible future needs of their own regiments while less fortunate Rebs suffered from deficiencies. North Carolina had forty textile factories in 1864, half as many as all the other Confederate states combined. She claimed the output of these almost exclusively for her own soldiers, despite the fact that she drew large quantities of wool and other raw materials from sister states.[21]

The most damning commentary on the disastrousness of such a shortsighted—though withal "constitutional" and well-meaning—policy is the fact that while Lee complained repeatedly of the raggedness and barefootedness of his men in the war's last winter, Vance hoarded in North Carolina warehouses "92,000 uniforms, great stores of leather and blankets, and his troops in the field were all comfortably clad." [22] This was State's Rights carried to its most costly extreme.

The combined—or perhaps it would be more accurate to say competing—efforts of Confederate and state authorities were unable to keep the majority of Confederate soldiers supplied with adequate and comfortable clothing. To meet deficiencies various expedients were invoked by Rebs themselves. One of these was to call on the folks at home. Letters to wives and parents, particularly those written during the winter months, were full of requests for garments of various sorts and for blankets.

In response to these importunities wives, mothers, and sweethearts, in co-operation sometimes with groups of slaves, brought forth spinning wheels and looms from outhouse and attic and set up home factories that rivaled the production of the more elaborate establishments of town and city. Jackets, trousers, hats, shirts, drawers, socks and other articles made by individual women and by soldiers' aid societies were packed in boxes and sent to camp on trains, or carried in small bundles by body servants or comrades on furlough.

Many soldiers preferred homemade clothing to that issued by the government, both for comfort and for durability. An Alabamian, who received garments from his wife regularly, wrote in the spring of 1864:

"Bettie I send you a couple of shirts and a pair of drawers. Use them as you please. I had rather wear your make. The reason I drew them was that they are so much cheaper than you can make them. You can use them in making clothes for the children." [23]

Soldiers who were short of clothing frequently borrowed the needed articles from messmates or kinsmen. A striking instance of fraternal assistance is revealed by the letter of a Texan to his sister in 1863.

"Me Joe and Grace all got together yesterday for the first time. Grace was the gladest fellow to see us that ever came a long he . . . is all most naked his Breeches is in strings all he has got fit to ware is a over shirt Joe gave him a par of drass [drawers] & shirt I gave him a par of breeches all I have except what I have on." [24]

When a Reb received fancy additions to his wardrobe from home-folk he was apt to be besieged for loans by socially minded fellows. A Mississippian wrote his mother in the spring of 1864:

"My Hat and boots are the admiration of all the Boys they all want them two of the Boys went out Courting the next day after I got here. I had to loan one my Hat and the other my overshirt." [25]

If a soldier had a little money to spare, he sometimes replenished his wardrobe by purchasing sundry items from comrades who were more amply supplied than himself. Now and then penny-wise Rebs capitalized on the near-nakedness of fellow soldiers by peddling among them at a profit clothing received from homefolk. A Virginian who had just returned from furlough with surplus apparel wrote to his wife:

"I sold my pants, vest, shoes, & drawers for sixtyone dollars so you see I am flush again. . . . You will have to make me more pants and drawers, if you can raise the material make two pair of pants & four pair of drawers & I will have A pair of pants & two pair of drawers for sale in that way will get mine clear . . . if you could make up a good supply of pants vests shirts and drawers, I could be detailed out to come after them."

A postscript was added cautioning her not to "tell any one what good pairs pants will bring in camp if they knew it they would go to peddling in clothes keep dark whether you make any for sale or not." [26] In some portions of the army the practice was followed of selling at auction the clothing of men who died in camp.[27]

A considerable portion of the Rebel clothing deficiency was supplied by the Federals. The cavalry branch of the service, because of its ability to make swift raids into Yankeedom, profited most in this respect. A Mississippian who was not inclined to exaggeration wrote his mother just after Christmas in 1862 that he had recently seen about six thousand cavalrymen pass his post and "every man had a complete Yankee Suit consisting of hats coats pants Jackets and boots." [28]

Infantrymen frequently did well by themselves in the wake of a battle. The writer's great-uncle told of a comrade who lost an arm on the night of the battle of Raymond, Mississippi, attempting to appropriate the uniform of one whom he thought to be a dead Yankee. The practice of reshoeing at the expense of dead and live Yankees was so common that the remark became trite among troops, "All a Yankee is worth is his shoes." [29]

Following the battle of Shiloh a newspaper correspondent wrote from Corinth that "other results of our victory are also everywhere visible. Unless he knew better, a stranger would mistake our army for first rate Yankees. Fully three-fifths of the men are dressed in Federal hats and overcoats." [30]

The practice of wearing Union uniforms was apt to be disastrous if persisted in during a period of active campaigning. General orders were issued repeatedly enjoining the custom, but seemingly to no greater avail than to have a portion of the forbidden articles laid aside. In many companies the combination of butternut jacket and Yankee pants came to be so prevalent as to be considered in an unofficial way as the standard uniform.[31]

The following general order issued by Forrest in December 1864 indicates one method which was used to make practicable the wearing of captured clothing:

"All men & officers belonging to this command who have blue yankee overcoats & clothing and who do not have them dyed by the 20th Inst *The Coats Especially* will be taken from them. . . . Division Commanders will order an inspection on the date above specified and see that this order is complied with. And in an instance when the Inspectors find the coats have not been dyed, they will be taken from the owners and turned over to the Qr M of The Division." [32]

But despite all the exertions of Confederate and state authorities, of soldiers and their families, and the enforced contributions of the Yankees, frazzled uniforms were much in evidence in Rebel ranks after the first half-year of conflict, and as a general rule raggedness increased as the war progressed. Rare indeed was that veteran who did not have occasion in 1863 and 1864 to inform his homefolk of embarrassing circumstances as to the seat of his britches.

"The 16th section of my uniform pants wore out," wrote one Reb to his wife, and another confided to his sister that he had been compelled to buy a new pair of trousers "as I had a 'flag of truce' hanging from a prominent part of my old 'uns." [33] But it remained for a Texan to sum up the situation in general. "In this army," he wrote from near Atlanta in June 1864, "one hole in the seat of the breeches indicates a captain, two holes a lieutenant, and the seat of the pants all out indicates that the individual is a private." [34]

A great many of the soldiers carried little sewing kits—called housewives—with which to keep their uniforms in repair. The results of rehabilitory measures were as amusing as they were varied.

"John Wilson and myself has been patching the seat of our britches this morning," wrote S. G. Pryor to his wife in the summer of 1861. "John puckered his patch bad but I got mine on finely as good as a heap of women would do that has a house full of children. . . . I can beat anybody that I've seen attempt it yet in camp." [35] "We are getting so we can do anything," boasted a Mississippian of Bragg's army. "Dr. Tankersly had a pair of Drawers that were too small and I had a pair that were too large. So we cut a piece out of mine and spliced his. So we have got a pair of Drawers better for both." [36]

Practice in patching undoubtedly led to improved technique among Rebel seamsters, and some attained such deftness with scissors and needle as to abandon the more prosaic modes of repair for fancy designs. One morning Ben Lambert appeared at roll call displaying on the seat of his britches a large red flannel patch, shaped after the fashion of a heart. This example unloosed a plethora of aesthetic efforts among Lambert's comrades of the Richmond Howitzers, and soon trousers that had a short time before been showing white in the rear were splashed with figures of eagles, horses, cows and cannon. One artist depicted on

one hip Cupid holding his bow, and just across on the other, in tribute
to the Love God's dead-eye marksmanship, was a heart pierced with an
arrow—all done in flaming red cloth.[37] Johnnies would have their fun,
at the expense of their woes.

But there were many soldiers who either spurned the use of the
needle or else felt unequal to its manipulation. Such men frequently
invoked the assistance of women living in the environs of camp or
sent tattered garments home for repair. In innumerable instances,
however, Rebs took no remedial steps whatever, but simply wore their
rags with the splendid indifference of seasoned campaigners.

To this spirit of indifference, indeed, must be attributed much of
the raggedness which Confederates suffered. The beginning of almost
every march was the occasion of a general discarding of surplus items
of clothing, for veteran soldiers made a fetish of traveling light.

The observation of a Georgia captain in early 1863 was widely
applicable. "The Company begins to look as ragged as ours ever did,"
he wrote; "the cause of it is that they have to toat their extra clothing
and rather than toat it they wont have it." [38]

The tendency to get rid of extra garments was accentuated during
the pressure of battle and of retreat. A Reb who during the withdrawal from the North Carolina coastal area in 1862 had lost everything but the sparse uniform he was wearing wrote significantly to his
mother:

"The fight we had the other day has taught me one thing, and that
is never to carry anything more with me than I absolutely need and
can carry on my back in case of necessity. It will not do to try to play
soldier and gentleman at the same time. . . . You must take it rough." [39]

Doubtless it was this philosophy that caused many Rebs to forego
without complaint some of the garments ordinarily deemed indispensable by civilized peoples. "I would like to have a pr socks," wrote
a Mississippian to his mother in 1862, but "I can dispense with
draw[er]s." [40]

A factor contributing markedly to the unhappy state of soldier
wardrobes was the infrequency of launderings. Negro body servants
and government-paid washerwomen may have been fairly ample for the
laundry needs of the army in the early months of the war, but after
1862 most of the common soldiers had to do their own washing.[41] The
situation was further complicated by a widespread scarcity of soap,

dating from early in the war. In the summer of 1862 a Reb wrote disgustedly to his mother:

"Soap seems to have given out entirely in the Confederacy & consequently it is almost impossible to have any clean clothes. I am with out drawers today both pair of mine being so dirty that I cant stand them." [42]

Cold water, no soap, and dirty clothes was a combination-complaint found in many soldier letters.

But possession of all the facilities for washing would have availed little during periods of active campaigning when men had to spend the daylight hours of week after week marching and fighting. If perchance there was a short respite, the need to rest was usually so strong as to make filth preferable to further exertion. If a Reb did muster the energy to seek out a creek and wash his clothes, he was frequently compelled by lack of a change to loll about unclothed until the laundered articles were dry enough to put on.

When these circumstances are considered, along with the fact that there were always some who were deterred from washings by sheer indolence, it is not surprising frequently to find in wartime correspondence instances of Rebs going for two, three and four weeks without once removing their shirts, trousers or underclothing. And there were cases of considerably longer duration. A Georgian wrote his wife in 1864 that some of his comrades had gone for two months without stripping, and a Texan testified early in 1865 that "something ner half of the command has not changed shirts for 4 or 5 months." [43] An inevitable consequence of practices such as these was a premature rotting of clothing that could ill be spared.

Deficiencies in clothing varied, of course, from time to time and from organization to organization. North Carolina troops seem generally, as a result of the jealous exertions of their governor, to have fared better than those from other portions of the country. Border-state troops probably suffered most of all, on account of inability of their home governments to supplement Confederate issues. An example of the extreme condition to which these orphan regiments might be reduced was the appearance at inspection on a cold November day in 1864 of a group of Missourians dressed in their drawers. [44]

Some articles of clothing were less scarce than others. Of socks, shirts and underclothing the central government seems to have had a fairly ample supply even in the winter of 1864-1865; want of these items must have been largely due, therefore, to failure of transportation or to delinquency of low-ranking quartermasters.[45] Overcoats and blankets were generally hard to get after the first year of war. Of the conflict's last winter a soldier stationed near Petersburg wrote: "I do not remember the issue of a single overcoat, and but a few blankets." [46] An Englishman who visited Lee's army during the Gettysburg campaign observed that many of the soldiers had blankets made of carpet strips, and that these gaily hued coverlets were adapted to use as overcoats in cool or damp weather by the cutting of holes in the middle, through which the men stuck their heads.[47]

When blankets of no sort could be obtained troops frequently resorted to the expedient of shifting the campfire just before bivouacking and lying down on the earth that had thus been warmed.[48] By occasionally adding rails to smoldering coals during the night, and by "scrooching" up close to his messmates, a Reb might fare tolerably well in dry weather. But rain rendered any degree of comfort impossible. The soldier's only recourse then was to huddle up to a tree and cat-nap as best he could between shivers and showers. "Cussing" the Yankees generally accompanied his sufferings, and his thoughts frequently must have been along the lines expressed by Private Bill Cody: "If we do strike them Yankees again," he wrote during a cool spell of late 1864, "they will get wone of the worst whippings they ever had for the most of the boys are mighty anxious to get a lick at them for some blankets." [49]

But the most pervasive and the most keenly felt of all deficiencies was that of shoes. The Rebel army was a walking army. Soldiers who followed Lee, Jackson, Bragg and other Confederate generals on their long and swift thrusts at the enemy won undying fame for themselves and their leaders. But the expenditure of leather entailed by these arduous marches was tremendous and, as circumstances proved, considerably beyond the producing and purchasing capacities of the South.

Shortage of shoes began to trouble generals and government officials before the war was a year old. Not long after First Manassas Joseph E. Johnston informed Quartermaster-General A. C. Myers that his army needed shoes. Myers replied that "we have sent to Europe for shoes, and I have officers travelling over all the Confederate States purchasing shoes, making contracts with farmers for leather, and with manufacturers for making leather into shoes." He expressed apprehension, however, that he would not be able to meet the demands of increasing mobilization.[50] His fears proved to be well founded. Several thousand pairs of the European purchase arrived in due time on Confederate shores. Contracts with Southern factories yielded considerably more. But the approach of cool weather in 1862 found troops in decidedly greater need of shoes than they had been the previous year.

Shortly before Lee began his march into Maryland a newspaper correspondent estimated that forty thousand pairs of shoes were needed by the army.[51] This estimate may have been exaggerated, but there can be no doubt that thousands of Rebs failed to participate in the fighting of September 16-17 because the condition of their feet made it impossible for them to march with their comrades.[52] It may easily have been true that the difference between a victory and a draw for Lee at Antietam was his want of a few thousand pairs of shoes.[53]

In October and early November, 1862, about ten thousand pairs of shoes were issued to the Army of Northern Virginia, but there still remained in Longstreet's Corps a shortage of over six thousand. A South Carolinian stationed at Culpepper wrote his mother on November 20, 1862:

"I thought that I had experienced a rough time of it last winter but that is nothing in comparison to what we have had to endure lately. There are men in my company who have been barefooted the last month, having to march all the way from Winchester to Culpepper (sixty miles) in that situation—cold and frosty mornings at that." [54]

Congress took cognizance of the deplorable state of affairs by authorizing the detail of two thousand men to make shoes.[55] Extraordinary efforts such as this, plus the reduced wear incident to winter quarters, resulted in a general improvement of the situation in the early months of 1863. But the strenuous campaigns of Gettysburg and Chattanooga played havoc with the government's leather supply, and the winter months of 1863-1864 brought a chorus of complaints from all quarters. An Alabamian wrote to his homefolk from camp on the Rapidan:

"The weather is as cold as the world's charity. I counted out on inspection yesterday, thirty-one men in Battle's Brigade who did not have a sign of a shoe on their feet, yet they are compelled to perform as much duty as those who are well-shod." [56]

A Louisianian serving in the Army of Tennessee noted in his diary of January 3, 1864, that about one-half of the men in his company had refused to do duty on account of being barefooted.[57] In some portions of Lee's army, men gathered up hides from commissary butcheries, traded them for leather, and made their own shoes; and the products of their handwork were said to be considerably better than those obtained from government contractors.[58]

In the Army of Tennessee men tried making moccasins from the raw hides, but results were not satisfactory. One Reb said of his experiment, "I made myself a pair & made a nice Job too they fit Splendid But behold after two or three days drying around the fire they were about two inches too Short behind."[59] Another soldier complained that his rawhide sandals "stretch out at the heel . . . the[y] whip me nearly to death they flop up and down they stink very bad and i have to keep a bush in my hand to keep the flies off of them."[60]

During the early months of 1864 good factory-made shoes were at such a premium that a lieutenant of Johnston's army declared, "It is not safe to pull off shoes & go to sleep or one would wake up minus a pair."[61]

The nadir of deprivation of shoes, and of other clothes as well, seems to have been reached by men who accompanied Hood on the Tennessee campaign during the war's last winter. Many of the troops began the northward movement in November with shoes so worthless that, according to a Reb who went along, they would not endure a week's marching. Consequently hundreds were barefooted before they reached Columbia, Tennessee; and in some brigades, one-fourth of the men marched barefooted over frozen roads from Franklin to Nashville through blasts of sleet and snow, leaving behind them smears of blood.[62]

Retrogression after defeat on December 16 was accompanied by perhaps even greater distress. The rapid marching, necessitated by pressure of Yankee pursuers, took an increasing toll of sole leather. To protect their bleeding feet from the frozen ground men contrived shoes not only of rawhide, but of hats and coat sleeves as well. But these Rebs could still sing, and as they dragged themselves along they lifted their voices in an impromptu adaptation to the old tune "The Yellow Rose of Texas":

> "And now I'm going Southward,
>   For my heart is full of woe,
> I'm going back to Georgia
>   To find my 'Uncle Joe.'

You may sing about your dearest maid,
    And sing of Rosalie,
But the gallant Hood of Texas
    Played hell in Tennessee." [63]

And a remnant did go back, to draw in Mississippi some "sorry" government shoes and in the spring many of them followed "Uncle Joe" Johnston into North Carolina to fight their last battle at Bentonville. By their grim perseverance these veterans of the Army of Tennessee and their comrades of other commands, who marched and fought with ever-dwindling protection from rain and snow through four years of war, achieved for soldiers of the Lost Cause a fame no less lustrous than that won by the heroes of Valley Forge.

CHAPTER VIII

TRIALS OF SOUL

THE South entered the war in the spring of 1861 with high spirit. The people were, with few exceptions, thoroughly convinced of the rightness of their cause—the defense of their homes against tyrannous and godless invaders. They were overwhelmingly confident of success. Men of the South, they thought, accustomed to an active outdoor life, were more robust than factory- and shop-bred Northerners. Southerners were also deemed tougher in temper than Yankees.

Overweening certainty of Rebel superiority was shown in wartime textbooks for the common schools. Johnson's *Elementary Arithmetic*, published in North Carolina, proposed these problems for patriotic youngsters:

"(1) A Confederate soldier captured 8 Yankees each day for 9 successive days; how many did he capture in all? (2) If one Confederate soldier kill 90 Yankees how many Yankees can 10 Confederate soldiers kill? (3) If one Confederate soldier can whip 7 Yankees, how many soldiers can whip 49 Yankees?" [1]

Southerners generally believed that the majority of Northerners were opposed to fighting, and those who were so foolish as to essay conflict with brave secessionists could not stand up under the rigors of battle. The war would doubtless be a short one, but short or long, most of the South's young men wanted to have a part in it—and many of the old ones.

In the flood tide of patriotism which rose during the first months of war there was an irresistible rush to arms. "All Mississippi is in a fever to get to the field, and hail an order to march as the greatest favor you can confer upon them," wrote Governor Pettus to President Davis in May 1861.[2] Everywhere men formed themselves into companies and regiments, with or without authorization, and importunately demanded immediate transfer to camps of instruction, or better still to prospective seats of war. Letters from state officers and from private citizens flooded Richmond authorities asking for induction into Con-

123

federate service, for arms and for assignment to active duty. Secretary of War Walker informed President Davis in July 1861 that applications on file in his office left no doubt "that if arms were only furnished no less than 200,000 additional volunteers for the war would be found in our ranks in less than two months." [3]

Some volunteers were so imbued with ardor that they not only equipped themselves, but also refused to take pay for their army services.[4] The revival-meeting type of zeal which characterized the first days of the Confederacy was further expressed by recruits choosing to sleep in the open when tents were available, and taking over the lowlier duties of army life. In a few instances this ardor ran to fantastic extremes. After one of the early battles a group of prowling Rebs came across a trunk full of United States currency. Such was the rampant state of their patriotism that, according to the recollection of one of them, they "scorned the filthy lucre and consigned it to the flames, only reserving a little as mementoes." [5]

Naturally the first swell of enthusiasm did not continue for long. In fact signs of defection made their appearance while ardor was still at flood stage. These were in connection with the length of service pledged by volunteers. When the war began Richmond authorities accepted troops for a twelve months' period, with equipment to be furnished by the War Department. Shortage of accouterments, combined with maturer consideration, caused Davis and his associates to revise this policy and to equip at Confederate expense only those volunteers who should enlist for three years, or the duration of the war. Twelve-month volunteers would be received, but only on condition that they provide their own equipment.

Announcement of this policy a short time after the fall of Fort Sumter aroused a widespread cry of protest. Some men of moderate means objected on the score that in view of the small compensation of soldiers they could not afford to pledge themselves to so lengthy a service. Non-slaveholders complained that rich men could enlist for the one-year period because of ability to equip themselves, while they, because of their lack of means, were required to enlist for three years or not at all.[6] Thus before a battle was fought, selfishness and class strife were fouling the pure waters of patriotism.

As weeks turned into months enthusiasm for military service gradually dwindled, and long before the passage of the first conscription act of April 1862 the initial flood of volunteering had ebbed to a mere trickle. The first draft law gave new life to volunteering, but it was of a

spiritless sort, occasioned primarily by the desire of men subject to conscription to escape the odium attached to forced service. Each subsequent conscription act was followed by a similar reaction. By August
1863 General Daniel Ruggles was constrained to write that "the spirit
of volunteering has ceased to exist," and the great bulk of available
evidence verifies the approximate correctness of his observation.[7]

After the first enthusiasm had spent its force, not even conscription
could bring the South's available man power into military service. The
policy of forcing enlistment by law was never more than a meager success. Its chief benefit was to hold in the army at critical times men
whose volunteer periods were about to expire, and to stimulate the
immediate enlistment of a small portion of civilians subject to draft.

Coercive acts of the Confederate Congress were subjected to sabo-
tage on every hand. State governors insisted on the exemption of local
defense troops, and thousands of militiamen of conscription age thus escaped Confederate service. Provincial-minded executives like Georgia's
Joe Brown and North Carolina's Zeb Vance went so far as to demand
immunity from draft of many petty officials, including justices of the
peace, on the claim that they were essential to the discharge of governmental functions. They also encouraged resistance to conscription
by declaiming the unconstitutionality of draft laws; and some state
justices added their influence by issuing writs of habeas corpus on
behalf of those held for their violation. Local physicians handed out
certificates of disability with great nonchalance which, until the law
was rectified, conscription officers were bound to accept at face value,
even when presented by the most robust individuals. In many communities public sentiment was so lethargic or so hostile during the last
two years of the war as to defeat all efforts to compel slackers to service.
Granted that the policy of conscription was impaired by defects in
administrative machinery and personnel, the main cause of its failure
must be found in the dwindling morale of the people.[8]

One of the most striking evidences of this was the practice of
evading military service by substitution. As early as the fall of 1861 the
War Department permitted release from the army of volunteers who
presented able-bodied proxies to serve in their stead. The first conscription act sanctioned the practice. A conscriptee, when summoned
to a camp of instruction, might take a substitute with him; if the proxy
upon examination proved to be of sound body and not subject to
military service on his own account, the "principal" was permitted to
return home and the substitute accepted in his place. Only one substi-

tution a month was allowed in each company, but this provision was frequently violated.

Objections to substitution were voiced soon after the policy was initiated, and the protest grew with the declining fortunes of the Confederacy. But the practice increased. Newspapers carried bids for the service of proxies, ranging from about $500 in 1862 to several thousand dollars in the latter part of 1863. Occasionally men not liable to conscription, induced by the lucrative hire and by the bounty which Richmond authorities allowed to enrollees, advertised their availability as substitutes.

Transactions were handled with the detached formality incident to regular trade, by banks, factors and merchants; laws of supply and demand eventually led to the setting up of substitute brokerages. Such a business was naturally accompanied by endless fraud and deceit. Men who were hired as substitutes frequently deserted, sometimes to multiply their gains by repeated substitutions under different names. By connivance with examining authorities, persons of unsound bodies were unlawfully accepted as proxies. Under the best conditions men thus inducted into service were not good soldier material. Many were aliens having little interest in the fortunes of the Confederacy. Most of them were mainly concerned with getting as much money and rendering as little service as possible. In a great many cases, by devising fraudulent papers, men who had no substitutes at all remained out of service on the pretext of having engaged them.

Substitution was originally designed to mitigate the apparent harshness of conscription, for it must be remembered that before the Confederacy's first law a general draft had never been resorted to in America. It was thought too that essential talent for home production would find the necessary release from army service. But the policy did not turn out as expected. Granted, as Howell Cobb pointed out, that a considerable number of men who availed themselves of proxies were substantial and patriotic citizens, all too frequently they were of another sort.[9] In numerous cases men who were released from service resorted to speculation and profiteering. Many of them revealed their true character by fleeing to the North when eventually ordered into the army or by procuring for "a consideration" some petty clerkship in the government offices at Richmond.

The presence of able-bodied men at home in large numbers, especially after Vicksburg and Gettysburg, was in itself the source of great dissatisfaction to men in the army and to their families; disgruntlement was particularly strong among the poorer classes who saw additional proof of their growing conviction that this was "a rich man's war and a poor man's fight." After frequent and futile efforts to purge the substitute system of its defects and abuses, Congress early in 1864 took the bull by the horns and abolished it. But even then there were many hangovers in the form of judicial claims of unconstitutionality.[10]

The number of men who purchased exemption from military service by substitution while the system was in force cannot be ascertained because the War Department records are inadequate. In the summer of 1863 General Bragg estimated the total at 150,000, but this outright guess was probably extravagant.[11] Secretary of War Seddon in his report to the President of November 1863 ventured an estimate of "not less certainly, than 50,000." [12] Seddon's figure is probably conservative. However that may be, the spectacle of nearly as many men as constituted Lee's effective force in the Army of Northern Virginia in the fall of 1863 escaping military responsibilities under the guise of purchased proxies—most of whom rendered poor service or none at all—is a shameful reflection on Confederate patriotism.[13]

While the morale of soldiers seems always to have been better than that of civilians, the army experienced a growing defection of spirit as the conflict went on. Expressions of war-weariness began to creep into their letters after Rebs had undergone only a few months of service. By that time it had become apparent that the Yankees were not to be whipped in one campaign, and camp life had lost the glamor of novelty.

Disillusionment sometimes found its first expression in advice to friends and relatives against volunteering. "I still advise you, and as strongly as ever," wrote an Alabamian to his brother in the spring of 1862, "to not come to the war. I tell you you will repent it if you do I do believe. You have no idea of what it is to be a soldier. . . . and be you assure[d] that if I had your chance to stay out of it I would do [so]. I do think that you would do very wrong to come unless they draught you." [14]

In not a few instances the change of tone as to the joys of soldiering was sudden, being influenced by some unhappy experience. Such was the case of Private Joe Shields.

In June 1861 he wrote enthusiastically from Vicksburg, "Dear Pa, we have arrived here all safe the troops are all in a jolly humor. . . . we are all well we had a pleasant time last night we sleep in the cabin on the floor. . . . I am in good spirits we have such a jolly crowd that a fellow cant have the blues."

A few days later he moved on to Memphis, where he and his comrades suffered disappointment in what they construed as inhospitable reception. Shortly after this experience Shields wrote his folk that "the Troops are all displeased at the treatment" and that "some are in favor of quitting & going either home or to Virginia."

He went to Virginia, but this failed to revive his spirit, for he wrote from Lynchburg on July 1, "Dear Pa . . . I hope you will stay at home for you could not stand it it is too hard a life. . . . I would advise all my friends unless they wish to live like negroes to stay at home I know if there is another war this chicken wont be thar when they enlist." [15]

But the most thorough case of disillusionment encountered by the writer was that of a young Mississippi aristocrat. In April 1861 this man wrote his sister that he had failed of admittance to the Washington Artillery because of his low stature but was drilling in New Orleans with a group of prospective infantrymen. "I am better-fitted for a soldier than anything else," he exulted. "I believe I am brave and not afraid to meet an enemy. . . . I am anxious to go—for I honestly and candidly believe that one Southern man is a match for any two Northern fanatics. . . . If they conquer us we can[t] be anything but rebellious provinces—And if we conquer them we will make them our slaves. . . . If I live I will hand down the name of Mandeville to posterity and to history—And if I perish it will be said I did so gallantly & not from a shot in the back. . . . When I go it will be to make a name."

He succeeded in getting in service a short time later and was sent to Virginia, where he was exposed to some strenuous marching. In August 1861, less than five months after having professed such enthusiasm for soldiering, he wrote his homefolk: "It is the opinion of the people here that we will be home by the first of October & I hope so for I am heartily tired of this life." [16] He died early in 1863, but whether under such circumstances as to make lustrous the name he bore is not known.

The long months of military quietude that followed First Manassas, with its introduction to the tedium of winter quarters, increased considerably the nostalgia and gloom of Confederate camps.

A Louisianian wrote despondingly to his mother in December 1861:

"As to the War I cannot tell when it will end . . . I wish . . . I was home by my own fireside. . . . I have seen quite enough of A Soldiers life to satisfied me that it is not what it is cracked up to be."

With the arrival of the Yule season his lot became almost insufferable, and in January 1862 he proposed to desert if his folk would but say the word.[17]

A homesick Alabamian wintering near Shelbyville, Tennessee, wrote mournfully to his father:

"My shoes is wering out very fast and my pants is warin out as fast as my Shoes is . . . I have bin troubble very bad lately I am heaire and my mind is wit you at home I wish the waire would stop fur I cant live in any pease attall heaire." [18]

A more comprehensive view of the decline in morale that came after a few months of comparatively inactive service was given by General Will T. Martin. In a letter to his wife, written from Virginia on October 20, 1861, he said:

"I am afraid there will be even worse complaints in the army than now exists. There is plenty already. The first flush of patriotism led many a man to join who now regrets it. . . . The prospect of winter here is making the men very restive and they are beginning to resort to all sorts of means to get home." [19]

Some soldiers seem to have experienced the depths of depression during the first winter, for then they felt homesickness at its worst, and they were not yet toughened to the hardships of war. As they became accustomed to separation from loved ones and more thoroughly inured to the discomforts of army life, they suffered less acutely, and consequently bore subsequent winters in camp with more fortitude than the first.

For most of the Rebs, however, greater depths of gloom were yet to come. Resort to conscription in April 1862 was a severe blow to their morale. Many objected to the policy as unconstitutional; others resented deeply the fact that the law deprived them of the privilege of visiting homefolk at the end of their year of volunteered service; still others found fault with the list of exemptions. Not a few saw in forced service an admission of despair on the part of government authorities. The reaction of a South Carolinian serving at Yorktown was typical:

"The Conscript Act will do away with all the patriotism we have. Whenever men are forced to fight they take no personal interest in it. . . . My private opinion is that our Confederacy is gone up, or will go soon. . . . A more oppressive law was never enacted in the most uncivilized country or by the worst of despots." [20]

Active campaigns in the spring, summer and fall of 1862 buoyed morale considerably, but going into winter quarters again, with its implication of another season of conflict, led to an unprecedented wave of war weariness. A Texan wrote his sister from Arkansas in late November, 1862, that he had "enough of Yanks." "I would to God," he added, "that I could do my share of fightin and come home though I see no chance for that." But he consoled himself with the observation, "There is one thing Sure the war cant go on always I will either go up the flew or come home before a graitwhile."

Several weeks later this man wrote another member of his family, "Well Leiza I wish I could tell when this custiard [cursed] war will come to an end. I fear the time is so fare off we will be a ruined people."

His brother was even more outspoken: "God speed the day when that time [war's end] shall come," he wrote, "for I am tired of camp life, especially in this country. it is no pleasur to be away from my folks and if this war dont stop before next fall I am coming home you can look for me in twenty days after white frost." [21]

This second winter's wave of despondency overwhelmed some who hitherto had shown great enthusiasm for army life. A case in point is that of E. J. Ellis of Louisiana. On June 9, 1862, Ellis had written to his mother:

"This war has done me good in many ways—It has taught me patence and endurance & 'to labor & wait'. . . . it has learned me to be less particular in a great many things—when I see dirt in my victuals, I take it out and eat on—If I taste it, I swallow & eat on. . . . If my bed is hard & my head not high enough, I content myself with the idea that it might be worse & go to sleep. . . . I think I have seen the dark side of soldiering and although it is tolerably hard, yet there aint any use of calling it intolerable."

In eight months this Reb's consoling philosophy had petered out, and he was singing a very different tune. "The fact is," he said in commenting on a slight but incapacitating injury suffered by a fellow soldier at Murfreesboro, "I would like first rate to get such a wound.

. . . Oh! wouldnt it be nice to get a 30 days leave and go home and be petted like a baby, and get delicacies to eat . . . and then if I ever run for a little office I could limp and complain of the 'old wound.' "

The passage of another month found him still harboring this idea, though the desired wound was increasing in seriousness. If "some friendly bullet" would "hit me just severely enough to send me home for 60 or 90 days," he wrote wistfully, "I would gladly welcome such a bullet and consider the Yankee who fired it as a good kind fellow." [22]

Numerous other Rebs indulged in similar musings, and according to a story circulating persistently through the camps, at least one soldier tried to carry out his wishes by taking a position behind a tree during battle and waving his arms up and down on either side. An officer who asked the gesticulator what he was doing allegedly received the amazing answer, "I'm feeling for a furlough." [23]

While soldier Ellis was pining for a wound, an Alabama comrade was speculating on the war's termination. "If the soldiers were allowed to settle the matter," he wrote in February 1863, "peace would be made in short order," and he expressed the hope that he and his family might eat watermelons together the next summer.[24] But instead of watermelon cuttings on home lawns, the summer of 1863 brought Vicksburg and Gettysburg. And before the year's end Bragg's Chattanooga battles filled the cup of Confederate disaster to overflowing. Many soldiers came now to despair of ultimate success.

A Georgia Reb home on sick furlough wrote to his brother in camp that his leave had already been extended twice, and if it was not renewed a third time he thought he would just stay at home anyhow. "There is no use fighting any longer no how," he said, "for we are done gon up the Spout the Confederacy is done whiped it is useless to deny it any longger." [25]

Another Georgian, serving in the Army of Northern Virginia, wrote his wife a few weeks after Gettysburg that "the men from N. C. held [a] meeting yes[t]erday I believe they will go back into the Union the men from Ga say that if the enemy invade Ga they are going home I dont believe an army will fight much longer. I know that miny will or would say that I am whiped . . . I would say to them if they would com and see and feel what I have they would feel as I do." [26]

A Mississippian who had heard reports of orders to destroy cotton wrote to his wife in December 1863, "As to cotton being burnt, I have but little to say as I think it & Confederate money will be worth nothing to me in a few months as I think our prospects are growing worse daily." [27]

In the spring of 1864 an Alabamian expressed conviction that "we never can whip the North Fer tha hav so meney moer men [th]an we hav got." [28]

No doubt some of those who succumbed to defeatism at this stage of the war were men who had never felt any strong enthusiasm for the struggle. But that troops of consistently good morale were also affected is seen in the case of Charles Moore, a young Louisianian. Moore, who served with the Army of Northern Virginia, was of unusual buoyancy of spirit. His diary fairly exudes cheerfulness and optimism during the first two years of war. A serious wound at Gettysburg, followed by amputation of his leg, evokes not a word of complaint or of pessimism. But on February 26, 1864, he enters in his journal the despairing note "no use of us fighting," and this was his first hint of despondency.[29]

Governmental and military authorities exerted themselves greatly to stay the tide of pessimism which besieged Rebel camps during the war's third winter. President Davis visited the Army of Tennessee and regaled the soldiers with optimistic sentiments. Confederate and state political leaders followed his example by visiting and addressing this and other portions of the Southern fighting force. The system of furloughs was broadened by some commanders. Sham battles were staged on grand and realistic scale to fire enthusiasm for spring campaigns.[30]

Officers high and low used the technique of suggestion and example with great effectiveness to induce en masse re-enlistment of men whose three-year terms were to expire in the spring of 1864. True, the continued service of these men was required by a recently enacted conscription law, but the gesture of voluntary action was desired as a fillip to general morale. A favorite device of officers to inspire pledges to further service was the assembling of men for dress parade, addressing them in patriotic vein, moving the flags up a few paces ahead, and then asking all those who were willing to re-enlist for the duration of the war to step up to the colors. When the lead was taken, whether by few or many, the impulse for all to follow suit was usually overwhelming.

Such action was recognized in a manner calculated to arouse the patriotism of other units. For example, on February 3, 1864, Lee promulgated General Order Number 14, in which he said: "The commanding general announces with gratification the reenlistment of the regiments of this army for the war. . . . This action gives new cause for the gratitude and admiration of their countrymen. . . . It is hoped," he added significantly, that "this patriotic movement, commenced in the Army of Tennessee will be followed by every brigade of the Army of Northern Virginia, and extend from army to army until the Soldiers of the South stand in one embattled host determined never to yield." He then proceeded to name the batteries, regiments and brigades that had initiated the movement "so honorable to themselves and so pleasing to the country." [31] Congress added the weight of its influence by voting resolutions of thanks to various organizations as they renewed their commitments. In the Army of Tennessee, furloughs at the rate of one to every ten men present for duty were promised to regiments that re-enlisted.[32]

The response of the soldiers delighted the officers. The enthusiasm that accompanied the pledging ceremonies was often unrestrained. Instead of promising renewal of service for three years or the duration, a few regiments of Johnston's army suggested avowal of forty- and fifty-year periods, while the Twentieth Mississippi Regiment proposed re-enlistment for ninety-nine years or the war.[33]

There are inklings, however, that the actual enthusiasm did not keep pace with these outward manifestations. When Georgia regiments accompanied their commitments to extended service with resolutions of censure of Governor Brown and the two Stephenses for non-co-operation with Confederate authorities, Brown retorted that the resolutions "were prepared by the officers before the men were convened, and that only a small portion of the troops attended the ratifying meeting, and of those present only a small part voted." [34] This must be taken with a grain of salt because of the Governor's tendency to extreme statements under duress.

More convincing is the testimony of a sergeant in the Forty-sixth Mississippi Regiment, Army of Tennessee. On March 31, 1864, he wrote in his journal: "On the night of the 25th a meeting of the . . . men of the regiment was called to consider the subject of reenlisting for the war. . . . We reenlisted . . . by adopting some very bold resolution of the original fire eating sort (but which I endorse) and were mustered in for the war." But he added significantly, "I am compelled to say that it was the immediate prospect of obtaining furloughs that induced many of the men to reenlist." [35]

There can be no doubt, however, that the various expedients invoked during the winter of 1863-1864 had a good effect on army morale. Grant's failure to take Richmond during the following summer also

raised the general spirit. But the evacuation of Atlanta, followed by
the march of Sherman's hosts through the heart of the Southland and
Hood's overwhelming disaster at Nashville, caused so deep a depression
in Confederate camps as to set at naught every effort to boost morale.[36]

The increasing despondency is vividly reflected by the tone of letters
coming from camp. "The soldiers are badly out of heart," wrote a
Georgian from Charleston in January 1865, "for they have been a
suffering for nearly four long years and there is no prospect of doing
better." [37] An Alabamian in Lee's army who had previously testified
to the good spirits of his comrades observed about the same time that
"the successful and . . . unopposed march of Sherman through Georgia,
and the complete defeat of Hood in Tennessee, have changed the whole
aspect of affairs." [38] A soldier of the Army of Tennessee returning
from furlough in mid-January was struck by the depression that had
overtaken his fellow soldiers. "When it comes to discussing the prosecution of the war," he said, "they are entirely despondent, being fully
convinced that the Confederacy is gone." [39]

On February 1, 1865, one of Lee's soldiers wrote that "the men is
not a gone [going] to stay in the field any longer for they Say that
they have fout longe a nuff and that they will not fight any more." On
March 19 another observed, "The campaign is a bout to open here and
I think there will bee hard . . . fighting here before they will give up
and it is a nuff to put enney boddy out of hart to think that we will
fight on when we can see at home and in the armey at this time that
we hant done eney thing with the enemy this winter." [40] In view of
the demoralization that pervaded the armies during the war's last winter, formal surrender in the spring had somewhat the character of a
postlude to defeat.

Several factors, in addition to reversals on the field of battle, contributed to the decline of morale in the Confederate Army. Important
among these was the poor quality and meager quantity of the rations.
Rebs proved in countless instances that men can march and fight well
on empty stomachs, but even so, the long continuing and gradually
increasing shortage of food, particularly of meat, was depressing.

"If I ever lose my patriotism, and the 'secesh' spirit dies out," wrote
a private to his homefolk in October 1862, "then you may know the
'Commissary' is at fault. Corn meal mixed with water and tough beef
three times a day will knock the 'Brave Volunteer' under quicker than
Yankee bullets." [41]

This Reb was hitting close to a bull's-eye. In the spring of 1863 some of Bragg's troops refused to drill because of the reduction of their fare to bread made of meal and water. They were put in the guardhouse, but one of their officers expressed apprehension that the Federals might ultimately triumph by starvation of the Southern armies.[42]

General Lee worried chronically about the dangerous consequences of empty haversacks. On January 22, 1864, he wrote the Secretary of War that "short rations are having a bad effect upon the men both morally and physically," and that desertions to the enemy were becoming more frequent as a result. A year later he implored an increase of the food issue to the Army of Northern Virginia in order to combat the alarming tide of absenteeism that had set in.[43] But his efforts were of little avail, and defection increased.

Shortage of clothing did its part. The long marches without shoes made straggling inevitable, and exposure of thinly clad men to the rigors of Tennessee and Virginia winters produced a high degree of discontent.

Even more depressing than their own hardship was the knowledge that wives, children and parents at home were deprived of sufficient food and clothing. An Alabamian wrote to his wife in October 1863 that he was going to try to get a furlough, but if he failed in his efforts he intended to come home anyhow, "for I cant Stand to here," he said, "that you and the children are Sufren for Bread." [44] And thousands of Rebs were moved by just such sentiments to set out for home without benefit of either furlough or discharge.

The conviction of soldiers that they and their families were being swindled by speculators, most of whom were thought to be slackers, was another factor working strongly against morale. The high prices that naturally followed inflation of the currency were widely believed to be the result of shady manipulations by heartless profiteers.

A Mississippian in Lee's army fairly boiled with rage when he heard that in his own community draft dodgers were "cramed down in every hole and corner speculateing and extortioning on those who try to live honest." "I believe," he said, "that such things are going on all over the C. S.," and that "impressing officers have pressed that to which they have no right for the intention of speculation." He decried the effect of such wrongdoing on the prospects of victory for, he opined, "the Old Book says that man can not serve both God & Mamon." [45] Doubtless most soldiers had exaggerated ideas about the prevalence of speculation, but whether they were right or not, their belief had a demoralizing effect on their patriotism.

Failure to receive their pay was another blow to the resolution of the men. The payment allowed by law for infantry and artillery privates was eleven dollars a month.[46] Even under normal conditions this was a miserly sum, but with the constant depreciation of money values the amount shrunk in 1864 and 1865 to the merest pittance. Congress failed to adjust wages to meet inflation. In fact no boost in pay was provided at all until June 1864, when the dilatory legislators at Richmond finally voted an increase of seven dollars a month for all non-commissioned officers and privates.[47] Payment was slow, and when it actually came the money was worth only a fraction of its original value. This fact did not escape pay-conscious Rebs. On March 4, 1864, William P. Chambers recorded in his journal:

"Yesterday we were paid up—wages to Jany. 1, 1864 and commutation for clothing for the year ending Oct. 8; 1863. As the 'old issue' of Confederate notes will soon be worthless, it seems the Treasury Department is very anxious to get rid of it—hence the large installment of wages we received." [48]

Letters and diaries of soldiers, as well as official communications of commanding officers, show that it was not unusual for pay to be six months behind, and in some instances troops went for a year without receiving any money from the government. In despair of getting their pay, not a few Rebs set up an informal business among their comrades in order to make enough money to buy tobacco, stationery and other conveniences. Some peddled eggs obtained from sources that probably would not have borne official investigation; others bought and sold fruit and vegetables. Still others had whiskey, food, clothing and other items sent to them from home for vending in camp. In the fall of 1862 such bargaining became so rife in the Army of Northern Virginia that General Lee issued a prohibitive order.[49]

For the most part discontent over delayed payment was expressed in mere grumbling—which according to one general was the soldier's greatest luxury—but in two cases at least it led to insubordination. A regiment of Pemberton's command in South Carolina gave notice in March 1862 that it would not obey an order to move to the support of Albert Sidney Johnston in Tennessee until it was paid; and two Mississippi companies stacked arms in February 1864 when the signal was given for dress parade, and announced that no more duty of any kind would be performed until they received at least a part of the wages due them.[50]

Photo by U. S. Army Signal Corps

DEAD CONFEDERATE SHARPSHOOTER AT THE DEVIL'S DEN, GETTYSBURG

It is said to be Andrew Hoge, Private, Company E, 4th Virginia Infantry. The identification appears in a note on a copy of this photograph on file in the National Archives Collection of Brady Photographs.

AFTER THE BATTLE

Photograph taken back of rail fence on Hagerstown Pike, September 17, 1862, after the Battle of Antietam.

Dissatisfaction in regard to pay was always widespread, and General Lee in 1865, after investigating the cause of increasing desertion in his army, concluded that "insufficiency of food and non-payment of the troops have more to do with the dissatisfaction . . . than anything else." [51]

The transfer of men to places far from their homes was a common cause of desertion. This was not true early in the war, because it was generally thought that the struggle would be short, and a trip to Virginia or Kentucky was regarded by Louisianians, Texans and others as a sort of holiday excursion. Nor were single men as much affected as those who were married. But after it became apparent that the war was to be long, and that various portions of the South were to be invaded, the thought of being far away from families who were helpless and in danger caused many a Reb to cast longing and uneasy glances toward home.

The question of furloughs also entered into the situation, for leaves seemed harder to get when the distance was great, and even if an absence of forty days was granted poor transportation cut short the stay at home. Then, too, homesickness from natural causes seemed to bear some relation to distance. However sound these latter deductions may be, there can be no doubt that after 1861 men objected strongly to transfers that took them far from home. An order of troop removal from Western Virginia to the vicinity of Richmond in December 1862 provoked wholesale desertion.[52]

A Mississippi regiment that was transferred from its native state to North Georgia in late 1863 made a similar protest. One of its members wrote that "the Ouls caught 45 of our men the night before we started and the next day and night they caught them at every Depot and on the wayside when they run slow I think about 125 of the Regt left us." [53]

But removals of soldiers from west of the Mississippi to points east of the river caused still greater demoralization. The mere rumor of such transfer produced great excitement in a Texas regiment, and the men swore that they would never cross the river. In another Texas group large-scale desertion followed such a report. A soldier of the latter regiment expressed himself thus:

"As for my part I take crossing in mine although it is a bitter pill. I cant believe the present Suffering of the Soldiers will last long this Hell roaring war cant exist long . . . it is rather cool for a man to leave his home exposed to the enemy an[d] go to protect one that is all reddy over run though I cant tell what is best neither do I give a darn blew button." [54]

One reason for the reluctance to grant furloughs to trans-Mississippians was the difficulty of getting them back across the river. A Louisianian said that a colonel of his brigade who was sent across the Mississippi from the Army of Tennessee in 1862 to collect absentees was able to assemble about four hundred men, but that when he started to recross the river with them, all but twenty-five escaped his custody.[55]

Another cause that contributed greatly to the decline of soldier morale was the consolidation of military units. With the dwindling of regiments, brigades and divisions through casualties and absences to small fractions of their full strength in 1863 and 1864, some adjustment had to be found. Recruiting was resorted to, to fill up the ranks, but with slight success. Conscripts and substitutes were frequently scorned by veteran volunteers, and these enrollees dreaded the prospect of being put in with men who would taunt and despise them.[56]

So with the failure to build up skeleton outfits by recruiting, Richmond authorities considered it necessary to combine them. But such a policy ran counter to the pride which old soldiers felt in their organizations, and this pride was too deep-seated to be readily laid aside. A regiment such as the Second Texas Infantry, for instance, jealous of the awe in which it was held by opposing Yankee outfits—as evinced after parole at Vicksburg by the respectful and admiring tone adopted by Federals when they said, "There goes the Second Texas!"—would naturally be unwilling to lose its identity, its battle flags and its hard-won reputation for gallantry on numerous fields of battle, by consolidation late in the war with a miscellany of regiments garnered perhaps from states other than the glorious Lone Star Republic.[57] And when such fusions were pushed down their throats, consequences were apt to be disastrous.

"Our Brigade has been cut up," wrote a Mississippian in 1862, "25 La. 30 Miss & 37 Miss . . . put into other Brigades and Anderson has taken 2 Florida Regts Our Regt is a brag Regt & . . . we are dissatisfied now." [58] Another Mississippian wrote early in 1865, "The boys do not like the consolodating of the companys . . . and . . . some . . . . has run away . . . I do not think [the others] will stay here much longer." [59]

In numerous cases officers testified to the harmful effect on morale of such combinations. "Both officers and men bitterly object," wrote an inspector of Gordon's division in 1864; "strange officers command strange troops," and "old organizations feel that they have lost their identity and are without the chance of perpetuating the distinct and separate history of which they were once so proud." [60]

The dismounting of cavalry outfits aroused even more discontent than the consolidation of infantrymen. Yet the heavy loss of horses through battle casualties, overuse and undernourishment made it necessary sometimes to convert cavalrymen into foot soldiers. The mere proposal of such an action, however, would almost invariably cause a wave of desertion.[61]

The matter of furloughs was a tremendous source of discontent. Any request for leave had to run a long gamut of approvals, and frequently action came only after months of delay. While soldiers waited they naturally chafed. When their requests were finally acted on they were generally refused. This led to a conviction that those in authority were heartless and unreasonable.

Then, there always seemed to be grounds for finding partiality in cases where furloughs were granted, and these were seized upon and magnified by those who were disappointed. Married men complained that single comrades were preferred, and vice versa; poor men were convinced that wealthy men were favored, privates grumbled that officers received a disproportionate share of leaves.

But the greatest dissatisfaction came from the failure of military authorities to grant furloughs which had been promised as rewards for re-enlistment, for procuring recruits and for returning deserters. The answer of those in authority to such complaints was that change in the military situation, increase of desertion, or overstaying of leaves that had been granted made impossible the fulfilment of agreements as made. But to homesick soldiers who after long effort had earned promise of á visit with homefolk, all such excuses seemed utterly invalid. The natural reaction was to "go anyhow," and thousands did.

Mistreatment by officers, fancied or real, in matters other than furloughs was often a factor in demoralization. One Deter Jochum wrote to his mother in 1864:

"The tiranny of officers is as great as can be the numerous desertions which occur at every retreat of ours is mainly caused by the tyranny of officers with their high pay they enjoy themselves no matter how high the prices while the poor soldier suffers." [62]

Sensitiveness to authority was unusually keen among the less literate classes of Rebs. The sharpness of reaction in such cases is vividly illustrated by a Texan's letter to his homefolk:

"We see hard times, and you can guess it is tolerable bad for me as I am Not allowed the chance of a dog I have come to The conclusion that I will stay and tuff it out with Col Young and then he can go to Hell for my part you know that if any one will try to do I can get along with Them but when they get Hell in their Neck I cant do any thing with them and so I don't Try if a man treats me well I will stick up to Him till I die and then see that my spirit helps him when I am gone to my long Home but he has acted the dam dog and I cant tell him so if I do they will put me in the Guard House . . . but I can tell him what I think of him when this war ends and as to go with him I wont do it to save his life . . . I will come [home] when my time is out or die I wont be run over no longer not to please no officers they have acted the rascal with me . . . I am so sick of war that I dont want to heare it any more till old Abes time is out and then let a man say war to me and I will choke him." [63]

Extravagant words, obviously, but there can be no doubt of the depth of his resentment and dissatisfaction, or of numerous parallels among fellow soldiers.

No small portion of the dissatisfaction in the Confederate Army must be attributed to the drabness of camp routine. Most Rebs were country bred, and to men accustomed to the freedom of field and farm an existence regulated in every detail by drum beats and bugle blasts was particularly distasteful.

"Oh how tiresome this camp life to me," wrote a Mississippian, in 1864, "one everlasting monotone, yesterday, today & tomorrow." [64]

Another had written several months previously, "I sometimes get very much vext at . . . [drill] orders and am all must fit to bite my lips. So very much so that I dont think I will ever waunt to hear of one a gain. nor hear the naim of officer dril are [or] Soldier gard or detail eny more after peace is made. Oh how glad I will be when the day comes that We . . . never . . . hear the Tap of a drum a gain which bids us rise and drill." [65]

Still another expostulated, "When this war is over I will whip the man that says 'fall in' to me." [66] The endless chore of guarding, marching, reveille and roll call made doubly sweet the prospects of home.

"If I was Jest free I would Com Back to old Coosy in a hery," wrote a nostalgic Alabamian. "I expect to spend my days in old Coosa if I get Back." [67] But this was only the summer of 1862, and for him and multiplied scores of chafing comrades, months of soul-trying monotony still lay ahead.

Added to military disaster, deprivation of food, clothing and pay, highhandedness of officers, loss of regimental identity, and the intolerable boredom of camp were still other factors tending to demoralize. Some soldiers whose spirit remained strong under all other hardships were revolted by the apparently futile slaughter of the war's last years; others were crushed by the repeated lamentations of their homefolk; still others were broken by the stench and filth of their surroundings; not a few were dispirited by squabbling and inefficiency among commanding officers and governmental authorities; and most depressing of all were the multiplying evidences of greed, selfishness, and ebbing patriotism that permeated army and citizenry alike after the summer campaign of 1863.

Declining morale revealed itself in several ways besides those already noted. One of these was the evading of responsibility by feigning sickness. This subterfuge, referred to as "playing old soldier" by Rebs, made its appearance early in the war.

In June 1861 William R. Barksdale wrote from a camp near Harper's Ferry that "many are reported sick who have little or nothing the matter but only desire to avoid drill. It reminds me of Jake and his chills to see some of these fellows drooping about here trying to look sick." [68] In spite of the efforts of officers and surgeons to put a stop to such shamming, it continued to flourish throughout the war. The prospect of a hard march, of a turn on picket, or of some other unpleasant duty almost invariably produced a swelling of the sick lists.

A less frequent resort to avoid service was the self-infliction of an injury of some sort. One Reb shot himself in the foot, and another in the hand, to escape service. A Louisianian amputated some of his fingers. A South Carolinian secured sick leave by making his arm sore, and extended his sojourn in the infirmary by tampering with the wound. Another South Carolinian managed to keep himself hospitalized for the greater part of the war by aggravating the infection of a toe.[69]

But physical disabling was a serious business. A much more common ruse to evade service was that of getting detailed to some softer assignment than soldiering. "When a person gets a Government contract or agency," wrote Lee to Seddon in 1863, "his first endeavor appears to be to get his friends out of the army in order to help him.

Then there are hundreds who go home on sick furloughs, and while there look out for places to which to be detailed, and forward petitions, stating in strong terms the necessity, &c, inclosing surgeons' certificates showing their competency for that work and no other. . . . There are some regiments reduced almost to insignificance by these details." [70]

After adoption of conscription many would-be slackers sought release from the army by claiming exemption on the basis of age, of election to state office, or of coming under the provision allowing immunity from service for ownership of fifteen or twenty slaves. And in numerous cases, by resort to the writ of habeas corpus, such shirkers were successful in obtaining discharges.[71]

A favorite practice was to secure transfer, by regular means or otherwise, to free-booting cavalry outfits or to state organizations in which duties were comparatively light. The prevalence of this practice is convincingly attested by the frequent complaints of departmental commanders and of other high-ranking officers that leaders of independent scouts, partisan rangers and home guards had recruited large numbers of infantry absentees. Such irregularities were invalidated and denounced repeatedly by Richmond authorities, but return of one of these infantrymen to his regular connection involved difficulties so vast that it was seldom accomplished. And the indications are that literally thousands of demoralized Rebs used these shady attachments to effect their escape from the full service due the Confederate Government.

Another method of dodging duty was abuse of the furlough system. Some soldiers, particularly those of partisan ranger companies, connived with their captains to secure leaves without authority from higher officers. Others purchased furloughs from comrades who had legally received them, for considerations ranging from twenty-five dollars to a horse. Others "bought" recruits—i.e. paid men to enlist in their outfits—so that they might secure the forty-day furlough authorized for each addition to the army. Still others told their parents to write letters to commanding officers telling of woeful conditions at home. And some Rebs went so far as to write their own furloughs, and "got by" with it.

Once arrived at home, they found great temptation to prolong the leave. And in countless instances some means of extension were found. A favorite technique was to get a local doctor to write a note saying that the absentee was ill, attaching a certificate of disability, and to mail this to army headquarters; another device was to overstay the furlough for a few days, then on reaching camp to tell of broken-down transportation, the rising of swollen streams or some other hindering act of man or God. Such events were actually frequent enough to make the stories plausible.

By far the most striking manifestation of sagging morale was the increase in the number of soldiers improperly absent from places of duty. Included among these were: first, men absent without leave, such as convalescents who failed to report for duty as ordered, troops who straggled from the ranks on the march, and those overstaying their furloughs; second, soldiers absent with leave, but not in accord with policies authorized by highest authorities; third, men absent under improperly granted detail; fourth, troops serving with organizations other than those to which they were regularly assigned; and fifth, men who without benefit of disguising techniques deserted to the enemy or to the protecting fastnesses of native mountains, swamps and forests.[72]

Unwarranted absentees, as all those who took leave of their assigned duties without proper authorization may be conveniently called, became a source of concern for Confederate leaders very early in the war. Their number was considerably boosted by the announcement in the spring of 1862 that all soldiers between eighteen and thirty-five years of age whose one-year terms of enlistment were about to expire would be held to continued service by conscription. This forcing of unwilling men to prolonged army connection, and induction after April 1862 of draftees whose spirits were already damaged by exposure to such epithets as slackers and conscripts, further enhanced the lists of improper leave-takers. General Lee was deprived of from one-third to one-half of his effective fighting force on the Antietam campaign by straggling; after his return to Virginia he wrote to Davis that "desertion and straggling . . . were the main causes of . . . retiring from Maryland." [73] Remedial legislation was sought by the President, and state governors were asked to co-operate in bringing shirkers to justice. But these efforts were only temporarily effective.

After the disasters of July 1863 leave-taking waxed greater in volume and boldness. Pemberton's men flocked home in such numbers following their parole at Vicksburg that Davis was forced to forego his desire to hold them together pending exchange, and instead to give the general leave-taking a semblance of validity by granting wholesale furloughs.[74] In the wake of Gettysburg the highways of Virginia were crowded daily with homeward-bound troops, still in possession of full accouterments; and, according to one observer, these men "when halted and asked for their furloughs or their authority to be absent from their commands, . . . just pat their guns defiantly and say 'this is my furlough,' and even enrolling officers turn away as peaceably as possible." [75]

The Assistant Secretary of War estimated at this time that the number of soldiers evading service by devious means, but chiefly by unauthorized absence, reached 50,000 to 100,000.[76]

Once arrived in their home country, these men from the mountains of North Carolina, Georgia, Virginia, Tennessee and Arkansas, from the piny woods of Alabama and Mississippi and from the lowlands of Florida, were wont to organize themselves into armed bands. In this way they were able to defy, with few exceptions, all efforts of Confederate authorities to bring them to justice. Secret societies, with imposing signs and rituals, were also formed for self-protection and for urging the cessation of war; to this latter end connivance with Federals, even to the extent of making friendly signs in battle to avoid being shot, was furthered.[77]

Many of the deserters were consistent Union sympathizers conscripted into the army against their will. Such was the case with a Georgia private who wrote his father in 1863:

"I am this day as strong a Union man as ever walked the soil of Va. I would hate to desert but if I ever get a good chance I will be sure to do it. I never expect to kill a Union man." [78]

Others were persons who, because of extreme youth or of little learning, had never gained a clear idea of what the war was about and consequently had little concern as to its outcome or little conception of the seriousness of desertion. Still others felt that they had to choose between continuing army service and returning home to rescue families from starvation, and they chose the latter. Some were cowards, but there were many whose bravery had been proved on the field of battle.

The defeats and privations of 1864 were accompanied by an alarming increase of unwarranted absenteeism. General Lee wrote apprehensively of the thinning of his ranks in August, and Secretary Seddon observed in September that "desertion is committed almost with impunity." [79] President Davis, according to the Richmond Enquirer of October 6, "emphatically announced the startling fact that two-thirds of the army are absent from the ranks."

The three months preceding Appomattox saw an ever mounting tide of leave-taking. Small groups of men assigned to picket duty slipped away nightly from their posts all along the Virginia front; scores of others took advantage of the cover of darkness to crawl from the trenches. In the retreat from Nashville Hood's troops straggled by the hundreds, never to rejoin their commands. Across the Mississippi 400 of General Price's men deserted in one day of February 1865.[80] Between February 26 and March 8, 779 men deserted from the Army of Northern Virginia, according to a report of General Lee, and from March 15 to 25, 1,094; in one instance an entire brigade deserted en masse.[81]

John S. Preston, Superintendent of the Bureau of Conscription, stated in February 1865 that there were over 100,000 deserters scattered throughout the Confederacy, and compilations from other sources indicate that his estimate is conservative.[82] But, as stated previously, figures for desertion tell only part of the story; unfortunately, due to lack of data covering absence other than desertion, the complete tale cannot be told.

There is significant information, however, in a composite tabulation prepared by the War Department from the last returns sent in by the various armies. This compilation shows a total of 198,494 officers and men absent and only 160,198 present in the armies of the Confederacy on the eve of surrender.[83] The figure for absentees includes of course those excused for wounds, sickness and other legitimate purposes, but even so, it is shamefully large. Interpreted most generously, available evidence is such as to merit the observation that months before Appomattox the Confederacy's doom was plainly written in the ever swelling tide of men who were unpatriotically taking leave of their comrades-in-arms.

But in the midst of all the defection that cursed the Confederacy, and in the face of increasing hardship, there were a large number of Rebs whose spirit remained strong. It is pleasant to turn from the woeful subject of evasion to consideration of those who stood firm at their posts of duty.

Morale seems to have been considerably better among the upper and middle classes than it was among less privileged groups. This better spirit can be attributed not so much to the greater material stake involved as to intangible factors of education, travel, experience and self-confidence. A broad background led to a more wholesome point of view and to greater adaptability. Aristocratic organizations like the Washington Artillery, the Mobile Cadets and the Richmond Blues were able to maintain a consistently higher morale than were the toughest of mountaineer troops.[84] And desertion was noticeably worse among soldiers of lower classes than it was among those of moderate and superior means.[85] But there were, of course, innumerable instances of strongheartedness among the humblest of Rebs.

A patriotic and optimistic attitude on the part of friends and relatives at home was a powerful stimulant to soldier morale. The will to persevere must have been strengthened by a note such as that penned by Mollie Vanderberg to her sweetheart in the army:

"Dear Henry,

"I feel more lonely and sad than I have been in some time—perhaps tis because the last companie have taken off nearly all of the gentlemen I respect in Texas. . . . Oh! that I knew what the termination of this awful conflict would be. Henry I want to see you but dont you come—join for the War if tis forty years if you get killed tis the most honorable death—if you escape I will rejoice. I love thee still." [86]

Likewise, the attitude of a father such as that of C. L. Stephens must have been an effective deterrent to desertion. "I have not tolde you Pa's sentiment about this war," wrote Stephens to his cousin in March 1865. "Some time he is in mighty good spirits and at another time he is out of heart but he does not believe in desertion atall he told me when I was at home [on furlough] that he did not want none of his boys to desert and ly in the woods . . . that he had reather [lose] our wate in gold than for any of us to runaway . . . I had rather die than to runaway myself." [87]

But the morale of many Rebs remained good in spite of expressions of gloom on the part of homefolk, as shown by statements of mild censure in letters sent home. "I am sorry . . . the people at home are whipped," wrote a Georgian to his father, in the spring of 1864; "Yes more than whipped. Some are both whipped and defeated. The army lacks a great deal of being whipped." [88] Several months later while dark clouds of defeat were overcasting Confederate skies a Mississippian observed to a fellow soldier, "Citizens seem very gloomy and desponding about our cause but this Army still retains its high spirits: we are all sanguine." [89]

Statements of soldiers about the general morale of the army cannot be accepted at face value when addressed to homefolk, because optimistic letters were sometimes merely attempts at lightening depression. But there is considerable significance in the very fact that men in the army must often rouse the lagging spirits of those at home.

The dogged and cheerful performance of duty in the most trying circumstances repeatedly testified to the staunch-heartedness of a portion of the army from beginning to end of the conflict. After the strenuous campaign about Yorktown in the spring of 1862 General J. B. Magruder reported that "from April 4 to May 3 this army served without relief in the trenches. Many companies of artillery were never relieved during this long period. It rained almost incessantly; the trenches were filled with water; the weather was exceedingly cold; no fires could be allowed; the artillery . . . of the enemy played upon our men almost continuously day and night; the army . . . subsisted on flour and salt meat, and that in reduced quantities, and yet no murmurs were heard . . . patriotism made them indifferent to suffering, disease, danger, and death." [90]

After the terrible ordeal of Vicksburg, where men lived for forty-seven days and nights under almost constant shelling, nourished by the scantiest of rations and by maggot-infested water, officers of several units testified to a dauntless spirit. Colonel Ashabel Smith of the Second Texas infantry said that "up to the last moment of siege the men bore with unrepining cheerfulness" the overwhelming hardships which they experienced. "When I think of their buoyant courage under these circumstances," he added, and "the alacrity with which they performed every duty, it appears to me no commendation of those soldiers can be too great."

General F. A. Shoup gave similar testimony of the spirit of his brigade. Concerning the capitulation he said:

"At 10:00 A. M. [July 4] we moved out of our trenches by battalion, stacked arms, and then returned to our old quarters in town. The men were full of indignation [because of the surrender]. . . . I have rarely heard a murmur of complaint. The tone has always been, 'this is pretty hard, but we can stand it.' " [91]

Admitting in these cases, as well as in others, a tendency of officers in official reports to overpraise the conduct of their men, there remains substantial evidence of the highest kind of courage and determination.

Shortly after General Lee had driven Meade back across the Rappahannock in the fall of 1863, he wrote to Secretary Seddon:

"Nothing prevented my continuing in his front but the destitute condition of the men, thousands of whom are barefooted, a great number partially shod, and nearly all without overcoats, blankets, or warm clothing. I think the sublimest sight of the war was the cheerfulness and alacrity exhibited by this army in the pursuit of the enemy under all the trials and privations to which it was exposed." [92]

One reason for this high morale in the face of great want was the inurement of the men to hardship, accompanied by a sort of do-or-die reaction. An Alabama captain noticed this tendency in his company. After the terrible suffering experienced by Longstreet's command in the war's third winter, he wrote to his father:

"If anyone had told me before the war that men could have borne for month after month . . . what we have, I would have thought it all talk. And I recollect when we first came into the service we grumbled at fare that we would now think the greatest luxuries." [93]

Three privates of Lee's army stated the viewpoint of common soldiers hardened to adversity. "I am in good spirits myself," wrote one in December 1863; "whenever I hear of a misfortune instead of its giveing me the blews it prepars me for battle & I feel like striveing to regane that which is lost." A second observed in May 1864, "As for myself, I am getting pretty tired of it, but am not ready yet a while to say Enought. I think I can stand thru three more years yet and I think before that time they [the Yankees] will get Middling tired of it." The third wrote during the latter stages of the Wilderness campaign: "I am been quite sick with fever for the last 4 or 5 days. They want me to go to Richmond but I am determined to see this fight out if it costs me my life." [94]

Even in the midst of all the shirking and defeatism that marked the last year of war there was much disapproval of the widespread defection. "Let a man try to 'play out' now by feigning disability," wrote a participant in the Atlanta campaign, "and he is jeered at and when exposed by the Surgeons he is greeted with shouts of derision." [95] A Louisianian aired his opinion against the seekers of soft appointments. "I have a profound contempt," he wrote, "for all men croakers who are hunting easy places at home to avoid the dangers of the battle field." [96] And, of course, good soldiers everywhere denounced the mounting tide of desertion that encompassed them.

Even in the hour of defeat the spirit of some was unyielding. Scores of Lee's men slipped away from Appomattox to avoid the intolerable humiliation of formal capitulation. And when General Bryan Grimes announced the surrender to his command, one Reb threw away his musket and with upraised hands cried out, "Blow, Gabriel! Blow! My

God, let him blow, I am ready to die." Another grasped his leader by the hand in farewell and sobbed, "Good-by, General; God bless you, we will go home, make three more crops, and try them again." [97]

Most soldiers of good morale were subject to occasional lapses of spirit, but there was one Reb of such consistent and high patriotism as to merit special mention. This man was J. T. Terrell, of Aberdeen, Mississippi. Though of superior background and education, he left military school to enlist as a private in the spring of 1861; and while he undoubtedly could have secured a lieutenancy through his influence, he never held a commission.

His letters fairly overflow with buoyancy from beginning to end of his service. On November 16, 1862, for instance, he wrote his mother:

"A soldier's life never was hard to me I can get along anywhere and under any circumstances. I have been in camp so long that I feel perfectly at home, and if I was anywhere else I . . . would have a natural feeling of not being in my proper place."

To his mother's suggestion after his sojourn in a Northern prison in 1862 that a substitute might be procured for him, he responded:

"I can say I do not want any as I think it is the duty of every man to bear an equal part in this struggle. . . . I think all men that own property to any extent and especially negro property Should take a part in this war as it has a tendency to encourage the poorer classes."

Just after re-enlistment for the duration of the war by his regiment in early 1864, he exulted:

"I tell you we are not by any means subjugated or despondent. There is life in the old land yet."

Two months later while on his way to participate in the defense of Atlanta, he wrote encouragingly to his mother:

"Hold up your hand and behold the Sky as it brightens. Day is fast dawning upon our infant Confederacy."

After the lapse of a few weeks he boasted:

"Our army is buoyant, enthusiastic, and hopeful in feeling. There is no better army anywhere nor is there any that is better officered. You need not fear the result when the Shock comes." [98]

Two and one-half months later "Tom" Terrell was dead—his brain pierced by a sharpshooter's bullet while on picket before Atlanta. After a few days his father at Quincy plantation in Mississippi received a letter from the hands of his soldier son's Negro body servant, Gabriel, telling of the tragedy. The missive, written by one of Tom's comrades on the very day of his death, is an eloquent testimony to unfaltering devotion to duty:

IN THE DITCHES ATLANTA GA.
Aug 22 1864

COL. B. M. TERRELL

My Dear Friend It becomes my duty to inform you of the death of your noble and gallant son. . . . Tom was a favorite with the whole regiment and all concur in saying that he was the best soldier in the regiment There can be said more for him than can be said for one in Ten thousand. he has never missed a roll call a drill a tour of duty never been absent a day without leave never reported to a surgeon nor has he ever slept out of camp unless on duty the loss of such men can not be supplied. Tom was strictly moral I never saw him out of humor in my life. . . .

Very respectfully your friend,
G. W. PENNINGTON [99]

If this tribute be accurate, Tom Terrell was truly "the good soldier" of the "lost cause."

How tragic for the Confederacy that there were not more like him. In the months that followed his death, the morale of both citizens and troops came to be in ever sharper contrast to the loftiness of spirit exemplified by Terrell, until on the eve of Appomattox evaders and absentees far outnumbered soldiers who were present for duty.

At the time of surrender an Alabama private addressed his captain on the sad fate that had overtaken the Southland. "Who was the cause of it?" he asked. "Skulkers Cowards extortioners and Deserters not the Yankees that makes it woss." [100] And in light of the shirking that surrounded him, this lowly Reb's observation carries an impressive conviction of truth.

CHAPTER IX

BREAKING THE MONOTONY

SOLDIERING can be a very dull job. Granting that "Old Peter" Longstreet, Stonewall Jackson, "Marse Robert" and most of the other generals managed to find an uncommon amount of scrapping for Johnny Reb to do, comparatively little time was occupied in actual fighting. The long hours in camp were wont to bear heavily on the Confederate private, as on soldiers of all armies since the beginning of organized combat. James Hampton Kuykendall, a Reb encamped in Texas, expressed a sentiment well-nigh universal among troops when he wrote in his journal on an autumn day of 1862:

"None can imagine, who has never experienced a soldier's life, the languor of mind—tediousness of time, as we resume—day after day the monotonous duties devolved upon." [1]

But Johnny Reb was, for the most part, a volatile, sociable person; his disposition, plus his innate love of fun, caused him to invent all sorts of escapes from the boredom of camp life. So frequent and varied were diversions, particularly during the first two years of conflict before deprivation and war weariness began to interpose so heavily, that a considerable number of men seemed to find more pleasure than hardship in soldiering. Some, indeed, after four years of campaigning could say convincingly that they enjoyed the war.

Perhaps the favorite recreation of the Confederate Army was music. In camp and on the march Johnny Reb found comfort in the sentimental melodies of the time. During the long wearisome stands on picket, he hummed or whistled softly to himself strains that recalled scenes of home and of childhood—or if his post was along the Chickahominy, the Rappahannock or the Chattahoochee, as it so frequently was, he might derive genuine pleasure from the playing by Yankee bands of "Cheer, Boys, Cheer," "Lorena," "Faded Flowers," and "Who Will Care for Mother Now." [2] But the greatest enjoyment came from informal singing about the campfire. Vocalizing in small groups seems to have been the general thing, but now and then mass singings on

151

such scale as to be called "musical sprees" or "jubilees" were staged. Once in a while song fests acquired additional zest by combination with convivial drinking.[3]

Johnny Reb had at his disposal an exceedingly wide repertoire of songs. Publishing firms, such as Blackmar and Werlein of New Orleans, Schreiner of Macon, and J. W. Randolph of Richmond, ground out a large quantity of sheet music, and Northern publishers sent Rebel tunes through the blockade.[4]

Much of the musical publishing, North and South, consisted of the reissuing of favorites, old and new; but a considerable quantity of fly-by-night trash came forth under the guise of patriotic melodies—items that frequently had more patriotism than melody. To supplement sheet music, Southern presses issued several pocket songbooks containing the words of sentimental and patriotic tunes. Among these brochures were the following: Songs of the South (Richmond, 1863); Stonewall Song Book (Richmond, 1863); Rebel Songster (Richmond, 1864); Army Songster (Richmond, 1864); Jack Morgan Songster (Raleigh, 1864); Songs of Love and Liberty (Raleigh, 1864); Southern Soldiers' Prize Songster (Mobile, 1864); Hopkins New Orleans 5¢ Song Book (New Orleans, 1861); Beauregard Songster (Macon and Savannah, 1864); General Lee Songster (Macon and Savannah, 1864); and Southern Flag Song Book (Mobile, 1864).[5] Letters, diaries and reminiscences of soldiers indicate that the great flood of new songs published during the war made little dent on Rebel ranks. The list of camp favorites was fairly small and it was made up to a large extent of melodies familiar before the war.

"Home, Sweet Home" was probably the most popular of all songs sung by wearers of the gray, but Payne's immortal work was closely pressed for top honors by two lugubrious ballads entitled "Lorena" and "All Quiet Along the Potomac Tonight." "Annie Laurie" and "Juanita" also ranked very high in soldier esteem. Other tender melodies heard frequently about the campfire were "Annie of the Vale," "Sweet Evelina," "Lilly Dale," "The Girl I Left Behind Me," "Bell Brandon," "Her Bright Eyes Haunt Me Still," "Listen to the Mocking Bird," and "Just Before the Battle, Mother."[6] The last-named song, like several others that were popular among Confederates, was borrowed from the Yankees.

An impressive portion of sentimental favorites had doleful themes. But soldiers had at their command also a number of rollicking songs that reflected lightheartedness and optimism. Sometimes as they

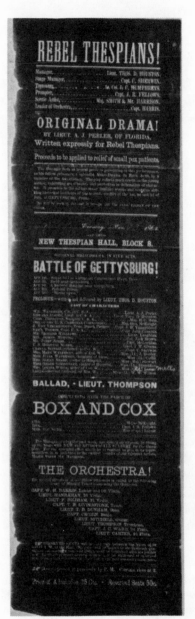

Courtesy North Carolina Historical Commission, Raleigh, North Carolina

CAMP THEATRICAL PROGRAMS

Programs for theatricals staged by Confederate prisoners at Johnson's Island.

THOMAS FONDREN McKIE, KILLED AT GETTYSBURG

"You recollect, Mother, we walked out into the garden and you cryed." From Maud Morrow Brown, *The University Greys* (Richmond, 1940). McKie was a private in the University Greys, Company A, 11th Mississippi Regiment. He was a Mississippian.

trudged along through mud and rain their voices rose in unison to a
verse that ran:

> So let the wide world wag as it will,
> We'll be gay and happy still.[7]

Another song heard occasionally among gray-clads contained this
thrust at the Yankees:

> The Sixteenth Louisiana charged them with a yell,
> Bagged the Bucktail Rangers and sent them all to hell.[8]

Soldiers of Bragg's army liked a saucy tune with this refrain:

> We are sons of old Aunt Dinah,
> And we go where we've amind to
> And we stay where we're inclined to,
> And we dont care a damn cent.[9]

A Tar Heel regiment had a rollicking ditty which paid tribute to the
girls back home:

> Ho for the maids of Kenansville
> A Song for Carolina's fair
> We'll sing a stan[za] with right good will
> To beaming eyes & f[l]owing hair
> To rosy cheeks & teeth of pearl
> And drink to each fair girl
> But who shall be the toast, I say,
> Who shall be the toast, Miss K?
> If eyes of azure & bright & beaming
> With angels smiles will set you dreaming
> Then indeed the toast shall be
> A bumper full for lovely Annie—
> If eyes as dark as the gazell's
> Brightly flashing warm your fancy
> Drink to ½ Doz belles
> But G may drink to lovely Nancy
> Too long 'tween drinks will never do
> My boys they're all too good for you
> Stay at your camp attend the drill
> Keep out of scrapes & Kenansville
> Fill up your glasses, hold your jaw,
> A toast to all hip-hip huzzah!
> A glass & cheer for each fair maid
> And a tiger give for our Brigade [10]

Camp repertoires in some portions of the army included indecent and ribald songs, but no documentary record of titles or content was found.[11]

Among patriotic songs "Dixie" was the most popular. Variations and parodies were numerous. One of these, found among the war letters of a Texan, is a sort of running commentary on Yankee leadership and fighting ability:

> I wish I was in the land of cotton
> Simmon seed and sandy bottom—away in Dixie.
> Stonewall Jackson have you any wool
> Yes my master *Baltimore* full.
>
> Burnside Burnside whither dost thou wander
> Up stream down stream like a crazy gander.
> Pope and McDowell fighting for a town
> Up jumped Lee and knocked them both down
> Nelson Bull Nelson fly away home
> Your army is scattered and your cannon all gone.
>
> I tell you what it is and what I am thinking
> Our Jeff Davis can whip old Abe Lincoln
> He whiped on the battle field I'll tell you the reason why
> He always makes the *Yankee* cowards run hog or die.
>
> There was a Yankee general by the name of Banks
> But he couldn't climb over a Stonewall fense.
> Lincoln! oh Lincoln how sad was the day
> When the Southrons did meet us in battle array
> They came in their power their might and their main
> And scattered our legions like sheep on the plain.[12]

Another parody, said to have been sung by the "Bienville Rifles" enroute from Louisiana to Virginia in 1861, bore the title "I wish I was in Richmond":

> I. From home and friends we all must go,
>   To meet a strong but dastard foe.
>   Look away, look away, look away to Richmond town;
>   And ere again those friends we see
>   We vow to die or all be free;
>   Look away, look away, look away to Richmond town;
>
>   . . . .

III. Old Abe they say is monstrous tight,
And cannot sleep a wink at night.
Look away, look away, look away to Richmond town;
But when he comes to Richmond City,
The way we'll cool him 'tis a pity.
Look away, look away, look away to Richmond town.

. . . .

V. We'll meet old Abe with armies brave,
And whip the lying scoundrel knave.
Look away, look away, look away to Richmond town;
As he pleads for terms and whiskey,
We'll give him hell to the tune of Dixie.
Look away, etc.[13]

Popular also, particularly during the early months of the war, was the "Bonnie Blue Flag," a composition inspired by the single-starred first flag of the Confederacy, and set to the music of an old Hibernian song entitled the "Irish Jaunting Car." The opening verse and chorus suggest the rousing appeal of this song:

We are a band of brothers, and native to the soil,
Fighting for the property we gained by honest toil;
And when our rights were threatened, the cry rose near and far,
Hurrah for the Bonnie Blue Flag, that bears a Single Star!

Hurrah! Hurrah! For Southern Rights Hurrah!
Hurrah! For the Bonnie Blue Flag that bears a Single Star.[14]

"My Maryland," written in 1861, was hardly less popular than "Bonnie Blue Flag." The heart of many a volunteer doubtless was fired with patriotic valor as he sang the memorable lines beginning:

The despot's heel is on thy shore,
Maryland! My Maryland!
His torch is at thy temple door,
Maryland! My Maryland!
Avenge the patriotic gore
That flow'd the streets of Baltimore,
And be the battle queen of yore,
Maryland! My Maryland!

and ending:

I hear the distant thunder-hum,
Maryland! My Maryland!
The Old Line's bugle, fife, and drum,
Maryland! My Maryland!
She is not dead, nor deaf, nor dumb—
Huzza! she spurns the Northern scum!
She breathes—she burns! she'll come! she'll come!
Maryland! My Maryland! [15]

Several regiments had glee clubs which gave occasional programs
for the entertainment of officers and men. One of the most famous of
these was composed of members of the Fourteenth Tennessee Infantry.
This club, organized in 1861 and maintaining an unbroken personnel
throughout the war, had some unusually talented singers who not only
presented camp concerts, but who also sang occasionally to comrades
on the march. June Kimble, the club's violinist, left the following
record of a memorable incident that took place as the army was head-
ing northward for the Chancellorsville-Gettysburg campaign:

"The time was about one o'clock A. M. Surgeon Wright, riding at
the head of his regiment caught the inspiration of the moment, took
his flute from his saddle pockets . . . and electrified his comrades . . .
with 'Home Sweet Home' . . . Instantly the other members of the
Glee Club gathered around him and in subdued tone joined in the
chorus. The effect was indescribable. The sweetness and beauty of it
all may never be duplicated in song or scene. Then followed 'Annie
Laurie,' 'Swanee River,' 'Massa in the Cold Cold Ground,' 'The Old
Kentucky Home,' 'Bonny Blue Flag,' and the climax 'Dixie Land.'" [16]

Instrumental music was another important source of diversion.
Regularly organized company and regimental bands provided marching
airs for drills and gave occasional night concerts. An Alabama brigade
which boasted two or three regimental bands was entertained with "the
best kind of martial music every morning and evening." [17] Selections
were of great number and variety. Captain D. S. Redding of the
Forty-fifth Georgia Regiment records in his diary that on July 3, 1863,
he heard the following pieces: "Shells of Ocean, Lone Rock by the
Sea, Dixie, Marseilles Hymn, They Told me not to Love Him, Bonny
Eloise, Fare thee well Kittie, Irish Emigrant's Lament, Prarie Flower,
Leila is Gone, Mocking Bird, Katie Darling, Old Hundred, Do They
Miss Me at Home, Grand March Innovation, Gentle Annie, Belle
Brandon." [18]

Captain Redding failed to remark on the skill of the musicians to whom he listened, but James J. Kirkpatrick of the Sixteenth Mississippi Volunteers suggested that the band of his regiment was distinguished more by zeal than by ability. On October 30, 1863, he made the following entry in his diary:

"Camp, 2 miles South of the Rappahannock. Drilling as usual. went over to the Band in the evening to hear some vocal and instrumental music. Our band is a great institution. It always keeps its numbers undiminished, and labors with the greatest assiduity at 'tooting'. Their music, however, is never the sweetest nor most harmonious." [19]

Difficulty of procuring instruments, scarcity of cultivated talent, and the stringencies of campaigning prevented the maintenance of high-class bands. European visitors to Southern camps were shocked by the "discordant braying" of some of the musical organizations, and there can be little doubt that the majority were of inferior rating.[20] But even so, their contribution to happiness and morale was considerable.

A South Carolina private who heard several bands play "Pop Goes the Weasel" at the conclusion of a public function in 1861 said: "I have never heard or seen such a time before. The noise of the men was deafening. I felt at the time that I could whip a whole brigade of the enemy myself." [21]

And General Lee, after listening to a brass serenade in 1864, remarked: "I don't believe we can have an army without music." [22]

In addition to regularly organized bands, many military units had informal groups of "artists" whose dominant motive was the entertainment of those who made the music. Such an organization was the minstrel band of Kennedy's Louisiana Battalion. Some of the instruments of this band were difficult to classify. There was a "cross fiddle" made of a drum head "nailed over half a whiskey keg with a rough pine neck, and strings and screws accordin"—but the melody achieved by the minstrels was such as to make them in great demand not only for camp "hoe-downs," but for civilian programs as well.[23]

Instrumental music that Johnny Reb used most frequently, and perhaps enjoyed most thoroughly came not from any organized group at all, but from one or two messmates who had brought highly cherished fiddles and banjos from home and who at night labored away at familiar tunes about the campfire. A good fiddler was a popular personage in any outfit, and a mess that could boast a violin-flute combination or a fiddle-banjo duet was the object of widespread envy. The favorite repertoires included such numbers as "Hell Broke Loose in Georgia," "Billy in the Low Grounds," "Arkansas Traveler," "Money Musk," "The Goose Hangs High," "When I Saw Sweet Nellie Home," "My Old Kentucky Home," "Oh Lord Gals One Friday," and "Dixie." [24]

In their home letters soldiers spoke often and appreciatively of the prowess of informal camp musicians. Edward T. Worthington, of a Mississippi company, wrote to his cousin from camp in Kentucky:

"We have a lively time here . . . every fellow full of life. . . . every night fiddlers are plentiful such as the break down and work out. When we want something nice we borrow the fiddle and go to our tent Will *tries himself* and draws a tent as full as they can stick around in it. . . . I wish . . . you could happen in sometime while Will Mason is playing the violin & see some of our capers." [25]

With fiddlers enjoying such popularity as this, it is not surprising that the price of instruments rose dizzily. An Alabama private, who must have been much better at music than he was at spelling, wrote proudly to his brother in October 1861:

"Tobe I have got the best violent in the Regiment Jo Jackson ses it is worth one Hundred dollars." [26]

A favorite exercise of musicians, both vocal and instrumental, was to go about at night serenading fellow soldiers of the encampment and young ladies of the countryside. These were occasions gala enough, but serenadings of popular officers seem to have elicited the maximum of jollity. Private J. E. Thornton wrote enthusiastically to his wife of an affair in Mississippi in which he participated in the fall of 1861:

"We had a great seranad the night after we were Transferred [from state to Confederate service] we all turned our coats rong side out and seranaded all the big officers we allowed to serenade Enterpris last night but General Oferil sent us word that he was sick and he rather we would wait till he got well So the eighth Regiment Seranad us last night it was a pretty sight all the Regiment together with pretty music." [27]

Officers thus complimented were expected to give tangible expression of appreciation. When Captain Thomas J. Key of the Army of

Tennessee was serenaded without prior notice by the band of General Polk's brigade ("composed of one cornet, one bass horn, two violins, two flutes, and one guitar"), a doctor friend came gallantly to his rescue by bringing out a bottle of whiskey, while the captain "refreshed the band by slicing up a loaf of light bread." [28] Few captains could have responded more nobly, even with forewarning.

Next to music, Johnny Reb probably found more frequent and satisfactory diversion in sports than in anything else. When leisure and weather permitted, soldiers turned out in large numbers for baseball. Captain James Hall of the Twenty-fourth Alabama Regiment observed that his men, while Joe Johnston was waiting at Dalton to see what Sherman was going to do, played baseball "just like school boys." The same could have been said of almost any other regiment of the Confederacy. The exercise might be of the modern version, with players running four bases, or it might be two-base townball. The bat might be a board, a section of some farmer's fence rail, or a slightly trimmed hickory limb; the pellet might be nothing better than a yarn-wrapped walnut; but enthusiasm would be so great as to make the camp reverberate with the cheers and taunts of participants, if not of spectators. And the game might become so rough as to necessitate precautionary steps. "Frank Ezell was ruled out," wrote a Texas Ranger in his diary, because "he could throw harder and straighter than any man in the company. He came very near knocking the stuffing out of three or four of the boys, and the boys swore they would not play with him." [29]

Football and cricket are mentioned by a few soldier correspondents, and there is one reference to a game called "hot jackets," in which each participant attacked his opponent with a limber hickory switch.[30] But common exercises were foot racing, wrestling, boxing, leapfrog, hopscotch, quoits, and marbles. Some Rebs played tenpins after a fashion ironically unique, by rolling cannon balls at the pins, or at holes in the ground.[31] Swimming was popular in encampments near the seacoast and streams; and Johnny Reb was not the sort of person who would halt his bathing for cold weather, particularly if the "gray backs" were gnawing in strong force. Water near camp sites was also utilized for fishing, seining and grabbling, though the sporting urge was frequently secondary to that of hunger. Hunting, likewise, was prompted by a double motive, and in many instances mess larders were enriched as a result of successful forays for quail, robins, turkeys, rabbits, squirrels, 'possums and deer. On many quests for game scarcity of ammunition plus greater effectiveness of other methods led to the laying aside of guns. Rabbits were stalked in wood or meadow and killed with rocks and clubs, or hemmed in and caught by hand. Hungry, emaciated Rebs could give almost any sort of edible animal a lively run, and their diaries and letters tell of amazing quarries. "The boys had lots of fun catching squirls clubing & shaking and yeling them out of the trees," wrote a Mississippian in 1862, and a comrade noted in his diary about the same time that "the soldiers of our Brigade chased and caught a Red fox. which was quite a myracle." [32] Shortly after the Antietam campaign a Virginian wrote his mother:

"Yesterday a covey of partridges was flushed in the Field where we camped, they grew bewildered & squatted about in the field; three or four were caught. I caught one plump & full grown; yes and eat him too, picking his bones clean." [33]

The most successful hunting-without-arms venture, from the standpoint of quantity of game brought in, is recorded by Private J. H. Puckett. Late one afternoon in February 1863 he and seven comrades slipped off from their camp near Shelbyville, Tennessee, and concealed themselves under a robin roost which had been visited with good results by other soldiers the previous night.

He wrote his wife this account:

"When night came, I could hardly believe my eyes. As far as I could see the heavens were blackened with these little Robins coming in to the Cedar brakes to roost. . . . When sufficiently dark, Book took 2 others and went way around, clum up bushes and whistled so as to let us know where to drive. We lit our torches and went thrashing through the bushes from one tree to another until they would light in the ones where our boys would be stationed and then of all the little chicken hollowing you ever heard, it beats all they come into the tree so fast and thick that they would [light] in our faces, on our heads feet hands and sometimes you can catch them with your mouth . . . [we] caught . . . in all about 50 . . . It took me ½ day to sew up my jeans pants where they bursted climbing through the thick cedar branches . . . but . . . I felt amply repaid when we set down to a big chicken stew made of Robins and they were the fattiest things I ever saw of the feathered tribe." [34]

Cavalrymen found diversion on occasion in staging "ring tournaments." [35] More exciting pastime, however, was gander-pulling. In this sport, horsemen riding at full tilt attempted to catch the head of a live gander that hung by its feet from a point barely within the rider's reach. Gander-pulling, when featured at dress parades, aroused great enthusiasm in both soldiers and civilians.[36]

Card games were another highly favored diversion in Southern camps. Indeed, accuracy would not be much stretched if the scriptural passage were parodied to read, "Wherever two or three Confederate soldiers were gathered together, there would a deck of cards make its appearance in the midst of them." Much of the playing, as has been previously noted, was for stakes, but many hands were held with fun as the sole objective.[37] Sessions were frequently of long duration—one mess habitually spent six hours a day playing cards—and interest of the players ran high.[38] Chess was not without its devotees in Rebel ranks, but it seems never to have gained any considerable popularity.[39] Draughts, or checkers, and a kindred game called "Fox and Geese" were played to a limited extent.[40]

Reading provided a source of recreation for many soldiers, though army routine was not conducive to a great deal of it. During the day, except in winter, there was little time for reading. In winter quarters there was usually ample leisure, but tents or huts were frequently so cold that soldiers sought comfort between blankets. At night fatigue, poor lighting and the activities of restless comrades made reading almost impossible. Also, interesting books and periodicals were hard to obtain. But in spite of these factors, there was a vast amount of reading done in the Rebel Army. Newspapers were the most eagerly sought of available reading materials. Frequent army movements and chronically deficient mail facilities made delivery of papers irregular and uncertain. But when subscribers did receive their journals from Richmond, Atlanta, Memphis, Jackson, or some other city, they read them avidly and then passed them on to a line of impatient comrades until the none-too-substantial pages were literally worn out. Periodicals such as the *Southern Illustrated News*, *Southern Field and Fireside*, and *De Bow's Review* also had a considerable circulation in the army.[41]

Better-educated and more fortunate soldiers procured and read books in considerable numbers. And there is evidence of good taste in numerous instances. W. M. Barrow, a Louisiana private with some college education, read, while in camp and prison, among other books, Thiers' *French Revolution*, Swift's *Gulliver's Travels*, and Dumas' *Count of Monte Cristo*. The camp reading list of Charles Woodward Hutson, a cultured young South Carolinian, included works of Shakespeare, Milton, Bulwer, Shelley, Scott, Coleridge, Beverly Tucker and

"Bill Arp," along with *Arabian Nights* and the New Testament.[42] Harry St. John Dixon of Mississippi read *Paradise Lost, David Copperfield*, Baldwin's *Flush Times of Alabama and Mississippi* and Fanny Fern's *Rose Clark*, but of Harriet Beecher Stowe's masterpiece he wrote: "[Spent] all day coughing & reading that d——d Yankee lie *Uncle Tom's Cabin*." [43] Edward A. Pollard, Cowper, Macaulay and J. J. Hooper were read by some, but their writings were not so popular as Hugo's *Les Misérables* and Scott's *Ivanhoe*. The most widely read of all books was the Bible.

As a rule even novels of indifferent interest and merit were eagerly read when available. But among some of the more serious-minded and religiously inclined troops there was a strong prejudice against fiction. Private H. A. Stephens of Mississippi reflected the attitude of this group in a letter to his sister:

"If you cant get good books to read do not read any. any composition of fiction falsehoods calculated to excite the mind, to a great extent should not be read by anyone. . . . when any one gets used to reading anything very excitable they cant read any other composition with intrst. . . . I have seen too many brilliant minds of young men almost ruined, Just in this way, during this war. one of my mess who had an excelant mind, read Novals a long time. he con clded a short time ago to study grammar if i would instruct him, & of cors i could not refuse, but it is the hardest work i ever saw for him to keep his mind on it he is a gorgian." [44]

Men of Stephens' serious bent of mind constituted a comparatively small minority of the army. Most Rebs looked at the lighter and brighter side of life. This tendency expressed itself in many forms of teasing and horseplay. If a comrade or visitor happened to make an appearance in some sort of unusual garb, he immediately became the object of a chorus of gibes.

Favorite greeting for a man with a large new headpiece was "Come out of that hat! I see your legs," or "Look out, that parrot shell you're wearing's going to explode," or "Take that camp kettle home, aren't you ashamed to steal a poor soldier's camp kettle?" [45]

And the donning of a new pair of boots would call for: "Come up outer them boots; come out; too soon to go into winter quarters; I know you're in thar; I see your arms sticking out."

A staff officer who rode through camp sporting a long and finely twisted mustache was apt to receive from behind tents and trees the irreverent suggestion, "Take them mice out'er your mouth; take em out; no use to say they aint thar, see their tails hangin' out." An unduly luxuriant beard might provoke the invitation, "Come out 'er that bunch of har. I see your ears a workin'." [46]

If some Reb happened to mimic a chicken, a cow, or a donkey the whole camp might break out in a frenzy of cackling, crowing, shooing, braying or bellowing. Let some visitor inquire as to the whereabouts of Company F, and a soldier down the line would yell, "Here's Company F"; others would take up the cry and soon the entire brigade would echo the refrain. When an old soldier on the march greeted a friend with "How are you, Jim?" fellow Rebs were almost certain to follow suit until Jim was overwhelmed with the salutations of a brigade or division.[47] Mischievous Confederates had a slang expression, "Here's your mule," which they bandied about in much the same fashion as American Legionnaires use the phrase "Where's Elmer?" [48]

Soldiers sometimes stole one another's letters, and discovery of a saccharine missive from some indiscreet sweetheart would immediately lead to making public the contents and ribbing the embarrassed or angry owner. A Texas private named J. W. Rabb one day received a poetically endearing letter from his sister Bet. When this note fell into the hands of Rabb's comrades they immediately concluded that Bet was his sweetheart and proceeded to tease him roundly. Rabb's barely decipherable narration of the incident to his sister gives a delicious insight into the bantering, fun-loving character of the Confederate soldier:

"You roat me such a good long letter i like it so much for The boys all thought that it was from my jularky and one little fellow develed me so much about Fly home to thy native home gentle dove he sayed that I looked more like a paterage." [49]

Another Texas private who had trouble with spelling wrote a friend back home about a trick of which he had recently been the victim:

"I mett with an accident yesterday it was my cook day and I was getting souper we had [a] pretty good size yong turky a cooking some develish fellows had been watching me when I put it in the pot well at souper time I went to take it out and put it on the table do you think I found the turky no by God it was nothing but the feather." [50]

Fondness of horseplay manifested itself in such activities as bumping comrades against trees, rolling them in mud, smoking them out of their tents, or loading their firewood with powder.[51] Putting a nervous recruit on picket with an unloaded gun—a fact concealed of course from the recruit—impressing on him the peril and responsibility of his position by telling him to die at his post like a man, and subsequently charging his station with hostile yells to see him run was considered a capital joke.[52] Little wonder is it that pranks innocently conceived sometimes had fatal consequences.[53]

A diversion from which soldiers throughout the South derived enjoyment was the staging of shows and stunts. These dramatic efforts were of great variety. Texas Ranger troops liked to indulge in circus performances.[54] The Richmond Howitzers' "Law Club" held occasional moot court sessions that were said to have been marked by brilliant discussions.[55] Many companies had lone artists who entertained their comrades informally about the campfire. The Kennedy Battalion of New Orleans enjoyed the occult tricks of "A no. 1 slight-of-hand man"; and another outfit boasted a "chin music" performer who for a jigger of whiskey would put his hand to his chin and make with his teeth "a sound like rattling bones, keeping time to his song and pat." [56]

A Texas Ranger told in his diary of an unusually versatile entertainer:

"April 12, 1862 . . . A fellow by the name of Vaughn is amusing the boys just now, he is a perfect curiosity—born in the city of New York, partly raised on the ocean, and having the advantage of general information, and personal observation gave him a decided advantage over us poor back woods fellows that was wonderful, he could sing funny Songs, dance clog, make funny speaches, play tricks, turn somer saults, and other things two numerous to mention." [57]

Frequently the talent of various organizations was combined for the preparation of elaborate minstrel or varieties programs. To these affairs the public was usually invited, and admission was charged for the benefit of wounded soldiers, impoverished civilians, or for some other benevolent purpose. The performances were staged in camp or in the theater of a town near by.[58]

If camp was the place of performances, considerable preparation was necessary to provide properties and accommodations for spectators. A location resembling a natural amphitheater was cleared of brush and rubbish. Seats were sometimes borrowed from a neighboring school or church, but more frequently soldiers had to stand, and visiting ladies were seated on boxes, barrels, planks, or "pinelogs, flattened on one side to prevent their rocking." The stage was usually of rough boards raised two or three feet above the ground, the "footlights" a dozen or so candles, the heating facilities a few log fires built around the edges of the location, and the curtain a tent fly or a blanket.[59] The program was made up of songs and instrumental music, magicians' tricks, clog dances by overly painted "Ethiopians," and ballets by terpsichorean artists whose heavy feet and large frames belied the crinoline that awkwardly draped them. But the inconsistency between dancers and apparel only added to the merriment. Pantomimes, tableaux, dialogues and plays completed the roster of offerings. These might occasionally have serious themes, but usually they were comic.

A program presented by Fenner's Battery at the beginning of the Atlanta campaign featured burlesques of the use of snuff by Georgia females, "the practice of soldiers shooting pigs and chickens, and visiting farm houses with doleful tales of hunger, the honesty of Quartermasters, and the inferior quality of Confederate whiskey." [60] Take-offs on officers were probably the most popular of all dramatic offerings.

A theatrical group from the Stonewall and Louisiana brigades wrote and presented a skit called the "Medical Board," satirizing the surgeons.

The rise of the curtain revealed a group of doctors sitting about a table playing cards and drinking brandy. Presently inquiry is made as to how such good liquor is obtained in these hard times.

The immediate answer is, "Oh, this is some that was sent down from Augusta County for the sick soldiers, but the poor devils can't need it, so we'll drink it."

Then a courier comes in with the message that a badly wounded soldier is outside. "Bring him in! Bring him in!" says the chief surgeon.

After a casual examination, the patient is told that his arms must be amputated. He inquires if he can have a furlough after the operation.

"Oh, no," replies the surgeon, who shortly announces that a leg also must be cut off.

"Then can I have a furlough?" asks the soldier.

"By no means," answers the doctor, "for you can drive an ambulance when you get well."

The surgeons now go in consultation and decide that the wounded man's head must be amputated. "Then I know I can have a furlough," observes the patient.

"No, indeed," says the chief physician. "We are so scarce of men that your body will have to be set up in the breastworks to fool the enemy." [61]

One of the most famous theatrical groups in the entire Confederate Army was that of the Washington Artillery. Variety shows staged by these players during the war's second winter were amazingly elaborate. Programs were printed in Richmond and distributed widely among soldiers and civilians. For the second performance, presented in February 1863 at camp near Fredericksburg, a special train was run from the capital; Lee, detained by business, sent a note of regret but Longstreet and other generals attended in full regalia; common soldiers flocked from all divisions, some coming on foot from points as far removed as twenty miles. Music was furnished by the combined bands of the Twelfth and Sixteenth Mississippi Regiments. The main feature of the show was a burlesque entitled "Pocahontas, or Ye Gentle Savage," and according to one who was present, "the house came down any number of times and the audience appeared delighted. Following the feature there was an after-piece called 'Toodles'. The program was brought to a rousing conclusion by a band rendition of 'Bonnie Blue Flag'." [62]

Theatricals not only afforded great amusement in the preparation and the showing, but also provided topics of conversation and subject matter of letters for days to come. After attending "a kind of Negro Show called the Lone Star Minstrels" in the Pine Bluff Court House by Flournoy's Texans, a member of that regiment wrote to his sister: "Bully for Flournoy's Regiment we are some punkins, Youll Bet." [63]

Occasionally a group of Rebs would break the boresome routine of camp life by having a party or spree. Return of a popular officer provoked one of these celebrations in the Ninth Texas Cavalry in February 1862. The soldiers staged an "uncommon big War Dance," according to a diarist of the regiment, "firing guns by platoons, anvils by the dozen, in fact alarming the whole country—& finally getting after the Dutch Sutler who they seem to think is extortioning in the prices he is charging . . . threaten to hang him . . . and finally taking 50 condemned wagons near by and piling them up all around his shanty literally causing the old fellow to leave in haste next morning." [64]

In another instance, a celebration in a Mississippi regiment had the nature of a command performance, according to Private C. W. Stephens. "Our Col. got drunk last Saterday night," he wrote his sister in October, 1863, "and had the boyes dancing off theare doble dutie he also danced and pated for them he told them that he intended to present our flag a monday and he said if theare was airie man in the Regt that did not intend to foler it he waunted them to be missing the next morning . . . we all a gread to foler it eny wheare." [65]

Sometimes when women were allowed to visit camp in sufficient numbers, bona-fide dances were enjoyed, but these occasions were so rare that dance-loving Rebs were impelled to stage womanless affairs. If bonnets and other articles of feminine attire could be had, they were donned by those soldiers playing the parts of the belles, but usually the boys paired off as they were and performed the convolutions of the waltz, or went through the mazes of the square dance to such tunes as "Gal on the Log," "Rackinsack," and "Leather Breeches." [66] The music was usually provided by a fiddler or two belonging to the participating outfits.

Occasionally there were disturbing religious qualms. "The Capt and myself had a regular concert," wrote a banjo-playing Reb, "winding up in a stag dance, the Capt being a member of the Methodyst church wouldnt play for the dance so the 'Ordinary Sergent' fiddled." [67] But another private who did not dance himself viewed tolerantly the capers of his comrades, on the score that he "like[d] to see the Boys have their fun." [68]

A birthday of a popular comrade would often call forth a celebration. Charles Moore entertained his friends on his birthday. "I invited my companions to assist me in Emptying 3 canteens of 'Oh! be Joyful'," he wrote, "then spent the balance of the evening Singing—until Tattoo then we parted in Good Spirits." [69]

Christmas and New Year almost always brought a round of parties, and when whiskey could be obtained it added to the jollity of the celebration. A Texan wrote to his brother in January 1863 that "we got 3 gallons and a half of whisky with our $140.00 and had a jolly time of it Christmas eve night," but added significantly, "I dont want you to say anything about our *Frollick, to any body*." [70]

The commissary department sometimes issued whiskey rations on festive days, but the amount was usually so small as to cause complaints of stinginess and favoritism.[71] Officers frequently took note of Christmas by serving whiskey to their men; that this was not always satisfactory is indicated by a soldier's report to his sister that "the General [Reuben] Davis sent up a barrel of whiskey to the camp, but it was such villainous stuff that only the old soakers could stomach it." [72]

Sometimes Rebs went to great pains to obtain whiskey suitable for a Christmas eggnog only to find that there were no eggs available. One soldier thus baffled wrote disgustedly: "If it were in my power I would condemn every old hen on the Rio Grande to six months confinement in close coop for the non-conformance of a most sacred duty." [73]

A regiment in the Army of Tennessee observed the Fourth of July, 1862, with a celebration featuring speeches and a barbecue. A member of the regiment passed off the incongruity of Rebels celebrating a "national holiday" with the remark: "Anniversary of our national independence we still struggling for the same, etc." His continuing observation overlooked another inconsistency: "Rev. Ransom preached . . . we had some good apple brandy to drink—all got lively, etc." [74]

Occasionally some statesman or eminent divine from back home would deliver an address to the soldiers in camp. No doubt such affairs were sometimes attended more from a sense of duty than of diversion, but there were many soldiers who, like Private C. W. Stephens, derived genuine enjoyment from almost any sort of oratory. In a letter to his father from Columbus, Mississippi, in November 1863, Stephens, struggling mightily with his spelling, observed:

"The ornerabel [honorable] C. K. Marshal addrest the peopel last night I listend to him 3 hours and as I was un well I retired I never heard a better speach fall from eny ones lips than that of his he could dive deaper in to the futer and farther back on the past than eny one I ever heard . . . I can hear speaking every night nearly . . . I like to heare the legislature members dispute which I can heare every day." [75]

Not a few Rebs found recreation in meetings of fraternal and benevolent associations. The Masonic order was particularly active among some portions of the army, and its sessions were apparently well attended by soldier members.[76] For still others the monotony was occasionally broken by visits from wives, sweethearts, parents and home acquaintances. When regiments composed of soldiers from the same neighborhood came into convenient proximity, there was an immediate and refreshing exchange of calls. Furloughs home and short visits to cities or to countryside acquaintances, whether obtained by authorization or by "flanking" sentinels, also had their part in the easing of army tedium. But opportunities for visiting and being visited came all too infrequently.

In moments when other resorts failed him Johnny Reb frequently fell back on the age-old diversion of "shooting bull." Topics ranged over an exceedingly broad field. The political situation and the war came in for a full share of attention, although discussion of military matters was frowned on by some groups.[77] If facts failed as topics of conversation, the soldiers could always turn to rumor to keep the conversational ball rolling.

Very early in the conflict the most fantastic tales began to pervade the Confederacy. Robert M. Gill wrote to his wife Bettie from Louisville, Kentucky, on April 29, 1861, in all seriousness, "It is reported by a gentleman here just from Washington City that Abe Lincoln had been drunk for thirty six hours & was still drunk when he left." And throughout the war, rumors of even more extravagant proportions from sources considered wholly reliable were accepted without question by campfire idlers and passed on with enriched detail and growing inaccuracy: General Kirby Smith in possession of Cincinnati; Lincoln and his whole cabinet captured by Jeb Stuart; General Grant killed; General Beauregard accompanied on the march by "a train of Concubines & wagon loads of champagne"; the Confederacy recognized by England and France; peace to be concluded in six weeks.[78]

For the most part these and other fictions were enjoyed, but one private was surfeited to the point of revulsion. "I never heard so many lies told in my life," he wrote to his aunt, "as are told in camp. I have got disgusted and quite [quit] lieing and . . . I find I get along bout as well as usual." [79]

At times the conversation around campfires took a serious turn to such topics as "wheather it is right that we men fight with the same Ardor while the young folks are dancing at home," "the proper mode of raising children," or the probabilities and consequences of McClellan's election to the presidency.[80] Again the talk would treat of such trivialities as who eats the most, or who had most of the blanket last night.[81] Not infrequently some gifted raconteur with a racy imagination would occupy the center of attention with stories of love and adventure. Unfortunately not all would-be storytellers were so accomplished, but it seems that even bores could command an audience in Confederate camps. Listeners had a particular fondness for stories that dealt with the supernatural. A soldier said in the fall of 1861 that he had told again and again the thrillers of Poe, Dumas and others.[82]

A few companies had mascots or pets which were the sources of much diversion. The Troupe Artillery of the Army of Northern Virginia had as mascot a small cur named Robert Lee. The dog lived up to his namesake in individual encounter, but in battle he utterly belied his illustrious name. At Chancellorsville he was observed skulking behind a tree exactly after the fashion of a demoralized man. But his survival gave point to the adage, "He who fights and runs away will live to fight another day."

Stonewall, canine pet of the Richmond Howitzer Battalion, was, in happy contrast to "Bob Lee," the very soul of heroism in battle. And he was idolized by the artillerymen, who would grab him up when orders came to shift position under fire and give him sheltered transportation in a limber chest. During periods of leisure one of the men taught Stonewall to attend roll call and to sit up on his haunches in line. He also made a little pipe for the dog. When the orderly sergeant, before commencing the roll call, would cry "pipes out," his trainer would stoop and transfer the pipe from Stonewall's mouth to his paw and the dog would sit rigidly at attention until roll call was over.[83] A considerable number of individual soldiers had gamecocks as pets.[84]

Another source of recreation was handicraft. Hour after hour the Rebs whiled away in camp and prison by making pipes out of cobs or clay, for themselves and comrades, in contriving rings from shells for wives, children and sweethearts, and in whittling countless gewgaws from pine boards for no one in particular. The urge to make pretty things was, in some cases, impeded only by lack of materials. Thomas Warrick wrote from camp in Shelbyville, Tennessee, to his wife in Alabama:

"Tell Mahaly that I will make her them Rings she Rote to mee to make as soon as I can get Something to make them out of. . . . Tell all of the girls that I will send them one." [85]

A few Rebs sought amusement in drawing, using camp scenes for themes and cartridge boxes for desks.[86] Others relieved the tedium by decorating their tents or equipping them with some of the comforts of home. In 1863 a group of Louisianians went so far as to plant a garden for the benefit of their regiment.[87]

Another unusual diversion was the publication of camp newspapers. Officers and men of John Morgan's command printed, at irregular intervals in 1862 and 1863, a sheet called the *Vidette* which told of battle exploits, announced general orders, and taunted the Yankees.[88] A similar paper, bearing the name *Missouri Army Argus*, was published for a while in 1861 and 1862 by some of Price's followers.[89] More pretentious in both format and content than either of these was a paper called the *Daily Rebel Banner* and printed apparently by members of Bragg's army.[90]

The vicissitudes of campaigning and the lack of facilities prevented the publication of printed papers in the great majority of Rebel camps. But in a few instances soldiers of strong journalistic bent partially overcame these difficulties by writing out or "pen printing" small news sheets. The first of these ventures seems to have been launched by a group of young Alabamians stationed at Fort Barrancas on the Gulf coast. On February 23, 1861, they released volume 1, number 1 of "The Pioneer Banner." Nine weeks later the second issue appeared. There may have been subsequent numbers, but no record of them was found.[91]

While at Camp Hudson on the western frontier during the early months of the war, the W. P. Lane Rangers circulated over twenty issues of "The Camp Hudson Times," and when they moved to Fort Lancaster about the first of February, 1862, they established "The Western Pioneer," which ran for an unknown length of time.[92]

Soldiers stationed at Port Hudson on the lower Mississippi during the war's second winter put out rival papers designated respectively as "The Mule" and "The Wood Chuck." [93] And in Lee's army a sheet called "The Waltonville War-Cry" and another entitled "The Rapid Ann" had brief existences.[94]

These manuscript papers were made up exactly after the fashion of a regular news journal. At the head of the first page the title was inscribed in large, ornate letters, accompanied in some instances by a decorative shield or a motto. The second issue of "The Pioneer Banner" contained a well-executed original drawing of Fort Barrancas by one of the "staff artists." Contents of the sheets were devoted to editorials, camp news and gossip, poetry, jokes, obituaries and advertisements.

"The Pioneer Banner" started out as a trimonthly affair, "for the Young Ladies of the Union Female College," but failing of its original schedule, the second issue was headed by a note announcing publication "semi-occasionally." It is doubtful, in view of the restricted reading-public anticipated by the editors and the exceedingly meticulous care devoted to preparation, that there were later issues of "The Pioneer Banner." But with what absorbing zest must the girls of the academy have read their copies for tidbits about individual doings in camp! And eventually one imagines the issues were treasured in the memory book of one of the most interested readers and cherished in the years that were to elapse before they found a final resting place in historical archives. Papers issued by the other groups were intended for wider circulation; consequently they were duplicated and given comparatively far-reaching distribution. A Lane Ranger said concerning publication of "The Western Pioneer" that first an original of each issue was prepared in complete detail; next, members of the staff made as many copies as they desired; and finally comrades who wanted duplicates to send home were allowed to write them off.[95]

Any cataloguing of kinds of diversion in the Confederate Army would be incomplete without a mention of tobacco. It is doubtful if any single item except food, water, and letters from home was so highly cherished by Johnny Reb as "the delightful weed." References to its scarcity, to its availability, to cost, to its quality and to its soothing powers appear repeatedly in soldiers' correspondence and diaries.

"Nancy what do you do fur tobacco to chew?" inquired a Reb of his wife; "I have to pay two dollars a plug fur what I chew." [96]

Another scribbled to his sister:

"Well Bet I herd you got three plugs of tobacco to go on I am glad to here that old Milan [his home county in Texas] can afford it. last Friday I got three plugs of No. one I cant sleep of nights Since for chewing $1.50 per plug and would not take twice the money for it . . . Tell Mass John that I am all right while my Tobacco lasts." [97]

A third wrote:

"Tell Bettie not to be uneasy about my using tobacco. I shall not chew it, nor hurt myself smoking it. I am convinced that it has been of some benefit to me." [98]

This was certainly a case of understatement. More enthusiastic was the Reb who observed "I . . . got my pipe and I woulddant take a dead negro for it," and another who boasted, "I am as Sassy as a big house Niggar got money and tobacco a plenty for the present." [99]

A note of despair creeps into Sergeant Frank Moss's communication to his sister "Lizer" when he observes:

"Tobacco is only worth $2.50 cts per plug and I have taken my last chew this morning So you may guess I will have a hard tim as I dont use that kind of tobacco." [100]

It is little wonder, in view of the exceedingly important roles played in army life by plug and pipe, that an anticipated cut in tobacco rations prompted more than one general to begin an impatient correspondence with the crotchety commissary general at Richmond; nor is it any wonder that many Rebs, who had resorted to everything from singing to smoking to make army life tolerable, should, on reaching home at war's end, inquire first, after the round of embraces, as to the prospects of the tobacco crop.

CHAPTER X

CONSOLATIONS OF THE SPIRIT

SOUTHERNERS of the nineteenth century were a religious people. Church affiliation was regarded as a badge of respectability; for both private functions and public enterprise the presence of the clergy was sought. The minister was preferred to the magistrate in the marriage ceremony, and community gatherings, whether picnics or political rallies, were usually opened with prayer. Most academies and colleges had daily chapel services which both faculty and students were required to attend. There was sometimes a wide divergence between the preacher's message and the laity's conduct, just as there is today, but religious sanction was demanded by the righteous—always a powerful minority—approved by the lukewarm and accepted by the wicked; all felt better to have had the blessing of the church.

It was only natural, then, that Johnny Reb should be sent away to war with a benediction. A vital part of most of the going-away ceremonies in 1861 and 1862 was a talk and a prayer by a local minister. In the knapsacks of many, if not most volunteers a Bible, donated by a mother or a sweetheart, was tucked away. When the Summit Rifles left their home community in Mississippi, a pretty girl handed each man a pocket Testament that had been bought by the Summit Bible Society.[1] Frequently one of the local ministers went along to look after the company's spiritual welfare.

In spite of these auspicious beginnings, religion did not thrive in camp during the first year or two of conflict. Sunday services were held irregularly and with small attendance. Testaments collected dust from disuse; many were lost or thrown away. In some quarters the faithful few who persisted in their devotions were scorned as weaklings. One soldier reported that a man of his encampment found reading the Bible was apt to be hailed with such remarks as "Hello, parson, you must be scared. I don't think there will be any fighting soon," or "Hello, parson, what time do you expect to start a revival?" [2]

Troops who wintered at Cumberland Gap in 1861-1862 were not sufficiently interested in religious services to provide shelter for them.

Concerning the general attitude of these men a chaplain said, "Very few of the commissioned officers were religious. The large proportion of the soldiers were wicked and many were reckless. For more than a year very few manifested any desire to become Christians save the sick or wounded." [3]

Throughout the army many men who at home took an active interest in church affairs lapsed into a state of indifference after a short time in the army. Some of the ministers who accompanied volunteer outfits to camp became so disheartened by the general spiritual desuetude that they despaired of their missions and went home. "Mr. Allen is going to quit the army," a Mississippian wrote in December, 1862; "he says it is an uphill and discouraging business preaching to Soldiers— I think so too—He hears nothing but the worst of language, his ears are greeted hourly with oaths." [4]

Among the factors contributing to the spiritual indifference which distinguished camp life in 1861 and 1862 was the festive spirit with which volunteers went to war. Few of the men realized that the conflict would be long and bloody. There was a widespread inclination to lay aside the inhibitions and conventions to which they had been accustomed in order to enjoy thoroughly the respite from quiet civilian life. By a majority, perhaps, soldiering was regarded as a grand lark and they wanted to derive the greatest possible pleasure from it while it lasted. Most of the soldiers were from the country, and the transition from farm to camp assumed to a large extent the character of a visit of rural youths to a city. They might have been good boys when they left, and they would be good boys after they returned, but in the meantime they wanted to have a fling at gambling, drinking and swearing, and they did not wish to be bothered with preachers.

Once this reaction got under way it was hard to stop. Chaplains were few in number and their efforts were not well organized. No agency existed for the promotion of wholesome recreation. After a while drill and camp routine became dreadfully monotonous. Fleas, lice, short rations, hard marching and ragged clothing taxed patience beyond endurance. For all these woes poker, keno, liquor and profanity appeared to offer the most convenient antidote. Those who wished earnestly for righteousness were often in despair. "I hope when you go to Pray you will think of me," wrote a discouraged Tar Heel in 1862; "I am a pore Harted sinner and never expect to Be no other way as long as I do remain Hear for agrivation is my Brexfus Dinner and supper." [5]

In the meantime church leaders of the South had come to a realization of the army's vast spiritual needs and had instituted movements that eventually were to be of tremendous influence. Among the most important of these was the setting up of agencies for the procurement and distribution of religious literature.

Shortly after the war broke out, Southern affiliates of the American Bible Society severed their connection with the parent institution and initiated the Bible Society of the Confederate States. This organization pledged itself to the publication and circulation of the scriptures among various groups, but principally among soldiers. Few Bibles were printed in the South before the war and the Confederate Bible Society had great difficulty in obtaining Testaments. Most of the Northern societies took the view that scriptures were contraband and stopped making their publications available for Southern distribution. The one great exception to the general rule was the American Bible Society. This organization made several donations of Testaments, including one of 100,000, to groups in the Confederacy active in servicing the army. Another outstanding benefactor was the British and Foreign Bible Society, which made large contributions and extended unlimited credit without interest for the purchase of Testaments.[6]

The various Protestant denominations were active in procuring and publishing Bibles, Testaments and other literature for soldiers. Southern Presbyterians sent M. D. Hoge to Europe to solicit and purchase religious materials. People at home were asked to contribute surplus Bibles for distribution in camp. When soldiers were killed their families were requested to permit the donation to comrades of Testaments belonging to the deceased. Chaplains and interested troops went over battlefields to gather up Bibles left by both friend and foe.[7] These several expedients yielded a large quantity of Bibles but never enough to meet army demands.[8]

In addition to providing Bibles, church organizations published religious periodicals for soldiers. The Evangelical Tract Society, an interdenominational body organized in 1861 at Petersburg, Virginia, which came to have a position in the South analogous to that of the American Tract Society in the North, issued the *Army and Navy Messenger*. The Presbyterian Board of Publication sponsored a monthly paper called the *Soldier's Visitor*. Southern Methodists published two semimonthly organs; the *Soldier's Paper* was issued from Richmond for troops in Virginia and the Carolinas, and the *Army and Navy Herald* from Macon, Georgia, for commands of the Southwest. Among papers initiated by the Baptists was a sheet published in Atlanta under the name of the *Soldier's Friend*. These and other periodicals designed specifically for camp readers were devoted largely to reading matter calculated to create abhorrence of evils most common to army life, and to inspire soldiers to Christian living.[9] The first issue of the *Army and Navy Herald* affords a good example of the general character and purpose of all. Included among article headings are these: "Come to Jesus," "A Model Boy," "The Whiskey Erysipelas," "Washington's Prayer," "The Scoffer Rebuked," and "The Soldier's Death." In an editorial the sponsors promised "to furnish the reader with such original productions and eclectic Christian literature as will in some humble measure compensate for the absence of books . . . and elevate his conceptions to the comprehension of a purer and more peaceful area . . . than the strifes of the times." [10]

The most numerous and most influential of religious publications issued to soldiers were those which came under the head of tracts. Every major sect, and several interdenominational organizations, issued these pithy leaflets in great quantity. The output of all sources totaled hundreds of millions of pages. The Baptists were particularly zealous in this work. The Virginia Sunday School and Publication Board alone published and distributed over thirty millions of pages of brochures. The Evangelical Tract Society and the South Carolina Tract Society were also exceptionally well represented in this field.[11]

Some of the tracts were reprints of those issued to English soldiers during the Crimean War. A few consisted solely of the Psalms, of the Gospel of St. John and of various other excerpts from the scripture. But the great majority were pointed spiritual essays prepared especially for Confederate soldiers by eminent Southern theologists. The publications were pocket-size and the usual length was four pages, though some contained as many as sixteen and a few ran as high as twenty-four. Some emphasized the importance of conversion; others told how to seek religion; many warned against specific sins; a few gave practical advice as to health of body and of mind; and a great number had as their central theme the danger of procrastination. A favorite technique was the use of personal incident and experience. Washington, Cromwell and various heroes of the Confederacy were cited as examples of Christian fortitude. Military allusions and analogies were frequently employed. The style of writing was usually unctious.

A recurring subject of the tract writers was the evil of cursing. The title of one leaflet was *Profane Swearing*, and of another *Why Do You*

Swear? The latter written by J. N. Andrews of North Carolina argued against profanity on the ground of its futility, its injury to self-respect, and its debasement of the user to the level of liars, murderers, thieves and adulterers. Still another tract captioned *The Silly Fish* charged the swearer with biting at the devil's bare hook on the ground that there was no possible satisfaction to be derived from the sin.

Gambling was another favorite topic. A tract entitled *The Gambler's Balance Sheet* listed the gains of the evil as: lewd and base companions; idleness and dissipation; poverty; and mental anguish. Losses are given as: time; money—"which ought to be sent home to your wife and babies, or to an aged father or a widowed mother"; feeling—"a young man in New York not many years ago played cards on his brother's coffin"; love of truth—the gambler will try to cover up his loss by a falsehood; self-respect; character—"your friends will disown you, your mother will be ashamed of you, your sisters will blush when your name is mentioned"; happiness; and soul. The balance, according to the author, could be nothing but "ETERNAL MISERY."

Drinking was a third target for writers of tracts. One of the most pungent of the brochures on this subject was that headed *Lincoln and Liquor*, written allegedly by a physician. It attempted to show the inconsistency of throwing off the Lincoln yoke and at the same time becoming enslaved to drink. It attributed recent defeats to liquor and predicted blighting drouths in the Confederacy if bountiful crops continued to be used in "distilled damnation." Finally it scorned the argument advanced by some that whiskey prevented disease, protected against cold, or was beneficial to those about to go into battle.

Another tract was devoted to the subject of *Depredations on Private Property*. Several were slanted to capitalize on the soldiers' repeated exposure to death; *Prepare for Battle* was the title of one of these, and *A Word of Warning for the Sick Soldier* that of another.

The hell-fire note was pressed in some; in *Sufferings of the Lost* a thorough roasting over the lake of fire and brimstone was promised in excruciating detail to unrepentant sinners.

The most popular of all the tracts was an eight-page pamphlet called *A Mother's Parting Words to Her Soldier Boy*. This work, by J. B. Jeter, was written in letter form. In the first year of publication about 250,000 copies were issued to soldiers. The style is direct, simple, crisp and unencumbered by the unctious sentimentality that mars many tracts. In the beginning a good tonic for morale is administered: The mother professes to give up her son without reluctance because he goes to support a righteous cause—"The great fundamental principle of the American Revolution that all authority is derived from the consent of the governed"; if she had ten sons she would sacrifice them with equal cheerfulness. In this sacred cause the mother implores her son to be a good soldier, obedient to his superiors and courageous in battle. She admits that the genius and spirit of Christianity are "utterly opposed to war," but says that the scriptures convince that "a just and defensive war" is not incompatible with righteousness. Then follows practical advice as to religion in camp: First, the son is urged to become a Christian lest his soul perish; but the argument is made with restraint and without appeal to fear. Second, he is admonished to keep his Christianity— "guard against drunkenness . . . as you would . . . against henbane" and avoid profanity. Third, the son is assured that piety is not effeminate—"some of the bravest soldiers of the world have been humble Christians; Cromwell, Gardiner, and Havelock . . . were as devout as they were heroic. . . . Washington maintained the claims of Christianity amid the demoralizing influences of the Revolution." Finally there is a benediction and a commitment of the son to the providence of the Almighty.[12]

Distribution of Bibles, tracts and other religious publications was accomplished through special agents called colporteurs, through chaplains and through interested soldiers. Usually the items were donated outright, but occasionally a small sum was required of recipients. A captain in the Twelfth Georgia Regiment testified that his company raised sixty dollars on a single day as a contribution to a regimental fund for religious literature.[13]

Hospitals were favorite resorts of colporteurs and no charge seems to have been made for literature distributed to the sick and wounded. Dearth of reading matter and the genuine interest of some in spiritual instruction made the disseminator of tracts a welcome visitor in camp. J. W. Jones said of his own experience:

"I had a pair of large saddle bags which I used to pack with tracts and religious newspapers, and with Bibles and Testaments. . . . Thus equipped I would sally forth and as I drew near the camp some one would raise the cry, 'Yonder comes the Bible and tract man,' and such crowds would rush out to meet me that frequently I would sit on my horse and distribute my supply before I could even get into the camp. . . . The poor fellows would crowd around and beg for them as earnestly as if they were golden guineas." [14]

Captain Lewis Minor Coleman testified that one of his men who made no pretensions to Christianity read the Psalms and the New Testament through twice during a month's encampment at Strasburg because he had nothing else to read.[15] Ministers sent out to raise funds for colportage had a good store of incidents at hand telling of the conversion of hardened sinners by tracts that came accidentally into their possession. Typical of these was the story of a wounded officer "who was awakened and led to Jesus while in camp by a 'fragment of a religious tract' which he picked up in an adjoining grove." [16]

By the beginning of 1863 distribution of religious literature had reached large proportions. By this time, likewise, efforts of the various churches to supply the army with chaplains and missionaries had attained considerable success. In the spring of 1863 there came the first of the great religious revivals which swept periodically over Confederate encampments.[17] The connection between this spiritual awakening and the high tide of pamphleteering and preaching was unmistakable.

The revivals apparently began in Stonewall Jackson's Corps in the latter part of March. On April 12, 1863, a private wrote from camp in Caroline County, Virginia:

"We are having a glorious time about now . . . we commenced a protracted meeting in this Brigade about four days ago. . . . Gen. Jackson (God Bless him) has given us the privilege to be exempt from Morning's Drill in order that we may attend preaching . . . we have two sermons each day & although we have no church to worship in we all sit around on the ground and listen to the sweet sound of the Gospel." [18]

About the same time another of Lee's soldiers told of the organization of an Army Christian Association that held prayer meetings three times a week, "sometimes in the quarters occupied by a captain—sometimes in the house occupied by a mess of privates—and all unite—without respect to rank or former denominational associations—in the worship of God"; he added that many soldiers had become zealous workers "who were never before connected with any church." [19]

The evacuation of winter quarters followed by the Chancellorsville and Gettysburg campaigns interrupted evangelistic activity. But in the autumn the flames were rekindled and during the winter of 1863-1864 the wave of revivalism reached unprecedented heights not only among troops quartered along the Rapidan, but also in the Army of Tennessee and in other commands throughout the Confederacy.

From a camp near Minden, Louisiana, a soldier wrote:

"A revival of religion has commenced in camps . . . I never saw such a difference in men in my life There is but one man in my knowledge who makes a regular business of swearing. . . . When I first came out in the army we could scarcely hear any thing else but profanity . . . over 250 have been converted since last summer in this divis[ion]." [20]

Another wrote from Bragg's headquarters in North Georgia:

"Thousands have professed Religion and the work is still going on . . . I do not think there is as much wickedness in our Regt as there used to be . . . it resembles more a camp meeting than it used to . . . around the fire you can see Groups of men singing." [21]

From Virginia one of Lee's veterans wrote:

"We have preaching in camp every day . . . & prayer meeting at night . . . I dont think I ever saw more interest taken in a protracted meeting." [22]

As winter came on soldiers built log tabernacles and equipped them with pulpits, seats and lights. In one instance there was apprehension that a theater erected by less pious comrades in the vicinity of their log church would lure away the congregation. But the minister, "Kentucky Andrew Broaddus," proved to be the greater attraction and, according to the report of a chaplain, "in the great revival that followed, the owners of the theatre and some of the actors, professed conversion, the 'plays' were suspended, and Brother Broaddus was invited to hold his services in the theatre as that was a larger and more comfortable building. . . . He readily consented to do so." [23]

Circumstances did not permit the building of tabernacles by all brigades, but the zeal of some worshipers was so great that they were not deterred from religious service by lack of shelter. One chaplain told of preaching to a group of Mississippians for forty minutes in a steady rain; "not a man stirred" and this despite the minister's suggestion that the congregation ought to disperse and seek cover. In another instance an exhorter preached to a large assembly of Virginia troops who stood in several inches of snow for the duration of his sermon; no less than fourteen of the men were barefooted. J. W. Jones testified that he saw shoeless men in attendance many times at services held on snow-covered ground.[24]

Word got around rapidly among civilians in the fall of 1863 concerning the outbreak of revivals in camp. This precipitated a rush to the front of prominent divines who welcomed an opportunity to abandon lukewarm home constituencies for eager congregations of soldiers. Such preachers as John A. Broadus, J. B. Jeter, J. B. McFerrin, Stephen Elliott, B. M. Palmer, J. C. Stiles, J. N. Waddell and a host of others equally eminent, thrilled to the response accorded their messages by tatterdemalion veterans; and by their presence and influence, as well as by the eloquence of their addresses, these men aided greatly the tide of revivalism.

Among the professions of faith received by outstanding ministers were those of Generals Bragg, Ewell, R. H. Anderson, Rodes, Pender, Paxton and Colonel Lamar.[25] Bishop-General Leonidas Polk in the spring of 1864 baptized Generals Hood, Hardee and Joseph E. Johnston. President Davis also became a communicant during the war. After these additions to the church, personal workers who approached lowly camp sinners were not lacking in examples to cite of lustrous association to be had in paths of righteousness.

The hard fighting about Atlanta and in the Wilderness naturally caused a decline of religious activity in the Confederacy's two principal armies. The abatement of services and the strain of campaigning were accompanied by a large-scale backsliding, though many converts were impelled to constancy by the ever-present prospect of death. In the Trans-Mississippi Department, where military duties were less arduous, revivals continued into the summer of 1864.[26] The winter of 1864-1865 witnessed a renewal of religious interest in the Army of Northern Virginia. About sixty chapels were built along the lines about Petersburg, and J. W. Jones expressed the opinion that revivals among Lee's troops during the last winter of conflict were as general and as powerful as at any prior time.[27] This conclusion may be correct, but it is probably not applicable to other commands. Certainly it was not true of the Army of Tennessee where Hood's disastrous Nashville campaign interfered greatly with the religious program. For the Confederacy as a whole the peak of revivalism was attained in the winter of 1863-1864.

Evangelistic outbreaks in the army seem to have been of a restrained character emotionally. Certainly they were accompanied by much less bombast than some of the revivals in hinterland areas earlier in the century. There were no evidences of such phenomena as "barking" or "jerking"; and very few correspondents mention the ecstatic hollering known as "shouting" so common at "big meetings" before and after the war. Perhaps audiences made up largely of hard-bitten campaigners were less susceptible than civilian congregations to such fervid exercises. Few camp ministers attempted to work up an emotional lather among their hearers. Seekers of religion were rarely brought to a mourners' bench and subjected to long sessions of praying, high-pressure exhorting and beating on the back. The most common procedure was for the declarations of repentance and faith to be made by the simple expedient of walking up to the rostrum and shaking hands with the preacher.

The factors that gave rise to large-scale revivalism among Confederates afford interesting ground for speculation, particularly in view of the fact that Federal armies experienced no such phenomenon. As has been previously indicated, one significant cause for the first series of eruptions in 1863 was the success at that time of efforts of Southern churches to provide the army with tracts and preachers. To a large extent the spiritual awakening was the result of extensive and well-organized denominational propaganda; and in a sense, the revival thus launched persisted for the war's duration, the recurrent waves being but variations of its intensity.

A second cause is to be found in the character of the Southern soldiery. Most wearers of the gray came from communities where the church was fervid, aggressive, and influential, and where revivals were common. True, there was a reaction against religion when men first went to camp, but by the beginning of 1863, this had exhausted itself and the normal susceptibility to evangelism had been restored.

A third and a very important cause lay in the state of mind which pervaded both the army and the citizenry after the second year of conflict. In 1861, 1862 and early 1863, optimism was rampant. Confederate armies were winning great victories and suffering few defeats. These successes, coupled with prospects of European recognition, seemed to assure triumph and independence. The favor of God was sought and acknowledged, but extreme confidence in human endeavor tended to belittle reliance on divinity, or make its expression perfunctory.

The series of setbacks that began with Gettysburg and Vicksburg produced a marked change of attitude. Both civilians and soldiers began to question the invincibility of Southern arms. Churches began to sound the note that military defeats were punishments inflicted by the Almighty as a rebuke to sin and to overweening reliance on the strength of man. The feeling gained wide currency that God would not permit the South to triumph unless and until her people humbled themselves, did genuine penance, and committed themselves to the keeping of providence.[28] This sentiment was particularly strong when the shock of military reversals first came, and it is significant that evangelism reached its peak immediately after Gettysburg and Vicksburg.

A fourth and final factor contributing to revivalism was the increasing prospect of death which confronted soldiers as the war went into its last years. Veterans who saw regiments dwindle in strength from hundreds to handfuls could not escape the realization that their chances of surviving the bloody battles yet to be fought were slim. The urge was strong, therefore, to escape damnation and to gain assurance of eternal peace by getting religion. From this and from other motives vast numbers of Rebs answered the call to salvation. According to a preacher-historian who made an extensive study of army revivals, no less than 150,000 soldiers made professions of faith during the war.[29]

Religious services in the Confederate Army consisted largely of preaching and prayer meetings. The usual time of the former was Sunday morning, but the demands of campaigning and a shortage of chaplains caused frequent changes in the schedule. When the army was on the march all services had to be held at night. In such instances the minister took his place in the open, with his congregation clustered about him on stumps, logs, or on the ground. Illumination was afforded by a flickering campfire or by the moon.

Prayer meetings were more frequent than sermons. They were usually held at night. Scripture reading, hymn singing and prayer usually constituted the bulk of the service. Occasionally there was a brief commentary on some Biblical passage or spiritual topic. These meetings were led by chaplains, missionaries, or visiting ministers when they were available, but in the absence of preachers some layman would be called on to direct the exercises.

Sometimes the meetings were very small and informal, having as their participants the six or eight men composing a mess, or other groups drawn together by convenience and congeniality. During periods of active campaigning chaplains often assembled their flocks very early in the morning for a brief session of prayer and scripture reading prior to the beginning of march. When a battle was immediately impending religious leaders attempted to invoke a benediction on troops before they went into action.

In a number of instances prayer meetings became the objects of enemy fire. Such situations produced a severe strain on religious faith. Robert Stiles told of the opening of Federal batteries on a service held during the Seven Days' campaign. When shells began to fall near by, Stiles peeked about to note the effects on the kneeling men. The simple-hearted worshipers felt that it would be sacrilegious for them either to open their eyes or to get up while prayer was in progress, yet their faith was not so great as to prevent their seeking shelter. Much to the amusement of their spying observer, therefore, they began to crawl about on hands and knees with eyes still closed, groping for trees, stumps, or any other available cover.[30]

During periods of revival, experience meetings were common. At these assemblages Christians would arise, either of their own initiative or on invitation of a leader, and tell of their spiritual experiences. If they were recent converts, their remarks would usually have to do with factors leading to profession of faith and the feeling which ensued as a result of their renunciation of evil. If sinners were present they might be given an opportunity to request the prayers of righteous comrades.

Every season of revival was accompanied by a succession of baptizings. These were usually featured by songs and prayers, but the main ceremony was the administration of the baptismal rites. If the candidates were members of denominations requiring immersion, a stream or lake had to be sought by those in charge of the service.

Sunday schools were also held in many camps. At one time it was reported that every company in Dole's Brigade of Lee's army had a Bible class. Sometimes these gatherings were conducted by a leader on a formal basis, in other instances they consisted simply of a group of worshipers gathering to hear the reading of a Testament by one of their comrades.[31]

Priests were active among troops who came from Catholic communities. When circumstances would permit, services were held each morning in tents used exclusively for religious exercises.

An Englishman who served in the Army of Northern Virginia during the early months of the war said that he frequently saw "General Beauregard and other officers kneeling with scores of privates at the Holy Communion Table." This authority paid particularly high tribute to the work of the Jesuits.[32]

In most services singing played an important role. Some of the tract societies compiled favorite hymns of the various denominations and issued them to the soldiers in pocket-size booklets. Among the most popular of songbooks were these: *The Army Hymn Book*, consisting of 191 selections, issued by the Richmond Presbyterian Committee of Publications; *The Soldier's Hymn Book* published by the South Carolina Tract Society, which in the second edition included 271 songs; and *Hymns for the Camp*, published by an unidentified agency and consisting in the third edition of 151 numbers.[33] Most of the selections were of a purely religious character, but patriotic songs were occasionally included. One booklet of Confederate imprint contained "America," without benefit of title, and for the phrase "Land of the Pilgrim's pride" the publisher substituted "Land of the Southron's pride." Other instances of specific adaptation to Confederate use are indicated by this stanza of a hymn classified under "Praise and Thanksgiving":

> "These Southern States at thy command
> Rose from dependence and distress;
> And stablished by thy mighty hand,
> Millions shall join thy name to bless."

and by a verse of a song set to the tune of "God Save the King":

> "Our loved Confederacy,
> May God remember thee
> And warfare stay;
> May he lift up his hand
> And smite the oppressor's hand
> While our true patriots stand
> With bravery." [34]

The favorite hymns of camp and field were not those contrived for the moment, but rather the old songs endeared by associations of home and childhood. Ranking particularly high in soldier esteem were such hymns as these: "All Hail the Power of Jesus' Name," "Amazing Grace, How Sweet the Sound," "How Firm a Foundation,". "Jesus, Lover of My Soul," "Just As I Am, Without One Plea," "Nearer My God to Thee," "O Happy Day," "On Jordan's Stormy Banks I Stand," "Praise God from Whom All Blessings Flow," "Rock of Ages," "There Is a Fountain Filled with Blood," and "When I Survey the Wondrous Cross." [35]

To promote spiritual fellowship and religious constancy "Christian Associations" were formed in many brigades. In addition to sponsoring services these organizations set up committees to distribute tracts, to organize prayer groups, and to perform various other helpful functions.[36] In some commands soldiers banded themselves together to oppose the use of strong drink. A convert to moderation wrote thus to his home-folk:

"I thank you very kindly for sending me the things . . . The whiskey you may depend will be used moderately as I belong to the Temperance society of whom Gen Braxton Bragg is president." [37]

In most army services, denominationalism was minimized. On one occasion a visiting minister reported: "We had a Presbyterian sermon, introduced by Baptist services, under the direction of a Methodist chaplain, in an Episcopal church." [38] But it was difficult for preachers who were steeped in sectarianism to avoid offending soldiers sensitive to doctrinal differentiation.

"I heard a sermoned the other night," wrote a Mississippi Baptist; "the preacher was a missionary and of corse preached Methodist doctrine but it is not my business to criticisize." [39]

A Reb of unknown affiliation made this guarded thrust at a Christian chaplain: "The Boys are taking fast with the Camelite persuasion . . . The preacher talks good sense and if He is right that is certainly an easy way to get to Heaven." [40]

Ministers who exhorted soldiers varied considerably in character and ability. The compensation provided by the government was not enough to attract men of talent. The law of May 31, 1861, authorizing President Davis to appoint and assign such chaplains as he thought necessary, provided a monthly salary of eighty-five dollars, and no allowances were made for food, clothing or other expenses. Two weeks later the stipend was reduced to fifty dollars. In the autumn of 1861 legislation was modified to permit chaplains to draw the same rations as privates. An act of April 19, 1862, raised compensation to eighty dollars and continued the ration allowance. In January 1864 Congress belatedly made provision for chaplains to draw forage for their horses.[41]

Men with families—and preachers were no exception to the rule of the period in the matter of large families—could not begin to provide for them from such meager salaries, and when pay was reduced from the original eighty-five to fifty dollars, many chaplains resigned and returned to their homes.[42] But some managed to get along by frugal living and by supplementing their salaries from other sources.

The life of a chaplain who worked conscientiously at his job was an arduous one. His usual constituency was a regiment, though in some instances a single preacher attempted to serve a brigade. In addition to holding services he attempted to talk individually with Christians to bolster their faith, and with sinners to persuade them to salvation; some kept records on every man under their charge in which they set down data as to home circumstances, church connections, change of religious status and other information pertinent to performance of their duties. Care and consolation of the sick and wounded was an important part of the chaplain's work. He had to write to the families of bedridden soldiers telling of their condition; in case of death, he addressed words of comfort to the bereaved. Illiterate Rebs often asked him to take down halting dictation of home messages. In some instances the camp minister took upon himself the organization and teaching of classes in reading and writing.[43]

The faithful chaplain shared the hardships of his flock. During periods of active campaigning he slept on the ground under the open sky. His fare was the scant ration issued to private soldiers. Some ministers had horses, but there were many who marched shoulder to shoulder with veteran infantrymen. When fighting began the chaplain usually took a position near the ambulances or the field hospital in order to have ready access to the wounded.

Dr. Charles Todd Quintard, of the First Tennessee Regiment, one of the most distinguished of all army ministers, was trained in medicine as well as in theology; when he moved among the wounded he filled the double role of doctor and preacher.[44]

In many instances chaplains thus engaged were exposed to Federal fire. Some, indeed, insisted on taking weapons and joining in the conflict.[45] At Chancellorsville, T. L. Duke, chaplain of the Nineteenth Mississippi Regiment, grabbed a musket, moved to the forefront of the line, and directed the movement of skirmishers.[46]

According to a newspaper report, Parson Brady of Tappan's Regiment, in an action near Columbus, Kentucky, shot a couple of Yankees and slashed the throat of another with his knife. His excitement then became so great that he forgot his ministerial vows and rushed after the retreating foe yelling, "Go to Hell, you damned sons of bitches"; this lapse caused him no end of teasing by the soldiers.[47] Several chaplains were cited in official reports for gallantry under fire, and a few were killed in action.[48]

The chaplain who braved the dangers of battle, whether with or without arms, lifted himself greatly in the esteem of the rank and file. R. H. McKim, who during the war laid aside the musket, took up the prayer book and assumed the chaplaincy of a Virginia cavalry regiment, related the following incident from his own experience. When the regiment moved forward to battle for the first time after he joined it, he took a position in the advancing column. This was a shock to the men and one called out:

"Hello, Parson, are you going with us into battle?"

"Oh, yes," replied McKim good-humoredly, "I'm an old infantry soldier—I don't mind these little cavalry skirmishes."

At this remark, a hard veteran rose in his stirrups, brandished his saber and yelled, "That's right, Paason. You stick to us, and we'll stick to you!"

And from that time, according to McKim, this rough trooper was a faithful friend.[49]

There were some chaplains who lacked learning, and others who lacked zeal; a few were deficient in both. The hardships of camp life eliminated the unconscientious, but in the early months of the war their number was considerable. An Englishman who had firsthand acquaintance with camp life said that a horde of incompetent ministers came to Richmond in the spring and summer of 1861 and were "saddled off on our regiments." These he characterized as "long-jawed, loud-mouthed ranters . . . offensively loquacious upon every topic of life, save men's salvation," and some of them "betrayed alarming proficiency in handling cards at a social game of poker." Such men, he said, "were seldom or never found administering to the sick or dying" and were rarely seen holding services; fortunately for the soldiers their sojourn in camp was comparatively brief.[50]

Native Rebs had occasion now and then to find fault with their spiritual guardians. "We have in our company two parsons," wrote a Mississippian in his diary; "truth forbids that I should say they are eminent or even thoroughly posted upon Biblical questions . . . The progress of religion amongst us is greatly impeded by this embarrassing fact." [51]

A Texan reported after listening to a camp exhorter, "I got enough . . . [preaching] in about 15 minutes to last me during the Campaign —he is a whale all but the oil—he pronounced servile, *serveile*—parental, *parentual*—said have came, etc . . . he gave the boys a regular rant." [52]

A Virginian complained that the regimental preacher "spoiled his sermon by whining & gasping it out." [53]

Other soldiers denounced their chaplains on the score of cowardice. "We got into a little row with the 'Yanks' a few days ago," wrote an

Alabamian, "and our parson . . . took to his heels when the shells commenced flying and I have not seen him since."[54]

A Reb who participated in the Atlanta campaign noted that while fighting was in progress the ministers attached to his brigade forsook the troops and went to the rear where they loitered about with cooks and quartermasters. "Surely," he said, "they will meet their reward."[55]

Some of the best and most effective preaching to which soldiers listened was that which came from officers active in the service. Bishop-General Leonidas Polk was able on occasion to exhort the men of his command. General William N. Pendleton, whom the rank and file credited with the exploit at Manassas of drawing a bead on the enemy and remarking, "Lord preserve the soul while I destroy the body," held services rather frequently during winter months. A sergeant who heard him speak in a log tabernacle in December 1864 wrote afterward: "I never listened to more solemn & impressing remarks."[56] General M. P. Lowrey and Captain Lewis Ball of Mississippi also preached to army audiences on numerous occasions. The former was a minister of notable eloquence.[57]

Sermons delivered to camp audiences, whether by chaplains, officers, or visitors, were usually couched in simple terms. Subjects receiving most frequent attention were the necessity of repentance, the uncertainty of life, the consequences of sin, the terrors of hell, the importance of Christian vigilance, the omnipotence of God, and the universality of divine mercy.

The diary of Bartlett Malone, a North Carolinian of Lee's army who faithfully jotted down texts used by camp preachers, reveals a close relation between camp sermons and military vicissitudes. In the spring of 1862 while McClellan's army was being assembled for the march on Richmond, Malone recorded listening to a discourse centering about 2 Kings 6:15-17—"Behold an host compassed the city both with horses and chariots. And his servant said unto him, Alas, my master! how shall we do? And he answered, Fear not: for they that be with us are more than they that be with them. And Elisha prayed . . . and, behold, the mountain was full of horses and chariots of fire round about Elisha." With what assurance must the minister have drawn a parallel between Elisha and the hard-pressed Confederates!

Shortly after the great Southern victory at Fredericksburg in December 1862, Malone heard a sermon on Psalms 126:3—"The Lord hath done great things for us; whereof we are glad." On the eve of the eventful Chancellorsville-Gettysburg campaign of 1863, the Tar Heel was impressed by an exhortation based on Proverbs 18:24—"There is a friend that sticketh closer than a brother." And on the very day of Stonewall Jackson's death a minister consoled Malone and his crushed associates with a message having as its text Romans 8:28—"And we know that all things work together for good to them that love God." [58]

Some officers manifested indifference toward religious activities, and a few openly opposed them. A brigadier general allegedly declared that chaplains were "the scourge of the army" and occasionally a colonel protested that emphasis on fear of divine punishment is detrimental to men in combat.[59] But the great majority of leaders approved of spiritual exercises. President Davis periodically ordered the observance of fast days. Lee and other commanding generals repeatedly enjoined unnecessary interference with Sunday services. The encouragement given by officers to the work of chaplains derived in great part from their own spiritual inclinations. But they undoubtedly attributed to religious influence a salutary effect on the rank and file, particularly in such practical matters as discipline, morale and conduct under fire.[60] If the leaders were correct in this view—and there seems to be no valid ground for challenging it—it is indeed regrettable that backsliding was as common as it was, and that a majority of Confederates made no profession of faith and had no church affiliation.[61]

CHAPTER XI

DEAR FOLKS

A VERY important part of the soldier's life was the exchange of letters with his family and friends at home. One of the first things he did after getting settled in camp was to collect pen, ink and paper and write his loved ones about details of his new existence. And thereafter, until death or war's end, he continued to write of things that he observed and experienced in camp, on the march, under fire and in prison. At the same time, he received missives—though not so often as he sent them—telling of crops, dogs, parties, gossip, health of the family and countless other details of life at home.

Never in the history of the South has there been such a tide of letter writing as that which was raised by the Confederate War, for on no other occasion has so large a proportion of the people been away from home for so long a time. Letters written by soldiers were more apt to be preserved than those received in camp, and these faded missives, now reposing by the thousands in private possession and in public depositories, constitute a valuable and largely neglected source for the South's social history.

It is a significant fact that during the Confederacy a large portion of the middle and lower strata of Southern society became articulate for the first time. Certainly from no other source can so much firsthand information be obtained of the character and thought patterns of that underprivileged part of Southern society often loosely called "poor whites."

Most Rebs enjoyed writing letters. The new world that was unfolded to them by travel to remote places, by association with many different kinds of people, and by contact with the horror of battle, gave them thrills and shocks that demanded expression. This flood tide of reaction found a natural outlet in correspondence with homefolk. The writer's vanity was flattered by his knowledge that the persons addressed had undergone no such experiences themselves.

But writing letters seemed less important than receiving them. Mississippian John Barksdale wrote to his brother in 1862:

"I do wish I could say something to provoke a reply. I care not how short it might be or long my say. I would be tempted to 'cuss' a little if that would produce the desired result or would breathe words soft as the memory of buried love if that would effect the object. . . . Leave the all engrossing cotton field for fifteen minutes, and write me at least one letter . . . you will certainly not loose more than the picking of twenty five pounds of staple and that you can have made up some other time; if not I will see that you are paid for it." [1]

Intense eagerness to get mail was almost universal. "Boys who will lie upon their backs with hardly energy enough to turn over," wrote an Alabamian, from Tupelo, "will jump up and hurry to the captains tent to get it." [2]

Another Alabamian, of very poor educational background, scribbled to his wife:

"Martha I waunt you to write often and send me all the nuse for I am one of the Glades[t] fellows that you Ever seen when I git a letter from you you dont no how much good it dus me to here from you."

Several months later he wrote:

"I haint got nary letter from you for somtime when you fail to Rite . . . it ceeps mee uneasy all the time." [3]

Yearning to hear from homefolk was so acute at times as to be pathetic. E. K. Flournoy wrote his wife in the spring of 1863 that he "was almost down with histericks to hear from home." [4]

Wilson Athey complained that he had "bin hear in camps three months and have never received but one letter from papy," and threatened to "take to righting to the girls" to see if they would quench his thirst for news.[5]

"To now be debared the pleasure of writing to you and hearing from those I love would be next to death," wrote William J. Whatley to his wife on one occasion. A week later he observed, after repetition of failure to hear from home, "I feel mightily down when the mail comes in and the other boys gets letters and I dont but it has not been that way often." [6]

The consuming desire to get mail led, in one case at least, to the repentance of a boy who had left home under a cloud of parental disfavor. After a few weeks in camp he wrote to his father:

"Wishing to hear from you I write you this, it being the fourth letter that I have written home and as yet have received only one from those I so dearly love. . . . It looks very hard Father and still I deserve it all and more too—but when you come to reflect that you have seen me for perhaps the last time on earth I feel as though I ought to hear from home at least once a week—but you may be right in this . . . after giving you the trouble and anxiety that I have, but father I ask I beg of you to forget and forgive all, and I promise to do better in the future. The time may come yet when you will be proud of your wild —reckless and disapated Son as I have been called, my mind is made up to be in the front rank if we ever get into a fight and there to make my mark." [7]

Such offense as the father felt must have been abated by this poignant missive, and his parental heart must have swelled with pride when he heard of the subsequent valor of his son in the baptism of fire at Fort Donelson.

The writing materials used by Johnny Reb varied greatly. When he first went to war he was able to procure elaborately ornamented envelopes and sheets. These, especially the envelopes, bore martial and patriotic insignia and poetry.

One of the most elegantly designed envelopes found by the writer was that enclosing a letter written by Ruffin Thomson of the Eighteenth Mississippi Volunteers. The cover, printed specially for Thomson's company, the "Brown Rebels," had on the left end an intricately drawn emblem showing among other things a bale of cotton, a steamboat, a cannon, a fort and a spray of stars. In the center was a flag-draped likeness of "Jeff. Davis, Our First President, Confederate States of America." Across the top of the envelope this verse appeared:

> When the tempest of war o'er shadows our land,
> Its bolts shall ne'er rend freedom's temple asunder,
> For unmoved at its portal, Jeff. Davis shall stand,
> And repulse with his braves the assault of its thunder. [8]

Patriotic verses on envelopes, and occasionally at the top of letterheads were very popular among soldier correspondents in 1861. Themes were varied but all were of an ebullient character. One was a rousing call to conflict:

> Men of the South, arise, arise—
> Hurl back the invading foe,

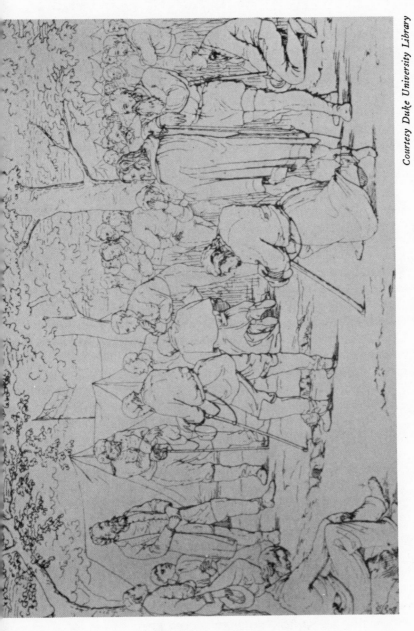

PRAYER IN STONEWALL JACKSON'S CAMP

From a wartime etching by Dr. A. J. Volck of Baltimore, Maryland.

CONFEDERATE COLOR-BEARER MOVING FORWARD IN BATTLE:
UNION SOLDIER'S CONCEPT

Drawing of Chas. W. Reed, soldier artist, Army of the Potomac. From
Chas. W. Reed Papers.

The sunny land must-aye-be free
Tho' blood of thousands flow:
Shall we who worship only God,
To a despot bend our knee?
No! No! men of the South arise,
AND SWEAR YOU WILL BE FREE.[9]

An unintended touch of irony was lent to these fire-eating sentiments by the postman's stamp, in bolder letters, of the words "Due 10."

Another exemplified the overweening confidence of the war's early days:

May those Northern fanatics who abuse their Southern neighbors,
Approach near enough to feel the point of our sabres;
May they come near enough to hear the click of a trigger,
And learn that a white man is better than a nigger.[10]

The oft-repeated themes of Yankee depravity and Southern pride appeared in this:

To arms! To arms! quick be ready
Think of what the South has been
Onward, onward strong and steady
Drive the vandals to their den
On, and let the watchword be
Country, home, and liberty! [11]

A fourth contained a note of desperate determination:

To arms! to arms! ye Southern braves
The avenging sword unsheath,
And 'round your heads or o'er your graves,
Entwine the laurel wreath.[12]

The strongest defiance was reflected in these lines:

Stand firmly by your cannon,
Let ball and grape-shot fly,
And trust in God and Davis
But keep your powder dry.[13]

These poetic efforts were usually accompanied by patriotic pictures and designs. In addition to the likeness of President Davis, the following were commonly used: the Confederate flag, a firing cannon, musket-armed infantrymen, a mounted cavalryman.

Sometimes these figures, separately or in combination, were used without accompanying poetry. One design consisted of a Confederate flag floating over a tree; from a limb Abe Lincoln is suspended by his feet, and about his neck an axe and a rail are tied; a Southerner viewing the scene stands on the Stars and Stripes.[14] Another decoration was simply the Confederate flag with the legend, "Remember Bethel, Sumpter, & Manassas, Forti et Fideli nil Difficile." [15]

Stationery of fancy design, while popular for a few months among the first volunteers, was rarely used after 1861. As the war moved into its second and third year, good paper of any sort was increasingly hard to get. In fact, the declining fortunes of the Southern Confederacy may be strikingly traced in the degeneration of the stationery used by ordinary soldiers. By the spring of 1863, and in many instances earlier, Rebs and their homefolk were writing on scraps of wrapping paper and resorting to many other expedients to keep up the flow of correspondence.

In accordance with a prewar custom many letters of the Confederate period were mailed without envelopes, the writing sheet simply being folded, sealed with wax and addressed on the outside. But the greater protection and privacy afforded by covers, and the inconvenience of keeping wax, tended toward a general use of envelopes in the army. In many instances soldiers made covers out of ledger sheets and wrapping paper. Occasionally they reversed an envelope of a letter received and used it for a missive of their own. Numerous covers were of wallpaper, the pattern being folded in. The most unusual container found by the writer was one made from a wallpaper issue of a newspaper. The outside of the wallpaper constituted the outside of the envelope, with the address written across the colored design, while the inside of both wallpaper and envelope was covered with French newsprint.[16]

But writing paper of any sort, in adequate quantities, was always harder to get than envelopes. The growing scarcity of paper, along with increasing inflation, boosted prices to a level almost beyond the reach of an ordinary soldier. Complaints occur repeatedly in the letters themselves. After paying a camp sutler five dollars for a quire of paper and three dollars for a bunch of envelopes, William R. Stillwell wrote to his wife, "How do you think that a soildier can save much money at eleven dollars per month?" [17] In November 1863 Thomas Caffey observed that the cost of a letter totaled fifty cents, and in midsummer of 1864, S. W. Farrow bemoaned, "Unless paper becomes more plentiful I shall have to quit writing it is worth a dollar a sheet." [18]

Johnny Reb had many devices to combat this paper shortage. One practice much in vogue was the inclusion of a request that the letter be passed around among various relatives and friends. A Texas private who worried chronically over the scarcity of writing materials began in late 1862 to reduce the size of his script, and after that time his handwriting, ordinarily difficult to read, was on such small scale as to be almost undecipherable. As an added conservation, he utilized canceled envelopes for writing paper.[19] Thomas Caffey, and doubtless others as well, erased the penciled messages of letters received and used the sheets thus cleared for the writing of answers, but with doubt as to its legibility.[20] Elers Koch instructed his parents, "When you write to me leave some blank paper for me to write back again."[21]

The desire to save paper, while probably not the main reason, doubtless contributed to the practice of writing joint or combination letters. The Moss brothers, Frank and W. M., often shared letters to their homefolk. Their co-operative technique varied. Sometimes Frank would fill the top portion of two sheets, front and back, and leave the lower portion for W. M. Again Frank would begin a letter, and W. M. would finish it. One missive was a multiple affair as to both the senders and addressees: W. M. wrote the first two pages to a sister; then Frank directed the third page to "My Dear Sisters"—there were three or four of them; the fourth page was written by Frank to a brother; and the envelope was addressed by W. M. to one of the girls.[22] The farthest limit of co-operation in this respect was reached by an epistle written seriatim to Bolling Hall of Alabama on September 15, 1863, by his five sons in the Confederate Army.[23] This item is indeed so remarkable as to be unmatched in Confederate letter writing, and perhaps in soldier correspondence of all time.

Envelopes and writing sheets were only a part of the problem confronted by correspondents. Ink became scarce, pale and expensive after the first year of the war. John Crittenden wrote to his wife in 1864:

"Bettie I have not been able to get any ink to write with yet . . . A Sutler here . . . has small Ink Bottles that will hold about three thimbles full. These he asks three dollars for could you fix me up some and send it to me?"[24]

Most Rebel ink users had long since fallen back on their own initiative. The greater portion of the soldier-made ink was derived from polk berries and oak balls. Pens were almost as hard to obtain as ink.

Substitutes for these were found in goose quills, cane quills and various other devices. A Texan scribbled to his sister in December 1864:

"I am writing with a corn Stalk pen when it wont write on one Side I turn over on the other. pen points are worth a dollar a peace Scarce at that." [25]

A great many writers resorted to pencils, but these, too, became expensive and hard to get.

Temporary relief was often unwittingly afforded by the Federals. Every Southern victory was followed by a flood of letters home written on elegant paper decorated with the Stars and Stripes.

After Chancellorsville a Georgian who had been lamenting the costliness and scarcity of stationery exuberantly informed his wife that he had captured from fifty to seventy-five dollars' worth of sheets and envelopes.[26]

And in the wake of the Rebel seizure of Plymouth, North Carolina, in April 1864, a Tar Heel lieutenant addressed his wife:

"I am seated in an old field surrounded by men . . . dividing out their captured spoils. I write to you on Yankee paper, with a gold pen, & Yankee envelope, with Yankee ink smoking Yankee cigar, full of Yankee sugar coffee &c with a Yankee sword, navy repeater & other 'fixins' buckled about me." [27]

When he was able to get his materials together, the letter-bent Reb still faced many difficulties. Writing desks were almost unheard of outside officers' tents and winter quarters. The usual writing platform consisted of a knapsack, a drum head, a canteen, a stump, or a board, and the seat was rarely anything but terra firma. Ordinarily the letter had to be composed in the hubbub of camp. Writing at night was made almost impossible by the scarcity of candles and by fatigue; and in the daytime there were frequent interruptions for drill and other camp duties. Under these circumstances the writing of a letter of any considerable length often extended over a period of several days.

In winter, when leisure afforded ample time for correspondence, extreme cold was a frequent handicap. One Reb wrote that "my hand keeps getting so cold that I have to stop and warm it in my pocket before I can go on"; and another complained that "for three days the weather has been so cold that . . . the ink froze on my pen as I wrote." [28]

A vivid picture of the difficulties which beset the camp correspondent is drawn by J. H. Puckett, in a letter to his wife dated June 27, 1862:

"I am seated in a beautiful grove of 'black Jack' with my back leaning against one, flat in the dust, short pencil, no board, nothing but my knee and finger to keep my paper straight, my face Southward, fires and smoke all about me, boys cooking dinner, crowds in talking distance discussing the great question [the war situation]. . . . You can give a pretty good guess what chance a fellow has to write sense. It is impossible to write a sentence without being disturbed." [29]

If the Yankees had just been firing away, this Reb must have experienced at one sitting practically every annoyance possible; and the Federals must not be forgotten, for more than one soldier interrupted his letter to answer the "long roll" and returned to complete it after the fight was over. Merely desultory shooting might or might not interrupt the writing.

A Tar Heel scribbling away under fire in the Petersburg trenches observed to his mother:

"I need not tell you that I dodge pretty often . . . for you can see that very plainly by the blots in this letter. Just count each blot a dodge and add in a few for I dont dodge for every shot." [30]

Another writing under similar circumstances from Atlanta remarked to his brother:

"The Yankees keep Shooting so I am afraid they will knock over my ink so I will close." [31]

Inability to pay postage often prevented letter writing. According to regulations of the time, payment could be made by the addressee, but this did little good in the many cases where homefolk were as short of money as the soldiers. Many Rebs did take advantage of the custom, however, including those whose families were well off; but the writer generally made some sort of apology for imposing on his correspondent.[32]

A great part of Confederate correspondence, perhaps the most of it, was delivered without benefit of postal facilities. Soldiers going home on furlough or on sick leave were almost invariably loaded down with letters of their comrades. Likewise relatives, clergymen, politicians, servants and other occasional visitors to camp were pressed into service. Soldiers home on furlough sometimes published notice in local papers that they were returning to camp at a certain time, and that they would be glad to take letters of friends and relatives of comrades belonging to their portion of the army. Rebs who sent letters home by comrades on leave frequently suggested in their communications that answers be returned by the same method. Through these informal means the correspondence of soldiers was greatly helped along.

In at least one instance a soldier was detailed by the military authorities for the specific purpose of carrying army mail. Absalom Grimes, a Missourian recently escaped from Federal prison, conceived, in the spring of 1862, the idea of gathering up letters among the friends and relatives of soldiers from the St. Louis area serving with Price's army in Mississippi and taking them across the Yankee lines. Through his daring and ingenuity, and with the assistance of influential friends in St. Louis, Memphis and elsewhere, he was able to establish a fairly regular mail service between troops and their correspondents in Missouri.[33] General Price was so impressed by the salutary effect on morale of Grimes's work that he had him commissioned official mail carrier for his command.[34] Subsequently Grimes made several trips between various Northern points and the Rebel camps with large cargoes of mail. Once he was captured with a carpetsack in his possession containing about three thousand letters addressed to Confederate soldiers and was sentenced to be shot, but with the characteristic boldness that carried him safely through four years of hair-raising adventure, he contrived his escape and resumed his perilous job. His most notable exploit was the establishment, in co-operation with a partner, Robert Louden, of mail service for soldiers under siege at Vicksburg.[35]

A pertinent reason for resort to irregular mail agencies was the notorious undependability of the Confederate Postal Department. As early as December 1861 a Richmond correspondent who had been instructed to post communications so that they would reach a New Orleans editor each Sunday wrote that the thought of such regularity was laughable. "Hang me if we've received a Western mail for the last four days," he remarked, "and the Southern, like the wind in Scripture, cometh and goeth where it listeth, and it listeth very much after the fashion of an awkward attack of ague and fever, the paroxysms of which occur on the second, third, or fourth, or fifth, or some other exceedingly incalculable day." [36]

But with the subsequent deterioration of the always overloaded transportation system, postal facilities continued to degenerate and deliveries became matters of the greatest caprice. Early in October 1863 a Mississippian serving in Virginia received a letter mailed by his wife on September 27. A short time later he received another dated August 10.[37] In April 1863 a Texan soldiering in Mississippi received a note written ten months before by his wife.[38] Many Rebs resorted to the practice of numbering letters by placing the figure 1, 2, 3, 4 and so on at the head of the missives in the order dispatched, so that correspondents might know with what regularity and in what proportion they were being received.

Soldiers chafed exceedingly at the tardiness of mails. "Just think," wrote a Georgian to his father from Petersburg in August 1864, "I have been from home five months and over, and have not received a letter from anyone of you."[39] About the same time, a Mississippian serving in Georgia remarked to his mother: "It is a constant incessant complaint in the army . . . in regard to not receiving any letters from home and their friends and relatives not receiving those they write to them. There is quite a defect somewhere, not to say gross negligence on the part of some one." [40]

Most soldiers, like these, attributed their failure to get mail to the postal authorities. But there were some correspondents who were inclined erroneously to lay the fault at the door of loved ones, who were thought to become delinquent in writing because of dwindling affection or carelessness. In such instances the note of hurt and despondency creeping into home letters was nothing short of poignant.

But in spite of all difficulties of writing and hazards of delivery, many soldiers continued to dispatch letters home with striking regularity until the end of their service. Some husbands wrote their wives once a week, usually on Sunday, regardless of conditions in the army. Others wrote more often, and not a few combined ingenuity with luck to secure the delivery of a large portion of their correspondence.

The writer has in his possession a file of 165 letters written by one Mississippi soldier to his wife from April 14, 1862, to August 28, 1864. These are letters that were delivered and preserved through the years. Doubtless some that the wife received were not saved. This soldier wrote on a rather flexible schedule approximating three letters a week. The average length was about three pages.[41]

The form and style of the letters naturally varied with the cultural background of the correspondents. Missives of well-educated men reflected the elegance and polish for which the letter writing of this period was distinguished. But as such men were exceptional, so were letters that approached excellence of composition. A good part of them were of fair quality in language, spelling and organization, being in general much like average letters of today except for their formal and euphuistic style. But a larger part were badly written from every standpoint of external form. Because of their prevalence, however, and especially because of their graphic detail, these more humble letters deserve particular attention.

Usually the correspondent opened his letter after the fashion of Private W. J. Honnoll: "My Dear cusin I Seat my Self down one time more to drop you a few lines to let you kno that I am in the best of helth I hope this will find you all enjoying the Same like blessing"; [42] or according to the manner of Private G. W. Athey: "Dear Mother I take my pen in hand to write you a few lines to let you no that I am well as common hoping that these few lines May come safe to hand and find you in Joying the best of helth Mother I have nothing of im portants to write to you at the presant." [43]

The introductory phrases "I seat myself" or "I take pen in hand" were widely used. Variations such as "I snatch my pen" and "I quickly draw my pen from its Scabbard" are found occasionally.[44]

One correspondent scribbled confusedly: "it is with pleasure this morning that I take my Seat and pen in hand to drop you a few lines." [45]

Good wishes for the health of the addressee and information about that of the writer were standard practices from which few deviated. Frequently occurring, too, was an apology for the absence of important information. Unless a letter was full of startling items, such as accounts of battles, it was apparently not considered newsworthy. One correspondent remarked: "I dont know that I can say Eny thing that is very Strange at this time." [46] Frequently Rebs who began letters by saying, "I haint got any thing of importance to rite" would proceed to the composition of several pages of material that must have been vitally interesting to the recipient.[47]

Difficulty of expression is shown by the recurrence of such statements as the following: "I have got so much to say But I Cant think of all that I doo waunt to say"; or "I dont know wife that I've got much news to write you—but I shall Keep Scratching a long untill I get Some more of this filled up." [48]

When the end of the letter was reached, the correspondent often closed with the stereotyped pledge, made ominous by the fact of war,

"I remain your Son untel death." [49] Thomas Warrick sometimes resorted to the variant, "I Ever Remain youre Husbin untell Deth when this you see Rem[em]ber me though meney miles a parte We Bee." [50] Another hackneyed phrase of prewar origin had particular point in the circumstances: "My pen is bad, my ink is pale; my love for you shall never fail." [51]

A striking characteristic of many letters is the inclusion of such formal and stilted expressions as "I can inform you that all goes well in camp," or "I am pleased to say to you that I am getting plenty to eat." There was gross inconsistency at times, as illustrated by a Reb who addressed his father as "Honored Sir," and later referred to him in letters to his wife as "the old man." [52]

"John I want you to write to me more plainer than you have bin a writing," complained Private Charles Futch to a brother serving in another portion of the army; he said further that he had recently carried a bundle of John's letters through two regiments and that "they was not a man that could read even the date of the month." [53]

And how fervently does the historian echo the wish that John Futch and thousands of his comrades had written more legibly! The handwriting of most letters was bad, but the spelling was worse. When these deficiencies are combined with haphazard punctuation, promiscuous capitalization, inferior paper and pale ink, the deciphering becomes indeed a task.

Concerning many Rebel letters this writer can repeat today the observation made of one particular missive by a correspondent in 1862: "I had not a like to a maid out half of yourre words theare is some that I hant maid out yet." [54] But modern scholars are drawn to these difficult manuscripts, if for no other reason than that of adventure. For the choicest originalities are often encountered just beyond the veil of apparent undecipherability.

Misspellings of simple words occur repeatedly. A few random samples will indicate tendencies:

accitment	for excitement	cear	for care
afeard	" afraid	ceep	" keep
agetent	" adjutant	cerce	" scarce
ancious	" anxious	Coossey	" Coosa
bin	" been	crawsed	" crossed
boath	" both	cullur	" color
bregad	" brigade	daingeroust	" dangerous
carey	" carry	dus	" does

eyedear	for idea	rickolect	for recollect
forchin	" fortune	ridgement	" regiment
furteege	" fatigue	rote	" wrote
furloe | furlow |	" furlough	sadisfide	" satisfied
		saft	" safe
garde	" guard	sirtenly	" certainly
horspital | horspittel | hospitly | orpital |	" hospital	sity	" city
		snode	" snowed
		sow	" so
		staide	" stayed
hurde	" heard	taulk	" talk
knews | noose | nuse |	" news	toilse	" toils
		tords	" towards
		unbenoing	" unbeknown
medison	" medicine	waulking	" walking
meney	" many	waunt	" want
mity	" mighty	wee	" we
moer	" more	wether	" weather
perperce	" purpose	wod	" would
pestearred	" pestered	wonst	" once
porchun	" portion		

When correspondents attempted to use long and unfamiliar words, they were apt to get unusual results, as shown in the following:

A brim ham lillkern	for Abraham Lincoln
Chic a har mana	" Chickahominy
comodate	" accommodate
coummling	" Cumberland
dyereaer	" diarrhoea
experdission	" expedition
Fluriday	" Florida
horspitibel	" hospitable
mungunry	" Montgomery
physitian	" physician
regislatury	" legislature
rumatis	" rheumatism

The ordinary Reb was nearly always subject to greater defeat by a word like *Chattanooga* than by the Yankees.

Difficulties with spelling caused some writers to combine two words into one, as *ought not* into "ortent," *roasting ear* into "roastinear," *a miracle* into "american," and *Irish potatoes* into "ashpotatoes"; or contrariwise to make two words of one, as "lew tennante" of lieutenant, "a nough" of enough, "comma sarry" of commissary, and "trance fur" of transfer.

A common practice was the prefixing of the archaic sign a to verbs, as "you ask how I was agetting along," or "I am agoing to Tennessee." Frequently the article a is combined with the adjective or noun following as "afew," "abig," "afurloe." Letters are sprinkled with other colloquialisms common among rural folk of English antecedents, such as "haint" and "hant" for have not or had not; "nary" for none or not any, "ary" for any or either, "hit" for it, "seen" for saw, and "fiten" for fought.

Occasionally rustic figures of speech were invoked. One Reb remarked that the Yankees were "thicker than lise on a hen and a dam site ornraier"; another said that his comrades were "in fine spirits pitching around like a blind dog in a meet hous"; and a third reported that it was raining "like poring peas on a rawhide." [55]

Poor spelling and writing were due in some measure to haste and carelessness. An Alabamian of fair education observed on one occasion: "I have written this Letter as well as many others I write in great hast Never haveing time to read them over." [56] That many other correspondents did likewise was evidenced by the fact that words spelled correctly at the beginning of letters were sometimes misspelled when repeated near the close.

To indifference and hurry also must be credited much of the repetition and incoherence that characterized soldier correspondence. The Alabamian referred to above said, "I have But Little system in Writing Letters the first thing I think of is the first thing I Write down, up one side of a sheat of paper and down the other"; and his method was by no means unusual.[57]

An interesting by-product of increased practice in letter writing was a marked improvement in quality. By 1864 soldiers who at first had experienced much difficulty in expression and penmanship were showing a noticeable progress in both handwriting and composition. Letters at this time are marked by less circumlocution, by greater ease of style and by increased coherence. But too much confidence caused some correspondents to overstep their abilities, sometimes with ludicrous results. A Tar Heel requested his folk to give kindest regards to all his "concomitants"; and a comrade who had heard rumors of an armistice said in all seriousness: "I hope they will have and [an] army mistress"! [58]

The two letters which follow will illustrate common characteristics of spelling and style. The first was written by a Louisiana soldier early in the war:

"*Dear Wife:* i take the opitunity to write to you to let you now that i am well an i hope these few lines may come safte to hand and find you injoying the same blesson we was sworen in the confedert states for durin the war i dont now when will see you i want to see you verry bad write to me as soon as you get my letter i send my best love to you and mark [a son] cis [kiss] mark for me i stod on gard las nite for the first time we fare tolible well yet we are now on rediness to go to new orleans they are therty five thousand yankes at chip ilant [Ship Island] now we are looking for a call every moment weare in the fiftenth regment tell mother i am well and i wold like to see her verry well tel her to write to me i have seen a great deal here they are fore regments here now . . . write to me as soon as you git my letter Dear wife my ink is pail my pen is bad my love to you shall never fail god bless you. cis mark for me and think of me as little as you can for i will never see no more pleser in this world i sent my likeness to you write to me if you got it or not i must come to a close remain your husband ontell death direct your letters to camp more in the cear of C E Hosea J. M Guess to Elminy Guess Remember me God bless the in cear of C E Hosea" [59]

The second was penned in the last year of conflict by an Alabamian:

"*Diere Sisteer* I Seat my Self this morn to Anter youer kine letteer which cam to han a bout ten Days a go this is the Fierst time I hav had the chance to Write this leave me on[l]y tole well I hoe this Few lins may cum to han An Fine you all well Dear Sisteer you want to no Soph a bout your husban he was well a Few Days go he cum out all Saft So fur I have cum out Saft So Fur but I am march Downn we hav bin run From the Yankey an Fiten them a bout 12 Days I am getin tierd of hit tha like to got me tha Shot a hole throw my Sacel an I had hit on my back but a mis is good as a mile Dear Sisteer I want you to write to me and giv me all the nus you hav got I can Say to you that brother James got woned in the thy Sly Jides darky got kill Stevn lyeman got woned I wod bee glad to see you all I hope this war will brake up Soon we never can whip the north Fer tha hav So meney moer men an we hav got I think we will move on to Atlant be Foer we Stop but I dout [t]hat tha will dow So I will close Fer I cant write I

dnt no [whet]her you can read this or not hit is bad dun I will mane
your Brother tel Deth write Soon"

"A WIDEMAN" [60]

These examples give point to the comment of a Texas soldier in
a letter to his sister, "tell Bob he need not quit writing I can guess at
his dutch if I cant read it." [61]

Soldiers who could not write called on acquaintances to take down
letters at their dictation. Sometimes company officers performed this
favor, but usually the scribes were messmates or relatives. Such service
was generally free of charge, but occasionally payment was made in
kind by performing camp chores, washing clothes, or half-soling shoes.
Secretarial duties in companies where there was much illiteracy were
apt to be heavy.

"Some body is nearly always after me to write for them," remarked
a North Carolinian; "this makes 8 letters I have wrote . . . I backs
[i.e., address] a good meny letters and reads letters to. I read 3 last
night." [62]

The spelling and handwriting of some who took dictation were so
bad as to suggest cases of the halt leading the maimed. Such a situation is indicated by the following postscript to a Georgian's letter:
"Rote by I. T. Hight for I. J. Owen to Anderson Owens & deny
Owens." [63]

Now and then an illiterate Reb learned to scribble out his own
letters. An interesting case of this kind was revealed in the statement
of Private W. W. Brown: "Mother when you wright to me get some-
body to wright that can wright a plain hand to read I Cold not read
your leter to make sence of it it wrote so bad I have lurned to do my
own wrading and writing and it is a grate help to me." [64]

What did ordinary soldiers write about in their letters home? The
answer must be everything, for there is hardly an item in the entire
range of human activity and interest that does not find some place in
their correspondence. Life, death, joy, sorrow, sin, righteousness, fidel-
ity, fornication, comedy and tragedy are all reflected and elaborated in
the letters which poured from Rebel encampments. Only a few
glimpses of this variegated subject matter can be given here.

A substantial portion of the average letter was devoted to a statement of things that the soldier wanted his correspondent to discuss in
later communications. First of all, if he was a father writing to his
wife, he wanted to hear about his children: what they talked about,

what new accomplishments they had achieved, or new tricks they had learned; whether they were obedient; if they were faithful in the performance of chores; how rapidly they were growing; did they show any increasing resemblance to their mother or father; what smart sayings had they uttered; were they making satisfactory progress at school; and did they recall their dad. One of the greatest apprehensions of fathers was that their young children would forget them.

"I often ask myself whether our little Callie speaks of her 'pa'," wrote Robert Gill to his wife. "Does she remember me? You must not whip her. I have a perfect horror of whipping Children." Later he remarked: "You say Callie is as pretty and Smart as ever, that May can walk and is just as Mama would have her to be. Are you not proud of them? What do you call them in your little talk to them, little Cherubs, or would that be sacraligious? Does Callie say her prayers right now or does She Still Say 'Punny's Soul' or 'Ma's Soul,' as the Case may be?" [65]

"I want to see the children very bad," wrote D. Hunter to his wife; "their is sevril men in the same fix that I am in that [they] hav young babs at home that they never saw." [66] In such cases as that of Hunter— and their number was large—interest in the appearance and doings of infants was unusually keen. A Georgian on receiving notice that he was shortly to become a father wrote teasingly to his spouse, "Molly you need not talk about and other boy war or not war I must have a girl if you go to talking that way I sal not lik it atall it must be a girl and its name must be Virginia [if] it is a boy I will call it Bull Run." [67]

Another Reb who chided his wife good-naturedly for presenting him with a girl instead of a boy received this mischievous retort: "I think you give your boys to some one else. I expect if I knew it you will have several boys scattered about against this war ends." [68] And a North Carolinian who had recently been visited by his wife inquired significantly of her "whether I done eny thing for you when you was out hear." [69]

Occasionally fathers in the army would address portions of their letters to their offspring. An Alabamian concluded a note to his wife thus: "I will say a few words to the Childern Willia I waunt you to Bee a good Boy and minde youre Mother Markus I waunt you and Willia to Bee smarte and make smarte men and all ways tell the Truth and mind what you are told and minde your'e Mother." [70]

Next to his children, the ordinary Reb was interested in hearing about other close relatives, about domestic pets, particularly his dogs,

and about crops, especially fruit, vegetables and other edibles that he
so longed for.

"How is the Crops?" inquired Jerome Yates of his mother. "You
must write me every particular of the Crop how high the cotton and
corn is where it is the Largest how fat the plow Horses are How the
Cows look How much milk you get How the Hogs look. How looks
the Colts . . . How many Chickens you have." [71] The minutiae of
home affairs and of community life were of vital concern to the soldier, and he liked for the narration of details to have some verve and
humor, as was suggested by a Texan's observation to his sister:

"Your very interesting letter . . . was written in a style that Suits
me exactly. I always like something Spicey, but these dry affairs that
are written on the old Sing, Song, style and that are utterly destitute of
Spirit never afford me any pleasure to read them I want something
funny, something that will make me laugh, haw haw Something that
will raise my spirits while sojourning in these low grounds of Sorrow." [72]

But the greater portion of letters received by Confederates fell considerably short of the standards desired by this soldier. Many were
written in the sing-song style that he decried, and the frequency of tact-
lessness in the choice of subject matter was amazing. In cases so frequent as to aggregate thousands, home folk elaborated their own hardship and gloom. They complained of bad crops, of fear of Yankee raids
or of havoc already wrought by Federal visitation, of trouble with overseers, of slothfulness and insubordination of slaves, of scarcity of food
and clothing, or of apprehension of such scarcity, of the undue pro-
longation of war, of the hopelessness of victory, of deprivation of the
company of their absent sons or spouses, of sickness or the anticipation
of it, and of innumerable other woes.

One wife, after apparently exhausting the supply of ordinary complaints, upbraided her soldier husband for fathering the several children
already born to her, and while complaining of his absence, expressed
dread of his return lest she again be subjected to motherhood. "Was
peace established & you at home," she wrote, "You know the horrible
nightmare which would always frighten away any little happiness that
might occasionally cross my path." [73]

A South Carolinian whose wife allegedly played the harlot with a
train of stay-at-homes, including "the preacher," had the scandal's
nauseating details revealed to him by neighborhood gossips.[74]

Communications carrying tidings of such unpleasant character as marital infidelity were exceptional, but those reciting other doleful subjects were regrettably prevalent. "You know not how . . . Depressing it is," wrote one Reb who was fortunate in having cheerful correspondents at home, "to get letters that breathe a spirit of Discontent. I tell you sister Scottie that one half of the Desertions from the southern army is caused by the letters they receive from . . . home." [75]

Another Reb, likewise fortunate, told his spouse of a comrade's correspondence: "A friend read me his wife's letters a short time ago. I was tired long before he closed. 'Oh do come home darling—oh for one hour with you—I would come to you if I could etc.' Now isn't that childish? Thank God you have more sense than that." [76]

Childish or not, there can be no doubt that letters of homefolk telling of dwindling larders, citing instances of immunity from arrest of army absentees, and openly urging return to families, played havoc with Confederate morale. [77]

There was apparently no systematic effort at censorship. People at home wrote what they would, and with impunity. [78] Troops were forbidden to disclose army strength, and private letters telling of current military operations were barred, but the ordinary Reb felt these restrictions to an insignificant extent. [79] Control of any sort over correspondence must have been difficult in view of the fact that such a large portion of the letters never got into regular postal channels. So Johnny Reb wrote with comparatively free rein to his homefolk. If he was tired of the war, he did not fear to say so, and in a considerable number of cases he announced to his relatives that he was coming home shortly, by regular means if possible, but he was coming anyhow.

Of the variety of subjects which filled the home letters of soldiers, none elicited such detailed treatment as battles. Rebs whose letters were ordinarily brief would extend themselves to many pages in narrating an experience under fire at Shiloh, Murfreesboro or Gettysburg. And frequently battle accounts would be carried over to a second and a third missive.

Food also occupied a prominent place in correspondence. Repeatedly the soldier told of the quantity of his regular rations, what he was procuring on the side by "foraging" activities, how present rations compared with past issues, what the prospects were for an increase or a diminution of food; how tough the beef was, how he was preparing his meals and who composed his mess. He kept close tab on fruits and vegetables in season at home, and on such epoch-making occasions as hog killing; if he was within convenient distance he sometimes requested that a portion of home abundance be sent to him; if not, he merely gave himself to expressions of wishfulness and regret.

Soldiers of slave-owning families made frequent mention of the servants. A very common postscript was "tell the Negroes howdy," or sometimes "give my respects to the colored members of the family." Occasionally a portion of the letter proper would be addressed to slaves commending them for good behavior, or warning them against failure in their duties during the master's absence. William J. Whattey wrote:

"I want you to tell the negroes, that if they dont go ahead with their work and do right and behave themselves while I am gone that I will certainly call them to an account when I come home; and I may be there before they look for me I am now having a harder time than any of them and if they wont behave themselves and work while I am gone that they need not expect any favors from me, tell Marshal that I will hold him accountable for his bad conduct." [80]

Descriptions of camp and of camp life were always favorite subjects. For instance a Texan wrote to his sister:

"Well lizeer I will tell you what is going on in camps today Jo is out on picket guard I am in the Tent writen on my nap Sack Dan Mayes & A Chatham geting diner A Norton has goan to Alins regment Dutch writin to Miss Mary Giles Glozner is Sick and Dolf waiting on him Jack Martin is ansurin his letter from Al that constitutes our famley A Granger I forgot he is playin marbles I would like to know whare we will be a month from today" [81]

Another Reb told proudly of the comfort he had achieved in bivouac: "We have a great invention for a bed. We put up 4 forks & lay sticks across them upon whitch are placed cane or reeds out of the river bottom and canes are lashed together with the inside of the paw-paw bark when a blanket is spread over these they make a sort of spring bed." And to make sure that the addressee obtained an accurate idea of his device, he made a rough sketch of it at the bottom of the page. [82]

Tidbits of camp gossip were frequently passed on, as well as asides on the conduct of men from the home neighborhood: this soldier under arrest, that one thieving, and this one guilty of deserting to the enemy while on sentry post. Such derogatory reports sometimes elicited disclaimers or explanations from those accused.

"I heard that Some boddy wrote to Coffeeville that all the boys here was a playing poker," remarked T. J. Newberry to his father. "I am in hops that you dont believe that I have come to that as much as you have cautioned me about it." [83]

Another Reb under censure of homefolk wrote to his wife: "You spoke in yours that William had written home that Crittenden Joe Batts and myself was all tight. . . . Wee had bought a bot of whiskey about that time, the first that I'd had for two months before and haven't seen any since I did not think that any of us felt that wee had drank so much I suppose he had nothing else to write." [84]

A third soldier who was being slandered by community gossips exclaimed disgustedly to his spouse: "The people . . . that . . . speakes slack about me may kiss my——— . . . Mollie excuse my vulgar language if you please." [85]

Unmarried Rebs were greatly interested in the doings of girls of their home neighborhood and their letters contain frequent inquiries about them: who was courting whom, what marriages had taken place, were the girls as beautiful as formerly, and were parties as well attended as before the war. Indirect messages of love-starved campaigners to sprightly maidens were numerous and varied: tell them that they all must not marry, as soldiers want some to be left for courting on their return home, or tell Miss So-and-So to be true to me and not marry a slacker. But of all such communications that of a rough and ready Louisianian was the most pungent: "What has become of Halda and Laura?" he inquired of a friend; "have you seen them and what did they have to say when you see them again give them my love—not best respects now but love by God." [86]

The ordinary soldier shied away from the subject of death in his correspondence, out of consideration for his anxious loved ones at home, and for the sake of his own morale. But occasionally he was forced to write a note of sympathy to the wife or parents of some comrade killed in battle. In such letters the bereaved family was informed in as great detail as possible of the circumstances of the casualty: at what time the deceased fell, where he was situated when he was struck, who saw him fall, whether he lingered or died instantly, what his last words were, and what disposition was made of his body and his personal effects. The letter usually closed with a eulogy of the man's character and bravery, and with expressions of condolence. In not a few cases, these messages were written by a brother of the fallen soldier who was serving with him at the time of his death. Such letters represent the height of sadness in soldier correspondence. Their tone and character is indicated by the following communication written the day after Antietam to a bereaved wife in Texas:

My dear afflicted Sister
    It gives me intensest pain to tell you of death of my dear brother, your devoted husband Andrew. Oh: how desolate is my sad heart at the loss of that brother twice indeared by the hardships and perils we have passed through togather. But if my heart is so sad, what must yours be my sister, deprived of a husband and a friend. I cannot comfort you, but can only commend you to the tender mercies of our Heavenly Father who hath said he doth not willingly afflict. He hath said he will be a Father to the fatherless, a husband to the widow. I pray him to have mercy on you and your little children. Our dear one suffered no pain in death for he was shot through the temples. He was killed on yesterday morning in the fight at Sharpsburg [also known as Antietam]. Of the conflict being undesided, his body has not yet been recovered, but Maj. George has promised to attend to his interment. I am too badly wounded to return to look after him. having been shot through the left arm and twice, slightly in the side. I cannot write more now, but will do so in a few days. My heart is too sad. To God I commend you my dear sister, Your sorrowing brother,
                                                        A. M. ERSKINE [87]

Johnny Reb was, with few exceptions, a sentimental person and this side of his nature often asserted itself in his correspondence. Thoughts of home and loved ones might inspire such an outburst as this:

"How pleasant are home and its associations. My Dear 'old log hut' how sweet are the memories that cluster around my heart at thy mention! how near to me Seem thy delapidated Strength, Even the Kitchen with its puncheon floor, the Cistern with oaken iron bound bucket, the ricketty old gail, and corn crib with cracks unstopped, Even old Becca's strained unmolodius tunes would be music to me. Then, how much dearer to me would be the playful laugh of Callie in her childish glee, the sweet & innocent smile of May, and the ever pleasant smile of Welcome Bettie!" [88]

Again tenderer emotions would seek expression in verse. Often this was nothing more than adaptation of trite jingle. One Reb complimented his wife with these lines:

"The Rose is red
The Grass is green
The days is past
That we have seen!" [89]

Another sent these surprisingly intimate stanzas to his spouse:

"The rose is red
The vilet is blue
Shogar is sweet
And so are you

"The sea is deap
And in your armes
I long to sleep
A heap Nancy" [90]

A third addressed his father:

"The night was cool
The day is hot
Our parting hours
Is not for got" [91]

A few soldiers composed original verses for their wives. The meter was usually unconventional, figures of speech were often strained and spelling poor, but even so, some revealed a genuine poetic feeling. A lowly Georgian wrote a poem captioned "Evening Moonlight" which had for its inspiration the familiar theme of home:

1 "this world is verry lonely now
Sens Im so fare from home
I have not a frind with me to bow
before my fathers throne
2 long and lonely have bin the days
Sens I have Seen my wife
the moon is dark it hath rays
and not much pleasure is my life
3 I am setting now in the broad moonlight
and thinking of the past
that awful and that solumn knight
you held me to your bosom fast

4 Our little boy was fast asleep
   I though he would not miss
   and while I stood by his bed to weep
   upon his cheek I plased a Kiss
5 I am going now wheer Iv often gon
   to appear before the throne
   and pray the father oh how long
   Before I shal see my home
6 the Lord has bin very good to me
   in all the conflicks past
   he has promised that a frind hed be
   and gide me safe to the last
7 Mollie you have my hart and life
   and if on the battle feeald I die
   you are my darling and my wife
   my only request is to by your side to lye" [92]

The poet also explains the circumstances of composition:

"Molly thar were several other verses but having to write it by moonlight and with a pensil I can not read them this morning I hav composed meny such sens I hav bin from home and as I walked my post at knight this will show you that not withstanding my long absens from home and has seen so much murder I still have the same tender feelings that I evar had." [93]

Another Reb, an Alabamian, sent a poem of exceptional tenderness to his wife:

"I'll think [of] thee when far-far away
And dwell with rapture on yore name
Oh! you for whom I write whoose harte can melt
At the Soft thriling voice of love.

"In pleasant dreames or Sorrows hours
In crowed hills or lonely bowers
The pleasure of my mind Shall be
Forever to remember thee.

"Aadress and compliment by vision
Make love and court by intuistion
Tis ore this Scene my me[m]ory wakes
And final broods with miser care

"Though fortune may frown me and frends forsake me
May banich me far from the presece of thee
Though wherever I roam and whatever is my lot
You will not you can not be for got

"May yore thought ever be of love
May your footsteps ever be a love sors
May your smiles ever be Smiles of love
May your tears ever be tears of Joy.
　　　　　Forget me not

"When that quenly orb of night
Throws back her veail of Ether blue
And fads in beauty and in light
I will gase on it and think of you

"No dearest I'll forget thee not
Tis traced too clearly on that brow
To think that thou will be forgot
Whilest memory clings to naught below

"Oh who the exquisit delight can tell
Or who can painte the charm unspeakable
Two Souls with one thought
Two hearts with one beat." [94]

When the transcription of this verse had been completed, the correspondent took his pen and painstakingly drew an elaborate though crude design of a leafy vine around the tops of the two pages, the pattern being different for each page. In each upper corner of the second page he sketched a figure resembling a potted plant. Hard-bitten, unlearned and backwoodsy though this soldier was, his character was rich with gentleness, and his spirit responded to beauty.

And like him were countless others who wore the gray. They were regrettably crude in speech, inept in writing, tatterdemalion in dress and rustic in background. On the march they were incalculably tough, and under fire they were a host of yelling savages. But their haphazard appearance, their rough ways, and their bloodthirsty demeanor on fields of battle belied their deeper selves. Basically and fundamentally they were, for the most part, men of warm affection, and susceptible to the tenderest of emotions.

CHAPTER XII

KICKING OVER THE TRACES

THE day was August 1, 1861. The scene, Camp Louisiana, headquarters of the battalion of Washington Artillery on the northern Virginia front. As the hour of ten o'clock approached, Private Napier Bartlett sat grimly in the tented hall of justice awaiting the convening of the special court-martial ordered the day before for his trial.

Presently the members of the court filed in. Private Bartlett recognized them immediately as officers of the first three companies of his battalion, namely, Captain W. B. Miller of his own Third Company who had been designated as the president of the court, Lieutenant C. C. Lewis of the Second Company, and Lieutenant J. B. Whittington of the Third Company. Lieutenant Whittington had been designated as judge advocate for the trial.

The accused did not have to wait long for proceedings to get under way. First Captain Miller read the order of the major requiring assembly of the tribunal. Then Judge Advocate Whittington swore in the other members of the court, and he, in turn, was sworn in by President Miller. Thereupon, the judge advocate, who acted in a role corresponding generally to that of prosecuting attorney in civil proceedings, read aloud the following charge against the accused.

"Charge—conduct to the prejudice of good order and military discipline. Specification—in this that he the said Bartlett of the 3rd. Co. B. W. A. being encamped on or about the 27th July 1861 near Centreville, Va. in the vicinity of the enemy, and he the said Private Napier Bartlett . . . being regularly posted as a sentinel did wilfully and deliberately lie down on his post and was found asleep. All this in camp near Centreville, Va. on or about the 27th of July 1861
            "John J. Garnett, Lieut. C.S.A. Comdg Section W. A.
"Witnesses: Lieut. John J. Garnett
            Corporal William Fellows Jr."

When he had finished reading the charge, the judge advocate faced the prisoner who had been led to the bar and said, "Private Bartlett,

217

you have heard the charge preferred against you, how say you—guilty or not guilty?" To which the accused, or his counsel, responded "not guilty."

Then Lieutenant Garnett was called to the witness stand by the judge advocate, sworn in and asked to tell what he knew of the charges against the prisoner.

Garnett said that he had been awakened about midnight of July 27 by the corporal of the guard who told him that a sentinel was asleep at his post. He arose and went with the corporal to a fence beyond the camp where he found Private Bartlett fast asleep. He shook the accused violently and said, "Bartlett, what are you doing?" or "What do you mean?" Bartlett replied that the corporal had given him permission to sit down at his post. Under cross-examination Garnett admitted that Bartlett may have said that the corporal told him to sit down.

The prosecution then swore in William Fellows who testified that he was corporal of the guard on the night of July 27, and that in accordance with instructions from Lieutenant Garnett he had assigned Bartlett to sentry post. A short time later he found the accused asleep. He then aroused Garnett and pointed out to him the condition of the accused. He testified further that at the time he posted the sentinels Bartlett had asked if he might sit down. He had responded, "Yes, but you must not go to sleep." Cross-examined as to Bartlett's condition when found, the witness said that the accused was "leaning against the fence asleep."

The defense then swore in Private Adams as witness. Adams testified that he heard Bartlett make some complaint to Corporal Fellows at the time he was posted on guard, but that he didn't recall its nature. Another defense witness said that he and Bartlett had been absent without leave during the night of the twenty-seventh, returning to camp about 11:15. During their walk of about six miles, to avoid the sentries, Bartlett had complained of a sore leg and had been forced on two occasions to stop for rest. When they returned to camp they were informed that they must immediately go on guard as punishment for their absence. He stated further that he heard Bartlett say to the corporal of the guard that he did not believe himself able to stand sentry on account of his leg.

The accused "made his statement and defence," either directly or through counsel, to which the prosecution responded. The court then found the accused guilty and imposed the following sentence: "That he be condemned to police his company's quarters every day for thirty days and . . . be debarred the privilege of leaving camp under any consideration for the same period of time."

There being no further business, the court adjourned. Subsequently the proceedings were written up, signed by Captain Miller and forwarded to the battalion commander for approval.[1]

The body that tried Private Bartlett was known as a special court-martial to distinguish it from a judicial organ of wider authority known as a general court-martial. Special courts-martial, consisting of three officers, were limited in jurisdiction to non-capital offenses of privates and subalterns. They were appointable by commanding officers of corps, regiments, barracks, forts, garrisons and other lesser posts of military service. They could not inflict a fine exceeding one month's pay, nor a period of hard labor or imprisonment exceeding thirty-one days.

The jurisdiction of general courts-martial included all persons and offenses subject to military law, including sutlers, drivers and all others receiving pay from the army. They were composed of from five to thirteen officers, preferably of rank higher than that of persons on trial. They were appointable by generals in the field, and by any other officers in charge of separate departments. A few weeks before Lee's surrender the authority to summon courts-martial was extended to include generals in command of state reserves.

The findings and sentences of both types of courts-martial were subject to the review of the officer by whose command the trials were ordered. Authority to review carried with it the power to execute sentence, to mitigate punishment, or to pardon. A simple majority was sufficient for conviction, save in capital offenses where concurrence of two-thirds of the court was required.[2]

Sentence in the case of Private Bartlett was strikingly out of proportion to the gravity of his offense. Mere confinement to camp and policing of company quarters for thirty days of a man found guilty of one of the most serious charges known to military practice, that of sleeping at post of duty in the presence of the enemy, was nothing short of preposterous. Under published regulations he might have been given the death penalty. Private Bartlett gave effective illustration of the evil consequences of easy sentences. For within six months of his first offense it became necessary to hale him again before court-martial, on the charges of feloniously taking away one of the government horses and remaining absent without leave for an entire night.[3]

But the leniency shown to Bartlett was apparently not out of harmony with early practices of Confederate courts-martial. Judicial sessions held at Corinth subsequent to Shiloh treated the offense of desertion with such lightness as to draw from Beauregard the following rebuke: "In those cases in which the charge of desertion has been established by the testimony . . . the sentence of the court is wholly inadequate to so grave an offense. In future the General Commanding will not approve of such trivial punishment." [4]

This tendency toward overleniency was perhaps a factor contributing to supplementation of the court-martial system in the fall of 1862; but the change came mainly from considerations growing out of the Antietam campaign. The jurisdiction of courts-martial did not cover adequately, except where martial law was proclaimed, offenses committed by stragglers beyond the boundaries of military encampments. Such cases were supposed to be tried by civil courts. [5] But in a borderland area, such as that traversed by Lee on the Maryland campaign, civil tribunals were apt to be so disorganized by removal of population and by other circumstances attendant on invasion, that their effectiveness was greatly hampered. Consequently crimes could be committed by roving soldiers with comparative impunity. Then, in the purely military realm, courts-martial were not adapted to conditions of active campaign, such as the Antietam movement. Time could not be taken out in the midst of operations for the convening of the court. And afterward witnesses might be either dead or so scattered as to make trials inconvenient and costly to the service. Delay incident to assembling and hearings, followed by review of findings by commanding officers, impeded the swiftness of action that was necessary to preserve discipline. In particular the wholesale straggling that marked the Maryland campaign presented a situation demanding immediate action that was impossible under the existing system. [6]

These considerations moved Lee in September 1862 to request remedial action of Davis. The president addressed the congress on the subject, and on October 9, 1862, a law was approved providing for the creation of special military courts. According to this law a court composed of three judges having colonel's rank and one judge advocate with captain's rating was assigned to each army corps. These courts were given extensive authority including the power to summon civilian witnesses. Their jurisdiction included that exercised by courts-martial and, in addition, offenses defined as crime by civil laws, but it did not apply to officers ranking higher than colonel. The new system was not intended to eliminate the function of courts-martial, but subsequent policy tended toward lessening of the latter's jurisdiction. [7]

Inauguration of the new judicial system appeared to produce salutary results. Secretary of War Seddon in 1863 expressed the conviction that the military courts had, by expediting court action, improved both discipline and morale. But the growing magnitude in 1864 of the related evils of straggling and desertion indicate a failure to achieve the ends for which Lee and others had hoped. James Phelan, one of the court members functioning in Mississippi, wrote a letter to President Davis on October 2, 1864, criticizing severely the exercise of pardoning power by corps commanders as allowed under the law creating the court system. When he assumed his judicial capacity, he said, he determined to create a wholesome respect for the new courts by dispensing emphatic justice to first offenders. But he soon found that it was very difficult to convict a soldier who had social position and influential friends. Two such soldiers arraigned before him, who by exertions of able counsel barely escaped conviction of desertion, were found guilty of absence without leave. Acquaintances set up a tremendous agitation for their pardon by the corps commander and "in a few days they were both parading the streets with their friends." In the meanwhile, some men of lesser social position, convicted at the same time, had not been favored by the interposition of wealthy and influential connections and were serving their sentences. Such discrimination, according to Phelan, was "a shame in the eyes of justice," and led to "the most hostile and unhappy spirit among the poor men of the army." Phelan's position and reputation were such as to give considerable weight to his statements.[8]

Rebs who were called before dispensers of army justice, whether courts-martial or special military tribunals, were charged with a great variety of offenses. A rather common cause of arrest was fighting. Most officers attempted to ignore minor altercations between their men, but occasionally contentions were of such a nature as to require official action.

Such was the case involving Privates Koss and Ryan of the Washington Artillery. Koss left his sentry post to warm himself at a fire surrounded by several comrades. Someone mentioned a previous disagreement between Ryan and Koss, whereupon the former spoke up and asked the latter if he wished to settle the matter then and there. Koss replied that he fought only with gentlemen, whereupon Ryan pitched into him.

The row took place near the officers' quarters, and Lieutenant Hawes, officer of the day, ran out to quell the disturbance. In restoring order Hawes struck Koss over the head with a saber and called the fighters "damned sons of bitches." Koss submitted written charges of cruel and unbecoming treatment against the officer, and the latter countered with action against Koss for fighting.

The regimental court-martial, convened to consider the case, found that Hawes used "strong language," but did not feel it necessary to administer any sentence. Koss was adjudged guilty of fighting and ordered to be privately reprimanded by the commanding officer of the battalion, but lest the major speak too harshly the court recommended the prisoner to his mercy.[9] No blood was spilled in this encounter, and had it not been for the conspicuousness of place and the submission of charges against a superior by Koss, it is doubtful if court proceedings would have been invoked. As one Reb correctly observed, the usual mode of discipline in cases where the "boys fall out and pass a few licks" was confinement in the guardhouse on the simple order of a commissioned officer.[10]

The offense for which Private Bartlett was convicted, that of sleeping while on post of duty, claimed the attention of courts with considerable frequency. And punishment varied greatly. Private C. A. Everett of the Washington Artillery, who was found asleep on picket in Virginia three weeks before First Manassas, drew a sentence of three days' close confinement in the guardhouse with bread-and-water ration. In passing sentence the court noted as extenuating considerations the facts that the accused had, prior to trial, been confined the full period allowed by regulations, namely eight days, and had shown "penitence for consciousness of the grievousness of the offense"; but the most amazing explanation of judicial clemency was the court's recognition of the circumstance "that on the night and time stated in the charge the accused had been induced to partake of an extraordinary quantity of liquor to which he was not accustomed." [11] The suggestion of this court would seem to be that men when confronted with a turn of sentry duty should take a heavy dram, compose themselves comfortably, and go to sleep, and if caught, to make demonstrations of abject contrition. A court-martial sitting at Macon, Georgia, in August 1862 handed down, in several cases of sleeping at sentry post, the extremely light sentence of forty-eight hours of double guard duty with public reprimand by a commissioned officer.[12]

Fortunately for Confederate discipline other judiciaries treated the offense more seriously. In 1862 a trans-Mississippi court-martial imposed a sentence of hard labor, with an eighteen-pound ball attached

Courtesy Confederate Museum, Richmond, Virginia

THE MISSOURI ARMY ARGUS

Camp newspaper issued for and by soldiers of General Sterling Price's Command.

Courtesy Military Records Division, Alabama Department of
Archives and History, Montgomery, Alabama

THE PIONEER BANNER

Front page of manuscript newspaper issued by soldiers in camp.

to the leg for the remainder of the war, and then dishonorable discharge.[13] Courts of Lee's army during the last six months of the war meted out such punishments as these: solitary confinement for fourteen days with bread and water diet; six months at hard labor; three months' imprisonment in the guardhouse with ball and chain; in three cases the death sentence was imposed, but interposition of Lee and the Secretary of War forestalled execution. The writer found no instance of a soldier being shot for sleeping at his post.[14]

For drunkenness while guarding prisoners at Tullahoma, Tennessee, in January 1863 Private Henry Jones was required to stand on the head of a barrel with a whiskey bottle hanging from his neck two hours each day for a month, and while not thus engaged to do hard labor.[15] But as a general rule cases of excessive drinking seem to have been disposed of informally without resort to court proceedings. In innumerable instances, however, intoxication was a contributing factor to some offense that did merit the consideration of judicial agencies. For instance, Sergeants Jules Freret and Gustave Aime, who made the mistake of demanding a drink of their captain and then proceeding to cut the ropes of his tent when refused, were given court-martial sentence of reduction of rank, fifteen turns of guard duty, and thirty days' confinement to camp.[16]

Theft and pillaging were, as previously noted, offenses of unusual prevalence, and punishments for them were of great diversity. A Texas private who stole a shirt from a comrade was sentenced to be placarded with the word "thief," mounted face backward on a mule with his feet tied under the animal's belly and paraded before his brigade to the accompaniment of discordant music of drums and bugles.[17] An Alabamian who helped himself to a citizen's honey was required to forfeit a month's pay, and during four hours of each day for ten days to stand on a conspicuously placed barrel wearing a board marked "bee hive." [18] One of Hood's soldiers who stole a saddle on the Tennessee campaign was made to march before his comrades with a large placard pinned on his breast and a saddle tied to his back.[19] Other thieves were given ball-and-chain assignments for periods of one to six months, or imprisoned with forfeiture of pay for varying lengths of time; in rare instances they were suspended by their thumbs for an hour or two with feet barely touching the ground.[20]

The punishment prescribed most frequently of all for pilfering was the barrel shirt. This consisted of an ordinary barrel, with openings at the end and on the sides for head and arms, slipped down over the shoulders and labeled usually with such descriptions of the crime as "stealing from a sick soldier," "robbing a comrade," or simply "thief." Culprits thus attired were made to march before their comrades at dress parade on successive days, sometimes to the tune of the "Rogues March," or "Yankee Doodle," played by regimental bands.[21]

Misbehavior before the enemy was another offense that came rather frequently to the attention of judiciaries. Military regulations authorized the death penalty for cowards but this was rarely invoked. In some instances courts-martial let offenders off with such light punishment as forfeiture of pay for two or three months plus the carrying of rails at dress parade for a few successive days. But the usual penalties were more severe. A Floridian who showed the white feather under duress was required to do hard labor for six months with a ball and chain attached to his ankle, and for the first week of each of the six months he was to be put on a bread-and-water diet. A craven Virginian was sentenced to hard labor for twelve months, with ball and chain, wearing on his back a placard inscribed "coward," and at the end of the year he was to be branded on the left cheek with the letter "C"—said letter to be one inch long—and then to be dishonorably discharged from the service. And for a South Carolinian who failed to stand the gaff of battle, this punishment was ordered: "To be publicly branded in the palm of the left hand with the letter 'C', one and one half inches in length; to have one-half of his head shaved; to be marched in front of his regiment at Dress Parade with a placard fastened to his back upon which shall be inscribed in legible words, 'I am a coward'; and to forfeit six months pay." [22]

It was apparently for cowardice also that one of the severest of all sentences encountered by the writer was handed down. The dictum of the court in this case was:

"He shall be marched bare-headed in a barrel shirt at the point of a bayonet in front of his Regiment on six successive dress parades. He shall be kept bucked and gagged [bucking consisted of setting the culprit down, tying his hands together, slipping them over his knees, and then running a stick through the space beneath the knees and over the arms; gagging was achieved by tying a stick or bayonet in the mouth] at all times when not on the march eight hours each day for 30 days, unless in the opinion of his commanding officer & surgeon, his life shall be so much endangered as to require respite, in which case, he may (for such time only as may be necessary to preserve life) be temporarily relieved of this kind of punishment by being tied to a tree or post in a standing position or be put to hard labor for a like time and purpose. He shall then at the end of his thirty days have a respite of seven days, and at the end of the 7 days shall again undergo the above punishment for a 2nd period of 30 days." [23]

Sentences for absence without leave varied more than for other infractions because of such diverse circumstances as the length of time the accused was away, whether he returned voluntarily and whether he left during a period of active compaign. Punishments decreed in 1862 by courts-martial of the Army of the Mississippi included: two months' confinement in the guardhouse for absences approximating two weeks where the accused returned of their own accord; and thirty days' assignment to stable cleaning, forfeiture of four months' pay, and ten days' wearing of ball and chain (twelve-pound ball, six-foot chain) for a four-day excursion to Memphis.[24]

A soldier detected in Natchitoches without a pass received in 1863 the unusual sentence of marking time on the head of a barrel two hours each day for five days.[25] In 1864 absentees for indeterminate periods from Lee's army suffered the following penalties: "head shaved, sit on a pole, ball and chain"; "head shaved, ball and chain, carry a billet of wood"; "forfeit two months pay, bread and water diet"; "marched once before the Regt wearing a barrel shirt with a placard inscribed 'absence without leave' "; "to cut and pack wood three months for his regiment, to stand on a block &c 15 days with a placard on his back labelled 'absence without leave' "; and at least two men who took French leave got off with a mere reprimand.[26] Several members of the Fifty-ninth Alabama Regiment, who in 1864 helped themselves to furloughs, were made to carry rails on their shoulders four hours a day for sixty consecutive days.[27]

Desertion seems to have demanded the attention of courts and general courts-martial more frequently than any other offense.[28] As has been previously intimated there was a widespread tendency early in the war to deal overleniently with this crime. In 1862 courts-martial of the Army of Tennessee let off some men found guilty of desertion with head-shaving, forfeiture of pay and a month's imprisonment with ball and chain.[29] And recurrently during the conflict there were noticeable softenings of punishments. Twice in 1863 Beauregard rebuked courts-martial for meting out light penalties to deserters; one court sentenced five offenders to periods at hard labor with ball and chain of from fifteen to thirty-two days, and a sixth, adjudged guilty of deserting in front of the enemy, was subjected only to four hours of hard labor a day for two months.[30]

Courts of Lee's army continued to hand down some easy sentences in the face of multiplied desertion. In the fall of 1864, for instance, one offender was sentenced to thirty days of hard labor with forfeiture of pay; another to deprivation of six months' wages; and a third to carrying a fence rail for sixty days and forfeiture of a year's pay.[31]

Throughout the conflict judiciaries showed the greatest reluctance to impose the death sentence. In 245 cases of conviction for desertion during the last six months of the war by courts belonging mainly to the Army of Northern Virginia, the extreme penalty was prescribed in only 70 instances. And 31 of these 70 sentences were invalidated by President Davis' general amnesty of February 1865.[32]

Commanding generals, with a few exceptions, were subject to squeamishness when it came to approving the shooting of deserters; and in a number of instances the Secretary of War interposed after sentences had been approved by Lee.[33] Sometimes executions were forestalled at the last minute with storybook flourishes of drama, as witness the entry in a Mississippian's diary:

"June 12, 1863, we were ordered out to our drill grounds this morning to witness the execution of a deserter from the Nineteenth Tennessee Regiment. As the poor fellow was seated upon his coffin, and everything ready for the command to fire, an officer rode up in great haste with a pardon. I was truly glad, but must say some of the boys were disappointed." [34]

Suggestion of the casualness with which desertion was regarded in some quarters is afforded by a letter written by a member of the Twentieth Mississippi Regiment to his father in January 1863:

"About noon today . . . was ordered to procede to Capt Hedden's Hdqrs . . . and there take charge of Six deserters and conduct them to . . . Hd Qr't's of General Tilghman. . . . After the General had given the men a little Fatherly advice—ordered me to march them back to Capt Hedden with orders for Capt H— to still keep them under arrest but to make them do camp duty." [35]

Evidence is not conclusive that this was the extent of their punishment, but such is strongly intimated; if the men were to be shot or dealt with in some other severe manner, why the fatherly advice? The impression of leniency is further supported by the statement of a

Mississippi district judge in 1864 that he knew many men "now in desertion for the fourth, fifth, and sixth times" who had "never been punished." [36]

In the great majority of desertion cases judiciaries invoked sentences lying between the two extremes of death and long-term imprisonment on the one hand and such trifles as carrying rails on the other. Before the passage of an interdicting law in April 1863, whipping was a common punishment.[37] Branding, usually with a red-hot iron, but occasionally with indelible ink, was also a frequently prescribed penalty; the marking was placed on the hip, in the hand, or on the cheek. Frequently whipping and branding were combined with other inflictions.

Private L. A. Childers, for instance, was sentenced "to be publickly flogged with fifty lashes on his bare back, to have the left side of his head shaved, and to be branded on the left hip with the letter 'D', which letter shall be four inches long and three inches broad . . . to wear a ball and chain . . . for six months, and at the end of that time to be dishonorably discharged." [38] Private S. B. Seymour received a similar sentence, with the exception that the ball-and-chain assignment was to run throughout the war, and that the whipping (39 lashes) was to be repeated at three-month intervals for the same period. Private C. H. Allbright of the "Montgomery True Blues" was to be branded, to have his head shaved, to receive ten licks with a paddle, and then to be drummed out of the service to the tune of the "Rogues' March." [39]

In the case of a Texas deserter the court specified, in addition to ball and chain, this interesting detail of punishment:

"He is likewise to ride astride a wooden horse for fifteen days two hours and a half each day, the riding to be done every day in the week except Saturdays and Sundays, the horse to be six feet high, the pole upon which he is to sit to be six inches in diameter . . . he to go through this exercise from two o'clock P.M. until half past four P.M." [40]

When the death penalty was administered to deserters, commanding officers usually staged executions in a manner planned to impress the soldiery. Usually the brigade or division to which the condemned men belonged were marched to the scene of execution and arranged in a hollow square so as to afford all a clear view of the proceedings. Frequently those destined to face the firing squad were required to ride through the encampment, and sometimes through an adjacent town, sitting on their coffins. Arrived at the designated place they were blindfolded and made to sit or stand on coffins, or tied to stakes, or compelled to kneel by open graves. Then amid the awful hush, a detail composed of perhaps twenty-four men was ordered to a position a few paces in front of the condemned. Only half of the guns were loaded, but no man among the executioners knew whether or not his was a blank charge. At the signal "Fire!" the ominous quiet was broken with the roar of muskets and the culprits sank in crumpled heaps to the ground.

A note of unintended horror was sometimes added to these occasions by factors of nervousness and chance. A case in point was an execution that took place in Bragg's army in late 1862. When the firing squad of twenty men, stationed twelve paces from the culprit, discharged its volley, little damage was done. Four men held in reserve against just such a contingency were then ordered to step up and shoot. The prisoner was still not killed. Finally all twenty-four executioners reloaded their pieces and administered the *coup de grâce*.[41]

Home letters of Rebs offer abundant proof that seeing the execution of comrades made a profound impression. And had the death penalty been applied with greater consistency, desertion would doubtless have been checked. The reaction of soldiers to the spectacle of deserter-comrades riddled by firing squads is well illustrated by Private Thomas Warrick of Alabama. On December 19, 1862, he wrote from Bragg's army:

"I saw a site today that made me feel mity Bad I saw a man shot for deserting there was twenty fore Guns shot at him thay shot him all to pease . . . he went home and thay Brote him Back and then he went home again and so they shot him for that Martha it was one site that I did hate to see it But I could not helpe my self I had to do Jest as thay sed for me to doo."

In August 1863 Bragg published Davis' order giving amnesty to all absentees who would within twenty days return of their own accord to posts of duty. Warrick and his comrades probably interpreted this as an indication that in future deserters would be treated with clemency. However that may be, when word came to the Alabamian in October that his family was suffering for food he wrote immediately to his wife that he would try to get a furlough, but that if he failed he would "com home Eny how." He was unsuccessful in his efforts to get leave, but in the weeks that followed he was compelled to witness further executions. To what extent these stringencies influenced him cannot be determined, but his change of tune in reference to taking leave is in interesting parallel to increasing harshness dealt out to deserters. In June 1864 he wrote his folks from Georgia: "I would be glad to see you all now but I recon that I have bin home my last time till this war closes." And he had.[42]

A great number of soldiers appeared before military tribunals on the charge of insubordinate and disrespectful conduct toward officers. Much of the trouble between privates and their superiors could be attributed to undue sensitiveness on the part of the former, and their lack of understanding of military usage. Too frequently men in the ranks were inclined to regard orders as personal affronts when they were issued in the brusque authoritative tone of superior officers. Such seems to have been the reaction of Private Charles Brown of the Washington Artillery whom Lieutenant Roper ordered to procure a missing halter just as camp was about to be moved from Richmond, in June 1861. Instead of obeying promptly the private dawdled away muttering. After a while Lieutenant Roper received word that Brown wanted to see him. When he approached the disgruntled private the latter spoke up in protest against his alleged mistreatment, saying that he wanted the officer to understand that he, Brown, was as much a gentleman as Roper or anyone else and that he was not to be ordered about in any such manner. The lieutenant repeated his order, and when Brown hesitated to comply Roper lifted his saber to enforce obedience. At the same time the private drew a sword that he was carrying. Roper then cursed Brown and struck him with the flat of his saber. The private endeavored to return the blow and then galloped away. Roper gave pursuit, overtook Brown and enforced compliance with his order at the point of his pistol. A court-martial imposed a sentence requiring that Brown have his name erased from the battalion roll, that his uniform be shorn of all distinguishing marks, and that in the presence of his comrades he be drummed out of camp.[43]

For a similar offense, that of resisting and drawing a saber on a commissioned officer, another Private Brown, belonging to the Second Texas Infantry, was sentenced in the spring of 1862 to hard labor for the duration of the war and then dishonorably discharged. But the same court-martial ordered only a public reprimand to a soldier "for severely kicking Sergeant Daniel"; still another who was found guilty of addressing violent and insulting language at his major, and then attempting to hit him, was let off with three months of hard labor. In sharpest and most incomprehensible contrast with other penalties imposed by this body was the death sentence given Private James R. Maxwell for resisting and striking the sergeant of the guard and two sentinels who took him in custody.[44]

The comparative impunity with which privates could address nasty remarks to superiors reflects discredit on the general state of Confederate discipline. A rampant Reb who, when accosted by a corporal on guard duty in downtown Galveston, called him "a damned son-of-a-bitch" received a milk-and-water sentence before his company by way of rebuke from the captain.[45] A Texas artilleryman who pleaded guilty to the charge of inviting his sergeant to kiss his backside was ordered merely to ask the aggrieved officer's pardon in the presence of his company commandant.[46]

One Private Neighbors who, when ordered to be bucked by his lieutenant for disobeying an order, said to that officer, "No one but a damned coward would have a soldier bucked; if you will pull off your insignia of rank I will whip you on the spot," had his ball-and-chain sentence remitted by Beauregard on the score of prior orderliness.[47]

Private James Sweeny who ran amuck with higher authority at Abbeville, Mississippi, striking his sergeant and designating him as a son-of-a-bitch, and telling an interposing lieutenant to "tie him up and go to hell," "kiss his ——," and so forth, drew the severer penalty of forfeiture of pay, confinement at hard labor with ball and chain for three months, and then a head shaving and drumming out of the service.[48]

Resistance and disrespect to officers evoked some unusual sentences. A Mississippian found guilty of insubordination was required to march before the guardhouse three alternate hours of each day for one month, bearing a weight of thirty pounds in a knapsack tied on his back, and during the hours intervening to be held in confinement.[49] A Louisianian who abused those in authority over him while in a state of intoxication had to wear a molasses barrel several times a day for thirty consecutive days.[50] And an artilleryman who violated the canons of respectfulness was ordered, in addition to wearing ball and chain, "to stand toeing a mark for 2 hours a day for the first ten days . . . without resting or changing his position."[51]

In addition to these common offenses there were a number of infractions that came occasionally to the attention of military tribunals. Among these were self-mutilation to escape service, selling whiskey, making seditious remarks, holding correspondence with the enemy, exciting or participating in mutiny, quitting post of duty without authorization, selling equipment, forging passes, breaking guard and refusing to perform some unpleasant task such as policing camp, standing guard, or doing fatigue duty. Penalties handed down for these breaches of discipline were varied, but they consisted mainly of types previously noted.

For offenses as a whole, the most common punishments prescribed by courts and courts-martial were these: (1) Confinement to the guardhouse (sometimes nothing more than a tent, a brush arbor or a circumscribed space which Rebs called a "bull pen"); (2) ball and chain—the ball weighing from six to thirty-two pounds and being attached to the prisoner's leg by a chain ranging in length from two to six feet; (3) wearing a barrel shirt, labeled usually with a description of the infraction; (4) hard labor; (5) carrying a weight, usually a rail or a stick of wood; (6) doing extra guard duty; (7) public reprimand by a superior officer; (8) bread-and-water diet; (9) stoppage of pay; (10) standing or marking time on a barrel, placarded with a description of his offense; (11) confinement in the stocks; and (12) branding.

Military judiciaries supplemented these common penalties with an impressive array of original and exceptional punishments. One offender was required to stand on the head of a barrel two hours a day for a week reading aloud from the articles of war; another had to wear for two months "a twelve-pound iron collar with three prongs round his neck"; a third was chained to a block for thirty days; a fourth was strapped astride a cannon barrel for sixteen hours; a fifth was bound to the wheel of a gun carriage; a sixth was forced to walk about with a log on his shoulder and with a bag of sand tied to each of his legs; a seventh was mounted on a rail, three empty bottles tied to his feet, placarded with the inscription "Ten cents a Glass," and drummed about the camp; an eighth was put to "filling a hollow sack with sand" two hours each day for a month; a ninth was marched in front of the guardhouse with a jug in one hand and a bed tick in another one-half an hour a day for two weeks; and a cavalryman was sentenced to walk from San Antonio to Austin, Texas—a distance of about eighty miles—in three days.[52]

War articles forbade a man being held to confinement longer than eight days without trial. Sometimes prisoners were held for the fullness of this limit before courts-martial were convened. But again cases were tried with the greatest dispatch. On the march a drumhead session might convene at night, try an offender and order his execution on the spot.[53]

An intoxicated Reb riding a boat en route to Portsmouth in June 1861 insulted and tore the dress of a passenger. He was seized by his comrades, placed under arrest just as soon as the vessel docked, and tried within a few hours. The next morning a placard reading, "A coward, but brave enough to insult a woman" was placed on his back, and fellow soldiers drummed him at bayonets' ends through Portsmouth and beyond while an accompanying band played the tune of "Yankee Doodle." [54]

Many trivial offenses committed by Rebs, and some serious ones as well, were handled by commissioned officers without resort to courts-martial or to other military tribunals. Assignment to extra guard duty was the penalty most commonly invoked by those in authority for minor aberrations. Rebs were wont to refer to this punishment as being "put on the roots." A diarist of the Texas Rangers cited an incident illustrating application of this corrective medium:

"March 23, 1862—Today we received news of a big fight in New Mexico, and Arkansas—Victories for the Confederacy, several of the boys were so overjoyed with the news, that they turned their horses loose, and got put on the roots for it, which came very near causing a small riot in camp." [55]

But Major General Hindman of Johnston's army frowned on this type of penalty. "Putting men on extra guard duty," he announced in February 1864, "as a punishment is prohibited. Standing guard is the most honorable duty of a soldier, except fighting, and must not be degraded." [56] Hindman's attitude, however, was exceptional.

Another penalty frequently imposed by company and regimental commanders for slight infractions was that of digging stumps. The number and the character of excavations varied with the gravity of offense and the temper of commanding authorities.

Captain C. R. Hanleiter of Thompson's Artillery, stationed near Savannah for an extended period, was one who favored this mode of punishment. His diary records that on December 8, 1861, he put three men "to grubbing for getting drunk"; and on April 1, 1862, he entered this statement: "Private Holmes having overstayed his leave of absence yesterday was required to extract a couple of pine Stumps—which he did quite scientifically." In the case of a man whom he apprehended under the influence of liquor, Hanleiter applied the unusual punishment of tying the victim with his back to a tree for several hours. He ordered other inebriates and fisticuff offenders to be confined in bombproof dugouts.[57]

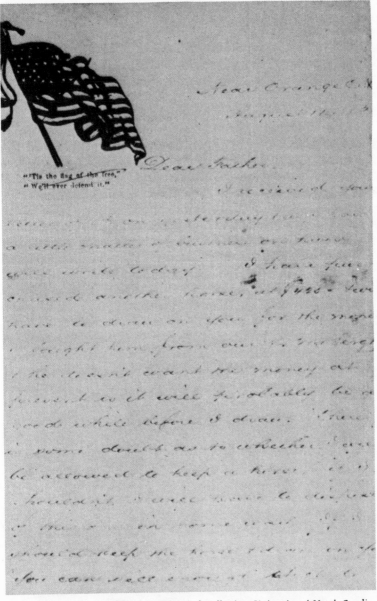

"'Tis the flag of the free,"
"We'll ever defend it."

LETTER WRITTEN ON "CAPTURED" STATIONERY

Letter written by Private Richard W. Waldrop, Company F, 21st Virginia Regiment. Note crossing out of flag and poetry. This is a sample of an educated soldier's writing. Manuscript, University of North Carolina.

sister i wan to pour
home worse than i eav
er did be fore but
when times gits bet ter
i will tri to come home
thare has ben a grate
meney soeldiers rain
ing a way lately but
i dont want to go tha
way if i can get home
any other way i saw
warren athey and andru
by hix the oth er day
i am go ing to sea them in
the mor ning they
are camp in about a mile of us
i wil come to a close Mr C Athey
to amily Athey

*Courtesy Military Records Division, Alabama Department
of Archives and History, Montgomery, Alabama*

A SOLDIER'S LETTER

A typical "poor white" letter written from a Confederate camp.

Early in the war officers had considerable difficulty in curbing reckless firing of guns.[58] The prevalence of this evil was due in part to the anxiety of volunteers to test their weapons when the long roll sounded, and also to the general excitement that prevailed as men fell in for their first encounters. Results were sometimes fatal. General Cheatham invoked the penalty of marking time from midnight to dawn in an effort to restrain nervous trigger fingers in his command.[59]

To a considerable extent this offense was due to the excessive jauntiness with which volunteers regarded camp routine. Summons to drill in the early months of war was apt to evoke hurrahing, brandishing of weapons, backslapping, ogling, and various other manifestations of horseplay. "General Whiting made some sharp remarks to our boys," observed a member of the Second Mississippi Regiment in 1862, "for hollowing & yelling when called into line he charged it to the new recruits and wants it stoped and no mistake as it is useless & unmilitary."[60]

Other forms of punishment applied by commanding officers included cleaning of camps, bucking, hanging by the thumbs, confinement to guard tents, and riding the wooden horse.[61]

A penalty resorted to by those in authority over the Twenty-seventh Mississippi Infantry deserves special mention for its uniqueness. The sight of swine was the source of great temptation to members of this regiment as to most other Rebs. When a hog was "captured," time and lack of facilities would not permit scalding and scraping according to the usual practice, but instead the victim had to be skinned. A piece of skinned pork came generally to be regarded as a telltale of pillage. When officers of this regiment nabbed pig thieves they took pieces of the skin, cut holes in them, slipped them over the heads of offenders, and required that the "hog-skin cravats" be worn all day in front of the provost guard.[62]

Occasionally the privates took justice in their own hands. A case in point was that involving soldiers stationed near Bowling Green during the war's first winter. One day a civilian came to camp on business. Some Rebs who engaged him in conversation were irked by the strong Union tone of his sentiments. "So without more ado they put him astride of a rail and ducked him in a neighboring pond."[63]

In 1864 members of a Virginia company became so disgusted with the misdeeds of a pestilential comrade that they voted unanimously to get rid of him. He was taken out of bounds, given thirty-nine lashes by a specially appointed executioner, and ordered never to show himself again in camp on pain of even worse treatment.[64]

In a third instance a Texas cavalryman apprehended in the act of rape was, even while officers were taking counsel as to his disposition, removed from the guardhouse by his comrades, hanged, buried, and his effects distributed among the most needy of the company.

In another case the wrath of this same outfit vented itself on an officer. A diarist-observer gave the following account of this incident: "Agt. B— . . . had been thrown out of office & Dud M Jones of Co. I substituted . . . B— was accused of abolitionism and Bigamy, the latter being pretty strongly proven upon him, the boys en masse took him out & hung him & gave his outfit to a poor boy a member of the same Co." [65]

It should be noted in explanation of the extraordinary severity of these last two instances that the period was early in the war, when military usages were not yet established, and in a location where ideas of frontier justice had not been abandoned.

The fact that military courts were overloaded, together with the difficulty of convening courts-martial, tended to place undue disciplinary responsibility on officers commanding companies, regiments and brigades. In the spring of 1864 Brigadier General L. S. Ross wrote to his superior complaining bitterly of inability to secure the co-operation of courts of any sort to check misconduct in his command. Some of the offenders he said had been in arrest for more than a year without trial, and others who had been tried had escaped the full measure of punishment because the courts had failed to publish their findings. "I have arrested and released . . . these men and officers," he added, "and returned them to duty so often without trial that military law has become obsolete." He concluded with the statement that "my command, influence, or authority over them does not depend on their respect for or fear of military law or authority, but simply their love for me as an individual." [66]

General Ross's situation was to some extent exceptional as to failure of judiciaries, in view of the fact that he was stationed in a peripheral area where court functions were more difficult than usual. But his observation as to control being determined by the personal influence which he had over his command applied in large measure throughout the Confederate Army. To a much larger extent than in most military organizations Rebel discipline was an individual matter between an officer and his men. This fact was noted by an inspector of Lee's army in the fall of 1864. In his report he pointed out that there was the greatest diversity of order and authority among the different brigades. One would be characterized by clean weapons, punctual response to signals and efficient performance of drill maneuvers, while another of the same division would be utterly shiftless and deranged. "The brigade," he said, "reflects the character and qualifications of its commander." "Indeed," he added, "the brigadier makes the brigade." [67] And this principle was prevalent on down the line of commands.

The factor of personal equation was at once the secret of the Rebel Army's brilliant achievement and the source of its greatest weakness. Given brave, efficient and respect-inspiring leaders from lieutenants to brigadiers—men who knew how to take into consideration individual pride and at the same time exercise a firm authority—Southern soldiers were insurpassable; but the same troops, when commanded by slovenly disciplinarians, were apt to straggle, pillage, evade drill, neglect equipment and skulk. Rebs might fight even under shabby officers, but too frequently such officers had lost the lion's share of their commands by straggling, overstaying leaves, sham sickness and other evidences of poor discipline before fighting began. In this connection the observation that Confederates were the best of fighters and the worst of soldiers is most significant.

What did ordinary Rebs think of their officers? The close relation between discipline and attitude toward those in authority merits consideration of this question. That there were innumerable soldiers who thoroughly disliked their superiors is indisputable. In letters to their folk they frequently aired their animosity. "Our Gen Reub Davis goes by the name of 'Henry of Navarre' among the boys," wrote a Mississippian, "from the long white plume he wears in his hat. . . . He is a vain, stuck-up illiterate ass, and I dont believe there is a man in the regiment who would willingly go into battle with him." [68]

The objection stated by this soldier to General Davis was one of the main causes of unpopularity. Rebs could rarely look with favor upon an officer whom they deemed guilty of "putting on airs." An Irish member of a Louisiana regiment, on beholding a lieutenant walking about in a resplendent uniform, gave vivid expression to an impression held by the majority of soldiers toward ostentatious officers when he remarked, "Oh Mike, look at that new lefttenant! Don't he think he is purtty wid the new chicken guts (narrow gold lace, insignia of rank) on his arms. Look at his strut." [69]

Another cause of dislike of officers was the belief that they were unduly severe or highhanded. When Colonel Lowry of Mississippi placed some men under arrest for falling out of line to get water while on the march, their comrades began calling him Corporal Lowry, and thereafter, until stern measures were invoked, every passage of the general through this portion of the line would elicit a chorus of shouts such as "Here comes the corporal!" and "Make way for Corporal Lowry!" much to the officer's embarrassment.[70] When commanders seemed to bear down on them too heavily, other privates were apt to complain to their homefolk that they were being treated like Negroes.

Resentment of easier circumstances enjoyed by officers was a fertile source of antagonism. "It is only the ones that wear grey coats and Brass Buttons . . . [who] are living better and wear better clothes than they did before the war," a Texan wrote peevishly to his wife in April 1864. "I do not blame them for keeping the war up as long as possible," he added, for "most of them are in no danger, they are always in the rear." [71]

Another Texan complained: "All of our commissioned officers are now absent. If one of them has the Belly Ache for a day or two he is posted off to the hospital. While the poor private who has all of the burden to bear, has to stay and tough it out." [72] A third Reb was angered by the belief that officers received their pay while privates had to wait endless months for theirs.[73] Still another couched his disgruntlement at the softer lots of provost guards and commissaries by dubbing them "bombproofs." [74]

Private T. W. Hall fulminated against officerdom in general. "Who is it that has the hardships to under go?" he wrote, "it is the privates." And "who is it that has bacon to eat, Sugar to put in their coffee and all luxuries of this kind?" he added, "the officers." [75]

Even the more intelligent men were susceptible to resentment of discrimination. "The only objection (or at least the greatest one I have) to the life I am now living," observed an Alabamian of unusually good background, "is the restrictions placed on the privates, when the officers can go to town at option, stay as long as they please, and get gloriously drunk in and out of camp when it suits them to do so. If I live through this campaign I for one am done 'sojering.' " [76]

Although there were many foreigners in the Rebel Army, prejudice against officers on the score of non-nativity was sometimes a factor in their unpopularity.[77] It might have been expected that the example of Davis in making Judah Benjamin his highest cabinet official and his closest confidant would have lessened anti-Semitism among soldiers, but such was evidently not the case. When a Texas regiment sent to Richmond in 1861 was transferred to Confederate service, the first colonel appointed by the War Department was a Jew. As the new officer rode up to take charge the displeased Rebs began to make comments in voices raised sufficiently for him to hear. "What?" said one. "What is it? Is it a man, a fish, or a bird?" "Of course it is a man," said another, "don't you see his legs?" The colonel withstood for a day the overt opposition confronting him on every hand, but when he waked next morning to find his horse shorn of tail he gave up his assignment as a hopeless one, and without a word he rode back to the city never to be heard of again by the regiment.[78]

The knowledge or belief that officers caroused, or yielded to the lure of high living, caused revulsion on the part of some men. A Louisianian noted in his diary in 1863 that a new brigadier had been appointed but that the officer was not very well liked. "From what I can learn," observed the diarist, "[he] is better able to command a bottle of whiskey than anything else." [79]

Sometimes intoxication of officers on duty worked a distinct hardship on Rebs, as when a Mississippi colonel abused his command on the march and another forced the men to accelerate their double-duty paces.[80] But again the results were opposite, as witness a comment of Private Jerome Yates: "Capt Davis . . . [is] two good when he is tight he lets us do as we please but when he gets sober he makes up for it." [81]

Inability of officers to perform in a creditable manner the duties of their positions was a cause of much dislike. "He is a man of but little Military capacity," wrote an Alabamian of a newly appointed colonel in the fall of 1861, "consequently a great many of the [company officers] . . . are resigning . . . we poor privates have to stick it out. . . . I dont want to be lead into Battle by an ignoramus, Col. Henry is fit for nothing higher than the cultivation of corn." [82]

Even greater contempt was voiced by a Floridian who said of his regimental leaders: "Our major is a fine man, the rest are not fit to tote guts to a Bear." [83]

The circumstance which caused officers to be held in lowest esteem by their men was any show of cowardice under fire. During the Atlanta campaign there were some instances of bad conduct on the part of company commanders, and these did not escape notice of Rebs. "The boys crack many a joke on some of the officers," wrote an Alabamian. "They were so scared that they went so far as to get their men to refuse to go back [to a charge]. They were afraid to refuse themselves for fear that they would be cashiered." [84]

A second lieutenant became panicky when assigned to a picket post at which a man had recently been killed. Several privates sent to deepen the trench where he was located were unable to get him out of the ditch long enough to permit execution of their assignment. "The boys plagued him a great deal about it," according to a member of the company, but "he had not a word to say." [85]

A most amusing and yet pathetic case of derision for a cowardly officer was an affair growing out of the battle of Secessionville in June 1862. The officer involved was one Lieutenant Doyle, who prior to his show of cowardice had aroused considerable antipathy by undue severity and highhandedness. "He puts on a great many airs . . . when . . . Drilling his company," related an observer. "With his hand grasp around the hilt of his sword and the blade parallel with the ground he would command them to left wheal, with all the cautionary remarks such as steady; steady; on the pivot come round like a gate now hepp. hepp and so on." When word spread about the camp after Secessionville that Doyle had taken to his heels under fire, the men gathered up kettles and other camp utensils and stacked them before the guardhouse. This miscellaneous heap they dubbed "Fort Doyle." Erection of this fort inspired a camp bard to write some verses commemorating the incident, and these when circulated elicited untold amusement. The poem was:

Latest From The War;
The last Fight at Secessionville!

We went to Secessionville a disturbance to quell
Where the Yankees were storming our batteries, in fact raising hell
The boys all pitched in as all who are brave
Not one of them flinching not one of them caved

Except one—Mr. Doyal who stopped when he saw
Shot falling so fast—for want of sand in [h]is craw
He turned on his pivot—swung around like a gate
And made strides from the field from six feet to eight

He left in a hurry, and we all really suppose
His time is the fastest on record—yet nobody knows
He went to the Surgeon and struck for a job
To act as assistant, or be placed in a squad

The Surgeon was busy, and made no reply
So Doyal left the line another place to try
He left swift footed, and we saw him no more
Untill the day was far spent, and the battle was oer

When he again turned on his pivot, swung around like a gate
Walked into supper—sat down and ate
So in honor of him, we've erected Fort Doyal
Costing large sums of money—besides great toil
   A gun shall be fired at the raising of each sun
   In honor of Doyal, who at Secessionville run

Now listen to me, take the advice of a friend
Be true to the country, you've taken arms to defend,
Let your motto be onward and go straight ahead
Though you march through blood and crawl oer the dead

So on ward it is dont flinch "nary" time
Glory, honor, and victory, shall surely be thine
Be kind to the boys, and treat them all well
Or they'll blow up the Fort—and send you to hell
            —Patriotic [86]

In happy contrast to leaders whose incapacity drew the scorn of ordinary soldiers was that very large group of officers who were able to command the complete respect of their men. Above all, men in the ranks appreciated willingness of superiors to share peril and hardship. When Captain E. J. Ellis of the Sixteenth Louisiana was moved by ill health in 1863 to write out his resignation, his company raised such a protest that he decided to stay on. His own comment on this reaction, given in the spirit of gratefulness rather than boasting, explains the unwillingness of his followers to part with him:

"We have toiled and suffered together, and together have faced the tempest of battle, they have divided their rations with me when they had not enough for themselves and the last drink of water from my canteen was freely and frequently given to them when I knew that many, weary, weary, miles of hot and dusty roads lay between me and the next water." [87]

Soldiers liked, too, ability of officers to blend severity with leniency, seriousness with humor, and willingness to close their eyes on occasion when circumstances required the setting aside of usual regulations.

They must have adored General C. Irvine Walker for his ineptness at distinguishing between scalded and skinned pork when rations were scant.[88] And the stories circulating through the armies of oversight, on the part of various generals, of incidents that deserved sharp rebuke testify to appreciation of this quality.

For instance there was a tale of General Wigfall finding a soldier on guard taking things with undue ease.

"What are you doing here, my man?" asked the general.

"Nothin' much," replied the man, "jes' kinder takin' care of this hyar stuff."

"Do you know who I am, sir?" asked the general.

"Wall, now 'pears like I know your face, but I cant jes' call your name—who is you?"

"I'm General Wigfall," said the officer irritatedly.

Without getting up or giving any other sign of being impressed the sentry extended his hand and said, "General, I'm pleased to meet you —my name's Jones"—and all this with impunity, according to the yarn.[89]

Another story concerned General Cheatham. He allegedly caught Private Jim Heath up an apple tree, on Bragg's Kentucky campaign. Heath was, in soldier parlance, "mortally scared to death" when he saw the general ride up under his perch. But Cheatham's address was, "Young man, drop me down a few of those fine apples."

"Yes, sir, and thank you too," said the private, with astonished relief.[90]

A third incident had to do with Stonewall Jackson. A Reb, beholding a figure slouched down on a horse, swaying precariously in the saddle as the general was wont to do when catching a nap on the march, cried out, "Hello, I say old fellow, where the devil did you get your licker?" As Stonewall, roused from his lethargy, looked up, a light of amazed recognition flickered over the soldier's countenance. "Good God! it's old Jack!" he exclaimed as he jumped a fence and headed for cover. When informed by the staff as to the cause of the Reb's discomfiture, Jackson, according to the story, only laughed.[91]

Soldiers also appreciated reluctance to shed blood, such as that manifested by Johnston before Atlanta. The writer has yet to find an unfavorable remark from a man in the ranks about this officer's Fabian generalship, while compliments are frequently found. Indications are that Hood, whom one soldier called a "butcher," assumed command in the face of an opposition so great as to cause serious apprehension. A Mississippi lieutenant wrote his wife on July 18, 1864:

"Hood is the most unpopular Genl in the army & some of the troops are swearing they will not fight under him. Brig Genls Cols & company officers have been called together to forestall anything like an outbreak Maj Genls & Brig & all regret that Johnston is gone, Johnston has made himself very dear to the soldiers." [92]

Simplicity and friendliness were also factors ingratiating officers with their men. Jackson, though a stern disciplinarian, was loved for his haphazard dress and his unpretentious conduct. This characteristic reaction to democratic conduct came from a Louisianian:

"General Steward often comes around to see how things are going. He was around yesterday by himself, no long train of beardles staff officers with their dazzling uniforms and [would-be] defiant looks attending him. he put me very much in mind of some old farmer, rideing around hunting up some stray cattle and couldnt find them. He is . . . very attentive to any request a private may make of him. . . . While other Generals headquarters are surrounded with Guards he has but one guard that is to guard his stables he is very popular with his command." [93]

Opinion of privates was of course an undependable criterion of a general's real capacity. The same is true to a considerable, but lesser, extent of other officers. In particular, adverse remarks from the ranks as to conduct of lieutenants, captains, and colonels were frequently without just foundation. In some cases these can be attributed to a universal tendency of subordinates to grumble; and in others they were due to false ideas of individual rights and to misconceptions of military usages.

But with due allowance for these considerations, there can be no doubt that much of the dissatisfaction with those in command expressed by ordinary Rebs was due to real incapacity of the officers themselves. The practice of electing company and regimental leaders and even subalterns, which prevailed during the first years of the war and persisted to some extent till near the end, frequently hampered selection of men best qualified for command; and officers once commissioned had an unhappy way of hanging on to their positions long after their incompetency had been proved.[94]

Resort in 1862 to a policy of examination for competency was effective, but in November 1863 the Secretary of War still found grounds to denounce election as giving "undue regard to popularity" and contributing to "a spirit of electioneering subversive of subordination and discipline." [95]

Reports of inspections made at various times of different portions of the army complain of laxity of officers in calling rolls, making reports, publishing and enforcing general orders, and attending to other important phases of camp routine; there is repeated reference also to the lack of sufficient distinction between officers and privates.[96]

Brigadier General John W. Frazier stated in an official report that men of the Fifty-fifth Georgia, which he "regarded as the best regiment for discipline and efficiency" of his command, did in 1863 "ride their colonel on a rail, which he [the colonel] never resented, but on promise to them of better behavior was allowed to resume his command." [97] And a Tar Heel private wrote in 1862 concerning his captain, "He put . . . [me] in the gard house one time & he got drunk agoin from Wilmington to Golesboro on the train & we put him in the Sh-t House So we are even." [98] What amazing commentaries on Rebel discipline!

There can be no doubt that the general state of discipline was notoriously bad in the early months of the war. There was altogether too much individualism. The editor of the Richmond *Enquirer* sized up the situation aptly when he said:

"Men in the army and out of the army thought for a long time the usual laws of discipline inapplicable to them. Were they not all gentlemen? And what gentleman would do a mean thing, steal a horse or plunder a chicken coop? Were they not all intelligent beyond other troops of the world? And what man in his senses would eat up the rations dealt out for five days in one or throw away his blanket because it was heavy? Were they not all brave and bold? And what brave man would linger behind on the march or turn his back to the enemy in battle. It was thought enough at first to operate upon the men by appeals to their zeal, their patriotism, and honor." [99]

This policy proved its error in countless instances and ways. Soldiers at Fort Jackson mutinied after passage of the Federal fleet up the river to New Orleans.[100] Troops of the Sixth Texas Cavalry refused to submit to Colonel Wharton's authority when he was assigned to command them.[101] A Virginia company balked at the use of muskets on the ground that enlistment had been for a "rifle company." [102]

Adjustment to military life, curbing of the evil of election, and other influences led to a noticeable improvement of discipline during the third and fourth years of war. Exceptions to this rule were detached cavalry units whose lack of order was ever notorious. But even after volunteers had become soldiers Rebel discipline fell to a level far below that anticipated by army regulations and thought essential to first-class performance in the field. The Inspector General of the Army of Northern Virginia reported in September 1864: "There is not that spirit of respect for and obedience to general orders which should pervade a military organization." As one evidence of general laxity he offered the item of straggling. "If the orders governing this subject were rigorously enforced," he said, "thousands of muskets would be heard in every fight that are now never fired." [103]

With this report in mind, and recalling the panics which had recently victimized Early's veterans in the Shenandoah Valley, Lee himself in February 1865 issued a circular pleading for the cultivation of discipline. Too much dependence, he said, had been placed on the soldiers' innate merit as individuals, and not enough consideration given to molding them into effective units. "Many opportunities have been lost and hundreds of valuable lives have been uselessly sacrificed," he added, "for want of a strict observance of discipline." [104] But his admonitions had scant opportunity to be carried out. For even as he spoke the shadow of Appomattox was descending on his army.

CHAPTER XIII

THE DEADLIEST FOE

ON AUGUST 9, 1862, an unsophisticated Tar Heel private stationed near Petersburg, Virginia, "took pen in hand" to address his homefolk. "T. G. Freman is Ded and they is Several mor that is Dangerous with the feever," he wrote; "they hev Been 11 Died with the fever in Co A since we left kinston and 2 died that was wounded so you now See that these Big Battles is not as Bad as the fever." [1]

Exactly one week earlier a well-educated Louisiana officer had written his brother from camp near Tupelo, "Look at our company—21 have died of disease, 18 have become so unhealthy as to be discharged, and only four have been killed in battle." [2] These two soldiers, one from the Army of Northern Virginia and the other from the Army of Tennessee, had each in his own limited sphere come face to face with an all-pervasive truth. The most destructive enemies of Confederates were not the Yankees but the invisible organisms which filled the camps with sickness.

Disease did not wait long to strike; and its initial onslaughts were the most devastating. During the first months of service it was not uncommon for half the men of a regiment to be incapacitated at one time by sickness, and frequently the ratio was higher.

In April 1862 Captain Alfred Bell reported that six out of every seven men of the Thirty-ninth North Carolina Regiment were ill. For this distressing situation Captain Bell blamed Lincoln, and he was firmly convinced that the Northern President "ought to be burnt in a hell ten thousand times hotter than fier." [3] Immunization and seasoning lessened the prevalence of sickness, but throughout the conflict disease continued to incapacitate a large number. Joseph Jones, one of the foremost authorities on Confederate medicine, estimated that on an average each Southern soldier was ill or wounded six times during the war, and that there were five times as many cases of sickness as of injury. He estimated further that for every soldier who died as a result of battle there were three who perished from disease. [4]

Various factors contributed to the excess of sickness which beset

244

Rebel encampments. Prominent among these was the character of men taken into the army. In the flush period of volunteering that followed Fort Sumter almost anyone who could stand on two feet was permitted to enlist. Henry M. Stanley of the Sixth Arkansas Regiment said concerning his induction, "We were not subjected to the indignity of being stripped and examined . . . but were accepted into the military service upon our own assurance of being in fit condition." [5] And what man under three score years was there in 1861 who did not consider himself able to do all the fighting necessary to whip the "craven Yankees"!

The indiscriminate policy of recruiting naturally brought into the army thousands of volunteers who were utterly unequal, because of age or frailty, to the hardships of campaigning. As a consequence many not only fell victim to disease themselves, but also, by the close association incident to camp life, communicated their maladies to hardier fellows.

Not until the fall of 1862, apparently, did Richmond authorities institute a program of physical examination for recruits. Even then there was not ample provision for eliminating the unfit. Examining officers were instructed to follow the general rule that a person who was equal to the active work of ordinary civil life was able to perform the duties of a soldier, and such defects as partial deafness, reducible hernia, muscular rheumatism, blindness in one eye, and loss of a couple of fingers were not to be considered as valid grounds for exemption.[6]

These regulations were of a decided benefit, but even so, great numbers continued to be inducted who were ill-adapted to the exposure, the deprivation, and the strenuous activities of life in the field.

Particularly susceptible to illness were the older men forced into the army by the conscription act of 1864. A surgeon who was put in charge of a regiment made up largely of enlistees under that law wrote in April 1864 that there "was more sickness in this regiment than in all the balance of the division." "It is a great pity that it was ever brought here," he said. "There are in it a great many old men of wealth and position at home who will die here. . . . Such men are entirely worthless here but would be very valuable at home." [7]

Of all the lessons taught by the Civil War, one of the most impressive was the fact that men of forty or over cannot be transplanted from the settled ways of civilian life to the strain and exposure of camp without exacting a heavy toll in sickness and death.

Most of the men who wore the gray were from the country, and this helps explain much of the sickness which plagued the Confederates. The country boys were tough, but they had not been immunized to the diseases common to children of towns and cities. Consequently they were besieged with these illnesses when they went to the army, while their city comrades of softer constitutions enjoyed comparatively good health. Pertinent also was the fact that townsmen knew better how to take care of themselves than the rustics did. Concerning some of the unsophisticates of the Alabama and Georgia hinterland, a North Carolinian wrote:

"They are like little children never away from home before, can't take care of themselves, and need someone to force them to wash themselves and put on clean clothing, when they start out to march they load themselves with more baggage than two men should carry. These are the men which for the most part compose our sick and fill up our Hospitals." [8]

Urban men also adapted themselves psychologically to the vicissitudes of army life more readily than those from the country, and this was a considerable item in physical well-being. From beginning to end of the war, the companies that were noted for the smallest sick rolls were crack outfits, made up of "gay youths of the cities," such as the Washington Artillery, the Richmond Blues, and the Mobile Cadets.[9]

Another factor which contributed to disease was exposure to rain and cold. Poets have delighted to dwell upon the tented field of Confederate days, but canopies were rarely to be found outside the imagination of the verse makers. During the terrible downpours in Virginia of March and April 1862, the great majority of Johnston's forces marched without raincoats and slept on the muddy ground without benefit of shelter; as a result hospitals were teeming with patients on the eve of Seven Pines.[10]

Later in the war oilcloths and tent-flies, both obtained largely from the Yankees, were in greater evidence, but even so, the soldier who had such protection was always the exception rather than the rule.

So habituated did Rebs become to mud and rain that some of them adopted a modified terminology, in which "dry" meant "not absolutely wet" and "perfectly dry" meant "somewhat damp, but not soaked through." [11] The huts built for winter quarters afforded some protection, but often winter quarters were postponed until January. In the meantime scarcity of clothing and lack of blankets combined with low temperatures and cold rains to inflict indescribable misery on the soldiers.

"It is really pitiable to see our boys at night sitting around their fires, nodding and almost asleep," wrote an officer on New Year's Day, 1864. "The ground is too cold for them to lie down on, and their one blanket is not warm enough for them to cover with. This is soldiering, this is." [12]

Suffering was often enhanced by inability to procure wood enough to keep the fires going. Shivering victims might draw some consolation from stories of Valley Forge, but philosophizing was of little effect in impeding the tides of sickness which always followed such periods of exposure.[13]

Much of the bad health must be attributed to an inadequate diet. Very seldom was there enough of vegetables in camp rations. During the greater part of the year fruit was unobtainable, and the day of "juices" had not arrived. When the soldiers did occasionally obtain apples and peaches, frequently they made no discrimination between the ripe and the green, and proceeded to gorge themselves. Rebs liked to brag about their culinary abilities, but the truth was that food prepared by troops was generally not of the most wholesome sort. A standard practice early in the war was to make flour up into slapjacks, and to fry these in a sea of bacon grease. Some regiments lived for month after month on a diet composed almost exclusively of fritters and fat meat.[14] Naturally the consequences were disastrous to digestive systems and to general health. "Much of the sickness our volunteers have suffered under," editorialized the Charleston Courier in 1862, "has been caused by half-done victuals—partially boiled rice and tough-baked bread." [15]

On many occasions impure water played havoc with army health. Troops stationed at Corinth depended in large measure for their water supply on shallow holes which they dug about the camps. Often these were placed so close to refuse deposits as to make contamination inevitable.[16] A newspaper correspondent reported that the water "smells so offensively that the men have to hold their noses while drinking it." [17]

In view of these circumstances it is not surprising to find that as many Confederates perished from disease during the seven weeks' encampment at Corinth in April and May 1862 as fell in the bloody fight at Shiloh.[18] These soldiers at Corinth were probably more careless about the sources from which they obtained water than Rebs generally were, but in all sections of the army and at all periods of the war the practice of drinking from rivers, creeks, badly situated springs and even from puddles was prevalent.

Another explanation of the numerous epidemics is to be found in the filth of many encampments. Ignorance, the overindulgence of elected officers, and the carelessness to which army life readily lends itself combined to defeat the earnest efforts of higher authorities to enforce sanitation. Latrines, or sinks as they were called by soldiers, were often placed too close to tents and bivouacs, and regardless of their location, there was a prevalent indisposition of Rebs to use them. Perhaps this was to be expected of a soldiery that came largely from a rural society in which men were accustomed to relieve themselves at whatever times and places the exigencies of nature overtook them. "Sinks not used," recurs with damning frequency on inspection reports, and in seacoast areas, the notation "beach used for sinks" is sometimes found.[19]

But the most extreme commentary on the nonchalance of toilet practices is that appearing in the diary of a Virginia private: "Dec. 3, 1863. . . . On rolling up my bed this morning I found I had been lying in—I wont say what—something though that didn't smell like milk and peaches." [20]

When soldiers were compelled to spend long periods in trenches, as at Vicksburg in 1863 and at Petersburg in 1864-1865, they were prone to litter the works with beef bones, melon rinds, fruit peelings, and other scraps.[21]

The scarcity of soap and the difficulty of bathing often added the factor of bodily filth. On January 19, 1865, Lee wrote the Secretary of War, "There is great suffering in the Army for want of soap. The neglect of personal cleanliness has occasioned cutaneous diseases to a great extent in many commands." [22] Even when soap and water were available there were always some soldiers who preferred personal filth to the exertion required for cleanliness.[23]

Swarms of pests worked in close co-operation with untidiness to communicate disease. Flies were a special nuisance. "When we open our eyes in the morning," wrote a Louisianian from Virginia in June 1861, "we find the canvas roofs and walls of our tents black with them. . . . It needs no morning reveille then to rouse the soldier from his slumbers. The tickling sensations about the ears, eyes, mouth, nose, etc., caused by the microscopic feet and inquisitive suckers of an army numerous as the sands of the sea shore will awaken a regiment of men

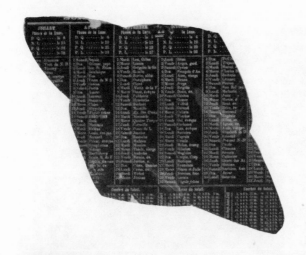

HOMEMADE ENVELOPE

Homemade envelope used by a Texas soldier,
Frank Moss. Outside of envelope is wall paper,
inside is French newsprint. The soldier made
the envelope from a Louisiana French newspaper
printed on wallpaper. From Barmore-Moss-Col-
clough-Rentfrow Papers, University of Texas Archives.

Courtesy Miss Brenda Thomson, Jackson, Mississippi

DECORATED ENVELOPE

Photostat of envelope for letter of Ruffin Thomson to his father of Terry, Mississippi, from Kingsville, South Carolina, November 15, 1861. From Ruffin Thomson Letters, manuscripts in possession of Miss Brenda Thomson, Jackson, Mississippi.

from innocent sleep to wide-awake profanity more promptly than the near beat of the alarming drum." [24]

Another Reb complained, "I get vexed at them and commence killing them, but as I believe forty come to every one's funeral I have given it up as a bad job." [25] Seemingly the only recourse was to swearing, but this did nothing to abate disease.

Even more noxious than flies were the mosquitoes that invaded Confederate camps from April to October. These pests, which in soldier parlance became "gallinippers," were declared by some Rebs to be more annoying than Yankee bullets. Naturally tall tales sprang up as to their size and achievements. One Johnny swore that his attackers were of a "preponderous size—almost able to shoulder a musket." [26]

Another—a Tennessean serving in the Mississippi lowlands—drew a comparison between those of his native state and those of his present acquaintance. "The Mississippi river fellow is far larger, has a longer and sharper bill," he observed, "and though he sings the same tune, he sings it with far great ferocity"; and whereas the Tennessee pests could muster only squads, those of Mississippi moved in regiments.[27]

Almost invariably comments on attacks by mosquitoes were followed in a few weeks by letters telling of epidemics of chills and fever. But people of Civil War times knew not the connection between the one and the other. Malaria was still attributed to the miasmas or poisonous vapors which rose from the swamps.

In some seasons and localities soldiers complained of the buffalo gnat, a pest described by one as a mischievous creature that "dives into the ear, nose, or anywhere on or under the skin and shylock like calls for blood." [28] "Blow-flies" and "chiggers" also came in for their share of denunciation. Fleas were even more of a nuisance. "I think there are 50 on my person at this time," wrote an Alabamian to his wife, "but you know they never did trouble me." Cryptically he added, "May I have thought of you often while mashing fleas; if you were here you could have your own sport." [29]

A Mississippian recently returned from furlough complained in 1862 of being singled out for special attack by fleas. "They hav most Eate me up since I came Back her," he said. "I was fresh to them so they pitched in." [30]

Another Reb testified that "they collect in companies at knight fall for the purpos of carrying us off . . . though like the Yankeys they are repulsed by desperate efforts & great patience." [31]

A more imaginative comrade declared:

"A great alarm was heard in the upper part of the regiment; hastening to the spot I enquired what was the matter. A man was asleep in his tent and a couple of fleas had taken holt on him and carried him half way to the river intending drownding [him] while asleep for he had sworn vengeance against them." [32]

But the tales of woe inspired by flies, mosquitoes and fleas were insignificant in comparison to those provoked by lice. Lice know no restrictions of time, place, or even of rank.

"There is not a man in the army, officer or private that does not have from a Battalion to a Brigade of Body lice on him," wrote an Alabamian in 1863. "I could soon get rid of them," he added, "but there is always some filthy man in camps that perpetuats the race." [33]

Both body lice, which roamed over the anatomy at large, and crab lice, which confined their attacks to hirsute areas, are mentioned—but the former, being the more numerous, came in for a lion's share of comment. They were dubbed with a great variety of grimly jocular names, such as "graybacks," "rebels," "zouaves," "tigers," and "Bragg's body-guard."

Military terms extended also to methods of extermination. Killing lice was referred to as "fighting under the black flag"; throwing away an infested shirt was spoken of as "giving the vermin a parole," and evading them by turning a garment wrong side out was called "executing a flank movement." [34]

When first infested with lice soldiers commonly experienced a feeling of disgrace; some even threw away their clothes. But as the curse became universal, shame gradually subsided. During periods of rest a few Rebs might always be discerned picking away at their shirts; others sought swifter riddance by singeing their clothes over campfires, a process that reminded one Johnny whose suit was "well stocked with big fat fellows" of popping corn. But respite once achieved was only temporary. Most veterans arrived at a state of splendid unconcern. One indeed claimed that he got to the point where he could not sleep soundly unless he had a few graybacks gnawing on him.[35]

Naturally there were many fantastic stories circulated about these unwelcome creatures. Several Rebs testified to catching lice with the letters C. S. (Confederate States) inscribed on their backs; one asserted that he saw a grayback adorned with the insignia I. W. (In for the War).[36] Another claimed: "I pulled off a Shirt last night and threw it down; this morning I saw it moveing first one way and then another;

I thought at first that there was a rat under it, but upon inspection found it was the lice racing about hunting for a Soldier." [37]

An Alabama rustic whose wife had suggested bringing two children to visit the camp wrote with a degree of seriousness advising against the proposal. "If you was here the Boddy lice would eat up Booth of the children in one knight in spite of all we could doo; you dont hav any idea what sort of a animal they are." [38]

But to Private Shield of the Virginia Light Artillery must be credited the most striking comment on record. One night as he prepared to retire he assumed a prayerful pose and recited:

> "Now I lay me down to sleep,
> While gray-backs oe'r my body creep;
> If I should die before I wake,
> I pray the Lord their jaws to break." [39]

Wonderful indeed was this ability of Rebs to make light of their woes. But unfortunately a sense of humor was neither a preventive nor a cure for the disease which followed in the wake of exposure, hunger, filth and pests.

Of the many illnesses which harassed Confederates, the first to attack in epidemic proportions was usually the measles. This disease was commonest among regiments composed of rural recruits. During the summer of 1861 one out of every seven of the men serving in Northern Virginia had measles, and total cases for three months exceeded 8,000.[40] In one camp of 10,000 recruits, 4,000 men were stricken.[41] So disruptive to the military program did this ailment become that the policy was adopted of withholding new troops from active duty until they were "put through the measles." [42]

Comparatively few men died from measles alone, but the mortality from subsequent complications was heavy. The tendency of patients to get up too soon was widespread, and the results were sometimes tragic.

Soldier correspondence of 1861 is full of such statements as this: "We have some 5 or 6 that is very sick ones in our company. . . . They all had the measles, & were getting well & they turn out to drill too soon after it and they all have relapsed. . . . Piercy and . . . Evans . . . died . . . both were hollering and dying at the same time." [43]

Shortly after the Seven Days' campaign, one of Lee's soldiers wrote his wife: "I have had good health since I left home with the exception of my bowels being disordered. But," he added, "it is a very rare thing to find a man in this army who has not got the diorreah." [44] This Reb was not exaggerating. Dysentery and diarrhea were the most prevalent of all camp diseases.

During the first nine months of the war the Confederate Army of the Potomac, the average mean strength of which was less than 50,000 men, reported 36,572 cases of these maladies. On the basis of figures compiled by Joseph Jones for forces east of the Mississippi, it appears that diarrhea and dysentery constituted no less than one-fourth of all the cases reported in 1861 and 1862.

At the Chimbarazo Hospital in Richmond, one of the Confederacy's largest military infirmaries, 10,503 cases of diarrhea and dysentery were treated during the war; this number represented one-sixth of all admissions for sickness; one out of every ten of the diarrhea and dysentery patients died. [45]

On the whole these maladies were less frequently fatal than some of the others, but allowance should be made for the fact that diarrhea by its weakening effects left the patient susceptible to diseases of a more serious character. Joseph Jones made the significant observation that while the deadlier ailments diminished as the war went on, chronic diarrhea and dysentery progressively increased, and that "more soldiers were permanently disabled and lost to the service from these diseases than from the disability following accidents of battle." [46]

Doctor Jones's statement gives point to a story told of an ordinary Reb. Near the end of the conflict this soldier, ragged, footsore and dysenteric, spied a Yankee cavalryman who seemed perfect in health and dress. "Oh my, oh my! you look like you wuz sich a happy man!" said the Southerner. "You got on sich a nice new-niform, you got sich nice boots on, you ridin' sich a nice hoss, an' you look like yer bowels wuz so reglar." [47]

Several factors, but mainly those of diet and exhaustion, made diarrhea and dysentery not only more prevalent but also much more often fatal among Confederates than among Yankees. [48]

Malaria was also a very common disease in Southern camps. Estimates of prevalency, elusive enough for all diseases on account of the fragmentary nature of health records, are particularly difficult in connection with malaria because of the widespread tendency of soldiers not to report mild cases.

The cause of the malady was not known, and many Rebs followed a practice that they had learned at home of simply knocking along as best they could without seeking medical treatment. If they were able to appear at roll call and carry on routine duties without interruption, as many were, no official cognizance was taken of their illness. [49] From such reported cases as exist, however, some general impressions may be derived.

In 1861 and 1862 malarial fever apparently constituted about one-seventh of all the cases of sickness reported by armies east of the Mississippi. During the first ten months of 1862 the Virginia Valley command, with an average mean strength of 15,582 men, had 3,885 cases of malaria. Soldiers serving in lowland areas fared much worse. The Department of South Carolina, Georgia and Florida, which had an average mean strength of 25,723 men, reported 41,539 cases of malarial fever from January 1862 to July 1863. And during the same period the force around Mobile which averaged 6,752 men had 13,688 cases. In all areas, malaria was much more prevalent during the summer than at other seasons. Fatalities from this malady were comparatively rare.[50]

Less frequent than malaria but far more fatal was typhoid. This ailment was said to have caused one-fourth of all the deaths from disease in the Southern armies.[51] Typhoid made its appearance very early in the war, and by August 1861 it had attained epidemic proportions among troops in Virginia. Large numbers continued to be stricken in the Confederate Army of the Potomac until December 1861 when a decline set in that lasted till May 1862. In June another outbreak occurred which lasted till September. In both instances the epidemics came in the wake of large-scale inductions of troops, most of whom came from rural areas.

Figures upon which to base estimates for the last two years of the war are not available. In all probability, additions to the army in consequence of the conscription law of 1864 caused a temporary increase of typhoid cases, but not to the extent of earlier outbreaks.

Joseph Jones made the statement several years after Appomattox that "typhoid fever progressively diminished during the progress of the war, and disappeared almost entirely from the veteran armies," and evidence drawn from Federal experience tends to prove his statement.[52]

Smallpox was apparently unknown in the Confederate Army during the first year of the war. The disease seems to have made its initial appearance in the Army of Northern Virginia, shortly after the Antietam campaign. This led to the belief that germs were brought from beyond the Potomac, perhaps on captured Yankee clothing, by soldiers participating in the Maryland movement. The theory gained credence from the fact that several hundred cases of smallpox had been previously reported in the Federal Army of the Potomac.[53]

Whatever its origin, the outbreak of this disease caused great alarm throughout the Confederacy. Figures as to the prevalence of smallpox are meager, but indications are that the epidemic which broke out in October 1862 in Virginia reached its peak in the early months of 1863. Several thousand cases were treated in the general hospitals of Lee's army in 1862 and 1863, and the rate of mortality was high.[54]

Vigorous measures were adopted by medical authorities to combat the spread of smallpox. Patients were isolated and a system of quarantine was instituted. Furthermore vaccinations were ordered throughout the army. In order to obtain an adequate supply of virus, surgeons were detailed to vaccinate healthy children who would pledge the donation of resulting scabs to army use. Experiments were also made for the procurement of virus from cows. In many cases soldiers were so thoroughly frightened that they did not wait for the doctors to act, but taking scabs from the arms of their fellows, they proceeded to vaccinate one another with pocketknives. The self-appointed inoculators were inclined to use the lancet rather generously because of a prevalent belief that the bigger the sore the greater the degree of protection. Within a short time after the flurry of vaccinations some of the sores presented a peculiarly loathsome appearance and refused to heal. These infections eventually became so widespread and aggravated as to impair seriously the strength of the army. At the time of the battle of Chancellorsville, 5,000 men were reported unfit for duty on this account. From these untoward circumstances there arose a great controversy over the causes of "spurious vaccination." The belief prevailed among soldiers that the phenomenon had a syphilitic origin, and this idea gained support from one Reb's admission that he had been vaccinated while on furlough by an accommodating inmate of an Augusta bawdyhouse. Most doctors discredited the theory of widespread venereal contamination, and while the argument was never completely settled, medical opinion generally attributed the infections to insanitary methods of vaccination, improper care of scars and lowered resistance in the persons inoculated.[55]

Pneumonia was very prevalent in Southern armies. Joseph Jones estimated on the basis of incomplete figures gathered during the war that for a nineteen-month period in 1862-1863, over 17 per cent of the Confederate forces were stricken by this disease. He found that soldiers in the Army of Tennessee were much more susceptible to the malady than those serving in Virginia, and that troops of the Department of South Carolina, Georgia and Florida were affected only to a slight degree. As a general rule, "Pneumonia prevailed to the greatest extent in the more elevated and northern regions of the Southern Confederacy, and in the armies which were subjected to the severest labors, privations, and exposures." The disease increased during the winter months and diminished in summer. During the period studied by Jones, approximately one out of every six cases proved fatal.[56]

Bronchitis, catarrh, scurvy, erysipelas and pulmonary tuberculosis patients were numerous at various times. In 1861 mumps was occasionally reported. Scarlet fever was rare.[57] Soldier correspondence contained references now and then to jaundice, which was erroneously regarded as a disease rather than as a symptom. In telling of jaundice Rebs often had trouble with spelling, but rarely with expression. "Henry has got the yellow Janders," wrote one; "he is as yellow as a orange and the white of his Eyes is yellow and he is yellow all over." [58] This certainly must have been a case of the obstructive type.

A malady that was rare, but which because of its peculiarity elicited much comment, was "night blindness" or "gravel." When soldiers whose vision in daytime was good first began to complain of inability to see at night, and started walking around holding on to comrades like blind men, doctors were inclined to think that they were shamming. But subsequent investigation proved that the disability was genuine. Connection with scurvy was noted in some instances, thus suggesting what apparently was the true cause of most cases, namely, dietary deficiencies coupled with undue exposure and exhaustion.[59]

Another ailment that gave doctors great concern because of the ease with which it could be feigned was rheumatism; but there can be no doubt that bona-fide afflictions ran far into the thousands.[60]

Syphilis and gonorrhea, though not widely prevalent, existed to some extent in most regiments. Venereal diseases usually increased when troops were stationed near cities, and when furloughs were increased.[61] Other occasional maladies mentioned by soldiers were delirium tremens, sore eyes, sore mouth, dropsy, toothache, and stomach-ache.

A skin disease called "camp itch," or simply the itch, was the cause of much complaint. This ailment was ordinarily of a trivial character, but complications arising from overzealous scratching sometimes were serious. Concerning itch Surgeon L. Guild wrote: "It is not Scabies but Lichen, and of so inveterate and obstinate a character in its chronic stage as to baffle all treatment whilst the patient remains in camp. Very many of these cases are therefore sent to General Hospital." [62] In view of such persistency, one is not surprised to find that one bedeviled Reb attributed his scratching to "the mange." [63]

Treatments for the various ills which beset the army were of the greatest variety. Contributing to this diversity was the tendency of soldiers to doctor themselves. Almost every recruit brought to camp a list of "sure remedies" gleaned from local tradition and experience; these were exchanged freely with cures of equal certainty contributed by comrades from other parts of the country. Editors and pamphleteers added their suggestions, and from this conglomerate of ideas Johnny Reb attempted to frame his prescriptions. For diarrhea and malaria a favorite treatment was hot tea made from the bark of such trees as slippery elm, sweet gum, willow and dogwood. A drink made of spice wood was administered to those suffering with measles. One Reb whose brother was stricken with cramp colic reported his experiments:

"I first gave him 2 doses of morphine, then a dose of my pills. He got no better. I then gave him a large drink of whisky & put a mustard poultice on his stomache. After which he got better & [is] now perfectly easy." [64]

Patients afflicted with chills were drenched with bitters and sundry solutions, the chief ingredient of which was rum, brandy or whiskey. In fact, alcoholic beverages were widely regarded as panaceas, whether taken straight or mixed. Mustard plasters were popular for chest and bronchial infections. One soldier who despaired of cure by his doctor sought haven in a private home where, according to his testimony, he "prety well burnt the pleurasy out of . . . [his] side with pepper and Number six and hot bricks." [65] Many Rebs wore flannel bands about their waist to fend off ill effects of exposure to dampness and cold.[66]

A sample of the advice received from pamphleteers is found in H. W. R. Jackson's brochure entitled *Historical Register and Confederates' Assistant to National Independence*:

"An Item Worth Noticing— . . . To guard against many diseases . . . volunteers should put a small quantity of tar—say a large spoonful —into their canteens. It has often been recommended as a preventative of chills and fever, measles &c. . . . After a day or two it detracts nothing from the taste of the water. . . .

"A good cure for a cold is to drink as much molasses and water (cold) on going to bed as one can swallow. Wrap up warm and rub off with a wet cloth in the morning. Another cure is to drink about a pint of tea made of roasted or baked apples . . . on going to bed, not forgetting the morning ablution. . . .

"Infallible Cure For Toothache—Take equal quantities of alum and common salt, pulverize and mix. Apply to the hollow tooth on a wet piece of cotton.

"A Good Cure For Cough—Vinegar and salt mixed together. A teaspoonful several times a day. . . .

"Remedy Against Fleas— . . . Fresh leaves of pennyroyal sewed in a bag, and laid in the bed will have the desired effect. In the absence of pennyroyal take green peach leaves.

"To Cure The Itch— . . . Take white elder flower ointment and flour of sulphur, each two ounces; oil of peppermint half a drachm. Mix and rub the body all over with it before a good fire for three nights before going to bed.

"Let your beard grow so as to protect the throat and lungs. . . . Keep your entire person clean. This prevents fevers and bowel complaints." [67]

Treatments administered by doctors were almost as diverse as those gathered by soldiers from tradition and almanacs, and in many instances they were almost as archaic. American medical practice was at that time in a state of transition from old to new methods, and confusion was inevitable. In the Confederacy the situation was complicated further by the blockade. Substitutes and variants had to be found for many of the usual medicines and treatments. Surgeon General Samuel P. Moore and his associates, many of whom were exceptionally able men, worked diligently to make the required adjustments. Dr. Francis P. Porcher was put to the task of preparing a 'treatise on the medical properties of the South's indigenous plants, and the results of his work published in 1863 under the title *Resources of Southern Fields and Forests* made available a storehouse of useful information.[68] But effective substitutes could not be obtained for some of the most essential medicines. And despite dramatic ventures in running Federal lines by patriotic women who concealed the precious medicines in their clothing, importations fell far short of army needs. To an increasing extent as the war progressed physicians depended on their own ideas and resources.

Treatments applied by doctors in diarrheal cases were particularly complicated. This was due partly to shortage of medicines but principally to confusion as to the cause of the illness and the inability to distinguish between dysentery and diarrhea. One Reb who went to the regimental physician "suffering violently with flux" was given some pills of calomel, quinine and opium. "I took them to my quarters," the patient said afterward, "threw them into the street, and . . . by dieting myself . . . [got well]." [69] Another soldier who had been plagued with diarrhea for some time was dosed with a miscellany of tartaric acid water, quinine, morphine and blue mass.[70]

In general, treatments for bowel complaints fell into two main categories: one stressed the use of astringents and the other advocated purgatives. Revealing insight into prevailing technique and procedure was given by a doctor who had ministered to Lee's men. "Early in the morning we had sick call," he said. "Diagnosis was rapidly made, usually by intuition, and treatment was with such drugs as we chanced to have in the knapsack. . . . On the march my own practice was . . . reduced to the lowest terms. In one pocket of my trousers I had a ball of blue mass, in another a ball of opium. All complainants were asked the same question, 'How are your bowels?' If they were open, I administered a plug of opium, if they were shut, I gave a plug of blue mass." [71] It is no wonder, in the light of such methods, that some Rebs called their doctors "damn quacks" and threw their medicine away.[72]

Scarcity of opium eventually forced army physicians to resort to substitutes that could be found near at hand. Blackberry, willow and sweet gum were used for intestinal astringents. Blue mass seems to have been available in fairly large quantities throughout the war, but in isolated instances of scarcity, vegetable cathartics of various sorts were readily obtainable.[73] Surgeons knew that scurvy was due to dietary deficiencies and in portions of the army affected or threatened by this disease, details of soldiers were sent into wood and field to gather wild onion, garlic, mustard, sassafras, pokeweed, artichoke, pepper grass, dandelion and other edible herbs. Vinegar was also used as an anti-scorbutic.[74]

Pneumonia was a great puzzle to Confederate physicians. On the theory that this disease was an "inflammation," many doctors resorted to bleeding. "Blagg was very sick," wrote a Virginian of a comrade suffering from pneumonia; "Byrd brought a Doctor down yesterday and he cupped him Severely & it relieved the Stitching in his Side immediately." [75] But death rather than improvement followed bleeding in such a vast number of cases that physicians generally abandoned cupping "in favor of a sustaining treatment of liquor, opium, and quinine." If drugs were not available, patients were given herbal preparations of various sorts along with local applications of time-honored mustard plasters.[76]

While the connection between mosquitoes and malaria was not known in Civil War days, experience taught that smoke smudges, dry camp sites and other expedients which gave relief from the former tended also to lessen the latter. Quinine was the generally recognized remedy for malaria, but as this was an imported drug it became increasingly scarce during the period of the Confederacy. Among the various substitutes brought into use were tonics made from the bark of dogwood, tulip tree (generally called poplar) and willow, with whiskey as the preferred agent. Surgeon General Moore recommended mixing the ingredients according to the following formula: "Dogwood bark, 30 parts; poplar bark, 30 parts; willow bark, 40 parts, whiskey 45 degrees strength. Two pounds of the mixed bark to one gallon of whiskey. Mascerate 14 days—dose . . . one ounce 3 times a day." Local application of turpentine was also used as an alternative treatment for malaria. According to Moore, experimentation proved this latter remedy "amply sufficient to interrupt the morbific chain of successive paroxysms—one application only being required in the majority of cases."

Early in the war quinine was widely used as a prophylactic, but its scarcity, coupled with a practice popular among soldiers of selling the drug instead of using it, eventually caused the substitution for this purpose of a tonic of native barks and whiskey.[77]

Itch was widely treated with internal dosages of a poke-root solution, and with external applications of an ointment composed largely of the same substance. Poke was also used in the doctoring of rheumatism, neuralgia and syphilis. One physician reported excellent results in treating gonorrhea with injections of ink ball; he also claimed that it could be cured by administering a combined dose of silk-weed tonic and pills made of pine rosin and blue vitriol.[78] For measles no satisfactory remedy seems to have been found, but in this, as in most other instances of uncertainty, doctors fell back on whiskey.

One of the greatest difficulties of the medical department was maintaining an adequate supply of alcoholic beverages. Ordinary Rebs thought the scarcity due to the insatiable thirst of army doctors. A skit in a camp joke book ran as follows:

What is the first duty of a surgeon?
Under the names of drugs and medicines to purchase a full
    supply of good liquors.

What is the second duty?
To cause all private cellars to be searched, and all the good
    brandies found there to be confiscated, lest the owners
    should smuggle them to the soldier, give them away and
    make the whole army drunk.
What is the third duty?
To see that he and his assistant drink up all of said liquors.[79]

The suspicions of the rank and file were not without foundation.
William H. Taylor admits in his memoirs that he and his fellow surgeons were accustomed to go on a spree the night following each
receipt of spirits and that they succeeded usually in "drinking up every
drop . . . before morning." [80]

Correspondence of high medical authorities indicates a considerable
leakage in the liquor dispensation and reveals the dismissal of at least
one surgeon "for appropriation to his own use of stimulants intended
for the sick." [81]

But impropriety of physicians was only a minor factor in the prevalent deficiency. The chief cause lay in the interference by state
authorities with distillation for Confederate use. Fears of grain shortage
and concern for states' rights were major reasons for this, but belief
that government contracts were used as a shield for manufacture on
private account was also a consideration. The Virginia Legislature
prescribed severe penalties for the fulfillment of any liquor contract
with Confederate authorities. Only by erecting its own distilleries was
the government able to obtain enough alcohol to meet a portion of its
most pressing needs.[82]

Lack of essential medicines, archaic methods of the doctors, laxity
of camp discipline and ignorance of the soldiery were the cause of an
untold amount of disease and suffering. But these constitute only a
part of the picture. Defective organization of medical personnel, incomplete transportation arrangements, and inadequate hospital facilities
also played an important role in multiplying the miseries of the sick.

These latter factors were especially important in the first part of the
war. Then it was that disease struck most heavily and that the country
was least prepared to care for the patients. The people were not lacking in willingness to provide for the sick, as witness the efforts of individual women and of volunteer relief societies.[83] The trouble was
rather in the enormity of the problem and in the lack of co-ordinated
enterprise. Both the citizenry and the army had to grow up to a realiza-

tion of the meaning of war in terms of disease, and to the ability to care for those who became ill.

Richmond papers and army medical records give a vivid insight into the great suffering experienced by the sick of Virginia commands in 1861 and 1862. In August 1861 it was reported that ailing troops were being transported in railroad cars previously used for hauling horses, and from which the manure and other filth had not been removed. Two months later the press told of several hundred sick soldiers being unloaded at Manassas. Rain was pouring down, but no provision had been made for their reception. After a long exposure to wet and cold, with no covering but their thin woolen blankets, the miserable Rebs were piled into cars, without receiving nourishment of any sort, and sent on to Richmond. At the capital there was no one to meet them, and they had either to lie helplessly at the depot until hospital authorities could give them attention, or to totter uncertainly about the streets in search of aid.[84]

It was not always easy for an ailing soldier to find hospitality. A Mississippian who in December 1861 rescued a suffering comrade from the sidewalks of Richmond, took him to a hotel where he offered to pay his room fee; he received a curt refusal from the landlord.[85] Later in the war various volunteer agencies established "Waysides" or "soldiers' homes" for the care of such cases as this, but some of these were denounced as humbugs by those who sought their shelter.[86]

Often the soldiers themselves, or their officers, were responsible for the neglect which they experienced. Surgeon General Moore complained repeatedly that large groups of ill men were sent from camps without prior notification to authorities who were to receive them, that those dispatched frequently exceeded the number reported, that sick cars were overloaded, and that officers ordered men removed from the army to the city who were so sick that they were on arrival "in almost a moribund state." [87]

The publicity given in late 1861 to shortcomings in the handling of the sick caused the War Department to institute an improved system which gave particular attention to transportation. But in early May 1862 a Richmond editor reported that a large number of ailing troops lay for hours on the sidewalk waiting for hospitalization.[88]

Later in the war, with the decline of the rate of illness and the expansion of facilities, such instances became rare. After 1862 hospital resources throughout the Confederacy seem to have been fairly ample for the care of the sick except in short periods following great battles when accommodations were unduly taxed.

In the camps sick soldiers continued to suffer from lack of attention throughout the conflict. There were never enough doctors and nurses. And the indifference bred by war caused troops to become neglectful of one another. It was not uncommon for ill men to lie for hours in their tents or in vacant houses without food or water.

"I did not believe men could be so selfish and indifferent as they have been in our regiment," wrote a Georgia captain on one occasion; "two thirds of them would not wait on the sick if they were not made to do it they would let them lie and suffer." [89]

The hopelessness of proper care and the high percentage of mortality caused most Rebs to contemplate illness with incalculable dread. The pervasive sentiment was well expressed by one who wrote from camp: "It scares a man to death to get sick down here." [90]

In most respects soldiers who were seriously wounded fared worse than those who were ill. The machinery for disposing of battle casualties was fairly simple. When a conflict was imminent, buildings or tents near the scene of contemplated action were designated as field hospitals and marked with flags. A small squad of men, preferably convalescents and others not in best fighting trim, was detailed from each company to remove the wounded to the field infirmaries. Each man so detailed was equipped with a knapsack containing dressings, stimulants and tourniquets; when fighting commenced, assistant surgeons, accompanied by the details, moved forward to dispose of the wounded. Assistant surgeons supervised the administration of first aid and told litter bearers which cases required removal to field hospitals. Regimental surgeons remained at the field infirmaries of their respective brigades to attend to the wounded as they were brought in. They operated immediately on the most urgent cases and directed removal in ambulances—which were simply canvas-covered wagons—of those that were to be transferred to interior hospitals.[91] Patients thus removed were sent first to receiving hospitals; from there they were distributed as soon as possible to the general hospitals located in most cities.

Early in the war the custom prevailed of permitting convalescents to go home as soon as they were able to travel, but consequent relapses from hemorrhages and from improper care, plus increasing reluctance of those on furlough to return to camp, caused an abatement of this practice after 1863.

The system which Confederate authorities set up for the care of the wounded was basically sound, but numerous factors hindered its operation. In the first place commanding generals sometimes failed to inform hard-pressed medical officers of contemplated campaigns in sufficient time to allow for adequate preparations. Lee's medical director complained on one occasion to Surgeon General Moore: "The movements of the army cannot be anticipated by me for the General Commanding never discloses any of his plans to those around him . . . every thing is done hurriedly and mysteriously." [92] Even when ample notice was given and advance preparation carefully made, medical authorities, because of limitations of personnel and essential facilities, were utterly unable to provide prompt and adequate care for the thousands of men who were wounded in every major encounter.

This was particularly true of the Confederacy's first great fights. At Shiloh many wounded lay in the mud of the battlefield all night under a cold pelting rain, without attention of any sort, even though infirmary corps moved about as rapidly as possible and doctors labored to the point of collapse. The falling back of the army necessitated a hurried removal, and shivering, moaning men were loaded into wagons, many of which were not equipped with springs, and hauled more than twenty miles over "the roughest and ruttiest roads in the Southern Confederacy" to Corinth. Here hotels, school buildings, churches and private homes were converted into hospitals, but all these did not provide enough shelter.

For days after the battle groaning men might be seen lying about the depot waiting transportation to improvised infirmaries at Memphis, Holly Springs and Oxford. Doctors came from far and near and made their contributions to the pile of amputated limbs that accumulated in the yard of Corinth's Tishomingo Hotel. Women came too, eager to render what assistance they could. One of them wrote in her diary:

"The foul air from this mass of human beings at first made me giddy and sick, but I soon got over it. We have to walk and when we give the men anything kneel in blood and water; but we think nothing of it." [93]

Less than two months after Shiloh the Seven Days' campaign around Richmond produced a tide of casualties such as the Confederacy had not seen before. Citizens of the capital and of Petersburg took omnibuses and private carriages to the battlefields and piled the injured into stores, tobacco warehouses, factories, residences and tents. But even these extraordinary measures fell short of the need. A newspaper appeal, dated three days after fighting ceased, stated that "hundreds and even thousands of . . . soldiers are lying wounded upon the battle-field waiting in extreme agony for some pitying hands to remove them to a place of refuge from the tortures which they endure." The grue-some results of this neglect were vividly suggested by an article on the treatment of flyblow. Other newspaper notices urged citizens to bring ice and food to the hospitals, to tear up old cotton clothes for bandages, and to volunteer their services as nurses and cooks. Not until more than two weeks after the last of the series of battles was the situation brought under control. In the meantime hundreds, if not thousands, of brave men whom timely attention could have saved had endured unspeakable tortures of hunger, thirst and pain, and had finally died.[94]

Even greater suffering was endured by some of those who a year later marched with Lee into Pennsylvania and fell wounded at Gettys-burg. The hasty retreat after the third day's repulse permitted little attention to the wounded. Those who were able to travel, and many who were not, were crowded into rickety wagons and started on the long and rough journey southward. A vivid picture of the tragedy which ensued was given by a high-ranking officer who participated in the retreat:

"For four hours I hurried forward on my way to the front of the wagon train and in all that time I was never out of hearing of the groans and cries of the wounded and dying. Scarcely one in a hundred had received adequate surgical aid. . . . Many . . . had been without food for thirty-six hours. Their torn and bloody clothing, matted and hardened, was rasping the tender, inflamed, and still oozing wounds. Very few of the wagons had even a layer of straw in them, and all were without springs. The road was rough and rocky. . . . From nearly every wagon . . . came such cries and shrieks as these

" 'Oh God! why can't I die?'

" 'My God, will no one have mercy and kill me?'

" 'Stop! oh! For God's sake, stop just for one minute; take me out and leave me to die on the roadside.' . . .

"No heed could be given to any of their appeals. . . . On! on! We must move on. . . . During this one night I realized more of the horrors of war than I had in all the two preceding years." [95]

When abandonment of positions came immediately after the battle as at Gettysburg, Antietam and Shiloh, the greater portion of surgery had to be postponed until the patients arrived at base hospitals in the interior. But under ordinary circumstances, most of the amputations and other emergency operations were performed at field infirmaries. These makeshift quarters, often situated in depressions bordering the scene of action, afforded only the crudest of facilities. Here amid the groans and screams of waiting patients, regimental surgeons wielded scalpels and saws for hour after hour on suffering creatures whose only anesthetic was frequently a drink of whiskey and sometimes not even that.

Surgeon Spencer Welch wrote on one occasion to his wife:

"I then went back to the field infirmary where I saw large numbers of wounded lying on the ground as thick as a drove of hogs in a lot . . . those shot in the bowels were crying for water. Jake Fellers had his arm amputated without chloroform. I held the artery and Dr. Huot cut it off by candle light. We continued to operate until late at night. . . . I was very tired and slept on the ground." [96]

E. D. Patterson, a private who was twice wounded at Frayser's Farm, committed to his diary such a vivid account of his experiences as to merit particular notice. "The first ball that struck me was so close that the musket's breath was hot on my face," he wrote while convalescing, "and I fell forward across my gun, my left arm useless falling under me. . . . I did not at the moment feel any pain, only a numbness all over the body. I felt as if someone had given me an awful jar, and fell as limber as a drunken man. I could not even tell where I was hit." As Patterson was contemplating dazedly the effects of his shoulder injury, he was struck again, this time in the thigh, by a ball that fairly lifted him from the ground. He bled profusely but did not lose consciousness. Through the remainder of the day and on into the night he lay in an open field. He had little hope of seeing the dawn of another day. "I thought of more things in one hour than I could write down in a year," he said. "I thought of a home far away. . . . I wondered if my fate would ever be known to them. I had a horror of dying alone. . . . I was afraid that none of my regiment would ever find me, and that with the unknown dead who lay scattered around me I would be buried in one common ground. . . . The thought was terrible. How I longed for day. Just that some one might see me die." He prayed, but with little faith, because of the realization that the supplication was prompted solely by the emergency. "The loss of so much blood had made me cold," he continued. "I shook until I almost feared that I would shake in pieces. . . . My limbs were as cold as ice and still I wanted water." A young Federal heard his cries for drink and came and ministered to him through the remainder of the night.

The next morning the ground on which he lay was repossessed by Confederates, and he was found by a cousin who was surgeon of a Georgia regiment. The doctor poured a couple of drinks of brandy down him, took him to a near-by house, and operated on his leg. Patterson requested chloroform, but the surgeon thought an anesthetic inadvisable. "I watched him while he laid open the flesh," the patient said, "and it reminded me of cutting fat pork, it cut so smooth and nice, and it hurt." Later Patterson was taken to a private home near Richmond where, after a second operation, he fully recovered.[97]

The permanent and semipermanent hospitals in the interior were of course better equipped than the field infirmaries. The best-administered institutions were usually the general hospitals of the larger towns. Richmond had more of these than any other city of the Confederacy. An effort was made in the capital to house the patients of each state in a separate establishment, and many of the hospitals bore the name of the state from which its inmates came.

One of the most famous and efficient infirmaries in Richmond was that of Sally L. Tompkins. This lady established a hospital on her initiative after First Manassas, and when later the government assumed control of all institutions ministering to soldiers, President Davis was reluctant to give up Miss Tompkins' services. To avoid the irregularity of having a person without title in an official position, he made her a captain and thus gave her the distinction of being the only woman ever to receive a regular commission from the Confederate Government.[98]

At various times of emergency, medical authorities were compelled to call on colleges and churches for use of their buildings. The University of Virginia, the University of Mississippi and the female seminaries at Lynchburg and at Corinth were among the educational institutions that provided facilities for the wounded. In these instances, and in most others, college and church officials contributed the needed shelter without hesitation. But occasionally there was opposition. A Virginia doctor wrote his superiors on one occasion that he had converted three Harrisonburg churches into hospitals, "but not without meeting . . . obstinate remonstrance bordering on physical resistance." [99]

After a Conference with Washington College authorities at Lexington, another doctor reported:

"There is not the slightest propect of obtaining the consent of the Trustees. . . . The salary of the most of the professors will be suspended if the exercises of the college are closed. Several of these professors are family connexions of the trustees who will most certainly protect their interests." [100]

Many soldiers looked with abhorrence on all hospitals, and there can be no doubt that they were justified. Operations were often rendered excruciatingly painful because of the scarcity of opiates and the dullness of scalpels. Some excellent sets of surgical implements were imported and others were captured, but there was never enough of these to go around; those manufactured in the Confederacy were characterized by Lee's medical director as "entirely useless." [101]

Post-operational care was inadequate. In Richmond, where conditions probably were better than average, the supervisor of hospitals reported on one occasion that 131 medical officers, many of whom were occupied with executive duties, were charged with attending 10,200 patients—a proportion of 1 to 70.[102] Inmates of hospitals complained repeatedly of an insufficiency of nourishment, and reports of medical officers leave little doubt that fare in some institutions was notoriously poor. Clothing and bed covering were frequently inadequate and sanitary conditions often left much to be desired.[103] At the Newsom Hospital in Chattanooga soldiers were given clean garments for the duration of their treatment, but on dismissal they were required to wear the filthy attire which they wore when admitted.[104]

"I beleave the Doctors kills more than they cour," wrote an Alabama private in 1862; "Doctors haint Got half Sence." And a Georgian expressed the opinion that army surgeons were the "most unworthy of all the human famaly." [105] These particular Rebs may have had no other foundation for their statements than the tendency of soldiers—well or sick—to grouse. But with full allowance for prejudices and overstatement, the conclusion remains inescapable that much of the suffering endured by the wounded was due to poor physicians. Examinations required of candidates for surgical appointments were sometimes no more than farces. One doctor said that his examining committee was composed of five members of whom one owed his position to the favor of kinsmen, another had failed to pass the course at the University of Virginia, and a third was very drunk.[106]

The practice of appointing surgeons with the understanding that they were to stand examination at a later time led to endless procrastination on the part of some who were of doubtful abilities. The category of doctors known as "contract physicians," who in times of emergency were called on for a considerable portion of army practice, apparently had to take no examination at all; these were, as a rule, utterly undeserving of professional status.[107] Many of the regular appointees of 1861 were young and inexperienced, a circumstance deriving largely from the fact that few of the established practitioners sought army positions.[108]

It would be erroneous to infer that the Confederate surgical corps was made up wholly of "culls," novices and quacks. The high-ranking officials were as a rule men of unusual talent and attainment; many of the regimental surgeons, and some of the assistant-surgeons, discharged their duties ably and conscientiously insofar as the nature of available supplies would permit.

The better class of surgeons, whatever their rank, were unusually resourceful. Of this type, a prominent medical director said:

"I have seen him search field and forest for plants and flowers . . . [that he] could use. The pliant bark of a tree made for him a good tourniquet; the juice of the green persimmon a styptic; a knitting-needle with its point sharply bent, a tenaculum, and a pen-knife in his hand, a scalpel and bistoury. I have seen him break off one prong of a common table fork, bend the point of the other prong and with it elevate the bone in depressed fracture of the skull and save life. Long before he knew the use of the porcelain-tipped probe for finding bullets, I have seen him use a piece of soft pine wood and bring it out of the wound marked by the leaden ball." [109]

Confederate surgeons, good and bad, were handicapped greatly by the undeveloped state of medical science which characterized their period. They believed that suppuration, or "laudable pus," was an essential feature with the healing process. They probed with ungloved fingers; they deterred recovery by tampering with wounds; they worked in soiled uniforms; they used bloodstained bandages; and they were only partially conscious of the importance of clean instruments. It is not surprising in view of these and other shortcomings that gangrene played havoc with their patients.[110]

The majority of surgeons seem to have been men of sympathy and of kindness. Sergeant William P. Chambers recorded in his diary an instance typical of many. When a doctor named Britts approached Chambers to operate he said: "You were soldier enough to get shot I reckon you are soldier enough to have the ball cut out." Chambers remarked that he had no choice in the matter of receiving the wound, and that he supposed the bullet must be extracted. Britts fumbled about uncertainly and said, "Chambers, I don't like to cut there," but presently he seemed to pull himself together, and with the advice "turn your head away, I don't want you to look at me," he began his unpleasant task. The first stroke of the knife struck the missile. When this proved to be only a part of the bullet Britts swore profusely. Not until after a considerable amount of probing, painful to the patient and grievous to the surgeon, was the remnant brought to the surface.[111]

Mortality from wounds, even from those in arms and legs, was woefully high.[112] Patients who recovered often experienced painful setbacks and distressing complications. Indeed no phase of Confederate history is so dark and tragic as that which reveals the incomprehensible torture endured by the sick and the wounded. And if glory be measured by suffering, the South's greatest heroes are not those who died at the cannons' mouth on Cemetery Ridge, or in any of the other gallant charges made by soldiers in gray, but rather those who, sorely wounded or desperately ill, lived to experience the unspeakable agony of hospitalization.

CHAPTER XIV

THE GENTLER SENTIMENTS

"I BELIEVE the biggest half of our Study here is about Something to eat and the other part is about wives and sweethearts," wrote a lonely Reb from camp in December 1862.[1]

His statement was not exaggerated, for woman was of tremendous moment in the life of the ordinary soldier. The reassurance of her smile and the fondness of her farewell warmed his departure from home, and the song which timed his step as he headed for the front was "The Girl I Left Behind Me." Memories of his sweetheart at home were with him ever after. He carried her portrait close to his heart, and the wreaths of smoke that curled from the campfire at night had an uncanny habit of shaping themselves into her elusive image. When exhaustion transported him to the realm of dreams he luxuriated in her fancied presence, and he resented the blatant morning call that took her away. As he prepared for battle his thoughts were mainly of her—it was for her that he must brave the roar and the carnage, for her that the enemy must be driven beyond Southern borders and independence achieved.

More romantically disposed Rebs saw the war as a composite of individual combats, with each soldier playing the knight for his particular lady. One wore a sprig of palmetto in his hat as a lover's token; others called their guns by their sweethearts' names.[2] Even the thoroughfares of camp were given such feminine designations as "Maiden Lane."[3]

Married Rebs thought of peace largely in terms of reunion with wives, and single men counted strongly on the resumption of courtship which should lead shortly to matrimony. "Kiss all . . . [the girls] for me," wrote an unattached soldier in 1862, "and tell them I shall be back some of these days and not one of them shall go uncourted."[4]

Another sent this message: "Tell . . . Miss Mollie when I come home if she wants to Marrie me all she has to do is to say so"; and a third said, "I am tired of camp life and thank God all Mighty if I live

270

through this war I will be stoped roving I intend to come home and marry Miss Lizzie Kemp." [5]

Thought of womankind was poor substitute for the reality. And as month after month passed with scarcely a glimpse of a woman, the craving for feminine association became well-nigh intolerable. "I have not seen a gal in so long a time that I would not know what to do with myself if I were to meet up with one," wrote a disconsolate Virginian, "though I recon I would learn before I left her. . . . I would be glad to [see] one more gal before the Yankees kill me." [6] Another wrote: "I havent hug a girl for so long I am out of practice." [7]

Some soldiers sought relief for their insatiable yearning by making long and reminiscent entries in their diaries.[8] Others took to verse. Of the latter class was an unsophisticated Tar Heel named William Malone in whose journal these poetic squibs were found:

"You are a charming little dandy
Sweeter than the sweetest candy

"Candy is sweet
It is very dear
But not half so sweet
As you my dear

"All I like of being a whale
Is a water Spout and a tail." [9]

The arrival at headquarters of an officer's wife—or even a comely washerwoman—would set a whole camp to gawking. Henry Kyd Douglas told of a visit to the army of the beauteous Hettie Cary shortly after her marriage to General Pegram. As Douglas escorted this lady from the parade ground after a review, an enraptured Reb was almost knocked down by her horse. When she began to apologize the awe-struck veteran lifted his shabby hat and said, "Never mind, Miss. You might have rid all over me, indeed you might." [10]

When soldiers on the march encountered a group of girls there was invariably a painful straining of necks, and if the gentle creatures were so thoughtful as to present pails of water, an overpowering thirst was sure to play havoc with the ranks. As the men waited their turn at the dipper they would ply the girls with questions, just for the sound of a feminine voice, and devour them with glances. A young soldier who was thus refreshed wrote the next day to his sister:

"One of them was a perfect wayside lily. . . . I could not help taking off my hat & bowing low to her as the bugle call forward was heard. I dont know her name & shall never see her again, but I am indebted to her for much more than a cup of water."[11]

Random observations in letters and diaries afford interesting insight into the qualities which Rebs esteemed in women. Femininity was regarded as the supreme attribute. Robustness was definitely objectionable, and big feet were almost disqualifying—"They are all too tremendous," complained one soldier of Kentucky girls, and another said disgustedly of backwoods Arkansas women who visited camp: "I have not seen one that would wear less than a number eight pair of shoes." [12]

Beauty was likewise an important consideration, though most soldiers had little use for the vacuous, inane type of beauty. Affectionate disposition and accomplishment in aesthetics were held very desirable. A Tennessean's description of a girl with whom he had been smitten reflects vividly the cardinal points of emphasis:

"She is a regular beauty, sings like an angel, dances like a sylph, talks like an authoress and . . . the English language is inadequate to express how much she does love. . . . Life has been but one dream of her since first I beheld her. The other night she came to the dance gaudy with nature's ornaments. She wore no jewels. Every gem she might have worn would but have hid a charm. Nature has completed for her a toilet which art can never rival. She seems to move in a halo of glory. She has a dowery of pearls but they are in her mouth . . . she . . . possesses a mind enriched with the gems of intellect, and a conversation brilliant with thought, repartee, and wit. She is indeed an angel on earth and no doubt will be an angel in heaven." [13]

Some soldiers revealed a distinct interest in the economic status of prospective brides. Private W. C. McClellan boasted of having found a "shore nuff Sweetheart" who was "worth $50 thousand dollers, a lady a fine sence and education" who lived "in a fine house surrounded by a fine plantation and innumerable slaves and hates the Yankees very much." [14]

Another Reb who aspired to the affection of a wealthy girl was not so fortunate as McClellan. In dejection he wrote to his sister that he had been "thrust through the little end of the horn with such violence as to almost cause contusion." In a fashion characteristic of jilted suitors he joined the ranks of woman haters, though not without a parting shot at the cause of his misery. His valedictory, written in verse, was as follows:

> "Depth of mercy, can there be
> Mercy yet reserved for me
> And I could say to that same woman
> Of all the etts
> I love Brunets
> Therefore you I adore
> But of all the Etts
> I hate coquets
> Therefore you I abhor" [15]

Men who wore the gray had an eye for shapeliness, and some were confessedly overwhelmed by voluptuousness.[16] But the great majority considered modesty an indispensable attribute. Rebs classed as forwardness the opening of conversation by girls to whom they had not been properly introduced.[17] There was one who took exception to the conduct of an officer's wife on the ground that she was "a perfect fidget." [18] Another had his faith in feminine virtue terribly jarred by a woman presenting him this conundrum: "If a Tumble Bug can role an ounce ball up a hill perpendicular how much can he sholder on a levell?" [19]

Amorous dalliance was deemed very *gauche*—one correspondent observed with disgust that he had "yet to find a lady about Fredericksburg that will not let a man kiss and hug them"—but formal betrothal was considered to sanction osculation. "I would have nothing to do with a young lady that would not kiss me . . . after we are engaged," remarked an Alabamian; "kissing is the truest [indication] of love, nothing more so, [not] even tears," he said, but before engagement "it is illegal." [20]

Other forms of conduct held in disrepute were noted by a South Carolinian who was quartered for a while with a private citizen having two daughters. The girls were pretty, he said, but "decidedly fast; the younger about 16, speaks of giving the dogs h-ll & slaps our faces when we kiss her; this same 'gal' climbs the trees for peaches, rides to mill on a horse bare back & not with both legs on the same side but one on each—astraddle." [21]

The "ideal girl" as envisoned by Johnny Reb was fairly well typified by a Petersburg belle, whom an adoring suitor described thus:

"She combines more attractions than any other I have seen—the crown of them all too, exceeding womanliness—as distinct from weak insipidity as manliness from bluster. . . . A person of middle size, formed like Hebe, and straight as poplar, graceful as willow, colour which comes and goes, skin clear white, hair black & abundant, always graceful however tossed, voice whose tones ripple soft but clear, and large eyes whose color varies as you look, but are finally seen to be steel gray—A face whose irregularity precludes the term beauty, but whose character makes insignificant a score of acknowledged beauties—Her eyes are . . . flood gates of light and they index the mind clear & quick." [22]

As a general rule soldiers had little opportunity for courtship. Cavalrymen, because of greater mobility and more flexible discipline, were able to get about to see the girls more than footsoldiers. But even the latter contrived occasionally to further their emotional interests. Rebs who received furloughs usually devoted a substantial part of their vacations to seeing the girls of their acquaintance, but Lee and other generals were woefully penurious with leaves. During periods of military inactivity women sometimes attended camp dances and parties, but such affairs were rare and restricted largely to officers.

Circumstances generally forced the ordinary soldiers to seek satisfactory social outlets by visits in the countryside. Many social excursions were accomplished under the guise of foraging for the supplementation of meager army rations, but once at large the provision hunters concerned themselves as much with needs of the heart as of the stomach, and while they were making inquiry as to the farmer's meat supply they were taking a firsthand inventory of his daughters. Not infrequently they succeeded in winning an invitation to dine; this was, of course, seized upon with alacrity, though maybe with a show of hesitation for politeness' sake. After the meal, singing was in order, with one of the girls pumping out tearful tunes at the melodeon. Then came a bit of talk about generalities, accompanied, if suitors were bold and parents had considerately excused themselves, by holding of hands and other mild forms of flirtation. In due time haversacks would be replenished and the foragers would take their leave, but not without seeking permission to make further calls.

Nocturnal absences from camp were rarely allowed, but resourceful soldiers were able to keep up their outside social connections by forging passes and by "flanking" guards. Occasionally a group of Rebs would favor their feminine friends with serenades. As acquaintances developed, parties would be arranged, and soldiers and girls would enjoy dancing and games. Frequently these casual associations ripened with remarkable swiftness into ardent romances.

The technique of Rebel suitors reflects the varied character of the Southern soldiery. Some attempted to enhance their prestige among the ladies by thinly veiled references to the old wound received at Bull Run. A few would boast openly of gallant actions in sundry battles. One pseudo-hero, who regaled wide-eyed listeners with glowing accounts of how he recognized and coolly bowed to acquaintances in enemy ranks amid a flood of bullets at Manassas, had the misfortune to be accused by other suitors of ingloriously absenting himself from the field before the engagement. When his disillusioned admirers subsequently questioned him on the point, he resorted to the explanation frequently used by cowards that the report of his absence was due to the fact that he got lost from his own regiment and fought with another; he also announced a wrathful determination to challenge his accusers.[23]

Suitors often made pretenses of great wealth and high social standing. One Reb of ordinary background had the girls all addressing him by the title of doctor.[24] Others talked of large cotton or sugar plantations, of fine carriages and of innumerable slaves. A Tar Heel private, who boasted of winning fifteen Virginia sweethearts by such exaggerations, wrote thus of his technique:

"They thout I was a saint I told thim som sweete lies and they Believed it all for they love a North Carolinian. I will tell you how I talk a round them After I got acquainted with them I would tell them I got a letter from home stating that five of my negros had runaway and ten of Pappies But I wold say I recond he did not mind it for he had plenty more left and then they would lean to me like a sore eyd kitten to a Basin of Milk." [25]

Rivalry was naturally strong where men were so numerous and women so few. Usually the competition was good-natured and aboveboard. There was some complaint among privates about officers monopolizing the field of courtship, but this they blamed on the girls as much as on the bombproofs. "The picnic was an exclusive affair," bemoaned a Virginian in 1863, "& I having neither Stars, bars, nor braid was not counted worthy to mingle in the very select company. . . . The ladies of this county are said to be addicted to Star-gazing & nothing of less brilliancy attracts their attention. What is a miserable private fit for? A man had as well be a dog." [26]

In rare instances underhand tactics were used by hard-pressed suitors. The meanest and the most effective of these stratagems was to charge a flourishing rival with having a wife and children at home.[27]

Timid Rebs were given to much indirectness in their approach. A delicious description is given in a letter of a girl who, with some feminine acquaintances, made a trip in 1863 chaperoned by an elderly male relative:

"Every stage, every bar, and boat were croudied with Soldiers, and they would talk and wrun on with us and would say . . . [to each other] 'That old man has got a heep prettie Daughters; lest go and talk to them. I know he wantes to get shet of some of them.' . . . there were some of the uglest ones that you ever saw . . . some very prettie soldiers too." [28]

Rebs frequently invoked the services of intermediaries to inquire into their standing with sweethearts. Some indeed were disposed to carry on all phases of the courtship by proxy. A good example of this is afforded by a private who wrote a juvenile kinsman:

"You kiss Soo for me and tell Soo to kiss you for me and by manageing the thing that way I will get two kisses, and tell Feb if he possible can steal me a kiss from Miss Bettie and after he kisses her tell her it was for me I would be very glad, indeed, I would." [29]

Occasionally suitors would slyly instruct agents d'amour to tell home sweethearts of their social triumphs while absent and to warn them of a loss of standing unless they showed more devotion.[30] The methods of some love-smitten Rebs were so indirect and their advances so halting that the war must have ended while their courtships were still in the most immature stages. Private G. W. Roberts of Mississippi was among these slow-moving suitors. While stationed at a parole camp near Demopolis, Alabama, in the spring of 1864, Roberts made the acquaintance of an overseer named Smith, whom he visited repeatedly. The soldier had a noticeable faculty for making an appearance just before mealtime, but his long stays afterward were due mainly to the presence in the family of an eligible daughter.

After a number of such calls Roberts mustered sufficient courage to write Miss Smith a letter asking for the privilege of corresponding with her. There was certainly no reason for resorting to the mails other than the Reb's timidity, for the girl lived within walking distance of camp and the writer had frequent access to her home. But when she received the formal missive her reaction was not one of amusement at Roberts's bashfulness, but rather one of displeasure at his forwardness. She answered as follows:

"May 19, '64 Sir—although it is the highest complement that can be paid our sex to receive offers calculated to leave a lasting acquaintance I must complain of its precipitate characters of your address to one, who till last March was a total stranger to you, without wishing to say anything harsh, I must confess that I do not feel any motive to entertain so hasty a proposal and have felt bound to lay your letter before my parents as I could not think of concealing from them any correspondence of such a Des[c]ription. Trusting that you will see this in its proper light, eagerly awaiting your Reply — D ——" [31]

The butternut Galahad took the cue of the letter's last sentence and responded promptly:

"May 19, 1864, Demopolis, Ala.:
"Miss D.S.: your letter Reach me safe this morning about 10 oclock which was notice with the highest esteem; By one who has made but a short acquaintance with thee. It was well peruse by the one who is writing to you now. I hope it will be received with pleasure. You stated in your letter that we had but a short acquaintance with Each other. I know that we have but a short acquaintance & that you are perfectly Right in laying my letter before your parents. I am willing as long as I communicate with you by letter for you to do so If I am not mistaken I ask you if I could write to you when I return to camps I have but one request to ask of you can I correspond with you or not. Hoping this will not concur any Dissatisfaction . . . only your highist Respect. G. W. ROBERTS." [32]

Unfortunately there are no later records on this affair, but it is difficult to believe that it ever reached a point where marriage could be plainly mentioned.

There were many gay youngsters in the army who were much more adept at courting than was Roberts. Some had sweethearts on every hill surrounding camp, and a few extras scattered in the valleys.

Harry St. John Dixon, a Mississippi cavalryman who entered the service shortly after leaving the University of Virginia, was among wooers of exceptional prowess. While at Pulaski, Tennessee, in 1863 he listed on a leaf of his diary "the girls I know here" as follows:

> "Miss Emma Rose
> "   Celest Rose
> "   Amanda Kenery le belle
> "   Manella Mosely
> "   Ida Caldwell
> "   Ala Petaway
> "   Eugenia McCord
>   &c."

This tabulation was postscribed with the comment: "O-o-o-o-o-how I lub you gals!!!—You sweet little criters." [33] Dixon had one romance after another of youthful fire and brevity. His journal, covering four years of war, is, in fact, little more than a cataloging of his affaires du coeur. At intervals he chided himself for his susceptibility to feminine wiles, as for example when he wrote: "I wish I was not such a fool about women. They have so much influence with me—it is so easy for them to gain the mastery over me." Then there were times when impetuosity combined with maidenly charm to produce temporary demoralization and a stricken conscience. Such an instance he recorded once in his diary:

"Jan 2, 1864 . . . attended a 'storm' [dance] at Miss Cuny's last evening . . . Took the 'little humming bird'—the little thing was chattering & smelling camphor all evening—Waltzed with Miss Annie Cozart till my right arm ached. What makes men so impure? Why cannot he have the manhood to resist temptation?—Her little bosom rested pantingly upon mine need I confess that I squeezed a little—just a little bit—soft, convulsive! And something else—our knees—Diable!"

On yet another occasion he wrote: "I see a pretty ripe, plump pair of lips—wish to kiss them—eminently natural!—Why not?" Dixon's flirtations kept him in emotional hot water a great deal of the time. He loved one whom he called his "pet" supremely, but in a weak moment he pledged undying affection to another.[34]

Even more of a social lion than Dixon was Private Joseph J. Cowand of the Thirty-second North Carolina Infantry. This gallant claimed to be engaged to six girls at one and the same time, and he declared his intention of adding a half dozen more to his list of betrothed.[35]

Many soldiers who played at Cupid's game were losers rather than winners. Sweethearts at home were stolen by militiamen, exempts and others who had the advantage of proximity. Camp romances cooled rapidly when fortunes of war transferred suitors to distant areas; and abandoned maidens quickly recruited new beaux to take the place of those removed. Victims of such emotional caprices reacted in various ways. Some poured out their woe to sympathetic relatives and friends; others took to cards and liquor; and still others addressed reproachful missives to those whose affections had paled. One disappointed Reb who chose verse as the medium of venting his spleen wrote thus:

"Miss—I'm raving I'm furious, I'm mad,
I'm Jealous, uneasy, disheartened and sad
I received information perhaps through the papers
Of your tricks and maneuvers, your pranks and your capers
You know when you left here I bid you beware
Of the fellows, Lieutenants and Captains up there
For you know that you promised that mine you'd be
That evening beneath the old Mulbery tree
When the moon in mid-heaven was shining so bright
And your dark eyes were radiant with love's mellow light
Then happy was I and how perfectly blessed
As your beautiful form to my bosom I prest
But my pleasure so full is now faded and yellow
For I hear that you're loving another young fellow
And if what people tell me so often is true
The courting is carried on chiefly by you
And if you deny it, I'd like much to know
Why so often to visit Miss Mary you go
And why when you meet him your eyes are so bright
With every expression of rhapturous delight
And even your voice ever changes its tone
As soft and as sweet as the turtle dove's moan
And then I'm told the opinion you harbour
The Lieutenant is the nicest young fellow in Barbour
But nice as he is if ever I meet him
As sure as his Bales, I'm going to beat him
But I'm not going to speak of the thing any further
Lest my passions should drive me to some bloody murder
But I'll give you my dear in the close of this letter
Some advice which may suit in the absence of better
For they tell me he's surely engaged to another
And if this is the fact (and I've no reason to doubt it)

Remember the Lamp and the Moth that was hovering about it
For in flying around him there's nothing to gain
But you might accidentally get burnt for your pains
"Yours in good will
"John Bunkam" [36]

Doubtless much of the heartbreak experienced by soldier suitors
was due to overzealous wooing. During the last years of the war many
Rebs became obsessed with the idea of getting married. Several factors
contributed to this. One was the fear that attractive and eligible women
would all marry civilians before the conflict ended. The matrimonial
flurries that swept over the South in 1863 and 1864 afforded a real
basis for this apprehension. Another consideration was the specter of
becoming so old and so worn by military service as to become undesirable as husbands. A third factor was the feeling of uncertainty and
insecurity engendered by war.[37]

Repeated exposure to danger resulted in a philosophy that said:
Get what you can of life and of love today, for tomorrow you may fall in
battle; partake, therefore, of married love while you can; if you die, you
will have had at least a brief knowledge of this happiness, and if you
live you will have a companion for years to come.

This reasoning, encouraged as it was by the granting of furloughs to
prospective grooms, caused many a sudden marriage.

"I never heard of so Much Marring in My life," wrote a Virginia
soldier to his parents in December 1863; "Chet Walker just got afurlough This morning of 10 days to go home to get Married. . . . I am
a great Mind to start courting Myself . . . to get me afurlough." [38]

In cases where officers refused to grant leaves without tangible proof
of forthcoming marriage, Rebs sometimes secured written commitments
from their brides-to-be. One such statement, addressed to an Alabamian, was as follows:

"If you come home, I'll marey you any time you come home. Love
has pierced me with his never erring dart, I yield to you my hart most
willingly in wedlock. I with you would gladly jine, and know fer [you]
that I never shall repine." [39]

A few who took war brides were not legally entitled to them. "Lit
Dooley was married last weak to a Miss Bailey," wrote a Reb from
camp in 1864; "he has a wife at home." [40] A Richmond paper found
occasion in 1863 to warn local readers that soldiers who had wives and

children in the deep South were escorting Virginia girls to the altar. An instance was cited of a recent case of bigamy involving a young lieutenant. This man had on the same day written a long and affectionate letter to his wife in Louisiana, and another of even greater endearment to his bride of a few weeks who lived near camp. By accident he put the letter of each in the envelope addressed to the other, and thus exposed his perfidy to both.[41]

At least one Reb who entered marital lists during the war did so unintentionally. Following an engagement with the Federals this soldier got drunk on captured whiskey. While in a state of inebriation he managed to strike up an acquaintance with a woman and before he recovered his sensibilities he swore to take her as his wife. In a subsequent explanation of the episode to his sister, he said that the bride was utterly unknown to him and that "w[h]en I woke the next mo[r]ning I was sick at my Stomake [because of] what I have don." He said further that he left her immediately and with the determination never to see her again, for "It wase knot lawfuel in the way it wase done." [42]

Most soldier suitors were compelled by circumstances to do a considerable part of their courting by correspondence. Their love letters were so strained by the stilted formality of the period as to be hardly worthy of the name. A Reb addressing his betrothed would tell of the weather, of the state of his comrades' health, of politics, of the probable course of the war, and of innumerable other trivialities of camp life, but very little of his love. The few allusions he did make to sentiment were frequently couched in such high-flown terms as to be without any resemblance to real-life romance.

Soldiers who wrote for the first time to feminine acquaintances filled their letters with apologies for presumptior. in opening correspondence. Some continued their apologies in subsequent missives. Attempts at discretion and dignity were sometimes so overdone as to become ludicrous.

The effort to use phraseology that was beyond the reach of the writer's orthography, if not of his vocabulary, produced similar results. One Reb began his letter: "Mutch Esteamed Miss I [s]natch my pen with acricy [alacrity?] to drop you a few lines." After wandering about uncertainly over varied topics he said: "I hope him who does all things well may Guide these few lines Saftly to your handes and may it find you and family all well." He then made the stock observation that he had nothing interesting to write. At the very end he approached a subject close to his heart, but his courage was not equal to a direct statement. "I suppose the youngsters is a marying as fast as tha come home," he said; "I think this is a vary good time to make a Selection, but not to perchous. I always like to hear of Some one doing well If I cant." [43]

Attempts to impart an idea of affection without making an overt commitment sometimes led to strange phrases. A Virginian wrote to his sweetheart that "I had rather see you than to see my Granfather or enny boddy else." [44]

Many letters were overladen with wild and incoherent platitudes. This type is well exemplified by the following excerpt from a missive addressed by a Mississippian to his fiancée:

"I can bare the Storms of the wintery Blast for thy sake oh Miss S.J.H be thou ever Bless as Butiful as thou art and idol to my throbbing hart oh had I the mind of the poet So that I could penetrate the verry depts of my hart but I can but express my Simple thoughts I am hear but my heart is Theire, we are in four miles of the yankees . . . could we not enjoy ourselves better if was at home with the girles . . . vainley I alas thou woulds soothe the pangs I feel, fond love betrayed what hopes I can poses Death alone my greaf may heal then farewell for ever more welth I have none they Farthers care thearefore I love one on Earth that I adore my only wealth is the love I bare then farewell perhaps for ever more never forsake me I Still will faithfull be Still on thy hand every bliss I will imploy Hence duty calls me they first my only love farewell perhaps for ever more but my hopes if far different I think will again meet if nothing happens more then I expect one thought from you would cheer my dropping mind I have more in my hart then ten thousand toungs can express if I had wings of and Eagle to the I would fly me thinks I can hear in my midnight drams thy Soft and gentle voice but alas when I awake I am in a Soldier tent I have nothing of importance to write you at this time but I will write soon and let you know all that happens . . ." [45]

Poetic utterance was a favorite resort for suitors who were hard put for appropriate expression. The ability to compose or to quote rhymes was considered a mark of good taste and of cultural distinction. Furthermore poetry was sufficiently ambiguous to permit whatever interpretation the recipient wished to give it. A suitor who was doubtful of his standing and uncertain of the propriety of affectionate address could, through the medium of verse, put out feelers without great fear of giving offense.

Sometimes the poetic phrases were written into the body of the letter without using verse form. One Reb wrote to his sweetheart:

"I'd mourn the hops that leave if thy smile had left me too I'd weep when friends deceived me if *thou wert like them* untrue The bee through many a garden roves and hums his lay of courtship ore but when he finds the flower he loves he settles there and hums no more." [46]

One of the most frequent and interesting users of the poetic technique was a timid Alabamian named Cribbs, who had a sweetheart as reserved as himself. Their bashfulness was indeed so great that the realization of mutual affection almost escaped them. He began writing to her early in the war that he had a sweetheart at home. Subsequently he described the object of his affections in considerable detail. At the same time she was telling him that she had a beau in the army, and that she would not marry until that particular soldier came home from the war. During the second year of conflict Cribbs finally got the idea across that his addressee was the sweetheart to whom he had been referring all along. But not until 1864 was he able to conclude definitely that the beau about whom she talked was none other than himself. The romance gathered considerable momentum with this discovery, but no records are available as to its outcome.

It was while Cribbs's identity as the beau of his sweetheart's correspondence was still in doubt that he wrote most of the poetry. In November 1862 he addressed these lines to his beloved:

"You do not know the many snares
Laid in this World for Thee
All lovingly I bid thee give
Thy sweet self unto me

"Then give to me love's magic seals
That all earth's joys eclipse
And close to mine in fondness press
Thy dewey coral lips."

In March 1863 he wrote:

"My love to you I cant unfold
It is like some lovly Ring of Gold
It is pure and have no end
So is my love to you Friend."

Two months later he resorted, for some unknown reason, to a crude code for communication of his poetic effusions. One verse appears thus in his cryptic medium:

"Why sh456d 3 b65sh t4 488. 3. 64v2
T3s 64v2 that 9563 th2 9267s 1 b4v2
Why sh456d 3 b65sh t4 sly t4 166
T3s 64v2 that h46ds 7y h219t 28 th9166"

which decoded reads:

"Why should I blush to onn I love
Tis love that ruls the relms above
Why should I blush to say to all
Tis love that holds my heart enthrall" [47]

Trite rhymes were much in vogue among less cultured correspondents. One of these ran thus:

"green is the vine
and read is the rose
how I love you
nobody noes."

Other examples are afforded by the following extract from a letter addressed by an uneducated woman to a soldier:

"i feel like a lonesome dove that has lost thair mate the rose is red an the villets blue an hant give me narry present that is purty like you as round as a ring has no end so is my love to you my friend when i am asleep i am dreaming bout you an when i am awake i take no rest ever mournin—my pen is bad my ink is pale my love for you shall never fale i want you to write to me i must come to a close so god bless your buttons—." [48]

Illiterate Rebs sometimes carried on correspondence with sweethearts through amanuenses. Private W. C. McClellan wrote love letters for several comrades in Company F of the Fourth Alabama Regiment. He also read to the suitors the answers which the letters received. McClellan must have been much in demand as a composer and scribe for according to his own statement he succeeded in getting three men engaged in the space of one month.[49] Unfortunately he left no record of his magic formula.

Courtship, whether conducted in person, by proxy, or by correspondence, was a factor of incalculable importance in army life. It had particular bearing on morale. The assurance of a sweetheart's confidence and affection had a buoying influence on a soldier's spirit. It tended to particularize the war and to give him a tangible and individual stake in its outcome. The association in the soldier's mind of women and of purity was a considerable factor in inspiring both single and married men to standards of wholesome conduct. There were, of course, many instances of opposite tendencies resulting from contact with a low type of woman, but all in all the influence of womankind over those thousands who wore the gray was ennobling as well as inspiriting.

CHAPTER XV

MUZZLE-LOADERS AND MAKESHIFTS

"WE CAN whip the Yankees with popguns," a Southern orator boasted in 1860. This was, of course, nothing more than platform exuberance, based on the theory that the North would not fight to preserve the Union.[1] But Fort Sumter and Lincoln's call for volunteers gave the lie to peaceable separation. And as the South prepared feverishly to resist Federal coercion it became strikingly apparent how little better than popguns were the weapons that she had.

Of shoulder arms, which must necessarily be the backbone of equipment in a shooting war, there were only about 150,000 in the whole Confederacy that were fit for use. About 20,000 of these were rifles. The others were smoothbore muskets, a considerable portion of which had been converted from the old Revolutionary flintlock type to percussion models. Both rifles and muskets were muzzle-loaders.[2]

Confederate and state authorities made heroic efforts to supplement this meager supply of guns. Before the outbreak of hostilities North Carolina, Mississippi and other states sent representatives to the North to purchase arms, and after the Confederate Government was organized, Montgomery authorities dispatched Raphael Semmes to New York for the same purpose. These missions resulted in gratifying contracts, but Federal officials clamped down on shipments before many deliveries could be made. Early in April 1861 Caleb Huse was ordered to Europe to buy equipment for the Confederacy. Eventually he succeeded in purchasing large quantities of guns, but shipments were slow in getting under way. Not until the fall of 1861 were there any deliveries to Southern shores.

When Josiah Gorgas was appointed chief of Confederate ordnance in the spring of 1861, he undertook immediately to promote the domestic manufacture of arms. One of the greatest handicaps was the lack of machinery, for such arsenals as existed in the South prior to the war were devoted almost wholly to storage. The seizure of Harper's Ferry by Virginia troops a few days after Fort Sumter's fall gave to the South a substantial amount of equipment for the fabrication of rifles and rifled muskets. A part of this was sent to Richmond and the remainder to Fayetteville, North Carolina. From the captured machinery a monthly output of 5,000 arms should have been realized, but various hindrances, particularly the inadequacy of skilled workmen, prevented the manufacture of more than about 2,000 rifles during any thirty-day period of the war. It was not until September 1861 that any production was realized from these factories.[3]

In the meantime both state and Confederate authorities had entered into contracts with numerous small-scale domestic manufacturers, many of whom had, before the war, been engaged in the fabrication of sporting arms.

McElwaine and Company of Holly Springs, Mississippi, is said to have been the first firm to receive an arms-making contract from the Richmond government. This establishment, known before the war as the Marshall County Manufacturing Company, was encouraged by the Mississippi Legislature in July 1861 to begin making guns of a type used in the Mexican War, a .54-caliber arm commonly designated as the Mississippi rifle. The next month the firm contracted to make 30,000 of these guns for the Confederacy.

Cook and Brother of New Orleans undertook the manufacture of Enfield model rifles for Gorgas, but fulfillment of contracts was delayed by forced removal to Athens, Georgia, before New Orleans was captured in April 1862.

The Shakanoosa Arms Manufacturing Company was organized at Dickson, Alabama, in 1861 to make Mississippi rifles for the state of Alabama. Its output, never very large, was hindered considerably by repeated removals before Federal invasion.

The S. C. Robinson Arms Manufacturing Company of Richmond made several thousand carbines for the Confederacy. Other firms that manufactured small arms for the Confederate or state governments were located in Tallahassee, Florida, and Montgomery, Alabama; Greensboro, Jamestown and Asheville, North Carolina; Columbus, Milledgeville and Macon, Georgia; and Tyler, Texas.[4]

Returns from both domestic manufacture and from foreign purchase were negligible during the war's first year. The original stock-on-hand of 150,000 guns was virtually exhausted before the battle of Bull Run. And still volunteers clamored to be taken into active service. "From Mississippi I could get 20,000 men," wrote President Davis to Joseph E. Johnston, July 13, 1861, "who impatiently wait for notice that they can be armed. In Georgia numerous tenders are made to serve for any

time at any place, and to these and other offers, I am still constrained
to answer, 'I have not arms to supply you.'" [5]

If the Confederacy had been able to place serviceable weapons in the
hands of these multiplied thousands of men who hoped so earnestly
for an opportunity to come to blows with the Yankees, First Manassas
might well have resulted in an overwhelming movement on Washington instead of in a stalemate.

On the day following the fight there squads of men were sent
to the battlefield to gather up guns and other equipment left by the
Federals. Back at home, state governments begged the citizens to send
or bring their shotguns, rifles and muskets to the county seats. Volunteers were urged to come armed to points of muster. The Tennessee
Legislature went so far as to authorize Governor Harris to seize all
private weapons for military use. Returns from these measures were
disappointing. People living in remote areas were unwilling to part with
their chief means of protection against brigands and beasts.

Competing activities of local and Confederate arms collectors raised
the issue of states' rights. Governor Clark of North Carolina was provoked to publish a notice saying that Confederate agents "have no law-
ful authority to seize your private arms, and you will be protected in
preserving the means of self-defense." [6] Jealousy of local authorities
was a serious deterrent to the armament program throughout the South
in 1861, and as conflict between central and state authorities sharpened
in the years that followed, the obstacle increased. [7]

Most of the guns collected in the months following First Manassas
were sent to state or Confederate armories for remodeling. Small-caliber
squirrel rifles were bored out to accommodate regular-size musket balls;
ancient flintlocks were adapted to the use of percussion caps; elongated
barrels of pioneer "shooting irons" were sawed off in the interest of
greater wieldiness; and in some cases bayonets were attached.

But the clamor for arms was abated little if any by these efforts. A
projected offensive on the Virginia front in the fall of 1861 had to be
called off because of inability to provide weapons for the necessary reenforcements. [8] About the same time Albert Sidney Johnston, commander of the Western Department, was reduced to the sad strait of
requisitioning additional flints for the firing of the obsolete muskets
carried by many of his troops. Across the Mississippi, almost half of
Price's force was armed with shotguns, fowling pieces and flintlocks.

At the battle of Mill Springs, Kentucky, January 19, 1862, the Confederates were hampered by the fact that rain made unusable the flint-

lock rifles with which many of the regiments were outfitted. Some of the Tennesseans, after several futile attempts to fire their dampened pieces, were seen to break them in exasperation over a near-by rail fence.[9]

Many of the defenders of Fort Henry were armed with shotguns and old sporting rifles; the Tenth Tennessee, described as "the best-equipped regiment of the command," had to depend on "Tower of London" muskets which had been carried by militia in the war of 1812.[10] Shotguns were taken into the action at Shiloh by a considerable number of troops. Some of the regiments engaged at Murfreesboro, December 31, 1862, had half of their men armed with smoothbore muskets. And not until the battle of Franklin, November 1864, was the Tenth South Carolina Regiment able to procure guns of uniform caliber.[11]

The Army of Northern Virginia fared better as to arms after 1861 than the western commands. This may have been due in some measure to favoritism of Richmond authorities, but it was primarily because the Virginia troops had greater access to that richest of all Confederate armories, the camps of the Federals. General Lee reported the capture of 35,000 stands of small arms as a result of the Seven Days' fighting, June 26-July 1, 1862. At Second Manassas 20,000 more were taken, at Harper's Ferry 11,000, and at Fredericksburg 9,000.[12] No figures are available for arms captured at Antietam and Shiloh, but these must have exceeded 15,000. On the Kentucky and Tennessee campaigns of August-December 1862 the Army of Tennessee took 27,500 muskets and rifles.[13] This brought the total of small arms captured in major engagements of 1862 to a figure well over 100,000.

At the beginning of 1863 the South found herself for the first time in possession of a surplus of shoulder arms. Chancellorsville netted an additional 20,000 pieces and Chickamauga 15,000, but losses sustained at Vicksburg, Gettysburg and Chattanooga, plus depletion from breakage and wear, wiped out the favorable balance; and from the beginning of 1864 till near the end of the war there were repeated complaints of deficiencies from all parts of the Confederacy.[14] The Trans-Mississippi Department seems to have experienced particular deprivation. In May 1863 General Magruder estimated his need at 40,000 small arms, and in December 1864 he expressed fear of inability to open the spring campaign unless the government could find a means of supplying his urgent requests for matériel.[15]

Throughout the war, shoulder arms carried by Rebs were characterized by the greatest miscellany of type and effectiveness. The gun in widest use during the first year of conflict was the .69-caliber smoothbore musket. This weapon was loaded either with a single round ball or with "buck and ball," that is three buckshot behind a regular-size ball. At close range the musket was formidable, but a Yank more than 100 yards away was comparatively safe. Repeatedly Federals, on ascertaining that their opponents were armed with this type of gun, exposed themselves and taunted the Rebs for the ineffectiveness of their fire. Muzzle-loading shotguns charged with buckshot were said to have rendered good service in closeup fighting at Donelson, but their exceedingly short range caused them to be discarded by all except the cavalry as soon as other arms could be procured.

The .54-caliber Mississippi rifle was a great favorite among early volunteers, and it had considerable use throughout the war. In 1861 some of the companies who went from the deep South to Richmond in the expectation of being armed with this type of weapon mutinied when told that they would have to accept smoothbores.[16] Such confidence in the Mississippi rifle was not without foundation, for in ordinary circumstances of distance and load it was a dependable arm. Hardly less effective were the .58-caliber Springfield and Harper's Ferry rifled muskets, a considerable number of which were in use during the early part of the war.

In the second year of conflict shotguns, smoothbores and flintlocks were largely abandoned for more modern types obtained from the Federals or from Europe. In innumerable instances the soldiers themselves made the substitution on the battlefield, a practice that caused no end of worry and difficulty on the part of those charged with the dispensing of ammunition. For the guns "borrowed" from Yankees were frequently of different caliber from those discarded, thus rendering unusable the bullets brought up from Confederate ordnance wagons. But Johnnies often solved the problem by appropriating the necessary cartridges from dead and wounded foes.

Another gun which had considerable use was the Austrian rifle. But it was despised because of its unwieldiness and ineffectiveness. A Reb who had the misfortune to draw one of these weapons remarked that the Europeans for whom it had been devised "must be hard, large-fisted fellows, used to playing with a pair of fifty-sixes," for he continued, "it is certainly the most ungainly rifle mortal ever used, being furnished with a heavy oak stock, and trappings of iron and brass, sufficient to decorate a howitzer."[17] When a soldier got ready to fire one of these monstrosities, he was apt to take a tight grip, brace himself for the shock, draw an uncertain bead, shut his eyes and pull the trigger.[18]

Even worse than the Austrian models were the Belgian rifles, which Confederates used in limited numbers. These were of such fragile structure as to be easily broken; the bore was uneven and the barrels of some were crooked. Yankee soldiers who had to use these shabby guns referred to them contemptuously as "pumpkin slingers." [19] Other types shipped to the South from Europe included the .70-caliber British musket and the Brunswick rifle. No report is available as to the reaction of Rebs to these weapons, but they were probably of an inferior quality.[20]

After 1862 the shoulder arms used by Confederate infantrymen differed little from those carried by the men in blue. The most common types in both armies were the .577-caliber long Enfield rifle musket of English manufacture, and the American-made Springfield rifle musket of caliber .58. Despite the slight discrepancy in the bore of these two guns, the practice prevailed widely of using the same cartridges for both. No doubt much of the clogging of which officers complained in official reports of battles was due to the loading of Enfields with ammunition made for Springfields.[21] The long Enfield rifle musket, over 100,000 of which were purchased abroad by Huse, was about the same size and weight as the Springfield rifle musket. It was perhaps the most popular gun in Confederate service and one of the most effective.[22]

Probably the most accurate of the muzzle-loading weapons were the Whitworth rifles. These excellent guns were used largely by sharpshooters. When equipped with telescopic sights, as they sometimes were, and placed in the hands of expert marksmen concealed in crags, trees and abandoned dwellings, the Whitworths were used with deadly effect on targets far removed.[23]

Comparatively few breech-loading small arms were used by Southerners. But of these the oldest was the Hall rifle invented in 1811. Basic defects of structure rendered this an unsatisfactory gun, and its use was very limited. The Morse rifle, patented in 1856, was manufactured in the Confederacy, and some muskets were converted by the inventor into breech-loaders; but these guns were impracticable because of the difficulty of procuring the special cartridges which they required. A Richmond firm undertook the production of a carbine designed after the fashion of the famous Sharps, but looseness at the breech caused these arms to spit fire into the eyes of their users, and they had to be discarded.[24]

Among cavalrymen the breech-loading Maynard rifles were held in high esteem because of their accuracy and range. But only a limited number of these could be obtained by Confederates. In the latter part of the war some Spencer and Henry repeating carbines were captured by Rebel horsemen, but these deadly guns—which, according to one gray-clad wag, contained so many charges that they could be loaded on Sunday and fired all week—like most of the improved types developed in the North, were of little use because of the difficulty of obtaining metal cartridges.[25]

Throughout the war Southern cavalrymen used extensively the short Enfield rifle. This was a dependable gun, but, like all muzzle-loaders, cumbersome to load, even when the ramrod was attached on a swivel hinge for convenience of horsemen. Until the very end the short double-barrel shotgun, loaded from the muzzle with buckshot, constituted one of the principal arms of the mounted service.

Rare was that colonel in either cavalry or infantry who had enough guns of any one type with which to arm his men. In the infantry a standard practice was to give the best weapons to flank companies because of the importance of their position, and to issue less desirable ones to those in the center. In some regiments there were several degrees of gradation. Colonel Walker of the Tenth South Carolina distributed his arms thus: Company A was equipped with Enfield rifles, Company B with Mississippi rifles, Company E with Harper's Ferry rifled muskets, and the others with smoothbore guns.[26]

The standard projectile for most Confederate rifles was the Minie type bullet. This missile, popularly but incorrectly called a ball, was a leaden cone devised by Captain C. E. Minié of France. Its distinctive feature was a hollow base—plugged sometimes with wood or iron—which expanded at fire so as to fit snugly into the riflings of the barrel. This not only gave greater force to propulsion but also increased the bullet's rotary action. Smoothbore muskets were loaded usually with round balls. A Confederate invention proposed to substitute for the ball an elongated projectile with a pointed lead nose and a base of wood or papier-mâché; the forward position of the center of gravity was calculated to cause the missile in flight to rotate on its axis like an arrow and thus to increase accuracy. But skepticism and red tape in the War Department seem to have prevented extensive trial of the new device.[27]

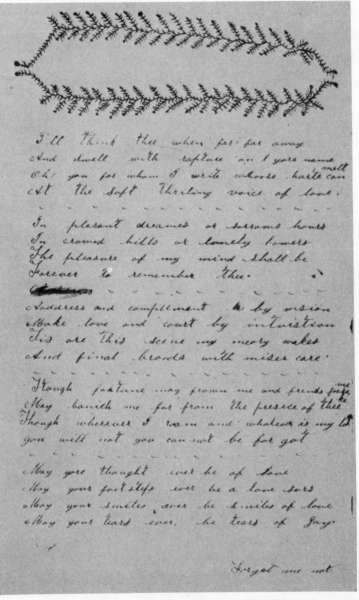

Courtesy Military Records Division, Alabama Department of Archives and History, Montgomery, Alabama

SOLDIER'S POETRY

Poetry written from Confederate camp by a poor white to his wife.

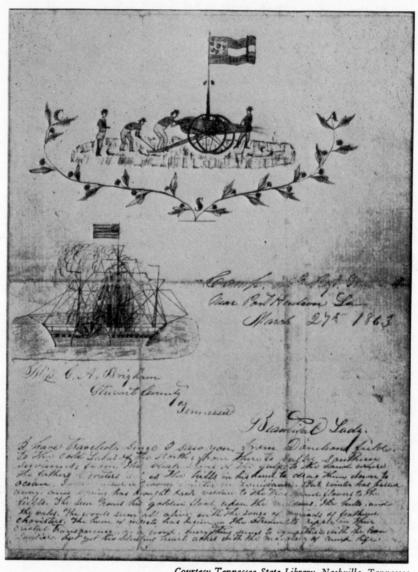

Courtesy Tennessee State Library, Nashville, Tennessee

A SOLDIER'S LETTER

Cartridges for rifles and muskets were usually made up in munitions plants, but early in the war soldiers in the field often had to fashion their own. One Reb gave the following description of the technique used in his company:

"We take a stick 4 or 5 inches long the Size of the Caliber of the Gun, Wrap around a piece of paper which we have prepared. A little of the paper Sticks over the end of the Stick & is tied with String the Stick is withdrawn the Bulit or Shot as the case may be inserted then a wad & next the Charge of Powder Accurately measured then the paper is nicely twisted to Keep the powder from leaking out." [28]

In a few instances soldiers made their own bullets from bulk lead in crude molds of wood or iron. A group of Missouri volunteers used sewing thimbles for molds. "While, the lead was hot," one of them wrote, "a sharp-pointed stick had been thrust into it. This gave the bullet the form of a minie ball which just fitted our guns and we could shoot through a boxcar three hundred yards away." [29] Expedients such as this became unnecessary after the first year of the war.

Most of the guns when issued to the soldiers were equipped with bayonets. These were of two principal kinds, the sword bayonet and the angular one. The former was a straight implement, used principally on cavalry arms; it was equipped with a handle to facilitate use as a detached weapon. The latter, designed primarily for infantry, was usually triangular in shape; it was fixed to the gun barrel by means of a socket which slipped over the muzzle.

Some of the early volunteers had their bayonets made by local blacksmiths from saws, butcher knives and files. But most of the supply was obtained by foreign purchase, by capture, and by government contract with domestic arms manufacturers.

Johnny Reb did not take readily to the use of the bayonet. It interfered with the loading of his gun. As he rammed home the charge in the excitement of battle it was very apt to prick or bruise his hand. He complained, with only half jest, that he could rarely get close enough to a "Blue-belly" to stick him. And when close quarters were achieved, most Rebs seemed instinctively to prefer grabbing their gun by the barrel and swinging the butt at Yankee heads to the gouging technique prescribed by the manual of arms. Certainly the inclination to regard bayonets as unnecessary equipment was so universal as to make it impossible for officers to maintain anything like an adequate supply of them.[30]

Almost as indispensable as a rifle, in the eyes of men who rushed to the colors in 1861, was a pistol of some sort. The pervasiveness of this attitude is indicated by the great number of pistols appearing in photographs of early volunteers. The size of these weapons ranged from delicate little instruments no larger than a pocketknife to awesome pieces having barrels almost as long as carbines. A few months' soldiering sufficed, as a rule, to convince the ordinary infantryman that a rifle was the only kind of gun he needed. Consequently pistols were rarely carried after 1862 by any except officers. But this was not true of cavalrymen, among whom pistols were popular throughout the war.

There was an even greater diversity of pistols than of muskets and rifles. Calibers ranged from .36 to .60, and firing capacity from one to nine shots. Some were muzzle-loaders and a few may have been flintlocks. Many were imported, more were manufactured domestically, and still more were obtained from the North by purchase and capture.

Probably the most popular and the most extensively used of all was the Colt's "six-shooter" revolver. The .44-caliber model of this gun had, in spite of its massiveness, gained a good reputation among Southerners who participated in the Mexican War. In 1861 agents were sent North to contract for large quantities of these and of the newer .36-caliber models. The manufacturers seemed not averse to supplying Southern needs, but Federal authorities prevented shipments of more than half of the number ordered. During the course of the war Rigdon and Smith of Georgia and other Southern manufacturers attempted with a fair degree of success to make revolvers after the fashion of Colt's. The total production of all types of Confederate Colts was small.

Revolvers obtained by capture, in addition to the Colt, included weapons made by Remington, Savage, Whitney, Beal, Joslyn and Starr. From England several brands of five-shooters were procured; among them were products bearing the stamps of Adams, Bentley, Kerr and Tranter, most of which were .44 caliber. Of the various types imported from France the most interesting was the Le Mat or "grape shot" revolver, invented by a New Orleans physician. In 1861 Dr. Le Mat signed a contract for delivery of 5,000 of these guns, to the Confederate Government. When he found that the necessary machinery could not be secured, he boarded the *Trent* with Mason and Slidell, proceeded to France, and set up his factory. The Le Mat was a nine-shot revolver with two barrels. It had a cylinder with chambers for eight .44-caliber bullets. The lower barrel fired a .60-caliber shot charge. Beauregard, Stuart and other Southern generals carried this type of pistol.[81]

Another weapon which the volunteer of 1861 frequently displayed when he visited the photographer—the usual term of the sixties was "daguerrian artist"—was a "Bowie" knife.[32] A favorite pose showed this ferocious-looking implement jabbed beneath the belt on one side and a pistol on the other. A variation depicted the soldier grasping the knife's handle. Whatever the position, the expression on the face was generally one of grimness if not of vengeance. If Northern appeasers had been given access to Southern photograph galleries of early 1861, they might have obtained convincing support for their argument to let erring Southerners secede in peace.

These pictures are not misleading. Long daggerlike knives were a prevailing fad among the Confederacy's first soldiers. A close observer of doings in Richmond said of the regiments who came to the capital from all parts of the Confederacy in the summer of 1861: "Every man you met, mounted or footman, carried in his belt the broad, straight, double-edged bowie knife." [33] And the Richmond Enquirer of September 27, 1861, noted that each man of an Alabama company was equipped with a two-and-one-half-pound knife having a blade nineteen inches long. Some of the models had serrated edges designed for tearing Yankee flesh. Others had curved blades and were made on such a generous scale as to suggest scythes to awe-stricken observers. These outlandish weapons may have proved of some benefit in culinary operations, but they seem to have had little use in battle.[34] As the volunteer became a veteran he sloughed off the Bowie knife along with other excess baggage.

Another unorthodox arm that received serious consideration in high places was the pike or lance. In the spring of 1862, when the Confederacy was facing her most serious shortage of guns, Stonewall Jackson wrote the governor of Virginia that soldiers on the field "must under Divine blessing, rely upon the bayonet, when firearms cannot be furnished." He suggested that companies of recruits be organized, equipped with long steel-tipped pikes and sent against the foe. General Lee indorsed the idea and requested that 1,000 pikes be forwarded to Jackson as soon as practicable.[35] A short time later Lee wrote General Humphrey Marshall that pikes were in production, and offered to honor his requisitions for this type of arm.[36]

Confederate victories in the summer and fall yielded such a rich harvest of arms as to render unnecessary the issuance of the emergency weapons; and army leaders seem to have dropped permanently the idea of using them. But not Governor Brown of Georgia. He was so thoroughly imbued with the vision of hordes of Southerners gouging their way to victory that he ordered the manufacture of thousands of pikes for the troops of his state. Variations of the weapon were developed, such as the addition of a hook with which to grasp and cut bridle reins from the hands of cavalrymen; deprived thus of the control of their mounts, the hapless riders would be easy victims of the pikemen's thrusts. Someone raised the question as to what the horsemen would be doing in the meantime; no answer was forthcoming, but the governor's enthusiasm lost none of its bloom. Some inventive genius carried the idea well nigh to its ultimate absurdity by designing a springed contraption by which the blade of the lance might be drawn back within the staff; when a victim came close the pull of a trigger would release the spring, and the blade would dart forth to transfix him. As far as can be ascertained, neither the simple version of this implement nor any of its variations ever came close enough to a Yankee to be put to a test, but relics in various museums, appropriately labeled "Joe Brown Pikes," bid fair to perpetuate eternally the memory of their fervid protagonist.[37]

Ordinary Rebs who belonged to the infantry did not carry swords, as these ornaments were reserved to the use of officers. But the saber was an accepted part of any cavalryman's equipment. During the early days of the war, state and Confederate authorities had great difficulty in supplying this type of weapon because of the lack of domestic manufacturing facilities. Caleb Huse shipped several thousand sabers from Europe in 1861 and 1862, and large quantities were obtained by capture and purchase from the North. After 1862, however, Southern firms were able to furnish most of the requisitions.[38]

The largest sword factory in the South was apparently that of Haiman and Brother of Columbus, Georgia. Clanton's cavalry regiment was armed throughout with sabers made by this firm. A Columbia, South Carolina, establishment turned out an excellent product fashioned after the North's regulation saber. Another Columbia manufacturer made for some of Hampton's cavalry "long, straight double edged swords, very serviceable and crusader-like with cross hilts." At Nashville a farm-implements concern reversed the Biblical command and turned plowshares into swords; the brass guards of these high-class weapons bore the appropriate markings "C.S.A." and "Nashville Plow Works." [39]

Other manufacturers were less successful in their efforts to provide serviceable weapons. Swords turned out by Froelich and Estvan, of

Wilmington, for the state of North Carolina were said to have been worthless.[40] Cavalry officers complained repeatedly that sabers furnished to their men were of such poor quality that they were thrown away. In this connection, however, it should be noted that there was a widespread indisposition on the part of Rebel horsemen to carry swords of any sort. They chose rather to depend on carbines and pistols, and many doubtless felt more at ease with shotguns than with all other weapons.[41]

The problem of supplying short arms and swords, great though it was during most of the war, was not so formidable as that of providing artillery. The taking over of various coastal forts in the early months of 1861 yielded a considerable number of heavy siege guns, but in none of the arsenals inherited by the Confederacy were there any batteries of light artillery. The only field guns in Southern possession when the war began belonged either to militia companies, such as the Richmond Howitzers and the Washington Artillery, or to the various states. Many of the latter were smoothbore iron guns of a vintage antedating the War of 1812.[42] And from the very beginning, state governors were inclined to hold the pieces in their respective arsenals with an embarrassing tenacity.

Most of the forty-seven artillery pieces in Confederate possession at First Manassas were old six-pounder smoothbores. All, save the four carried into action by the Washington Artillery, belonged to the state of Virginia. Twenty-eight cannon, mostly of rifled bore, were captured by Confederates in this battle.[43]

During the months that followed First Manassas President Davis and his associates made Gargantuan efforts to supply the South's artillery needs. As in the case of small arms, three principal sources were utilized, namely, European purchase, domestic manufacture and capture from the Federals.

Caleb Huse succeeded in making contracts for large quantities of guns in England, deliveries of which began in 1862. During the first two years of the war, Huse's purchases totaled 129 pieces, nearly half of which were bronze six-pounder smoothbores. Other imported types included Blakely rifles of 2.10, 4.5, and 8-inch calibers, Whitworth rifles of various sizes, 8-inch Armstrong rifles, small-caliber bronze howitzers, and twelve-pounder steel rifled cannon. Most of these were muzzle-loading models, though a considerable number of the smaller rifles were charged from the breech. The most widely heralded of all the importations were two enormous Blakely guns bought for £10,000 in 1863 for the defense of Charleston. These titans weighed twenty-three tons each, used a forty to fifty-pound charge of powder, and fired a round shot weighing about five hundred pounds. They were loaded at the breech by means of a screw plug. One of them brought untold grief to the hearts of its purchasers by cracking at first trial. But the damage proved reparable and both cannon were placed in service, though with charges so reduced as to lessen considerably the maximum range.[44]

A delightful story went the rounds of Rebel camps in the latter part of the war about a North Carolinian who was captured at Antietam. As he was being marched to the rear he noticed a number of Yankee fieldpieces. He paused and began to read aloud the marking "U.S." on each gun.

"Well, what now, Johnny Reb?" one of his captors asked good-naturedly.

"I say mister—you-all has got as many of these U.S. guns as we 'uns has," replied the Tar Heel.[45]

The story was not without point. In the halcyon days of 1862 and early 1863, scores of Federal cannon took up forced residence in the Confederacy. Following the Seven Days' fighting Lee reported capture of fifty-two pieces of artillery, and Bragg took eighty-one on his Kentucky-Tennessee campaign. Further accessions at Second Manassas, Harper's Ferry and elsewhere brought the total of artillery prizes for the year 1862 to a figure exceeding 250.[46] There were also substantial captures at Chancellorsville and Chickamauga, but these were counterbalanced by losses at Vicksburg and Chattanooga. After 1863 the South had to look principally to her own resources for the strengthening of the "long arm."

Domestic artillery production was slow getting under way. At the outset of the war there was only one plant in the South capable of turning out large cannon; this was the Tredegar Iron Works of Richmond. The situation as to light artillery was not much better. But Josiah Gorgas and his associates tackled the problem with characteristic vim. Contracts were arranged with a great number of foundries, including Noble Brothers of Rome, Georgia, Leeds and Company of New Orleans, T. M. Brennan of Nashville, and the Columbus Iron Works of Columbus, Georgia. In addition the government developed its own works at Augusta and at Selma. In order to secure the necessary iron, steps were taken to stimulate mining activities in Virginia, North Carolina, Tennessee, Georgia and Alabama. Copper-producing facilities in Eastern Tennessee were expanded, and in Georgia an order was issued for the seizure of copper stills. Public appeals were made all over the South for candlesticks, hearth irons and other items of brass. General Beauregard, inclined toward the dramatic, in March 1862 issued a call for bells belonging to churches and plantations. Braxton Bragg deemed this step sensational and unnecessary, but Richmond authorities and the country at large indorsed the action of the hero of Sumter and Manassas, and bells of all sorts and sizes came pouring into Southern depots for conversion into weapons of war.[47]

All of these efforts eventually yielded results which, in the light of limited resources, shortage of skilled labor, inadequacy of transportation and interference of state governors, were nothing short of remarkable. In the year ending September 30, 1863, the Ordnance Bureau issued 677 fieldpieces, and the Richmond arsenal alone distributed during the period from July 1, 1861, to January 1, 1865, 341 large siege guns, 1,306 pieces of field artillery, and large quantities of caissons, gun carriages, ammunition, friction primers, fuses and other accessories; most of the artillery issued was made at the Tredegar Iron Works. Considerable ingenuity was displayed by ordnance authorities in using substitutes for scarce materials and in developing new techniques of manufacture. Toward the end of the war the Tredegar Works succeeded in making a twelve-inch gun by the water-cooled hollow casting procedure, a method that produced a weapon of great strength and of unusually smooth bore.[48]

But by no means all of the artillery produced in the South was of good quality. Some of the early products were so poor, indeed, as to invoke the utter scorn of generals in the field.

D. H. Hill wrote the Secretary of War repeatedly from the Yorktown defenses complaining of the inaccuracy, short range and fragile construction of the guns of his command. "There must be something very rotteh in the Ordnance Department," he blurted on April 24, 1862. "It is a Yankee concern throughout, and I have long been afraid that there was foul play there. Our shells burst at the mouth of the gun or do not burst at all. The metal of which the new guns are made is of the most flimsy and brittle character, and the casting is very bad." [49]

The frequency with which guns burst when exposed to the strain of repeated firing was enough to test faith in the loyalty of their makers. Many of those issued in 1862, and some that were turned out late in the war, were more dangerous to friend than to foe. At Fredericksburg a large Parrott gun exploded in such close proximity to Generals Lee and Longstreet that they seemed to be spared only by the interposition of providence.[50] An additional danger came from the instability of gun carriages. General Magruder wrote from Yorktown that some of his cannon would "dismount themselves after a few fires." [51]

Complaints were also registered against Southern-made guns on the ground of defective boring. This weakness sometimes resulted in woefully inaccurate performance. An artillery sergeant of the Army of Tennessee recorded in his diary on August 6, 1863:

"We are testing our guns today. The target was placed at 1,000 yards; we fired seven shots, not one of which struck the target. As we have splendid gunners, Col. Polk had the rifle guns condemned." [52]

There was a gradual improvement in the quality of domestic-made artillery during the third and fourth years of the war. But new difficulties arose in the form of the dwindling of the horse supply and the scarcity of accessory equipment. At no time after 1861 was this branch of the service able to compete on anything like equal terms with that of the Federals except in personnel.[53]

From beginning to end the Confederates used many different types and sizes of artillery. The biggest guns were the coast and river Columbiads and Blakely's of calibers ranging from thirteen inches on down to eight. But cannon of this size were too cumbersome for field purposes. Gettysburg affords a good example of the artillery in most general use in land engagements. Of the 244 pieces taken into Pennsylvania, 103 were three-inch rifles, 107 were twelve-pounder Napoleons, thirty were twelve-pounder howitzers, and four were small-caliber Whitworth rifles.[54]

Other rifled pieces which had wide use in the Confederacy were the ten-pounder iron Parrott (caliber 2.90 inches), the twenty-pounder iron Parrott (caliber 3.67 inches), the thirty-pounder iron Parrott (caliber 4.20 inches), and the bronze mountain rifle (caliber 2.25 inches). The Parrott guns' distinctive feature was a thick wrought-iron band shrunk around the breech to prevent them from bursting. The scheme was originally devised by Colonel R. P. Parrott of the United States forces, but after the outbreak of war John M. Brooke, designer of the *Merrimac*, perfected a similar technique for the Confederacy.[55] The mountain rifles were so called because they were of a construction sufficiently light to be carried on horseback over precipitous terrain. For the most part, however, they were transported on light carriages.

With the introduction of trench warfare on a large scale in 1864, the use of short "dumpy" pieces, called mortars, became extensive. These were set at a pronounced elevation so as to lob shells over into the opposing earthworks. In a few instances regular-size guns were adapted to this function by tilting back the mounting for greater elevation and lightening the charge.

Perhaps the most interesting of all the pieces used by Confederate artillerymen was a crude type of machine gun. In fact it is claimed that the first machine gun ever used in battle was the Williams repeating cannon taken into action at Seven Pines. This gun had a four-foot barrel and shot one-pound projectiles. Its firing mechanism was very much like that of a Colt's revolver, except that the cylinder was turned by a crank. Ammunition was fed from a hopper placed above the chamber. Newspaper reports of testings of this gun claimed that it shot eighteen to twenty balls a minute and that it was accurate for a range of a thousand yards. Several other types of automatic cannon were mentioned by the Confederate press, but details are too scant to permit an adequate idea of their appearance and function. Another interesting gun of the Confederate period was a double-barreled cannon.[56]

But far and away the most popular of the Confederate fieldpieces were the twelve-pounder Napoleons. These guns which, in the latter part of the war came to have such wide use as to constitute the backbone of the light artillery, were smoothbore muzzle-loaders of caliber 4.62 inches. Shortly after Fort Sumter, Colonel Andrews of Baltimore went to the Pikesville Armory near that city and copied drawings of the recently tested Napoleons. Immediately thereafter he took the plans to Virginia and persuaded Governor Letcher to order the manufacture of some of these guns on state account. A few were completed in time for use at First Manassas. In the months following, scores of Napoleons were cast for the Confederacy by Tredegar and other domestic establishments. At first they were made solely of bronze, but after brass became scarce an iron model, strengthened at the breech with a jacket, was put into production. Both domestic and imported Napoleons were well suited to Confederate needs because of simplicity of operation, ease of transportation and accuracy at medium ranges.[57]

Grouping of guns into batteries varied considerably with time and circumstances. Early in the war the six-gun arrangement was the most common, four of the pieces being smoothbore six-pounders and two being twelve-pounder howitzers. As three-inch rifles became available they were substituted for the six-pounder cannon. In the last year of the war many batteries were made up wholly of Napoleon guns. The six-gun grouping was modified also, batteries ranging in size from two to eight guns, until late in the war when four guns became the standard. Six-horse teams were usually needed for the handling of the larger fieldpieces. One of the most effective of field units was the horse artillery. Used in conjunction with regular cavalry, the horse artillery was indeed the forerunner of modern "panzer" outfits.[58]

Missiles fired from artillery pieces varied greatly with the type of gun and the purpose of fire. It has been estimated that about seventy different types of projectiles were in use at one period of the Confederacy. If the principal objective was the battering down of a fort, solid shot was used, and in the Confederacy the most common form of solid shot was the iron "cannon ball." For field purposes, where the primary aim was the destruction of men, a bursting charge was preferred. But Confederates used spherical shot to a considerable extent in smoothbore fieldpieces.[59]

Bursting projectiles were of two main kinds: in one, fragmentation was produced at the mouth of the cannon by the explosion which hurled the missile forth; in the other, the shot remained intact until a time fuse or a percussion fuse set off an inner charge. Projectiles of the first kind, while restricted to short ranges, included two of the deadliest agencies known to the Civil War period, namely, canister and grape.

Canister consisted of a large group of small balls inclosed in a cylindrical tin cover, or "can," plugged at the ends with discs of iron or of wood. When thrown from the mouths of advantageously placed cannon, as at Fredericksburg, they rained death upon the advancing foe.

Grapeshot were composed of a group of iron balls, usually about two inches in diameter, but frequently smaller, held together by a series of round discs transfixed with a bolt. These clustered charges were used with terrible effectiveness at ranges extending to several hundred yards. If canister, grape, or other orthodox charges were not at hand, Rebel operators of smoothbore guns did not hesitate to load their pieces with trace chains and other available miscellanies.

Among the exploding type of missiles conical shells were the most common. Shrapnel were also used; these were shaped like shells, but the walls were thinner and the interiors were packed with small balls which scattered like birdshot when the projectiles burst in flight. Some of the spherical shot were loaded like shrapnel and functioned in the same manner. Confederate shells were frequently fitted at the base with bands or sabots of lead or of soft iron to make possible a snug following of the cannons' rifling. Some of the hideous screeching that filled the air during battle and caused such widespread comment on the part of both sides was produced by the ragged edges of the leaden jackets. Colonel J. W. Mallet, one of the most outstanding of the South's ordnance officers, invented a shell with a cavity fashioned so as to assure fragmentation into a definite number of pieces when explosion occurred.[60]

Explosion on contact with the target was obtained by the use of percussion fuses. When the purpose was best served by causing the shell to burst while in flight or after it landed, time fuses were applied. The period of delay was controlled by the length of the fuse. Neither type was very satisfactory. The time fuse often failed of ignition when fired from the piece; or if it was ignited the spark was frequently extinguished by flight through the air or by the shock of landing. The triggers and fulminates which were supposed to set off percussion fuses were similarly disarranged. Such undependability brought constant complaint from officers in the field. In October 1861 Magruder wrote Gorgas from Yorktown that about half the shells fired by his command exploded at the guns' muzzle; and an artillery chief, reporting on the performance of his batteries at Chancellorsville, estimated on the basis of careful observation that only one out of every fifteen of the shells that were fired exploded at all. "I was compelled to watch closely the effect of all the projectiles," he said, "as if we were using entirely solid shot." [61]

The lamentable ineffectiveness of Southern artillery in the first years of the war was due in considerable measure to the poor quality of powder used in fuses, primers, shells and cannon. When the Confederacy was organized there was in all the South's arsenals no more than 60,000 pounds of serviceable powder. Agents were rushed to the North to buy up all that was available, and deliveries were being made in large quantities when Fort Sumter was attacked. Thereafter importations from the North ceased. Blockade runners brought in large shipments from Europe in 1862 and 1863, but to a great extent the Confederacy was compelled to depend upon her own production.[62]

Eventually ample quantities of a high-class explosive were obtained, but the intervening period of experimentation and development was filled with anxiety and error. Scarcity of powder in the fall of 1861 compelled those in charge of defenses at New Bern, North Carolina, to fill shells with sand and use them as solid shot. The commander of the batteries along the Potomac during the war's first winter said:

"The ammunition found in the magazine for the large guns was very indifferent. The powder was a mixture of blasting with rifle powder. Sometimes the Armstrong gun at the same elevation would not throw a shell more than halfway across the river; then again far over the river."

A similar situation was reported by the commander of defenses below New Orleans in the spring of 1862, after his unsuccessful attempt to turn back the Yankee gunboats:

"Generally our shots fell short for lack of elevation and in consequence of the inferiority of our powder. Even our nearest gun, a 10-inch sea-coast mortar, would not reach his boats with the heaviest charges." [63]

Fortunately for the South, President Davis was able to secure for the supervision of powder manufacturing G. W. Rains, a West Point graduate and a man of unusual ability. Colonel Rains's first efforts were devoted to the stimulation of the few small powder mills which existed in the South when war broke out. He then proceeded to develop niter mining in Tennessee, Georgia, Alabama, Arkansas and Texas. At New Orleans he was able to obtain several hundred tons of sulphur that had been imported originally for a sugar factory.[64] He constructed a saltpeter refinery at Nashville which attained a daily production of 3,000 pounds. The principal government establishment, however, was located at Augusta, Georgia. Through a stroke of good luck, Colonel Rains came into possession of a booklet by an Englishman describing the processes and machinery employed at the British Gunpowder Factory at Waltham Abbey. From the information thus obtained Rains and a few talented associates designed with remarkable ingenuity both the Augusta plant and the machinery installed therein. Through subsequent experimentation various short-cuts and improvements in the manufacture of explosives were developed. During its three years of operation the Augusta plant produced 2,750,000 pounds of powder. The cost of manufacture was a little over a third the price paid for powder brought in by blockade runners, and the quality of the domestic product was as good as the finest output of the English mills.[65]

The procurement of sufficient quantities of niter was the source of great concern to ordnance authorities. To supplement the supply obtained from limestone caves in various parts of the country, the earth in cellars and under outhouses was dug up and leached. Niter beds were established in large numbers near cities and towns. These beds were composed of a variety of vegetable and offal substances and when worked for a period of two or three years, yielded several ounces of niter to the cubic foot.[66]

One of the items utilized in the production of niter was human urine. Jonathan Haralson, Agent of the Nitre and Mining Bureau at Selma, Alabama, ran a notice in the newspaper requesting the women of the town to save all the "chamber-lye" accumulating around their premises so that it might be collected in barrels sent around by the Bureau. This advertisement allegedly inspired a local wag named Wetmore to write some naughty verses chiding Haralson for ungallantry, which in turn elicited a poetic defense from the accused. The poetic exchange was supposed to have been printed in broadside form and circulated among the soldiers in the Petersburg trenches, much to their merriment. Be that as it may, there are innumerable copies of the poems in circulation among descendants of those who wore the gray, but unfortunately the content is not of a publishable character.[67]

There was apparently no time during the last two years of the war when the available supply of powder was not equal to the needs of the armies. In April 1865 the Augusta plant had on hand a stock of 70,000 pounds.[68] This progress from nothing to abundance, which Gorgas, Rains and their associates were able to accomplish in the face of formidable difficulties, was one of the most admirable achievements of the Confederacy.

While guns and ammunition were of first importance in a soldier's equipment, there were certain accessory items which were hardly less dispensable. Among these was a container of some sort for drinking water. Tin canteens, fitted with a strap to hang over the shoulder, were ordinarily employed for this purpose, but in 1861 these were hard to get. As a consequence many of the early volunteers quenched their thirst from clay jugs, from straw or leather-covered bottles, and from homemade contraptions fashioned of cedar or cypress.

The most common type of wooden vessel was constructed like a barrel. It was about eight inches in diameter and about two and one-half inches thick. The mouth was plugged with a cork or twig. The owner's name, company and regiment were sometimes carved on the side. Metal canteens were of a variety of shapes and sizes. Probably the greater portion of those carried by Rebs came from their opponents. The standard type of Federal canteen was of tin and resembled two small dinner plates stuck together, only the bulge was greater. Many of them had cloth covers to keep out the heat. Other models were in shape and size very much like the wooden containers previously described. A few were smaller, bearing close resemblance to the medium-sized fruit and vegetable cans seen on grocery shelves today, though somewhat shorter, and equipped with nozzles.[69]

The hard school of experience, such as that conducted by Jackson in the Valley, Bragg in Kentucky, Early in Maryland, and Hood in Tennessee, caused some soldiers to discard canteens as needless encumbrances and to rely solely on the tin cup which, when not in use as a mess pot, dangled conveniently from the belt. On the march or even on the battlefield an ingenious veteran could usually find an opportunity to seek out some branch or spring from which to fill his cup. If not—well, a good soldier could shift his saliva and push on doggedly till the scurry of comrades up ahead gave promise of better luck.

Knapsacks were another item with which enlistees of 1861 and early 1862 equipped themselves. These satchels were designed for carrying not only surplus socks, drawers and shirts, but also such sundries as writing paper, toilet articles, chewing tobacco and cherished miniatures of folk at home. Some were of leather, but the great majority were made of heavy cloth, treated in some cases with enamel or rubber for sturdiness and weatherproofing. Knapsacks were usually fastened on the soldiers' backs by means of straps. Many of the homemade products resembled very much the cloth satchels in which rural school children of today carry their books.

Knapsacks had comparatively little use among Rebs after the first year of the war. Deprivation and inclination combined to reduce extras, whether drawers or daguerreotypes, to the barest minimum. The prevailing practice among veterans was to wrap essential oddities of wardrobe and toilet in a blanket, tie the ends together, cover with an oilcloth captured from the Yankees, and drape this wheel-like traveling bag from left shoulder to right hip.[70]

Rebs carried their rations in kits which quartermasters listed as haversacks, but which camp parlance dubbed with a variety of designations ranging from war bags to mess boxes. Some were made of leather and others of metal, but canvas seems to have been the material in widest use. In shape and structure many of the food bags differed little from knapsacks. As a rule soldiers who discarded the latter carried some of their "little conveniences" in haversacks along with bread and bacon. Of course there were always a considerable number of Rebs who insisted on getting along without either haversack or knapsack.

Included in the impedimenta of most Rebs were two other important items: the cartridge box and the cap box. The former was a rectangular container made of leather of a size sufficient to accommodate at least forty rounds of paper cartridges. The latter was a small square-shaped pouch in which percussion caps were carried. Both types of boxes were commonly attached to the belt. The cartridge container, because of its size and awkwardness, was irksome to many soldiers, and a pervasive practice was to transfer the contents to the pocket, throw the box away, and report it as "lost." [71]

From beginning to end of the war the average Reb went through a combined hardening and shedding process. And the veteran who emerged in the spring of 1865 was as far removed from the volunteer of '61 in accouterments as he was in sinew. One Reb wrote:

"Reduced to the minimum, the private soldier consisted of one man, one hat, one jacket, one shirt, one pair of pants, one pair of drawers, one pair of shoes, and one pair of socks. His baggage was one blanket, one rubber blanket, and one haversack." [72]

His weapon, if he was a walking soldier, was one gun, more than likely a muzzle-loader, sans bayonet. He was the ultima persona of the rule laid down in May 1862 by General "Dick" Ewell to those who were to follow him in the campaign against Banks:

"The road to glory cannot be followed with much baggage." [73]

CHAPTER XVI

BLUE BELLIES AND BELOVED ENEMIES

IT WAS a hot July day in 1862. A Confederate soldier of twenty-three years sat beneath a tree on a hill near Richmond guarding a group of Yankees captured during the recent Seven Days' fighting. Ordinarily this Reb—whose name must remain in the realm of the unknown because of the incompleteness of his records—was a buoyant, zestful character, but on this particular day he was morose and inconsolable. He had just read a list of the casualties of Mechanicsville, Gaines's Mill, Frayser's Farm, and Malvern Hill. Included among the dead were a number of boys with whom he had frolicked during days of peace. But now they were gone.

As he mused over the loss of his comrades this young soldier laid aside his gun, drew from his pocket the small leather-bound diary that his sweetheart had given him when he left for camp, and began to write:

"July 10, 1862 . . . May God avenge us of our infernal enemies— and if I ever forgive them it is more than I Expect. 'Forgive your Enemies' is the Divine precept—a hard one to obey—How can one forgive such enemies as we are contending against? Despoiling us of our property, driving us from our homes & friends and slaying our best citizens on the field are hard crimes to forgive—At any rate let me have a chance to retaliate & then I can forgive with a better grace. I hope to see many such epithets as this:

> 'The Yankee host with blood-stained hands
> Came Southward to divide our lands
> This narrow & contracted spot
> Is all this Yankee scoundrel got'

So May it be." [1]

Most soldiers in the Rebel Army had feelings toward the Yankees very much like those expressed by this unidentified Virginian. There were some who excelled him in the pungency with which they recorded their antipathy. "I hope that we may slay them like wheat before the sythe," wrote a North Carolinian to his homefolk; "I certainly love to live to hate the base usurping vandals, if it is a Sin to hate them, then I am guilty of the unpardonable one." [2]

A Mississippi private who had heard that his homefolk were being despoiled by the invaders blurted out, "I intend to fight them as long as I live and after this war stops. . . . I intend to kill Every one that crosses my path." [3]

Not a few Rebs got so worked up over Yankee meanness that they swore to perpetuate hatred of the foe in generations to come. Typical of this group was the Georgian who wrote his wife in the spring of 1862:

"Teach my children to hate them with that bitter hatred that will never permit them to meet under any circumstances without seeking to destroy each other. I know the breach is now wide & deep between us & the Yankees let it widen & deepen until all Yankees or no Yankees are to live in the South." [4]

Hatred of Southern soldiers for those of the North was due to a variety of reasons. In their letters and diaries very few of the rank and file mention violation of states' rights as a cause of their antipathy. While most of them had heard small-fry politicians denounce the Lincoln government on this score, it is doubtful whether many of them either understood or cared about the Constitutional issues at stake. The threat to slavery was resented rather widely, not so much as an unwarranted deprivation of property rights, but as a wedge for "nigger equality."

Common soldiers hated the men in blue primarily because they thought them to be an unsavory sort of people who came from a low and vulgar background. It is amazing how many Rebs commented on the crudity and obscenity of letters found on the battlefields addressed to Union soldiers. One Confederate who read a number of letters found in the Atlanta area in 1864 wrote to his wife, "I would send you a sample of them, but I am ashamed they are so vulgar. . . . I do not believe God will ever suffer us to be subjugated by such a motly crew of infidels." [5]

Another Reb confided to his wife that he had seen a great many letters written by wives of soldiers in Sherman's army, and that they were full of such profane expressions as "d—n liar—damed theaf &c." and that "one who wrote a soft & affectionate letter told her husband that some 'bad talk' about her could not be helped." [6] Other Johnnies, with striking unawareness of their own orthographic and grammatical shortcomings, made fun of the Yankees' inability to write and to spell.

The conviction was rather prevalent in Southern ranks that Federal soldiers made a fetish of money. One Reb cited an instance of this quality which he accepted as being typical:

"One of our boys, in conversation with one of the wounded prisoners who had both eyes shot entirely out, remarked to him that his wound must be very painful. The Yankee replied: 'I don't mind the pain so much, sir, but I wouldn't have both of my eyes shot out for twenty-five dollars.' " [7]

The Federals were also thought to be a bunch of thieves, having little regard for the rights of private property, particularly if that property happened to belong to Southerners. The robbery and despoliation that accompanied Union invasion was, indeed, one of the greatest of all causes of hatred. A Mississippi soldier whose home had been visited by raiders wrote to his mother as his regiment headed Northward on the Gettysburg campaign:

"I can fight so much Harder since I have got a gruge against them it is my Honest wish that my Rifle may Draw tears from many a Northern Mother and Sighs from Many a Father before this thing is over." [8]

Rebs liked to point out the superior regard of their own army for civilian rights. Whenever they invaded the Northern or border country, they were amused at the fear of brigandage manifested by the inhabitants along the way. "Poor fools," remarked a soldier marching with Bragg through Kentucky in 1862, "the Yankees treated them so badly, they thought we would do the same. They soon found out that there is a great difference. The Yankee army is filled up with the scum of creation and ours with the best blood of the grand old Southland." [9]

This Reb's observation gives a clue to an impression that was widely prevalent in the Southern ranks, and accepted by them as a partial explanation of the low character of Union soldiery; namely, that the majority of the Federals were recruited from the lowbred immigrant class which swelled the population of the East and the Midwest. It was pointed out repeatedly in home letters that prisoners encountered by the correspondents could not speak the English language. There can be no doubt that a particularly strong prejudice against foreigners in the South increased hatred of the Yankee soldiery. The comment of a sergeant of Bragg's army is typical of a general attitude. "Quite a number of Northern bums, called U.S. soldiers passed our camps," he wrote; "most of them were imported from Germany." [10]

Another cause for hating the Federals was found in the conviction that they were tricky and deceitful. This was applied more to the native breed than to foreigners—a wartime variant of the ancient concept that New England peddlers foisted wooden nutmegs on unwary Southern purchasers. Rebs cited numerous instances of Yankees using flags of truce for reconnoitering purposes; and of crying out "we are friends" during battle to stop opposing fire or to gain safe entrance into Confederate positions. Early in the war a few metal breastplates were found on the bodies of captured or slain Federals, and the belief was current in Southern ranks that they were worn by many members of the opposing army.[11] Both the public press and private correspondence denounced these protective devices as emblems of Yankee trickiness. A similar view was taken of a contraption found in the trenches before Atlanta with which Yankee soldiers, by the use of mirrors, were able to take pot shots at the Rebels without showing their heads above the parapets.[12]

Some Rebs carried their resentment of Yankee "slickness" to humorous extremes. An Alabamian, for instance, was provoked to write his brother:

"I desire above all things on earth to drive a Bayonet to the heart's Blood of some of the Hell bound invaders of the North. They resort to every mean trick that can be conceived of to Whip us, such as hoisting our colors, concentrating there froces upon us where we are weakist." [13]

The concept of heartlessness or brutality swelled considerably the hatred springing up in the hearts of the soldiers of the South. Atrocity stories circulating through the camps told of the bayoneting and shooting of Rebels after they were captured; of helpless Confederate wounded having throats slashed and tongues cut out; of gray-clads shot in the act of ministering to suffering Federals lying between the lines; of Yankees using poisoned bullets; and of the denuding and abuse by Northerners of defenseless Southern women in areas of invasion.[14]

Warriors of all ages have been quick to resent affronts to women. The South, with its chivalric traditions, was unusually touchy on this score. It was this oversensitiveness that caused the Northern general

B. F. Butler to be so thoroughly despised. For his alleged thievery
the General was derided as "Spoon" Butler, but it was his notorious
Order No. 28, in which he threatened to regard as harlots some New
Orleans ladies who were "acting up" under his rule, that gave him the
sobriquet of "Beast."

Rebel leaders promptly utilized the propaganda value of Butler's
order. Beauregard made it the subject of a general order to his troops,
pointing up its provisions as an indication of the sort of warfare that
the North was waging; and not without results.

"Have you seen Butler's proclamation?" wrote one of his soldiers
a short time later; "Don't it make you Shudder? Can such a people
rule over us. Forbid it almighty God!" [15] Another Confederate, whose
anger was uncontainable, resorted to an acrostic:

> "I sing the Chieftain, whom from Boston's shore,
> S ome Yankee Captain to our city bore
> B rutal and vulgar, a coward and knave,—
> F amed for no action, noble or brave,
>
> "B eastly by instinct, a tyrant and sot,
> U gly and venemous—on mankind a blot—
> T hief, liar, and scoundrel, in highest degree,
> L et Yankeedom boast of such heroes as thee!
> E very woman and child will for ages to come
> R emember thee, monster—thou vilest of scum!" [16]

Hatred for Sherman, Sheridan and other generals was hardly less
than that for Butler. Lincoln was likewise regarded as low and brutish,
so much so in fact that even intelligent soldiers regarded his demise as
a blessing, as witness the entry of April 19, 1865, in the diary of Private R. W. Waldrop: "Everything in mourning today for old Abe who
ought to have been killed four years ago." [17] The attitude of the man
in the ranks toward those of the North, both high and low, was aptly
if not accurately summed up by the Virginian who wrote his mother
that "the Yankee horde have forgotten the laws of war & have not
natural honour and chivalry enough to suggest them on the conduct
they enforce. . . . They are like ferocious monkeys which I believe
the Spanish proverb makes the most cruel, wicked, and capricious of
tyrants." [18]

Another factor which contributed much to Johnny Reb's loathing
of the Yankees was the conviction that the men in blue were lacking

in courage. This belief had a powerful hold on Southerners before hostilities began; it gained wider currency after the battle of Bull Run, and continued to flourish till the end of the war. Occasionally a soldier's letter or an officer's report of a battle conceded gallantry to the foe. After Missionary Ridge, for instance, Lieutenant James Hall wrote to his father that the scaling of the heights by the Federals "was a sublime spectacle and I could not withhold my admiration." [19]

In similar vein wrote Captain B. E. Stiles after an encounter on the Virginia front in 1862. "It is all stuff saying that the Yankees are cowards," he concluded.[20] "They fought as boldly as men ever fought and they fight well every time I'v been in front of them," was the testimony of still another officer after Second Manassas.[21] But complimentary expressions such as these are amazing for their rarity.

Derogatory sentiments on the other hand were often recorded. "I saw a house full of Yankee prisoners," wrote a Texan in 1861; "they were large hardy looking men, but as you know they lack the courage." [22]

A short time later an Alabamian boasted to his brother, "We whip them everytime We meet, no matter how great their Numbers, or how few ours. The infernal Scoundrels cant stand the Bayonet—they Scamper like a herd of cattle." [23] A year and a half later this Reb held his antagonists in the same low esteem. "I hope it wont be long," he wrote then, "untill fighting Jo Hooker will be able to advance . . . with his army of white livers and give us a chance to enrich some of the poor land of old Virginia with their corrupt Bodyes." But, on second thought he retracted the statement attributing fertilizing qualities to Federal remains, recalling that a farmer whose property included a portion of the Manassas battlefield had told him that "one Yankee body will kill an acre of land whereas a Southerner's bones will enrich it for all time to come." [24]

Sometimes when Johnnies felt constrained to concede particularly desperate fighting on the part of the Federals, they offered in explanation of the valor their conviction that the bravery had been imbibed. Men of intelligence on more than one occasion recorded with all seriousness such statements as "Grant had made his men drunk," or, "Those Federals whom we capture are all drunk, and they tell us all are made so to get them to advance." [25]

It might logically be expected that Confederates would have taken note of the improved fighting quality of their opponents as experience molded men of the Union ranks into seasoned veterans—experience that brought them to the point where they could pin their names to their backs in order to facilitate identification of their bodies, and charge to certain death as Grant's troops did at Cold Harbor. But this was not the case. Evidently prior conceptions could not give way, and if letters and diaries are an accurate indication of attitudes, the overwhelming majority of Confederates remained firm to the end in the conviction that the majority of Yankees were lacking in the stuff that it takes to make good soldiers.

The opinion of Private W. C. McClellan of the Ninth Alabama Regiment was as representative as it was vivid: "Poor deviles," he wrote in 1863, "you have got no sand in your craw. . . . You d—n cowardly Scoundrels [you can't] face the music you blue bellys." [26]

And Private McClellan stood ready to back up in a personal way the contempt he expressed. For in a previous communication of disparaging tone he inserted this sentence: "Some Yankee may get hold of this letter before it gets to its destination [The Federals were moving about in the area of his home]; if so all I have to say is I can whip the hind legs off him before he can say God with his mouth open." [27]

Antipathy toward ordinary Yankees was deep and pervasive, but it was mild in comparison with the hatred which most Rebs felt for Negroes who wore the blue. All in all some 200,000 Negroes were taken into Federal ranks during the war. These colored soldiers did not get to do their full share of fighting, but they did figure prominently in a few engagements, including Port Hudson, Fort Pillow, Brice's Cross Roads and the Crater.[28] The mere thought of a Negro in uniform was enough to arouse the ire of the average Reb; he was wont to see in the arming of the blacks the fruition of oft-repeated Yankee efforts to incite slave insurrections and to establish racial equality. Anticipation of conflict with former slaves brought savage delight to his soul. And when white and black met on field of battle the results were terrible.

Negroes were taken prisoners in several engagements, but if the wishes of the private soldiers who fought them had prevailed, no quarter would have been granted. Most of the Rebs felt as the Mississippian who wrote his mother: "I hope I may never see a Negro Soldier," he said, "or I cannot be . . . a Christian Soldier." [29]

On more than one occasion Negro troops were slain after they were captured.[30] Following the Crater affair a Reb wrote his homefolk that all the colored prisoners "would have ben killed had it not been for gen Mahone who beg our men to Spare them." One of his comrades

killed several, he continued; Mahone "told him for God's sake stop."
The man replied, "Well gen let me kill one more," whereupon, according to the correspondent, "he deliberately took out his pocket knife
and cut one's Throat." [31]

But the War of Secession was not all hatred. Many Rebs whose
anger flashed to white heat in battle, became indulgent and generous
toward the foe when fighting subsided. Others felt little or no hate
for the men in blue, even while they were pinning writhing bodies to
the earth with their bayonets. To these latter, fighting Yankees was
regarded more or less in the light of a regular chore—disagreeable, indeed, but unavoidable.

The war of the sixties has been called a "polite war," and in a sense
the designation is apt. The conflict followed generally the pattern of a
series of battles. Men of the opposing armies when not actually engaged in a shooting fray were wont to observe niceties that in twentieth-
century warfare would be regarded as absurd. And even during combat
there were occasional exchanges of courtesy. The conduct of the war
in its entirety had something of the flavor of a medieval tournament.

The chivalric concept manifested itself at the very outset of the
war. When Beauregard's aides were conferring with Major Robert
Anderson in April 1861 on the eve of Sumter's bombardment, one of
the Union officers complained jokingly to A. R. Chisolm that the garrison's supply of cigars was woefully short. The Rebel officers said
nothing, but when they returned to the Fort for further conference a
short time later they brought to the Yankee garrison not only a generous supply of cigars but several cases of claret as well. Before the
night was over, these same Rebs gave the order to the batteries to open
fire on the Fort—an order calculated to reduce the bastion to utter
ruin.[32]

This Fort Sumter incident was but the precursor of thousands of
acts of mutual kindness. In many instances the motive was sympathy
for an unfortunate antagonist. A Rebel cavalry company while on a
scouting expedition in the fall of 1861 surprised a group of Yanks and
took several prisoners, including a lieutenant in his late 'teens. The
leader of the Confederates wrote his wife the next day that he could
have killed "the handsome little fellow," but that he had not the heart
to shoot him when he saw his beardless face. So he pulled his youthful
prize up behind and as they rode along they "got to be quite good
friends." When this officer overtook his company he found to his surprise that the other prisoners had likewise captivated their captors, for

"every rascally Yankee was mounted and my men on foot." And thus they proceeded to camp.[33]

During the second battle of Bull Run in 1862, W. F. Jenkins, a seventeen-year-old private of the Twelfth Georgia Regiment, was severely wounded. At nightfall two of his comrades came to take him to the field hospital. As they struggled along through the darkness, they were halted with the query, "Who are you?"

"We are two men of the Twelfth Georgia, carrying a wounded comrade to the hospital," they replied.

"Don't you know you are in the Union lines?" asked the sentry.

"No," answered one of the Rebs.

"You are. Go to your right," said the Federal.

"Man, you've got a heart in you," said the second Reb as the little party turned to the right and headed for the Confederate lines.[34]

In other instances Federals were the recipients of kindnesses. At Vicksburg, at Fredericksburg and at Cold Harbor, Yankee wounded who cried piteously for water as they lay between the lines were given succor by Rebs who dared to run a gantlet of fire to fulfill errands of mercy. During the engagement at Kenesaw Mountain in June 1864 a copse which sheltered some wounded Federals caught fire, threatening the helpless soldiers who lay there. Colonel W. H. Martin, of the First Arkansas Regiment, immediately jumped to the parapet, waved his handkerchief and cried out to the enemy, "We won't fire a gun until you get them away." Shooting on both sides ceased instantly, and the wounded men were removed from danger. At the end of the brief truce a Federal major gave his own fine pistols to Colonel Martin in appreciation of the humane action.[35]

In the wake of many battles the wounded of both sides had their sufferings mitigated by the tender offices of their antagonists. Parched lips were refreshed by pulls from enemy canteens; positions were made more comfortable by the contriving of pillows from overcoats or blankets; piercing pains of shattered thighs were dulled by administrations of copious draughts of brandy. Farewell messages to the folk at home were penned by fingers that a few hours before had wielded hostile weapons; and sincere prayers were offered for the soul's salvation of enemies who lay on the verge of death.

Often the friendly relations between Yanks and Rebs derived solely from convenience. On the night following the battle of Jonesboro, Georgia, in 1864, the armies were in such close proximity that the blue and the gray floundering about in the darkness garnered firewood from

TRAFFIC BETWEEN THE LINES DURING A TRUCE

Drawing by W. L. Sheppard, one of Lee's soldiers, from *Battles and Leaders of the Civil War*.

Courtesy Confederate Museum, Richmond, Virginia

HANDMADE POSTCARD

On the back is a delightful note, in poetic form, chiding the lady for her flirtation. The card is made in color, evidently by a soldier.

the same rail fence, and knelt to drink on opposite sides of the same narrow stream; the men were conscious that the proceedings were unorthodox, but they said nothing of it.[36]

In Virginia in 1862, and in Mississippi the next year, informal truces were called to give soldiers opportunity to pick the luscious blackberries ripening on the no man's land that lay between the lines.[37]

Occasionally the spirit of mutual helpfulness was carried to amusing extremes. During the Georgia campaign of 1864 Rebel soldiers on picket, lacking digging implements to make rifle pits, were forced to beg spades of Yankee vedettes opposite them; and the Yanks were graciously accommodating.[38] This politeness had a parallel on the Virginia front, but with the men in gray filling the role of lenders.[39]

An instance of noblessee oblige more striking than these, however, grew out of the fight at Munfordville, Kentucky, in the fall of 1862. After this engagement Colonel Wilder of the Federals proposed a truce for the burying of the dead. General Chalmers of the Confederates immediately acceded, but to his dismay he found that his men were not equipped for the digging of graves. After brief deliberation he decided to call on the Yanks for assistance. Colonel Wilder very considerately lent spades for the burial of the Rebels.[40]

The spirit of friendliness that sprinkled Yankee-Rebel relations had no more eloquent expression than the musical fetes in which the two armies occasionally participated. Sometimes Federal bands played for the Rebels, as at Fredericksburg during the war's second winter when a crack group of Union musicians posted on the Northern bank of the Rappahannock staged a concert unique in the annals of war. The program began with a medley of Northern airs—patriotic tunes and war songs. This was well enough for the listeners in blue, but not to the complete liking of that part of the audience stationed on the Southern bank.

"Now give us some of ours," shouted Confederates across the river.

Without hesitation the band swung into the tunes of "Dixie," "My Maryland" and the "Bonnie Blue Flag." This brought forth a lusty and prolonged cheer from the Southerners. Finally the music swelled into the tender strains of "Home, Sweet Home," and the countryside reverberated with the cheers of thousands of men on both sides of the stream.[41]

At other times bands of the opposing armies participated in unpremeditated joint concerts. At Murfreesboro, for instance, on the night before the great battle, a Federal band began just before tattoo to play "Yankee Doodle," "Hail Columbia" and other tunes popular in Northern camps. After a little while the Union musicians yielded to the Rebel band which played a group of Southern favorites. These voluntary exchanges had continued for some time when one of the bands struck up "Home, Sweet Home." Immediately the other band joined in, and in a few moments the tune was picked up by a multitude of voices of both camps. For the brief period that the countryside reverberated with the notes of Payne's cherished song the animosities of war were lost in nostalgic reveries, and the fading away of the final notes found tears on the cheeks of scores of veterans who on the morrow were to walk unflinchingly into the maelstrom of battle.[42]

The element of competition was occasionally introduced into these informal concerts. A Confederate band would run through a tune. Then a Federal band would attempt to give a better rendition of the same piece. In these contests—forerunners of present-day "battles of bands"—the Yankees usually came off with the honors.[43]

In the absence of bands the joint fetes often took vocal form. Men on opposite sides of rivers bordering the Confederacy on several occasions united in the singing of "Home, Sweet Home." When in less mellow mood, their efforts were inclined to greater levity. In January 1863, for instance, Lieutenant W. J. Kincheloe of the Forty-ninth Virginia regiment wrote to his father: "We are on one side of the Rappahannock, the Enemy on the other. . . . Our boys will sing a Southern song, the Yankees will reply by singing the same tune to Yankee words." [44] The lieutenant's observation is substantiated by the fact that several Civil War songs had both Yankee and Rebel versions.

One co-operative venture on the Rapidan was of a religious character. Private Goodwin of a Southern regiment, following the example of many of his fellow soldiers, "got religion" during the war, and a group of about fifty of his comrades escorted him down to the river's edge to be baptized. The procession attracted the attention of the Federals, and a considerable number of them came ambling down to the opposite bank to view the proceedings. Presently the Confederates launched into the hymn, "There is a Fountain Filled with Blood." This was a tune familiar to soldiers of both armies, and many of the Yanks joined in the song. Private Goodwin was duly dipped to the satisfaction of all.[45]

This religious collaboration had an unhappy counterpart in interarmy gambling and drinking. There was a little island out in the middle of the Rappahannock where soldiers from both banks were wont to meet now and then to drown their woes in a draught of liquor.[46] Gaming between pickets, and between other troops, was rather frequent. A Rebel officer making an unexpected tour of inspection one night on the Petersburg lines was shocked to find a considerable stretch of the trenches devoid of men. On close inquiry he discovered that the absentees were, by previous arrangement, in the Federal ditches playing cards.[47]

Joint swimming parties were sometimes indulged in by troops stationed along rivers.[48] These were apt to be accompanied by a great deal of "ducking" and banter. In fact, in whatever circumstances Rebs and Yanks came into proximity, there was usually not a little of "smart talk" or "jawing."

The boys in blue would sometimes shout across a Virginia river to inquire how "old Jeff" was getting along. The Rebs would retort by inviting the Yanks to come to Richmond and see, reminding them of several previous unsuccessful efforts to reach the Confederate capital. At Vicksburg the Federals would yell out, "Haven't you Johnnies got a new general—General Starvation?" The men inside the works would come back with the queries, "Have you Yanks all got nigger wives yet? How do you like them?" Before Atlanta the Federals would cry out from their trenches, "What is Confederate money worth?" or "How much do you ask for your slaves?" From the Rebel ditches would come the taunt, "What niggers command your brigade?" or "Have the niggers improved the Yankee breed any?" [49]

A Yank who placed himself in a vulnerable position by shouting to a bedraggled Reb, "Hant you got no better clothes than those?" received the pungent answer from Private Tom Martin: "You are a set of damned fools—do you suppose we put on our good clothes to go out to kill damned dogs?" [50]

On yet another occasion a Federal holding confab with an antagonist between the picket lines said sentimentally, "Why can't this war stop? I love you like a brother." The Reb's reply, in the words of a comrade, was: "You can say more for me than I can say for you for I haven't a dambed bit of love for you." [51]

Good-natured raillery might be provoked by the most unexpected occurrences. One morning early in 1865 a large hawk came flying along over the lines before Petersburg. Soldiers from both sides immediately forgot their potshooting at each other and opened fire on the bird. It became bewildered by the cross fusillade and lit in a tall poplar tree halfway between the trenches. When finally it was shot down, both

Yanks and Rebs let out a tremendous whoop, each side claiming the honors of marksmanship and demanding possession of the prize.[52]

By far the most common form of fraternizing was the exchange of small articles of various sorts by men of the opposing camps. Throughout the war, in all portions of the armies, traffic flourished, and this despite the efforts of superior officers to put a stop to it. The usual method of procedure was for the men to meet at some intermediate point between the lines and there to swap tobacco for coffee, peanuts for pocketknives, pipes for stationery, and Southern for Northern newspapers. A Mississippian wrote his sister in 1864 from Petersburg, "We read each other's Papers in 15 minutes after the News Boys bring them from the Office." [53]

These barter sessions were frequently the occasion of mutual cussing of "bombproof" generals, of grousing over troubles—which were very much the same in both armies—of talk about home affairs, of display, with polite comment, of daguerreotypes of sweethearts, and of expression of hope for a speedy end to the war. Now and then the parley would end with a generous snort of "tanglefoot," drawn perforce from the Yankee canteen. In more than one instance the participants in these get-togethers were members of the same family—brothers, or father and son, drawn to different allegiance by the fortunes of war.[54]

Serious-minded Rebs were sometimes conscience-stricken as a result of these interminglings. A Mississippian who wrote his family of "our boys and the Yankees mixing up and talking together on friendly terms," remarked apologetically, "I threw an old dirty Yank a piece of Tobacco and He threw me a little sack of Coffee—I did not have any chat for them." [55]

A Tar Heel who had trafficked recently with the Feds confided to his father:

"I tell you the Yankees assembled around me like a parcel of buserdes [buzzards] would around a lot of dead horses I chatted [with] them about ½ hour and left I tell you I dident feel rite no way." [56]

Rebs and Yanks separated by narrow rivers developed an ingenious device for carrying on trade. Little boats, some two or three feet long, were made of bark or of scrap lumber, fitted with sails, loaded with coffee, tobacco and papers, and the sails set in such fashion as to carry the craft to the opposite shore. The recipients of the cargo on the other side would in turn load the vessel with items of exchange and head it back to the port of origin.[57] A soldier in Lee's army records the fact that on pleasant days during the spring of 1862 the waters of the Rappahannock near Fredericksburg "were fairly dotted with the fairy fleet." [58]

During the war's last winter, pickets facing each other along the lines before Petersburg, when denied the privilege of trade and communication, resorted to the expedient of tying small articles and messages to grapeshot or shell fragments and tossing them over to the rifle pits of their opponents. In this way they "flanked" the interdiction laid down by superiors. [59]

Now and then a couple of Rebs would go over and spend the night in the Yankee camps, returning just before daylight. In such instances the Yanks might give expression to their good will by filling the haversacks of the parting visitors with coffee and other delicacies rarely seen by men in gray. [60] Rebs likewise played host on occasion. A Delaware lieutenant who made a "hollering" acquaintance with a group of Confederates on picket was invited by them to a party behind the Southern lines. The Rebs called for their guest in a boat, outfitted him with civilian clothing, escorted him to the dance, introduced him to the country girls as a new recruit, and before dawn deposited him safely back on the Federal side of the river. [61]

It would be easy to exaggerate the significance of the fraternizing that dotted the Confederate war. Hatred and fighting far outweighed friendliness and intermingling. But the latter always existed in such proportions as to worry high officers. The fact that the men on both sides spoke for the most part the same language, plus the fact that many had mutual acquaintances or relatives, tended to draw them together. This, coupled with curiosity, war-weariness in both camps, failure to comprehend clearly the issues of the conflict, and the desire to trade, made it increasingly difficult to maintain a definite line of demarcation between the two camps. In the last months of the war, as defeat became more and more apparent, Rebs who went out to swap or to parley with the Yankees failed in increasing numbers to return to their side of the lines.

This inescapable urge of blue and gray to intermingle and to exchange niceties suggests that—grim war though it was—the internecine struggle of the sixties was not only in some aspect a chivalric war but that it was in many respects a crazy and a needless war as well. There is some point, at least, to the observation made by a Reb after a conference on a log with a Yankee vedette. "We talked the matter over," he said, "and could have settled the war in thirty minutes had it been left to us." [62]

CHAPTER XVII

WHAT MANNER OF MEN

THE men who marched under the Stars and Bars were impressively diverse in character. The full range of their variation can never be known, however, because one of the most fruitful sources of information—the original muster and descriptive rolls—is so incomplete. For some companies such rolls were not even prepared; for many, only a part of the required data was given; and for hundreds of others the records were lost or destroyed. But from rolls that are extant, from comments of travelers, from court-martial proceedings, memoirs, diaries and personal letters, a general idea of the South's soldiery may be obtained.

Scattered through the camps of the Confederacy were men of widely varied birth and race. The great majority of the rank and file were Southern-born, of course, but the non-native element was large enough to figure prominently in the general pattern. A considerable proportion came from the country north of Mason and Dixon's line. A random sampling of 42 descriptive rolls covering 21 regiments from six Confederate states yields the names of 86 privates born in eleven northern states.[1] Of these, 37 were natives of New York, 10 of Illinois, 9 of Pennsylvania, 7 each of Indiana, Massachusetts and Ohio, and the rest came from Connecticut, Maine, New Jersey, Vermont and Michigan. An estimate of the total number of Yankee-born men who served the cause of the South could be no more than a guess, but the figure must have run into the thousands.

The foreign-born element in Southern ranks was also large enough to demand attention. A number of companies were made up entirely of foreigners, and several regiments were composed largely of this class.[2] In some Louisiana camps orders on the drill ground were given in French to polyglot organizations containing Irish as well as Latins; and one of the most amazing incidents of the war was the objection raised by a lusty son of Erin to a dictum requiring officers to give their commands in English instead of in French—"I don't know what Oi'll do,"

322

he said to his lieutenant. "You want us to drill in English and the devil a wurd I know but French." [3]

Early in the war, Georgia rustics listened with openmouthed awe to Colonel Polignac drill his French-speaking battalion at the Richmond fairgrounds. "That-thur furriner he calls out er lot er gibberish," said one onlooker, "and thum-thur Dagoes jes maneuvers-up like Hell-beatin'-tan-bark! Jes like he wus talkin' sense!" On more than one occasion when Federals and Confederates bivouacked on adjacent sites, Germans of the opposing camps united to sing in their native tongue songs dear to the Fatherland. [4]

Louisiana, whose population in 1860 was more than one-tenth foreign, contributed more non-natives to the Southern cause than any other state. Some regiments recruited from New Orleans were made up largely of Irishmen, others of Germans, and still others combined these two groups with a miscellany from every part of the globe. Company I of the Tenth Louisiana—which Professor Lonn calls "the Cosmopolitan Regiment"—was composed of men from no less than fifteen countries; and in the First Louisiana Regiment thirty-seven nationalities were represented. [5]

Texas was next in the number of foreigners supplied for Confederate service. Several infantry and cavalry companies from Comal, Gillespie, Fayette and Colorado Counties were German. Some of the Texas Germans were notoriously unsympathetic toward the Southern cause, but many served faithfully and gallantly. From the Lone Star State likewise came companies made up largely of Irish, Mexicans and Poles. And here, as in Louisiana, many of the organizations were composed of a mixture of nationalities. [6]

Alabama had a number of companies consisting almost wholly of foreigners. Company I of the Eighth Alabama Regiment, known as the "Emerald Guards," listed 104 men (from a total of 109) who named Ireland as their birthplace. The uniform in which this company went to war was dark green, and the banner showed on one side the Confederate colors with Washington in the center, and on the other a harp enwreathed with shamrock and flashing the inscription "Erin-go-Bragh." Another Alabama company known as the "Scotch Guards" was composed largely of Scotchmen. Still others, principally those from Mobile, had large representations of Frenchmen and Germans. [7]

Virginia and South Carolina contributed many foreign-born soldiers to the Confederacy, most of whom were Germans and Irishmen from Richmond, Charleston and other large towns. In Tennessee, Memphis and Nashville each furnished several companies of foreigners. In fact there was no Southern state that did not count among its enrollees for Confederate service foreigners ranging in number from several hundred up into the thousands. Even North Carolina, which boasted the highest percentage of native population, had several companies composed almost exclusively of Germans or of Irishmen or of mixed nationalities.[8]

Most of the foreigners who fought for the South were infantrymen, though there were considerable numbers in all branches of the service. Of the various nationalities represented, the Irish were most numerous. Frequently they were rough, quarrelsome, plunderous and impervious to discipline, but for the most part they were blessed with a redeeming good humor. They adapted themselves well to the hardships of camp life, and they enjoyed an excellent reputation as fighters. Next to the Irish in number were the Germans. Their love for music enlivened the atmosphere of many encampments, and when convinced of the rightness of the Confederate cause, as they doubtless were in a majority of cases, they acquitted themselves creditably on the firing line. The British, the French, the Poles, the Canadians, the Dutch, the Austrians and the many other nationalities represented in Southern ranks all made their distinctive contributions to the Lost Cause. The total number of foreigners enrolled in the Confederate Army unfortunately must remain unknown, but there can be no doubt that the figure ran well up into the tens of thousands.[9] To this host of immigrants who wore the gray, particularly to those thousands who yielded up their lives in the service, the South owes an incalculable debt of gratitude and honor.

Another of the diverse groups in the Confederate Army was the Indian. Shortly after the formation of the Secession Government Albert Pike was sent to the trans-Mississippi country to make treaties with the various tribes residing in the red man's territory. The emissary's efforts, notably successful, prepared the way for actual recruiting. In November 1861 the Department of Indian Territory was established with Pike as commanding officer. It was Pike's intention to use Indian soldiers largely for defense of their home area, but his plan was overruled by other considerations.

When General Van Dorn began his campaign for the relief of Missouri in early 1862, four regiments and two battalions had been formed from among the trans-Mississippi red men and half-breeds. Later a fifth regiment and several battalions were created. In the latter part of 1864 the Indian troops were organized into three brigades. These were: The First Brigade, composed of Cherokees, Chickasaws and Osages, commanded by Chief Stand Watie, a valiant officer of whom General S. B. Maxey said, "I wish I had as much energy in some of my white commanders as he displays"; the Second Brigade, made up of Choctaws, led by Tandy Walker; and the Third Brigade, of Creeks and Seminoles, headed by D. N. McIntosh.[10]

A few Indians were scattered among white regiments serving east of the Mississippi. The Sixty-ninth North Carolina, recruited from the mountain district of East Tennessee and western North Carolina in 1862, had two Indian companies made up largely of Cherokees. Most of the commissioned officers were white men, but there was one lieutenant named John Astoo-ga Sto-ga, a warrior of imposing physique and good education. One of the Indian companies had a sharp encounter with Federals at Baptist Gap in the latter part of 1862. The red men were victorious, but Sto-ga was killed. His followers scalped several of the fallen Yankees.[11]

The first engagement in which trans-Mississippi Indians participated was the affair at Wilson's Creek in the autumn of 1861. The number of red men involved was small, and their chief contribution seems to have been the rousing war whoop which they had taught to their paleface comrades. In a charge led by Colonel Greer, the savage shriek, issuing from both Choctaws and Texans, blended with the Rebel yell to create surprise, if not alarm, in Union ranks.[12]

The only major encounter in which western Indians took part on a large scale was the Battle of Pea Ridge in early March 1862. As the vanguard of Pike's command came up to join Van Dorn on the eve of this fight, the red men presented a picturesque spectacle. Speaking primarily of the Cherokees, a member of the First Missouri Brigade said:

"They came trotting by our camp on their little Indian ponies, yelling forth their wild whoop. . . . Their faces were painted, and their long straight hair, tied in a queue, hung down behind. Their dress was chiefly in the Indian costume—buckskin hunting-shirts, dyed of almost every color, leggings, and moccasins of the same material, with little bells, rattles, ear-rings, and similar paraphernalia. Many of them were bareheaded and about half carried only bows and arrows, tomahawks, and war-clubs. . . . They were . . . straight, active, and sinewy in their persons and movements—fine looking specimens of the red man." [13]

But the performance of those who took part in the battle revealed patent deficiencies. The discipline of most units was unworthy of the name. General Pike permitted some, in deference to native character and inclination, to go into action with bows, arrows and hatchets. Those who had guns were little better off, on account of the inferiority of the weapons which the government had issued to them. Some who essayed forward movements were demoralized by Federal artillery, which they called Yankee wagon-guns. Their best work was accomplished under cover of trees; some, indeed, climbed up among the branches to fight.

Colonel Watie's half-breeds rendered helpful service as scouts, but the most notable episode of Indian fighting was the capture by a group of Texans and Cherokees of a Union battery. The red men in high elation took one of the pieces, surrounded it with brush and applied the torch; as the flames leaped up they danced about the conflagration and filled the air with savage yells. But the festivity was brought to a premature and tragic end. The gun was loaded, and when it became hot it went off with a resounding explosion, killing and wounding some and thoroughly frightening the rest. In the wake of the battle a few of the Indians reverted to the primitive practice of mutilating the dead. This act was condemned by the great majority, however, and by both native and white leaders.[14]

Following the Battle of Pea Ridge, activities of the red men were limited largely to raiding and scouting. In September 1862 a force led by D. H. Cooper engaged a group of Federal Indians commanded by William A. Phillips. The Confederates were victorious, but both sides acquitted themselves with credit.

The following July another clash came at Honey Springs. The Confederate regiments of Indians were led respectively by Stand Watie, Tandy Walker and D. N. McIntosh. Fighting was stubborn at first, but early in the action red men on the Southern side discovered that their powder was worthless and began to throw their guns away. Demoralization thus begun spread to the other troops and the result was defeat for the Confederates. In the Camden, Arkansas, campaign of 1864, Choctaws commanded by Tandy Walker rendered minor but valiant service.[15]

The Cherokees and Seminoles were never unanimous in their support of the South, and as Confederates suffered reverses large numbers went over to the Federals. The Cherokees were particularly susceptible to discouragement and defection. On two occasions groups belonging to the command of Colonel John Drew abandoned Confederate ranks under duress and went over to the Yankees en masse; the opinion was widely prevalent in the South that John Ross, principal chief of this nation, conspired with the Yankees for his capture. But many of the Cherokees remained loyal to the Confederacy throughout the war, and their troops were among the best of the Indian fighters. The Choctaws and the Chickasaws were overwhelmingly faithful to the Southern cause.[16]

The Indian soldiers of the Confederacy were victims of shabby treatment by their white superiors. General Pike strove assiduously to secure a square deal for them, but he was far removed from Richmond, and opposed by leaders like Van Dorn, Hindman and Holmes, who were concerned primarily with the protection of white areas and who apparently cared little for the welfare of the red men. Pay, food, clothing and weapons intended for the Indians were diverted by these commanders to other troops. Corruption and fraud were rife in the filling of contracts, and in other phases of government service. A general reorganization of late 1864 resulted in some improvement, but the change came too late to be of much benefit.

Treatment of the Indians was, indeed, one of the darkest and most regrettable episodes of Confederate history. While the contribution of the red man to the Southern cause was admittedly insignificant and marked by large-scale defection, it appears, nevertheless, that on the whole he rendered a better measure of service and honor to the Great Father at Richmond than was accorded to him in return.[17]

The visitor to Southern camps in the first year of the war might expect always to encounter a large number of Negroes. These, to be sure, were not soldiers, but their relation to the fighting force was so vital and so intimate as to merit consideration as a part of the army. Conspicuous among the Negroes attached to military personnel were the body servants. When members of slaveholding families enlisted in 1861 it was quite common for them to take along black members of the household to serve them in camp. Some of the wealthier volunteers had more than one servant, but the usual practice was for a single slave to minister to his own master or to a mess of from four to eight men; in the latter case all members "chipped in" to bear the cost of his maintenance. Non-slaveholders sometimes hired Negroes to act as body servants. The duties of these Negroes consisted mainly of cooking, washing, and of cleaning quarters. Those attached to cavalry companies were required to look after their masters' horses. Many became adept at foraging—a term frequently used in the army to dignify the practice known among civilians as stealing—to supplement the usual leanness of rations issued by commissaries.[18]

During battles the body servant usually remained in the rear out of reach of Federal shells. But a few became so thoroughly imbued with the martial spirit as to grab up muskets during battle and take pot shots at the enemy. There are several instances on record of servants thus engaged killing and capturing Federals. On at least one occasion Confederate domestics made prisoners of Negroes serving Yankee officers. When fighting abated, the colored aide usually loaded himself with canteens and haversacks and went in search of his master. If the latter was wounded, the servant carried him to shelter and sought medical assistance; if he was killed, the domestic made arrangements for his burial or escorted the body home. The relation between master and body servant was usually marked by genuine affection. Frequently intimate association extended back to childhood days. When Confederate masters were ill, they were nursed by their black companions, and when the latter were stricken, they sometimes were attended by their owners with the tenderest solicitude. There were some instances of unfaithfulness and of cruel treatment, but the circumstances of the soldier-servant relationship made these much less frequent in the army than on the plantation.

The life of the body servant was generally not a hard one. He seldom lacked for food, and he usually recouped his wardrobe in the wake of each battle from Yankee sources. He had opportunities to earn money by doing odd jobs for his master's comrades, and the stake thus acquired could be increased or diminished by sessions with fellow servants at dice or cards. Occasional visits home for provisions made it possible for him to play the hero among less fortunate inmates of the slave quarters. In camp his ready laugh—whether inspired by genuine amusement or by a keen sense of appropriateness—was a valuable stimulant to soldier morale, as was his proficiency with song and guitar.[19]

It was with real regret, therefore, that most private soldiers dispensed with the service of their colored associates during the second and third years of conflict. But the increasing scarcity of provisions in the army and the greater need of their labor by civilians made it necessary for the Negroes to be sent home. Those who remained in camp after 1863 were largely the servants of commissioned officers or were employed by the government as musicians, cooks, nurses, hostlers and wagon-drivers.[20]

The largest group of Negroes connected with military affairs were those employed for the construction of fortifications. Early in the war great numbers were hired to throw up works in seacoast and river areas and in other strategic portions of the Confederacy. The intrenchments used in resisting McClellan's peninsula movement were largely the work of Virginia slaves. At first planters responded generously to government calls for laborers, but in the second year of the war impressment sometimes had to be used, and in 1864 levies became the general rule. In February 1864 a Confederate law was passed authorizing the Secretary of War to conscript 20,000 Negroes for military labor. This was only partially due to dwindling patriotism of slaveowners, as many planters felt that their Negroes were neglected and abused while in government employ. The controversy between state and national authorities as to the constitutionality of impressment also colored the picture. Opposition to compulsion eventually reached such proportions as to hinder greatly the program of defense.

Planters who objected to the use of slaves for government work were not without grounds for their attitude. The labor was unduly strenuous. In marshy areas and in rainy weather Negroes suffered from exposure and from disease. Food was often inadequate and poorly prepared. Medical attention was frequently deficient. Supervising authorities were sometimes delinquent in releasing laborers at the end of their period of service. All in all the lot of those who toiled on fortifications was a hard one, and "the 'pressin agent" who was sent around to collect the required workers was dreaded by masters and slaves alike.[21]

Negroes served as soldiers in both the Revolution and the War of 1812, and when the Confederacy was created there was a disposition in some quarters to take free men of color into Southern armies. A regiment was organized in New Orleans, but it was not accepted for Confederate service. In 1863 a proposal to arm slaves was launched by the press, but after a brief discussion the subject was dropped. In January 1864 General Patrick Cleburne revived the question by advocating to a group of fellow officers the enlistment of a large force of slaves and offering them freedom as a reward for faithful service. When Cleburne's action came to the notice of President Davis he ordered suppression of the whole matter. But as the gloom of defeat settled down over the South, sentiment favoring the enlistment of Negroes increased. In November 1864 Davis intimated a willingness to consider a limited use of blacks in the ranks. Finally in March 1865 Congress passed a law authorizing the President to call for as many as 300,000 slaves to serve as soldiers. No assurance of freedom was given. In the month that followed a few companies were organized. Colored recruits attired in resplendent uniforms paraded the streets of Richmond only to be splattered with mud thrown by contemptuous white urchins.[22] The ironic spectacle of Negroes fighting for the cause of Southern independence and the perpetuation of their own bondage was prevented from materializing by Lee's capitulation. Slaves rendered tremendously valuable service to the South by their labor on farms, in factories and on fortifications. There were many Confederate leaders who thought they would also give faithful assistance on the field of battle. But the alacrity with which the great majority seized freedom when it was brought to their reach by Federals gives rise to serious doubt of their fighting long for the Confederacy on any condition save that of general emancipation.[23]

Soldiers who marched in Rebel ranks belonged to a wide variety of occupations and professions. This is brought out by examination of the company rolls. One hundred and seven of these representing 7 states, 28 regiments and 9,000 private soldiers, well distributed as to locality, revealed over 100 occupational classifications. Over half of the enlistees —5,600 out of 9,000—listed themselves as farmers.[24] Other well-repre- sented groups in the order of their numerical strength were: students, 474; laborers, 472; clerks, 321; mechanics, 318; carpenters, 222; mer- chants, 138; and blacksmiths, 116. Other vocations having fifty or more representatives were: sailors, 88; doctors, 75; painters, 69; teachers, 68; shoemakers, 57; and lawyers, 51. Among lesser groups there were 48 overseers, 39 printers, 36 masons, 35 tailors, 31 millers, 31 engineers, 23 coopers, and 21 bakers. Listed also were apothecaries, artists, barbers, bookkeepers, butchers, carriage makers, colliers, cooks, dancing masters, dentists, distillers, drummers, fishermen, horse traders, jewelers, manu- facturers, ministers, musicians, patternmakers, peddlers, photographers, planters, publishers, sheriffs, stage drivers, tanners, weavers and wheel- wrights. Surprises are occasionally encountered in the list. One recruit is put down as a convict, another as a gambler, a third as a rogue, a fourth as a speculator, and several as gentlemen.

The ages of those who wore the gray were no less diverse than their vocations. Descriptive rolls usually gave the ages of recruits at the time of their induction, and a sample taken from these records, consisting of 11,000 infantry privates most of whom enlisted in 1861-1862, and representing 11 states, 94 regiments, and 141 companies, revealed a personnel varying from mere boys to old men.[25] One recruit on the list was a lad of 13, 3 were 14 years of age, 31 were 15, 200 were 16, and 366 were 17. Boys under 18 years constituted approximately one-twentieth of the 11,000 cases examined. With the 18-year-olds the figure jumped sharply to 971, the highest of all the age groups, and within the limits of 18-25 over one-third of the total cases were included. A decline set in with 23-year-olds, but each age was well represented on through the 20's, and the number of cases included within the 18-29 range was approximately four-fifths of the total. Men in their 30's comprised approximately one-sixth of the aggregate and those in the 40's, one-twenty-fifth. Eighty-six of the 11,000 fell in the 50-59 group, 12 were 60-69, 1 was 70, and the oldest was 73.

The distribution suggested by this sample is applicable primarily to the first year and a half of conflict. The second conscription act may have increased the relative strength in the army population of the 36-45 age group, but the ratio of men above 45 and of boys below 18 was probably higher in 1861 and early 1862 than at any other time. The tidal wave of enthusiasm that swept hundreds of old and young into the ranks at the war's beginning lost its force with the passing of time, and many of extreme ages, beset with debility and with camp-weariness, returned to their homes after a year of service. The conscription law of February 1864 comprehended 17-year-olds and men from 46-50, but these were to be employed only as a reserve force. The great majority of additions to the army after 1862 came from the 18-45 group, through upward extension of the conscription age and revocation of exemptions, substitutions and details.[26] There is apparently little foundation for the charge made by Grant late in the war that the Confederacy was robbing the cradle and the grave to sustain its forces. The overwhelming bulk of the Southern Army from beginning to end appears to have been made up of persons ranging in age from 18 to 35.

Some of the oldsters of the Confederate Army rendered distinguished service. Private George Taylor of the Sixtieth Virginia Infantry, whose three-score years earned for him the sobriquet of father of the regiment, was cited for gallantry at Frayser's Farm. A Mississippian of advanced age named John Thompson, who enlisted as a private when the war began, fought so valorously at Belmont and at Shiloh as to win a commission. After his death at Chickamauga General Patton Anderson paid him high tribute in an official report as a man and as a soldier.[27] But in all probability most men of fifty years or more who had to march in the ranks were more of a burden than a benefit to the cause which they so patriotically espoused. Exposure, inadequate nourishment, and the strain of campaigning combined with ripe age to acquaint them better with hospital and wagon train than with the field of action. The fate of elderly Rebs is well exemplified by the case of a private, E. Pollard, of the Fifth North Carolina Regiment. This soldier, whose seventy-three years entitle him perhaps to the distinction of being the oldest man regularly enlisted in Confederate service, was taken into the army as a substitute in July 1862. In September 1862 a surgeon who examined him reported that he had been unfit for duty three-fourths of the time since his enlistment. Shortly thereafter he was given a discharge for being "incapable of performing the duties of a soldier on account of Rheumatism and old age." [28]

The boy soldiers made a good record. There were a number of instances of teen-age Rebs receiving mention for bravery in official reports and orders. Following an engagement in early May 1862, General Beauregard said in a general order:

"The Commander of the Forces desires to call the especial attention of the Army to the behavior of Private John Mather Sloan of the 9th Texas Vols., a lad of only 13 years of age who having lost a leg in the affair . . . near Farmington exclaimed 'I have but one regret I shall not soon be able to get at the enemy.' "

The general stated his intention at some future time of publicly decorating the hero with a badge of merit. If this occasion materialized, how the heart of Private Sloan must have thrilled to be thus honored by the "Grand Creole." [29]

At Shiloh fifteen-year-old John Roberts was frequently in advance of his company, according to the subsequent report of his commanding officer, "was knocked down twice by spent balls," "had his gun shattered to pieces," and "throughout the whole action . . . displayed the coolness and courage of a veteran." [30]

During an engagement before Atlanta in July 1864, Eddie Evans, a mere boy of the Twenty-fourth Mississippi, asked for the privilege of carrying the colors, and he afterward "bore them with such conspicuous coolness and gallantry," according to the statement of his colonel, "as to elicit the admiration of all. At one time he took his stand in advance of the line without any protection in an open field, distant from the enemy's line not more than fifty yards, waving his colors defiantly and called upon his comrades to rally to the flag." [31]

Some of the youngsters seen about Southern campfires were buglers and drummer boys who had regularly enlisted. Others were unattached waifs adopted by the troops as mascots.[32] A most interesting group having semiofficial capacity were the drillmasters borrowed temporarily from the cadet corps of Southern military schools to assist in the instruction of raw recruits. Most of these boys were quite young but they called out their orders with impressive manliness.

A North Carolina historian, writing of the Hillsboro Military Academy contingent, said:

"It was certainly a novel sight to see the little cadets from thirteen years old and upwards, each tramping his squad of grown and sometimes grizzled men, over the parade ground and to witness the grim seriousness with which the future veterans took their military subjection to their juniors in years." [33]

The work of these youthful instructors and of their co-workers from the Virginia Military Institute and from a number of other campuses was invaluable.[34]

Naturally boys who came into such close contact with army life were fired with a burning desire to smell the smoke of battle. After brief and trying sessions with their studies most of them realized their ambitions. A few of the strongest-willed contrived means of entering immediately into active service. Among these was Charlie Jackson of Memphis, Tennessee, who served as drillmaster for a company raised by his father. When the troops departed for Shiloh, Charlie would not be left behind, and against his parents' entreaties he took an undersized musket made specially for his use, and went with his erstwhile pupils into battle. He served gallantly until near the end of the first day's fighting when a mortal wound brought an end to his career as a soldier.[35]

Under a program sanctioned by government authorities late in the war, students of various Southern institutions were organized into companies and held for reserve purposes.[36] The crowning achievement of college boys on the field of battle was that of Virginia Military Institute cadets in the affair at New Market, May 15, 1864. When General Breckenridge engaged the Federal forces led by Sigel, his command consisted in part of a battalion of over two hundred boys from the Virginia college under one of their professors. As the fight progressed the cadets marched steadily forward under heavy fire to a position beyond the town. There they were called on to join with a Virginia regiment to take a battery that was inflicting serious damage on the Rebel lines. In the advance that ensued the college youths, because of their greater endurance and ardor, outdistanced their veteran comrades, and as a consequence they had to stand in a rain of bullets until the older men could come up for the final dash. But they held their formation and when the order came to charge at double quick they rushed gallantly forward. The guns were soon captured, and when a cadet mounted one of the captured pieces and .waved the Institute flag there was a wild yell of triumph. In this notable victory at New Market, the boys won for themselves and their school an undying glory, but at great cost. When the casualties of battle were counted, it was found that the toll of dead and wounded included fifty-four cadets, eight of whom were killed.[37]

Considerable argument has been exchanged as to the age and identity of the most youthful person to serve as a full-fledged Confederate soldier. In 1901 a Floridian wrote the editor of the *Confederate Veteran* stating that when he surrendered in April 1865 he lacked one month of being fifteen years old, and that his service dated back to 1861. If this man's claim be true, he would appear to have undisputed title to the distinction of being the youngest Rebel.[38]

Occasionally, but very rarely, a woman was to be found in Confederate ranks posing, of course, as a man. The motive of some who laid aside skirts for uniforms was immoral, but in other cases the action was prompted by desire to be associated with their husbands. Such was the case with Malinda Blalock, of the Twenty-sixth North Carolina Regiment. When James Moore, recruiting for Company F of this organization, proposed to enlist Keith Blalock, the husband swore not to enroll unless his wife was allowed to join the army with him. Moore agreed to take them and to keep in confidence the identity of Malinda. The latter enlisted under the name of Sam Blalock. For two months she drilled and did all the other duties of an ordinary soldier. Her disguise was not revealed until Keith Blalock was given a discharge for physical unfitness; Malinda then informed Colonel Vance of her true status and was sent home with her husband.[39]

A story so remarkable as to create a doubt of its authenticity is that of one Madame Loreta Velasquez as told by herself. Born in Cuba in 1842 of Spanish parentage, she was sent to New Orleans to complete her education. After some months in school devoted, it seems, more to dreaming of exploits of Jeanne d'Arc and other adventurous characters than to serious study, she eloped with a young United States Army officer. When secession came she persuaded her husband to cast his

lot with the South. She also confided to him her own determination to
join the army. He tried desperately to dissuade her, but when he had
departed for camp she donned a uniform, after fitting herself with a wire
frame so shaped as to give her figure a masculine appearance, glued on
a false mustache, adopted the title of Lieutenant Harry T. Buford, and
set out for Arkansas where she recruited a company of volunteers. As
an officer unattached, she took part in the battles of Bull Run, Ball's
Bluff and Fort Donelson. At intervals she resumed feminine garb and
worked as a spy. In the spring of 1862, after fleeing from New Orleans
authorities who had discovered her sex, she enlisted in the Twenty-first
Louisiana Regiment. She fought in the battle of Shiloh and was
wounded while helping to bury the dead of that engagement. This
misfortune revealed her disguise a second time. But afterward she
frequently posed as a man, and for the remainder of the war she was
engaged in spying and plotting. If Madame Velasquez's account be
true, her career was indeed a phenomenal one; if it be false, she deserves
high rating as a fictionist.[40]

The variation in education and culture which characterized army
personnel has already been noted to some extent in other connections.
Here and there among the rank and file were to be found men well
versed in the classics and in other branches of learning. Robert Stiles
told of a comrade who kept a diary in modern Greek.[41] Other reliable
sources reveal instances of private soldiers poring over Latin readers and
Greek grammars, or reading the writings of the literary masters.[42] A
South Carolinian wrote his mother that he had been reading Macaulay's
history but that he had been unable to get to the fifth volume. "I wish
to survive this war," he said, "if only to have that pleasure." [43]

The number of well-educated privates scattered through the ranks
was larger in 1861 than at any later time because, as a general rule,
unusual abilities won promotion in a fairly short time, and recruits of
this type were not frequently available as replacements. But in certain
choice organizations made up largely of men of means and culture this
was not the case.

The First Company of Rockbridge Artillery had on its roll four
masters of arts, twenty graduates of Washington College, forty or more
students of this institution and of the University of Virginia, and many
more who had attended other colleges. Company E of the Eleventh
Virginia was composed, for the most part, of boys from Lynchburg
College, and its first captain was one of their professors. The First
Maryland Infantry, Hampton's Legion, the First Virginia, the Third

Alabama, Company F of the Twenty-first Virginia, the Richmond Howitzer Battalion, the Oglethorpe Light Infantry of Savannah, the Washington Artillery and several other volunteer organizations also had a large proportion of well-bred and educated men.[44]

Cavalry and artillery units seem to have held special attraction for scions of first families. In instances where large numbers of exceptional men belonged to the same company, only a few could hope to win commissions within the organization, and many frowned upon the idea of leaving their congenial associates to seek offices elsewhere. In other words the opinion prevailed in these select circles that it was better to be a private in the Richmond Howitzer Battalion or in Hampton's Legion than a lieutenant in most other groups. This sentiment, coupled with the difficulty of getting transfers, explains to a considerable extent the continued presence in the ranks throughout the war of many men of good education and of high social standing.

But the number of these men, like other pleasanter concepts of Southern history, has been exaggerated. The error may be attributed in part to writers of the moonlight-and-magnolia school who saw in the old South a society richly endowed with wealthy landowners who devoted their leisure to the classics. But a more immediate basis for the misconception is to be found perhaps in the greater articulateness of the men composing the choice companies. As a general rule the most interesting and the most widely read of regimental histories and personal memoirs were written by members of the Rockbridge Artillery, of the Richmond Howitzers, and of other exceptional organizations. These books naturally emphasized the cultural and social attainment of the authors' particular groups.[45] There was a tendency for readers to infer that the companies thus described were representative of the army as a whole. Veterans of more ordinary groups either remained silent or wrote volumes of less charm and of a more limited circulation. The result was distortion in favor of the select few.

At the opposite end of the scale were the illiterate, and their number was considerable. When Company A of the Eleventh North Carolina Infantry was mustered into service 27 men of the 100 enrolled had to make their marks when called on to sign the descriptive roll. In another Tar Heel company 36 out of 72 privates signed with an X; in a third, 30 out of 80, in a fourth 54 out of 100; and the average for 14 companies of thirteen different regiments was 40 out of 100. The ratio of illiteracy in these units was undoubtedly higher than in the general run of Confederate organizations, but the great majority of companies

A BOY SOLDIER

Randolph Fairfax, killed at the battle of Fredericksburg, December 13, 1862. He enlisted in August 1861 at eighteen as a private in the famous Rockbridge Artillery. The picture was probably taken shortly after his enlistment.

BOY SOLDIERS OF THE CONFEDERACY

John Kennedy (left), Company A, 3rd Tennessee Regiment, and Enoch Hancock, Company A, 3rd

throughout the army had anywhere from one to a score of members
who could not write their names.

Soldier correspondence and other firsthand evidence indicates that
most of the Rebel rank and file lay between the two educational extremes. They were neither learned nor illiterate, though it must be
admitted that those who were barely literate were much more numerous
than those of fair education. Their schooling, like their culture, reflected in a general way the yeoman society to which most of them
belonged.[46]

The thought patterns of common soldiers were interesting and
varied. Prejudices were numerous and strong. Antipathies of the poor
toward the rich and of the well-born toward the underprivileged were
not so much in evidence as other aversions, but caste consciousness was
present to a limited extent, and class friction occasionally provided the
spark for disturbances in camp. Yeomen resented the special status
enjoyed by planters under the fifteen and twenty-Negro law. A North
Carolinian wrote his wife in the fall of 1864 that she might expect him
home soon because "all of the gentel men has got out of it [the war]
and i don't intend to put my Life betwen them and their propty." [47]

A Texas private attempted to incite his comrades to desert in September 1863 by saying publicly to them, "It makes me mad to hear
poor men that have nothing and are living in small huts, and on other
peoples' land, hold up for the South." [48] The feeling that soldiers who
owned slaves received better treatment by company officers than that
accorded the poor caused another Texan to raise such a row as to receive a severe court-martial sentence for mutiny.[49]

Sensitiveness to class seems to have been voiced more frequently by
the rich than by the poor. George Cary Eggleston recalled an instance
in a Virginia company where a young private of superior social standing
forced a public apology from a lieutenant of ordinary background who
had dared to put him on double duty for missing roll call. A Georgian
refused in 1861 to obey an order on the ground that the officer issuing
the command was no gentleman. Corporal John Hutchins on being
called to task for a minor infraction said to his superior, "God damn
you, I own niggers up the country," and when private John Shanks was
ordered from the drill field to the guardhouse for inebriation he blurted
out to his captain, "I will not do it. I was a gentleman before I joined
your damned company and by God you want to make a damned slave
of me." [50]

A Mississippian who was invited by a colonel to dine at his mess was enraged when he found out that the officers had already eaten and that he was expected to share a second meal with a clerk. The aggrieved soldier wrote later to his wife that he told the colonel's aide "that I considered myself a gentleman, treated every body gentlemanly & demanded the Same of every body & that I eat at Nobodys Second table, not even Gen'l Beauregard." Eggleston testified that he personally knew of "numberless cases in which privates . . . declined dinner and other invitations from officers who had presumed upon their shoulder straps in asking the company of their social superiors." [51]

The aversion of aristocratic privates to plebeian officers sometimes extended to men of high rank. A case in point is that of a young Mississippi gentleman whom the fortunes of war in 1864 placed under the authority of Nathan B. Forrest. The chagrined grandee wrote in his diary:

"The dog's dead: finally we are under N. Bedford Forrest . . . [a circumstance that] I have dreaded since the death of the noble Van Dorn. . . . 'The Wizzard' now commands us . . . and I must express my distaste to being commanded by a man having no pretension to gentility—a negro trader, gambler,—an ambitious man, careless of the lives of his men so long as preferment be en prospectu. Forrest may be & no doubt is, the best Cav officer in the West, but I object to a tyrannical, hotheaded vulgarian's commanding me."

Subsequent entries in this soldier's journal indicate no abatement of his antipathy to his commoner general.[52]

The more frequent manifestations of class prejudice on the part of aristocrats were not due solely to greater touchiness on the subject; another factor was the greater impunity with which they could express their sentiment. An Englishman who served in the Confederate Army told of an officer—unpopular because of his assumption of airs—slapping a soldier with a sword during drill. The recipient of the blow threw down his rifle, stepped from the ranks and stabbed the officer to death with his Bowie knife. The company "looked on and applauded; the culprit quietly wiped his knife, resumed his place in the ranks, and dress parade proceeded as if nothing had happened!" Incidents such as this were reckoned as affairs of honor, according to the Englishman, and courts-martial took no cognizance of them.[53] This statement is probably exaggerated, but it derives partial substantiation, at least, from the complaint of a prominent military judge to President Davis that "to convict a soldier of any offense, who has social position, friends, and influence is but a mockery of form." [54]

Flare-ups of prejudice were less frequent as the war progressed. The tightening of discipline required increasing submissiveness of insubordinate aristocrats; common exposure of rich and poor to the dangers of battle and the hardships of camp enhanced mutual respect, and in some cases produced intimate friendships between men of social extremes. A glimpse of the metamorphosis is afforded by the statement of a Low Country youth who served in Hampton's Legion:

"It would have seemed strange to me once in my ignorance of the world to have found literary taste among mechanics and tradesmen; and yet I have found instances in my own company . . . of admirable taste and large reading." [55]

Prejudice of rural troops toward those from the city was evidenced by the bandying of such sobriquets as "parlor soldiers" and "kid glove boys." [56] Metropolitan dandies retorted by ridiculing farm youths for their rusticity. Provincialism likewise found expression in the nicknames applied by soldiers of one state to those of another. Virginians were called the "Buttermilk Brigade"; South Carolinians, "Sand Lappers"; Alabamians, "Yellow Hammers"; Georgians "Goober Grabbers"; and Louisianians, "Tigers."

Local attachment was so strong that Confederate authorities were forced to keep troops of the same state brigaded together, even when military expediency called for their separation. Concession to particularism was carried to the extreme of providing separate hospitals for the sick and wounded of each state. Difficulties between soldiers of different localities were frequent. Mississippians who were put in the same brigade with Florida troops for the Perryville fight accused their unwelcome associates of shooting at them instead of at the Yankees; when subsequently this hybrid organization passed a Mississippi division on parade, men of the latter yelled out the greeting, "Come on out of that Brigade—we won't fire on you." [57]

Troops of the various states were very jealous of their reputation in battle, and woe to that officer or newspaper representative who seemed in his report to favor Tennesseans at the expense of Texans or to give less than a full measure of glory to each of the units composing the Confederacy.[58] One of the factors which caused so much opposition to consolidation of skeleton regiments was dread of the loss of state identity.[59]

The tendency was widespread for soldiers composing one army to disparage those of another. Rebs who followed Bragg and Joe Johnston referred to those of Lee's command as "Jeff Davis pets"; and they attributed victories on the Virginia front to the fact that Yankees in that locality did not fight so hard as those opposed to Western commands. Lee's men in turn berated the fighting qualities of the Army of Tennessee.[60] Shortly after Pemberton's capitulation an Alabamian serving with Lee wrote in disgust of "the imbecility of officers and the cowardice of our men at Vixburg." The surrender of that city was, in his opinion, "the most disgraceful affair in the history of our country," and his chief consolation was that he was not involved in the shame. "If I live to be a hundred year's old," he said, "I shall always be proud to know that I once belonged to the Army of N. Va." [61]

After Chancellorsville another of Lee's soldiers wrote to his father in North Alabama:

"Tell old Bragg for God's sake not to let the Yanks whip him as he usually does when this army gaines a victory . . . If the armys of the West were worth a goober we could soon have piece on our own terms." [62]

When Longstreet was sent to the assistance of Bragg late in 1863, the troops composing his command took a condescending attitude toward their comrades of the Chattanooga encampment. One of Longstreet's men began to pine for his Virginia connection shortly after his arrival in the West, but he professed himself "willing to help Bragg out of the mud before we go." After the battle of Chickamauga another railed out against Bragg's troops for their failure to back up the Eastern units. "Had we some of the Va army to have supported us," he said, "There would have been no trouble; these Western troops dont know how to fight Yankees." [63]

One of the aversions most frequently expressed was that of infantrymen for cavalrymen. The term "buttermilk cavalry" had almost universal use among walking Rebs as a derogatory sobriquet. The connotation was apparently twofold: softness and thievery—foot soldiers envisaged equestrians lolling about on their mounts begging or stealing buttermilk and other delicacies while they themselves toiled along for endless miles on half rations. An Alabamian expressed a widespread

sentiment when he said that every cavalryman ought to have a board
tied on his back and the word "thief" written thereon so that good
people might be on guard against their depredations. But this branch
of the service was more usually condemned for uselessness and cowardice.[64] Whenever a cavalry unit rode by a group of infantrymen, the
latter would almost invariably turn loose a flood of invective and derision.[65] One hard-bitten marcher said that the mounted service steered
so clear of dangerous combat as practically to constitute a life insurance
company.[66]

After one of Early's Valley disasters in the fall of 1864, another infantryman expostulated:

"Our cavalry lost all their artillery . . . I do wish that the Yankees
would capture all the Cavalry. . . . They never will fight So I think it
is useless to have them in the Army Eating rations." [67]

General Longstreet was alleged to have made the statement following Chickamauga that it was on this battlefield that he first saw a dead
Rebel with spurs on.[68] But there was frequently a note of envy in dis-
paragements such as these. The dream of countless footsore infantrymen as they trudged along through the mud stooping beneath the
weight of equipment, their impoverished "innards" murmuring protest
at every step, was a transfer to the cavalry and the sweet life that would
thus be achieved—relief from the grime, sweat and the pain of walking,
abundant opportunity to forage, periodic visits home for new horses,
pretty girls far and wide brought within easy reach, and virtual certainty
of arriving at the nether end of the war in safety and in soundness.

Such was the cavalry as the ordinary Reb envisioned it. And if
he had a younger brother at home yearning for the army, he forgot his
aspersions and wrote to his parents:

"Tell Him . . . to Join the cavalry . . . if He can not get into
the Commisary or Quartermasters Department to never Join as a private . . . but by all means to Join the Cavalry—and bear in mind that
a private in The Infantry is the worse place he can possibly be put into
in this war—so if he wants to have a good time Join the Cavalry." [69]

And hundreds if not thousands of Rebs made their dreams come
true by deserting the infantry and enlisting with Forrest, with Wirt
Adams, and with other mounted leaders.[70]

Antipathy of cavalry toward infantry was inconsiderable, though the former did apply to the latter the uncomplimentary term of "web feet," and there was some resentment of the scorn which the foot soldiers expressed for their conduct as fighters. As a general rule, however, equestrians shrugged their shoulders good-naturedly at revilings and congratulated themselves on their good fortune at being able to do their campaigning on horseback. Typical of many was the attitude expressed by a Lone Star cavalryman who wrote when he heard of the commissioning of an infantry acquaintance: "I wood rather be corporal in company F of the Texas Rangers than to be first Lieu in a flat foot company." [71]

There was a pervasive feeling among volunteers that conscripts were second-rate soldiers, and manifestations of this attitude tended undoubtedly to injure the service. When recruits were inducted under the draft legislation they were already in a bad frame of mind because of the stigma attached to compulsion; the scornful glances and the contemptuous remarks which greeted them in camp were ill-adapted to the making of fighters. [72]

Many conscripts, particularly those brought in by the laws of 1862, were good soldier material, and had they been accorded a wholesome reception by volunteers, the majority of them might have fitted congenially and usefully into the military organization. Some developed into first-class troops in spite of the antipathy which encompassed them. After Fredericksburg General James H. Lane reported that conscripts recently added to his brigade conducted themselves creditably, and General A. P. Hill made the significant observation that in this affair they showed an earnest desire to win the respect of their veteran comrades. Major John Harris who commanded a Tennessee brigade at Murfreesboro paid high tribute to the performance of conscripts who served under him in that battle. [73]

But the great majority of testimony, both of officers and of privates, bristled with such uncomplimentary epithets as cowards, skulkers, shammers, useless and worthless. One colonel declared that he would rather have his regiment reduced to a battalion and his rank to that of a major than to replenish his organization with men forced into service. [74] There was undoubtedly a factual justification for much of the criticism, but few veterans realized that their own unfriendliness contributed markedly to the unhappy situation of which they complained.

The contempt for conscripts was mild in comparison to that provoked by militia and reserves. Kate Cumming told of hearing a soldier mimicking "Joe Brown's Pets," as Georgia militiamen were called, from the top of a boxcar in Marietta. This Reb told piteously of his treatment; how he had been in the service for two whole weeks and as yet had not received a furlough; and how he and other brave reservists were nobly defending the rear of Bragg's army.[75]

An Alabamian reported that when a militia unit was assigned to guard duty in the vicinity of the camp, soldiers of his regiment would go out, take away the guards' guns and compel them to sit for long periods on logs.[76] As for fighting, few full-fledged Rebs expected that of "Bob-tail militia." "They had just as well stay . . . [home]," wrote one of Joe Johnston's veterans in 1864; "they aint worth a low country cow tick." [77] And when one of Lee's men heard that state troops had participated in the defense of Petersburg late in the war he exclaimed: "The militia fought! Long be it remembered." [78]

Another object of great contempt was the staff officer. When Rebs saw young aides dashing about in fine uniforms carrying messages and performing other duties with airs bespeaking a sense of unusual importance, they were annoyed. The feeling that such officers used family influence to get soft positions caused them to be designated by some as yellow sheep-killing dogs, which term was soon shortened to "yaller dogs." When one of these officers rode by, Rebs would begin whistling and whooping as if they were calling hounds.[79] As Hood's army was falling back from Nashville after severe fighting in December 1864, a staff officer who came up ostentatiously to a mud-splattered infantryman and ordered him to halt and face the foe received the significant reply: "You go to hell. I've been there." [80]

In the canine category also were placed those ordinary soldiers who because of pretended ailments hung back with the wagon train on the march or during battle. The epithet applied to these shammers was wagon-dogs, and when Terry's Texas Rangers rode by them they raised a song, written allegedly by a cavalryman; it ran like this:

> Come all you wagon dogs, rejoice—
> I will sing you a song,
> If you'll join in the chorus—bow wow wow;
> When we go to leave this world,
> We will go above with sheets unfurled—
> bow wow wow.[81]

Court-martial proceedings indicate that prejudices of nationality sometimes figured in disturbances among enlisted men. Private Henry Brandes of Hampton's Legion received a prison sentence for calling a sentinel an "Irish son of a bitch," and another South Carolinian was punished for denouncing a corporal of the guard as a "blind Dutch son of a bitch." [82] Mississippi regiments stationed at Iuka early in the war were opposed to the induction of Irish levee-builders into their organizations, and when officers forced acceptance of the foreign recruits a free-for-all fight ensued.[83]

Certain random types that appeared in Rebel ranks require special notice. Almost every regiment had a braggart who regaled his comrades at every opportunity with tales of his magnificent doings from early childhood down to the present. His accounts were sometimes listened to because of lack of other diversion, but again he would be taunted into silence. Closely akin to the boaster was the self-seeker—the man who in private life had perhaps made a splash as a petty politician, and who in the army became hell-bent for promotion. This type, too, was the butt of many scornful remarks. The dandy was also in evidence. He sported foppishly cut coats and fancy boots, combed his long hair back over his ears, pinned up one side of his hat, donned a feather and imagined himself a cavalier.

Occasionally there was a snob, such as a youngster from Natchez who refused to join one company because it was composed of commoners, and who, when he finally joined another, looked down his nose at most of his associates. "We are two distinct parties," he said on one occasion, "the Aristocrats and the democrats," and he professed nothing but disdain for the latter. He took offense at his colonel for "putting on airs," ceased saluting him, and swore to call him to task after the war for failure to proffer the recognition due one of his high social standing. His attitude was identical with that of another snob who wrote:

"It is galling for a gentleman to be absolutely and entirely subject to the orders of men who in private life were so far his inferiors, & who when they met him felt rather like taking off their hats to him than giving him law & gospel." [84]

Now and then a brute was found whose soul was so hardened as to make him seemingly impervious to ordinary human emotions. Such a character was a Tennessean who sang in battle from sheer joy of slaughtering, and who would yell out with utmost indifference, "Good-by, Jim," or "Good-by, Sam" as comrades fell one by one at his side; likewise the Louisianian who ran his bayonet through a pig on the march, tossed the gun across his shoulder as if nothing had happened, and bore the squealing animal aloft while it died a slow and painful death.[85]

Another type was the arch-plunderer, a good example of which was Sam Nunnally of the Twenty-first Virginia. Periodically Sam would disappear from camp for interims varying from one to three days. At the end of these absences he would return as mysteriously as he had vanished, but invariably with a plausible excuse and a load of spoils. He was particularly adept at playing wounded after a fight to rifle the pockets of the dead. After one night of such lurid activity he came sneaking into camp with three watches, several knives, some money and various other articles. On another occasion, a foraging excursion among the living yielded not only a large supply of food and other provisions, but a horse for transporting the thief and his prizes.[86]

Almost every regiment had a prankster who was quick to make fun at the expense of the unwary. If a hirsute comrade wished to borrow a razor, he would refuse him positively, but at the same time he would slyly offer his tonsorial services. If the proffer was accepted, the self-appointed barber would shave one half the customer's face with great care, then pocket his razor and take to flight in a roar of laughter.[87] Usually there was a greenhorn for every such mischief-maker—the mentality of a few Rebs ran so low, indeed, as to require their discharge from the service—and the lot of these dullards was as cruel as it was amusing.[88] One such creature was honored with sham election to the post of fifth lieutenant. After the balloting he inquired with all seriousness into the nature of his duties. His electors professed ignorance on the score, and sent him to the lieutenant. This officer, sensing the hoax immediately, replied without hesitation: "His duties are to carry water and catch fleas out of the soldiers' beds." The unsophisticate proceeded to conform in good faith to these instructions until someone convinced him that the whole thing was a joke.[89]

In another instance a recruit of very short stature was brought into camp. Some of his comrades, adjudging him too small to carry a musket, assumed the role of doctors, stripped him, tapped his chest, went through various other motions of a medical examination, and wrote out with charcoal on a scrap of newspaper a certificate of physical disability. The examinee, according to instructions, presented this to his colonel, who laughed and forwarded the case to the brigade surgeon. As a consequence of the joke the recruit received a long furlough.[90]

Eccentrics of various sorts were scattered among the rank and file. An old country gentleman who enlisted in the Twenty-first Virginia took an umbrella to camp, and in sun or rain, on the march and in the field, he insisted on seeking shelter beneath this canopy. His comrades jibed him freely, but to no avail; the parasol remained a constant companion for the duration of his service.[91]

Some of the troops who hailed from the West were very rough in appearance. A Louisianian who in 1863 watched a group of 400 Texans ride by his plantation reported that they bore no resemblance to soldiers. "If the Confederacy has no better soldiers than those we are in A bad roe for stumps," he said; "they looke more like Baboons mounted on gotes than anything else." [92]

Rough-looking likewise were the Mississippi flatboatmen and wharf hands from the waterfronts of Memphis, New Orleans, Mobile and other cities of the Confederacy.[93] Among these, as well as among other groups of formidable mien, there were many individuals whose chief crudities were those of external appearance. But it cannot be denied that the Southern Army had its share of rogues and desperadoes. In Mississippi, Governor Pettus pardoned a number of convicts on condition that they would join the army.[94] From among Federals in Southern military prisons several companies of troops were recruited, and these "galvanized Yankees," as they were called, were generally a tough lot.[95] But cutthroats, robbers and knaves were by no means found only among those who came from behind prison walls. Inspection reports and court-martial proceedings cite numerous instances of brigandage and criminality among recruits drawn from the country at large. Some of the irregular cavalry units operating in border districts appear to have been composed largely of thugs.

Another type encountered with regrettable frequency was the loafer. Rebs of this species imposed on their messmates by seeking the lighter duties of cooking, bringing water and cutting wood. They evaded the hardships of campaigning by malingering. When the order came to march they would rush to the surgeon with some complaint calculated to secure assignment to "Company Q," as the sick list was called, so that they might ride the wagon train and be near the food supply. Some of them succeeded in being sent to infirmaries, and loafers once thus ensconced developed one chronic malady after another—though never quite sick enough to miss a meal—until their attachment to the hospital became more or less permanent. Those who thus evaded duty bore the opprobrious designation of "hospital rats," but they were so degenerate as to be utterly beyond shame.[96]

In happy contrast to these faithless wretches were a group who because of their selflessness and their exceptional devotion to duty were worthy to be called patriots. They consistently bore the hardships of camp without complaint; they insisted on taking their place in line of battle even when they were unwell and when their feet were without the protection of shoes; they were always present at roll call; they refused to seek promotion, and they manifested a cheerful spirit in defeat as well as in victory.

But all these were exceptional types. The average Rebel private belonged to no special category. He was in most respects an ordinary person. He came from a middle-class rural society, made up largely of non-slaveholders, and he exemplified both the defects and the virtues of that background. He was lacking in polish, in perspective and in tolerance, but he was respectable, sturdy and independent.

He was comparatively young, and more than likely unmarried. He went to war with a lightheartedness born of detachment and of faith in a swift victory. His morale wavered with the realization that the conflict was to be long and hard. He was nostalgic and war-weary. He felt the blighting hand of sickness, and it was then that his spirit sank to its lowest ebb. His craving for diversion caused him to turn to gambling and he indulged himself now and then in a bit of swearing. But his tendency to give way to such irregularities was likely to be curbed by his deep-seated conventionality or by religious revivals.

He complained of the shortcomings of officers, the scantiness of clothing, the inadequacy of rations, the multiplicity of pests and numerous other trials that beset him, but there was little depth to his complaints, and his cheerfulness outweighed his dejection. Adaptability and good-nature, in fact, were among his most characteristic qualities. He was a gregarious creature, and his attachment to close associates was genuine.

He had a streak of individuality and of irresponsibility that made him a trial to officers during periods of inactivity. But on the battlefield he rose to supreme heights of soldierhood. He was not immune to panic, nor even to cowardice, but few if any soldiers have had more than he of élan, of determination, of perseverance, and of the sheer courage which it takes to stand in the face of withering fire.

He was far from perfect, but his achievement against great odds in scores of desperate battles through four years of war is an irrefutable evidence of his prowess and an eternal monument to his greatness as a fighting man.

NOTES AND ACKNOWLEDGMENTS

ACKNOWLEDGMENTS

The author wishes to express appreciation to the following persons and firms for permission to reprint material as indicated:

D. Appleton-Century Company, New York, *Battles and Leaders of the Civil War*

Bobbs-Merrill Company, Indianapolis, *The Story of the Confederacy*, by Robert Selph Henry

Dietz Publishing Company, Richmond, Virginia, *Ham Chamberlayne— Virginian*, C. G. Chamberlayne, Editor

E. P. Dutton and Company, New York, *Scraps of Paper*, Marietta M. Andrews, Editor

Longmans, Green and Company, New York, *A Soldiers' Recollections*, by Randolph McKim

University of North Carolina Press, Chapel Hill, North Carolina, "The Diary of William Bartlett Malone," by W. W. Pierson (in vol. 16 of *James Sprunt Historical Publications*)

Yale University Press, New Haven, Connecticut, *Absolam Grimes, Confederate Mail Runner*, M. M. Quaife, Editor

Robert Laurence, New York, *Catalog of the George Walcott Collection of Used Civil War Patriotic Covers*, Robert Laurence, Compiler

Albert Shaw, Jr., New York, *Photographic History of the Civil War*, F. T. Miller, Editor

NOTES

Chapter I

OFF TO THE WAR

[1]Frank P. Peak, "A Southern Soldier's Views on the Civil War, 1860-1862," manuscript in private possession.

[2]Magnolia Plantation Record Book, manuscript, Southern Historical Collection, University of North Carolina. All U. N. C. manuscripts cited hereinafter are from this collection. I am indebted to the late U. B. Phillips for my first knowledge of the item quoted. Intersectional recrimination of the forties, fifties, and early sixties is brilliantly treated in Avery O. Craven's The Coming of the Civil War, (New York, 1942).

[3]A. T. Barclay, "The Liberty Hall Volunteers from Lexington to Manassas," Washington and Lee Historical Papers, No. 6 (Lynchburg, 1904), 124-127. P. A. Bruce, History of the University of Virginia (New York, 1921), III, 256-340.

[4]Diary of Duncan McCollum, entries for April and May 1861, manuscript in private possession.

[5]Arthur M. Shaw, Jr., Centenary College Goes to War (Shreveport, Louisiana, 1940), 6-7.

[6]J. B. Mitchell to his father, Feb. 23, 1862, typescript in Military Records Division of Alabama Department of Archives and History, Montgomery, Alabama.

[7]Dorothy Stanley, ed., Autobiography of Henry M. Stanley (New York, 1909), 165-166.

[8]Ibid., 140-220.

[9]Henry Graves to his mother, from camp near Wilmington, N. C., May 7, 1862, typescript, Georgia Archives.

[10]Ruffin Thomson to his father, Jan. 10, 1861, manuscript in private possession.

[11]Index of Local Organizations, manuscript, War Records Division, National Archives.

[12]New Orleans Daily Crescent, April 29, 1861.

[13]Ibid.

[14]Ibid., May 20, 1861.

[15]George Whitaker Wills to his sister, Sept. 10, 1861, manuscript, University of North Carolina.

[16][Napier Bartlett], A Soldier's Story of the War, Including the

Marches and Battles of the Washington Artillery (New Orleans, 1874), 16.

[17]*Ibid.,* 18 ff.

[18]O. T. Hanks, "Account of Civil War Experiences," 3, manuscript photostat, University of Texas.

[19]*Ibid.,* 3-4.

[20]*Ibid.,* 7 ff.

[21]W. W. Heartsill, *Fourteen Hundred and 91 Days in the Confederate Army* (Marshall, Texas, 1876), 4-5.

[22]*Ibid.,* 6 ff.

[23]The bandages were presented to the Second Company of Orleans Cadets by a committee of ladies from New Orleans. New Orleans *Daily Crescent,* May 9, 1861.

[24]Diary of A. L. P. Vairin, entries of May 5-9, 1861, manuscript, Mississippi. Archives; Thomas Caffey to his sister, May 7, 1861, "War Letters of Thomas Caffey," Montgomery *Advertiser,* March 28, 1909; Diary of James J. Kirkpatrick, 1861-1864, 4, manuscript, University of Texas.

[25]*Ibid.; Battle-Fields of the South* (London, 1863), I, 13-14; James J. Hall to his children, June 11, 1861, manuscript, University of North Carolina; *Official Records of the Union and Confederate Armies* (Washington, D. C., 1880-1901) ser. 1, LI, pt. 2, 114 (to be cited hereinafter as *O. R.*). Drinking seems to have been more universally indulged in while soldiers were en route to war than at any other time; for sample comments on this point, see: Charleston *Daily Courier,* August 24, 1861; Samuel E. Mays, compiler, *Genealogical Notes on the Family of Mays and Reminiscences of the War Between the States* (Plant City, Fla., 1927), 30-32; J. W. Reid, *History of the Fourth Regiment of South Carolina Volunteers* (Greenville, S. C., 1892), 11.

[26]J. E. Hall to his sister, May 31, 1861, manuscript, among Bolling Hall Papers in Manuscripts Division of Alabama Department of Archives and History.

[27]H. Browning to his sister and brother, Aug. 28, 1861, typescript among Crittenden Papers, University of Texas.

[28]J. B. Lance to his father, Nov. 10, 1861, manuscript, Louisiana State University.

[29]W. G. Evans to his brother "Faulk," July 25, 1861, manuscript, Evans Memorial Library, Aberdeen, Mississippi.

[30]Frank P. Peak, *op. cit.*

[31]Journal of W. R. Howell, entries of May 12, 13, 1861, manuscript, University of Texas.

[32]Manuscript, Mississippi Archives.

Chapter II

THE BAPTISM OF FIRE

[1]G. L. Robertson to his mother, Jan. 19, 1862, Robertson Letters, manuscript photostat, University of Texas.

[2]J. E. Hall to his father, July 1, 1861, manuscript, Alabama Archives.

[3]O. R., series 1, X, part 1, 465.

[4]G. L. Robertson to his mother, Jan. 19, 1862.

[5]Diary of E. D. Patterson, entry of May 6, 1862, typescript in private possession.

[6]New Orleans Daily Crescent, August 5, 1861, quoting Charleston Courier.

[7]S. G. Pryor to his wife, Oct. 5, 15, 1861, typescripts, Georgia Archives. Pryor was a lieutenant.

[8]William G. Stevenson, Thirteen Months in the Rebel Army (New York, 1864), 70-71. Of muskets collected after Gettysburg, 12,000 contained two charges, 6,000 had from two to ten unfired cartridges, and one was loaded with 23 charges rammed down one on top of the other. F. A. Shannon, Organization and Administration of the Union Army (Cleveland, 1928), I, 137.

[9]Robert M. Gill to his wife, May 21, 1862, manuscript in author's possession.

[10]George Baylor, Bull Run to Bull Run (Richmond, 1900), 21. A Mississippi captain wrote in 1864: "I have seen whole regiments and brigades deliver their fire when I was sure that they did not even wound a single man." Richmond Daily Dispatch, April 12, 1864.

[11]John L. G. Wood to his father, July 4, 1862, typescript in Georgia Archives.

[12]A. N. Erskine to his wife, June 28, 1862, manuscript, University of Texas; New Orleans Daily Crescent, Aug. 5, 1861, quoting Charleston Courier; T. C. DeLeon, Four Years in Rebel Capitals (Mobile, 1890), 130-131.

[13]Marcus D. Herring, "War Experiences," typescript in private possession.

[14]O. T. Hanks, "Account of Civil War Experiences," 33, manuscript photostat, University of Texas.

[15]W. A. Fletcher, Rebel Private Front and Rear (Beaumont, Texas, 1908), 20.

[16]John C. Jenkins to his aunt, Feb. 14, 1862, manuscript, Louisiana State University; S. G. Pryor to his wife, Oct. 4, 1861, typescript, Georgia Archives.

[17]A. N. Erskine to his wife, June 28, 1862.

[18]S. G. Pryor to his wife, May 18, 1862.

[19]Thomas Warrick to his wife, Jan. 11, 1863, manuscript, Alabama Archives.

[20]W. C. Athey to his sister, Sept. 29, 1863, manuscript, Alabama Archives.

[21]Manuscript, Confederate Memorial Hall, New Orleans.

[22]E. J. Ellis to his mother, Oct. 21, 1862, manuscript, Louisiana State University; O. R., series 1, XVI, part 1, 1117.

[23]Robert M. Gill to his wife, Aug. 16, 1864; J. W. Jones, Christ in Camp (Atlanta, 1904), 259.

[24]J. E. Hall to his sister, May 29, 1864.

[25]Diary of E. D. Patterson, entry of April 4, 1862.

[26]Henry Graves to his father, June 16, 1862, typescript, Georgia Archives.

[27]John T. Sibley to E. P. Ellis, March 10, 1863, manuscript, Louisiana State University.

Chapter III

BESETTING SINS

[1]O. R., series 1, XIX, part 2, 722.

[2]G. L. Robertson to his mother, Feb. 12, 1864, Robertson Letters, manuscript photostats, University of Texas.

[3]Diary of G. W. Roberts, entries of May 12, 27, 1864, manuscript, Mississippi Archives.

[4]T. C. Holliday to his brother, Dec. 13, 1863, manuscript in private possession.

[5]There are various samples of Confederate playing cards in the Confederate Museum at Richmond, and in the Keith M. Read Collection at Emory University. All Emory University items cited hereinafter are from the Keith M. Read Collection.

[6]Richmond Daily Dispatch, Jan. 5, 1863; R. E. Yerbey to his mother, Dec. 18, 1861, typescript, Georgia Archives; Thomas Warrick to his wife, Dec. 24, 1862, manuscript, Alabama Archives.

[7]A. E. Rentfrow to his sister, Feb. 11, 1862, manuscript, University of Texas.

[8]Manuscript among James Buckner Barry Papers, University of Texas.

[9]Theodore Gerrish and John S. Hutchinson, The Blue and the Gray (Bangor, Maine, 1884), 441; Richmond Daily Dispatch, Nov. 13, 1861; Sam R. Watkins, Company Aytch, Maury Grays, First Tennessee Regi-

ment (Chattanooga, 1900), 46; Diary of Harry St. John Dixon, entry
of June 16, 1864, manuscript, University of North Carolina.

10[Napier Bartlett], op. cit., 24.

11W. J. Worsham, The Old Nineteenth Tennessee Regiment,
C.S.A. (Knoxville, 1902), 62, 185; John C. West, A Texan in Search
of a Fight (Waco, Texas, 1901), 103-104.

12Henry Kyd Douglas, I Rode with Stonewall (Chapel Hill, North
Carolina, 1940), 197.

13Ruffin Thomson to his mother, Dec. 1, 1862, manuscript in private possession.

14Samuel Hankins, Simple Story of a Soldier (Nashville, no date),
11-13.

15Theodore Gerrish and John S. Hutchinson, op. cit., 305.

16Romans 11:33.

17Jones, op. cit., 267, 268.

18Clipping from newspaper scrapbook in Alabama Archives.

19O. R., series 4, I, 834-835.

20Jones, op. cit., 268. Bragg wrote President Davis on Dec. 1, 1863:
"The warfare has been carried on successfully, and the fruits are bitter.
You must make other changes here, or our success is hopeless. Breckin-
ridge was totally unfit for any duty from the 23d to the 27th—during all
our trials—from drunkenness. The same cause prevented our complete
triumph at Murfreesborough. I can bear to be sacrificed myself, but not
to see my country and my friends ruined by the vices of a few profligate
men who happen to have an undue popularity. General Hardee will
assure you that Cheatham is equally dangerous." O. R., series 1, LII,
part 2, 745. A similar intimation is contained in correspondent "Sallust's" communication of Dec. 2, 1863, to the Richmond Dispatch
(issue of Dec. 11). "You will be surprised and mortified to learn," he
wrote, "that this army is not free from the vice of intemperance. I refer
to the painful subject here merely to warn those officers who are guilty
of this abominable offense that, if I forbear for the present to publish
their names, it is only to give them an opportunity to reform their habits,
and do their duty. If they persist in their criminal courses no power on
earth shall prevent their exposure, if life be vouchsafed to me and you
will print my letters."

21Quoted in New Orleans Daily Crescent, Feb. 7, 1862.

22Diary of A. L. P. Vairin, entries of Nov. 27-30, 1862, manuscript.
Mississippi Archives; Diary of Robert E. Jones, entry of Nov. 8, 1863,
typescript in private possession; O. R., series 1, XLV, part 1, 1259, re-
port of Capt. Wm. A. Reid, to Col. E. J. Harvie, Inspector General,
Army of Tennessee, Nov. 29, 1864; Henry Bryan to Gen. L. McLaws,
March 28, 1861 [1862], manuscript, Heartman Collection; John Crit-

tenden to his wife, Feb. 13, 1864, typescript, University of Texas; C. W. Stephens to his father Jan. 21, 1864, manuscript in private possession.

[23]Mobile *Daily Advertiser & Register*, Feb. 4, 1864, quoting Augusta *Chronicle and Sentinel.*

[24]John Brynam to Thomas Morris, March 22, 1862, manuscript, Louisiana State University.

[25]New Orleans *Daily Crescent*, Sept. 26, 1861, correspondence of Israel Gibbons.

[26]*Confederate Veteran*, V (1897), 276.

[27]Stevenson, *op. cit.*, 46-47.

[28]Quoted by the *Army and Navy Herald*, Oct. 15, 1863.

[29]Anonymous diary of a Louisiana soldier, entry of Oct. 3, 1862, manuscript in Heartman Collection; New Orleans *Daily Picayune*, Aug. 7, 1861; diary of D. P. Hopkins, entry of April 12, 1862, typescript, University of Texas; Daily Richmond *Enquirer*, Sept. 17, 1864; Eppa Hunton, *Autobiography* (Richmond, Va., 1933), 55-56.

[30]O. R., series 1, XI, part 3, 526.

[31]See letter of Marcus D. Herring to editor of Jackson (Mississippi) *Clarion Ledger*, [undated but evidently May 1927], in scrapbook of Marcus D. Herring. This item is in private possession.

[32]V. S. Rabb to his brother, Jan. 4, 1863, manuscript photostat, University of Texas.

[33]Robert Fore to James Reding, Jan. 2, 1863, manuscript, University of Texas.

[34]Letter of Robert M. Gill, manuscript in author's possession.

[35]O. R., series 1, XLV, part 1, 1255; part 2, 783; LI, part 2, 222, General Order No. 57; Richmond *Daily Dispatch*, Feb. 8, 1865.

[36]O. R., series 1, XXXI, part 3, 622; XXXII, part 2, 622-623; XXXIV, part 2, 942-943; XLIV, 412; XLV, part 2, 688-689, 798-799; XLIX, part 1, 1010-1011; part 2, 1124-1125; and series 4, II, 289, 1061; III, 763.

[37]William W. Christian to Carrie Harmon, April 27, 1861, manuscript, Duke University; Frank Richardson to his sister, Dec. 6, 1861, manuscript, University of North Carolina; Edwin Tillinghast to his sister, Aug. 24, 1863, manuscript, Emory University; J. P. Cannon, *Inside of Rebeldom* (Washington, D. C., 1900), 163.

[38]Diary of W. S. Rinaldi, entry of June 1, 1862; O. R., series 1, XX, part 1, 726.

[39]Baylor, *op. cit.*, 179.

[40]William R. Stillwell to his wife, July 8, 1864, manuscript, Georgia Archives.

[41]W. C. McClellan to his sister, July 9, 1863, manuscript in private possession.

[42]Diary of J. B. Clifton, entry of June 28, 1863, typescript, North Carolina Historical Commission.

[43]William N. Berkeley to his wife, June 27, 28, 1863, manuscript, University of Virginia.

[44]Thomas F. Boatwright to his wife, July 9, 1863, manuscript, University of North Carolina.

[45]Adrian Carruth to his sister, Aug. 4, 1863, manuscript in private possession. There were, of course, a great number of instances of soldiers eschewing profanity because of religious conversion, and for other reasons. H. A. Stephens wrote his sister Nov. 22, 1863, "I have quit cursing and taken up smokeing. I find that it is of benefit to me or I would not do it. tell Ma I will quit it when the war is over." Manuscript in private possession.

[46]Confidential letter dated May 2, 1863, typescript in private possession; the chaplain of a Tennessee regiment wrote in 1864 that he had heard more cursing in twenty-four hours in the army than he had heard in all his prior life. "The air, indeed, is so filled with profanity," he said, "that it seems to swear without a tongue." Joseph Cross, Camp and Field (Macon, 1864), Book I.

[47]Brig. Gen. William Nelson, Commanding Fourth Division U.S. Troops, in his official report of Shiloh said: "The men lay upon their arms. Lieutenant Gwin, of the Navy, commanding the gunboats in the river, sent to me and asked how he could be of service. I requested that he would throw an 8-inch shell into the camp of the enemy every ten minutes during the night, and thus prevent their sleeping, which he did very scientifically, and, according to the report of the prisoners, to their infinite annoyance." O. R., series 1, X, part 1, 324.

[48]See Robert M. Gill to his wife, June 10, 14, and July 25, 1864. Gill was a lieutenant at the time these letters were written.

[49]General Orders, Department of South Carolina, Georgia, and Florida, Confederate Archives, chapter II, volume 42, p. 57 and volume 43, pp. 137-138, manuscript, National Archives.

[50]William R. Barksdale to his brother, June 11, 1861, manuscript in private possession; Harry St. John Dixon of the 28th Mississippi Cavalry wrote in his diary March 21, 1864; "Oh! if I could see the little girl this morning instead of . . . listening . . . to boisterous laughter over obscene brutal jokes." Manuscript, University of North Carolina.

[51]Orville C. Bumpass to his wife, Sept. 18, 1864, and March 2, 1865, manuscripts, Evans Memorial Library.

[52]For example, see J. M. Jordan to his wife, Dec. 17, 1863, typescript, Georgia Archives.

[53]E. P. Becton to his wife, Oct. 26, 1862, manuscript photostat, University of Texas.

[54]J. M. Jordan to his wife, Feb. 8, 1864.

[55]New Orleans *Daily Crescent*, Jan. 8, 1862.

[56]General Order, dated Sept. 1, 1862, Headquarters of Heavy Artillery, Vicksburg, Mississippi, document in Heartman Collection. Army Regulations permitted each company to have four laundresses, but required that they furnish certificates of good character. J. W. Randolph, editor, *Confederate States Army Regulations, 1863* (Richmond, 1863), 12, 77.

[57]W. C. McClellan to his sister, March 16, 1863, manuscript in private possession.

[58]S. A. Boston of a Virginia regiment wrote to his sister June 24, 1861, concerning the "Louisiana Tigers": "A woman dressed in the same uniform [striped male attire] is one of their Lieutenants & two other girls act as markers. Of course they are women of no standing." Manuscript in private possession. Colonel Arthur Fremantle said that a nice-looking woman was pointed out to him on the train between Chattanooga and Atlanta in June 1863, who had fought as a private soldier at Perryville and Murfreesboro. "Several men in my car had served with her," he added, "and they said she had been turned out a short time since for her bad and immoral conduct. They told me that her sex was notorious to all the regiment, but no notice had been taken of it as long as she conducted herself properly." Arthur J. Fremantle, *Three Months in the Southern States* (London, 1863), 173.

[59]Manuscripts from confidential sources.

[60]Army of Tennessee, Letters, Orders, and Indorsements, Confederate Archives, chapter II, volume 15½, pp. 142-143, manuscript, National Archives.

[61]Richmond *Daily Dispatch*, May 6, 1862.

[62]*Ibid.*, May 18, 1862.

[63]Daily Richmond *Enquirer*, Aug. 22, 1864.

[64]Richmond *Enquirer*, Nov. 6, 1863 (semiweekly edition).

[65]Manuscript, Mississippi Archives.

[66]Letter of Oct. 22, 1864, manuscript, Evans Memorial Library.

[67]George M. Deckerd to "Rehum," manuscript photostat among Reding Papers, University of Texas.

[68]Wirt A. Cate, editor, *Two Soldiers* (Chapel Hill, 1938), 20-21.

[69]Letter of June 6, 1863, typescript in possession of Prof. Glover Moore, Mississippi State College.

[70]These reports covering sixty-two regiments are filed with Confederate Regimental Records in the War Records Division of the National Archives.

[71]Letter of June 11, 1861, manuscript in private possession.

[72]Daily Richmond *Examiner*, Dec. 5, 1862.

[73]Letter to his wife, Oct. 22, 1864, manuscript, Evans Memorial Library.

[74]Diary of L. G. Hutton, entry of Nov. 9, 1862, manuscript, University of Texas.

[75]Undated letter of J. M. Guess, manuscript in Miscellaneous Collection, Confederate Memorial Hall, New Orleans.

Chapter IV

IN WINTER QUARTERS

[1]New Orleans *Daily Crescent*, Feb. 14, 1862.

[2]O. R., series 1, V, 941-942, 951, 1014; XLII, part 2, 1261.

[3]Cavalrymen rarely built huts, as the nature of their duties required frequent moving about even in winter, and their greater mobility made it possible for them to disperse themselves to such an extent as to procure accommodations from civilians. Gen. Will T. Martin wrote to his sister Jan. 31, 1863, from Morristown, Tenn.: "The infantry is all in winter quarters. The cavalry in our army never goes into winter quarters." Typescript in private possession.

[4]G. L. Robertson to his mother, Jan. 4, 1862, manuscript photostat, University of Texas. In some instances the hut's walls were built by driving timbers into the ground after the fashion of a stockade. George Whitaker Wills to his sister, Nov. 19, 1862, manuscript, University of North Carolina.

[5]William M. Owen, *In Camp and Battle With the Washington Artillery* (Boston, 1885), 68-69.

[6]Montgomery *Daily Mail*, Feb. 17, 1863.

[7]G. L. Robertson to his mother, Jan. 4, Feb. 12, 1862.

[8]William R. Stillwell to his wife, March 7, 1863, manuscript, Georgia Archives.

[9]Thomas Caffey to his sister, Dec. 19, 1861, in "War Letters of Thomas Caffey," Montgomery *Advertiser*, April 9, 1909; diary of James J. Kirkpatrick, entry of Dec. 18, 1861, manuscript, University of Texas.

[10]Theodore Mandeville to his sister, Jan. 3, 1862, manuscript, Louisiana State University.

[11]New Orleans *Daily Crescent*, Dec. 11, 1861, correspondence of I[srael] G[ibbons].

[12]Peak, *op. cit.*; Theodore Mandeville to his sister, Jan. 3, 1862.

[13]New Orleans *Daily Crescent*, Dec. 11, 1861, correspondence of I[srael] G[ibbons].

[14]J. E. Hall to his brother, Bolling Hall, Jan. 28, 1865, manuscript, Alabama Archives.

[15]Hanks, *op. cit.*, 120.

[16]Carlton McCarthy, *Detailed Minutiae of Soldier Life in the Army of Northern Virginia 1861-1865* (Richmond, 1882), 87, 89.

[17]Diary of James J. Kirkpatrick, entries of Feb. 19, March 23, 1864; G. L. Robertson to his sister, Jan. 15, 1862, manuscript photostat, University of Texas.

[18]C. Irvine Walker to Ada Sinclair, April 15, 1864, typescript, University of Texas.

[19]T. B. Hampton to his wife, March 24, 1864, typescript, University of Texas.

[20]William R. Stillwell to his wife, Feb. 17, 1863.

[21]Diary of T. Otis Baker, entry of March 22, 1864, manuscript, Mississippi Archives.

[22]Journal of E. Mussence, entry of March 31, [1863?], manuscript fragment among Washington Artillery Papers, Confederate Memorial Hall, New Orleans.

[23]O. L. Barnett to his family, April 4, 1864, manuscript, Emory University.

[24]Grant D. Carter to his sister, March 24, 1864, typescript, Georgia Archives.

[25]Hanks, *op. cit.*, 120-121.

[26]Diary of Charles Moore, manuscript, Confederate Memorial Hall, New Orleans.

[27]*Ibid.*, entries of Feb. 28-April 28, 1863.

Chapter V

HEROES AND COWARDS

[1] O. R., series 1, X, part 2, 389.

[2]Forty rounds was evidently the capacity of an ordinary cartridge box. After the battle of Gettysburg the War Department sent out a circular to army and departmental commanders enjoining the practice, except on special order of the general commanding, of issuing on the eve of battle twenty rounds of ammunition, "over and above the capacity of the cartridge boxes." O. R., series 1, XXVII, part 3, 1091.

[3]This summary of pre-battle instructions is derived from various sources. For examples, see O. R., series 1, X, part 2, 325-326, 535, and XI, part 3, 410-411. State pride was sometimes appealed to in these addresses. George Whitaker Wills to his sister, June 28, 1862, manuscript, University of North Carolina. General T. C. Hindman sought on one occasion to invoke hatred of the enemy as a pre-battle conditioner: "Remember that the enemy you engage has no feeling of mercy," he

said. "His ranks are made up of Pin Indians, Free Negroes, Southern Tories, Kansas Jayhawkers, and hired Dutch cutthroats. These bloody ruffians have invaded your country, stolen and destroyed your property, murdered your neighbors, outraged your women, driven your children from their homes, and defiled the graves of your kindred." Broadside, dated Dec. 4, 1862, Emory University.

[4]T. W. Montfort wrote to his wife from Ft. Pulaski, April 5, 1862: "There is something sad and melancholy in the preparation for Battle. To see so many healthy men prepareing for the worst by disposing of their property by will—to see the surgeon sharping his instruments & whetting his saw . . . men engaged in carding up & prepareing lint to stop the flow of human blood." Typescript, Georgia Archives.

[5]Journal of William P. Chambers, entry of May 18, 1864, Mississippi Historical Society Publications, Centenary Series, V, 321. This source will be cited hereinafter as P.M.H.S.

[6]Robert M. Gill wrote to his wife from line of battle in Georgia, June 23, 1864: "I saw a canteen upon which a heavy run was made during and after the charge—I still like whisky but I do not want any when going into action for I am or at least was drunk enough yesterday without drinking a drop." Manuscript in author's possession.

[7]J. H. Belo, Memoirs (Boston, 1904), 40.

[8]For example, see O. R., series 1, XXX, part 2, 237.

[9]O. R., series 1, XXI, 664. A Virginia veteran attributed the greater resonance of the Southern battle cry to the rural background of most Confederates. In isolated areas, he said, hallooing was a necessary means of communication, while in the cities and towns from which a substantial portion of Yankees came, there was hardly ever an occasion for shouting. In comparing the sounds of the two yells, he said that the Federal cheer was a repeated "hoo-ray," with prolonged emphasis on the second syllable, while the Confederate cry was a series of "woh-who—eys" with a heavy subsiding accent on the blended "who" and "ey," the effect being a sort of "whee." J. Harvey Dew, "The Yankee and Rebel Yells," Century Magazine, XLIII (1892), 953-955. Other veterans referred to the Yankee shout as a practiced "hurrah," or a concerted "hip, hip, huzza, huzza, huzza," and to the Rebel Yell as a "yai, yai, yi, yai, yi," but nearly all stress the individual informal quality of the latter. W. H. Morgan, Personal Reminiscences of the War of 1861-1865 (Lynchburg, 1911), 70; A. P. Ford, Life in the Confederate Army (New York, 1905), 58. Douglas Freeman told the writer in an interview that the Confederate cheer was a battle-field adaptation of the fox hunter's cry, which cry the Richmond News Leader designated in the Aug. 17, 1936, issue as a wild "y-yo yo-wo-wo." The writer leans toward the theory that the "who-ey" version was the one most commonly used.

[10]Journal of William P. Chambers, entry of Aug. 4, 1864, *P.M.H.S.*, Centenary Series, V, 332.

[11]*O. R.*, series 1, XXXVIII, part 3, 922.

[12]For example, see *ibid.*, series 1, XXXIV, part 1, 752.

[13]*Ibid.*, series 1, XXXIV, part 1, 849.

[14]Robert M. Gill to his wife, July 28, 1864.

[15]*O. R.*, series 1, X, part 1, 583; XXXVI, part 1, 1093-1094.

[16]Morgan, *op. cit.*, 200; E. D. Patterson, in his diary entry of June 28, 1862, says that at Gaines's Mill when he and his comrade went over a ridge they encountered such heavy fire "that the whole brigade literally *staggered* backward several paces as though pushed back by a tornado." Typescript in private possession.

[17]*O. R.*, series 1, XXXVI, part 1, 1093-1094, General Samuel McGowan's report of the "Bloody Angle" phase of Spottsylvania Court House; McGowan says further that a 22-inch oak tree was cut down by the heavy musket fire, injuring several soldiers when it fell. *Ibid.*

[18]John L. G. Wood to his aunt, May 10, 1863, typescript, Georgia Archives; Robert M. Gill to his wife, Oct. 6, 1863; diary of Maurice K. Simons, entry of May 31, 1863, manuscript photostat, University of Texas.

[19]*O. R.*, series 1, XXX, part 2, 305, Gen. T. C. Hindman's official report of Chickamauga; XXXIX, part 1, 821, Maj. E. H. Hampton's report of Allatoona; XXXI, part 2, 726, 750-757, Gen. John C. Brown's and Gen. P. R. Cleburne's reports of Lookout Mountain; XXVII, part 2, 486-487, Maj. Samuel Tate to Gov. Z. B. Vance, July 8, 1863, concerning Gettysburg; A. C. Redwood, "Jackson's Foot Cavalry at the Second Bull Run," *Battles and Leaders of the Civil War* (New York, 1887-1888), II, 535-536; Walter Clark, editor, *North Carolina Regiments, 1861-1865* (Raleigh and Goldsboro, 1901), II, 376.

[20]*O. R.*, series 1, XXXVIII, part 3, 689.

[21]For condition of troops before and during the Shiloh fight see *O. R.*, series 1, X, part 1, 454, 464, 498, 499, 522, 547, 569-570, 586; and XVII, part 2, 641.

[22]A young Georgian, writing of his experience at Manassas, said, "As we were retiring I stopped to take a mouthful of mud—scarcely could it be called water—my mouth was awfully hot and dry." *New Orleans Daily Crescent*, Aug. 8, 1861.

[23]Thomas Warrick to his wife, Jan. 11-13, 1863, manuscript, Alabama Archives.

[24][Bartlett], *op. cit.*, 192-193.

[25]For instances of scattering of regiments under fire, see *O. R.*, series 1, X, part 1, 467, 584; XXV, part 1, 984-985; LI, part 2, 199. Also John Crittenden to J. S. Bryant, Jan. 29, 1863, typescript, University of Texas; and J. E. Hall to his father, June 3, 1862, manuscript, Alabama Archives.

[26]Heartsill, op. cit., 159; Hanks, op. cit., 29, manuscript photostat, University of Texas; Henry L. Graves to his aunt, Aug. 7, 1862, typescript, Georgia Archives; G. A. Hanson, Minor Incidents of the Late War (Bartow, Florida, 1887), 36; O. R., series 1, XXX, part 2, 418.

[27]J. W. Rabb to his mother, Jan. 14, 1863, manuscript photostat, University of Texas.

[28]John L. G. Wood to his wife, Dec. 18, 1862, typescript, Georgia Archives.

[29]Robert Stiles, Four Years Under Marse Robert (New York, 1903), 219-220.

[30]Harmon Martin to his sister, Aug. 25, 1863, typescript, Georgia Archives.

[31]George W. Athey to his sister, (no date, but Dec., 1864), manuscript, Alabama Archives.

[32]Hanks, op. cit., 35.

[33]Diary of E. D. Patterson, entry of June 2, 1862.

[34]O. R., series 1, XX, part 1, 957; M. D. Martin to his parents, May 8, 1863, typescript in private possession.

[35]James Mabley to his sister, May 16, 1863, manuscript, Emory University.

[36]Harry Gilmor, Four Years in the Saddle (New York, 1866), 141.

[37]Diary of E. D. Patterson, entry of Aug. 31, 1863.

[38]Stiles, op. cit., 116-117.

[39]O. R., series 1, XII, part 2, 736; W. W. Heartsill, op. cit., 159; Robert M. Gill to his wife, July 25, 1864.

[40]Diary of Maurice K. Simons, various entries, May 17-July 3, 1863.

[41]Ibid. River water next to the east bank became contaminated with maggots from the great number of dead animals thrown in, and cisterns were either polluted or exhausted. O. R., series 1, XXIV, part 2, 392.

[42]Diary of Maurice K. Simons, entry of June 13, 1863.

[43]Ibid., entries of May 27, 31, 1863.

[44]Diary of James J. Kirkpatrick, entry of Aug. 5, 1864; Robert M. Gill to his wife, July 9, Aug. 16, 1864; Bolling Hall to his sister, Laura, Sept. 20, 1864, manuscript, Alabama Archives.

[45]Crenshaw Hall to his father, Oct. 16, 1864, manuscript, Alabama Archives.

[46]Crenshaw Hall to Laura Hall, Feb. 20, 1865. A Virginia officer charged with building a redoubt on the Petersburg line kept a man posted to call out the Yankee shots. At each flash of their guns he would call out "down" and the men would fall flat in the trench. The Federals got on to the trick and resorted to the device of setting off a blaze of powder to deceive the Rebs, and then giving them the real load as they rose up from their shelter. C. G. Chamberlayne, editor, Ham Chamberlayne—Virginian (Richmond, 1932), 267-268.

[47]J. E. Hall to Laura Hall, Oct. 15, 1864, Feb. 8, 1865; Crenshaw Hall to Laura Hall, Feb. 20, 1865.

[48]O. R., series 1, X, part 1, 589; XI, part 1, 950.

[49]Ibid., XX, part 1, 730, 747, 867.

[50]Ibid., XII, part 2, 593; XXX, part 2, 379.

[51]Ibid., XXX, part 2, 190, 379-380.

[52]Ibid., XXV, part 1, 1003.

[53]Ibid., XI, part 1, 950; XIX, part 1, 933; Clark, op. cit., II, 350-354.

[54]Ibid., XVII, part 1, 400; XIX, part 1, 875.

[55]Ibid., XX, part 1, 719, 852.

[56]Ibid., 931.

[57]Ibid., X, part 2, 528; XI, part 2, 992-993; XX, part 2, 494; Robert Ames Jarman, "History of Co. K, 27th Mississippi Infantry," 10, typescript in private possession.

[58]James A. McCord to his brother, Dec. 3, 1864, manuscript photostat in private possession.

[59]O. R., series 1, XXVIII, part 1, 418-419, 524.

[60]Mays, op. cit., 36; O. R., series 1, XI, part 2, 563, 612; part 3, 506, 571.

[61]O. R., series 1, X, part 1, 391, 432, 571-572, 576-577. For other evidences of reprehensible conduct under fire at Shiloh see ibid., 401, 501, 507, 546, 570, 589.

[62]Ibid., XX, part 1, 761, 879.

[63]Ibid., XXIV, part 2, 88.

[64]Anonymous diary of a Louisiana soldier, entry of Nov. 25, 1863, manuscript, Confederate Memorial Hall, New Orleans.

[65]O. R., series 1, XXXI, part 2, 665-666; see also Bate's General Order of Nov. 28, 1863, ibid., 744. News correspondent "Sallust" wrote from a point near the battlefield at midnight of November 25: "The Confederates have sustained today the most ignominious defeat of the whole war—a defeat for which there is but little excuse or palliation. For the first time during our struggle for national independence, our defeat is chargeable to the troops themselves and not to the blunder or incompetency of their leaders. It is difficult for one to realize how a defeat so complete could have occurred on ground so favorable." Richmond Daily Disptach, Dec. 4, 1863.

[66]Stephen Ramseur to his wife, July 23, Aug. 3, 1864, manuscript, University of North Carolina.

[67]Pulaski Cowper, compiler, Extracts of Letters of Maj. Gen. Bryan Grimes (Raleigh, 1883), 69-70.

[68]G. P. Ring to "My own Darling," Sept. 21, 1864, manuscript, Confederate Memorial Hall, New Orleans. General Grimes also mentions the pleading of the women. Cowper, op. cit., p. 70.

[69]Cowper, op. cit., 77-78; O. R., series 1, XLIII, part 1, 598-600; R.

W. Waldrop to his father, Oct. 21, 1864, manuscript, University of North Carolina.

[70]O. R., series 1, XLI, part 1, 637, official report of General Price.

[71]*Ibid.*, XXXVIII, part 3, 835; part 4, 766-767.

[72]*Ibid.*, XLV, part 1, 660, 747, 749, 750.

[73]Cate, *op. cit.*, 169.

[74]Fletcher, *op. cit.*, 84.

[75]C. Irvine Walker to Ada Sinclair, July 28, 1864, typescript, University of Texas.

[76]Stiles, *op. cit.*, 135.

[77]O. R., series 1, XXX, part 2, 183-184; part 4, 715.

[78]*Ibid.*, LI, part 1, 273; William R. Stillwell to his wife, May 2-3, 1863, manuscript, Georgia Archives; Thomas Caffey to his sister, Feb. 16, 1863, "War Letters of Thomas Caffey," Montgomery *Advertiser*, April 25, 1909.

[79]For example, see Fletcher, *op. cit.*, 84.

Chapter VI

BAD BEEF AND CORN BREAD

[1]Jerome Yates to "T. O. D.," Jan. 18, 1864, manuscript, Heartman Collection.

[2]O. R., series 1, X, part 2, 571. The prescribed ration, taken from the 1857 U. S. Army Regulations, was: "Three-fourths of a pound of pork or bacon, or one and a fourth pounds of fresh or salt beef; eighteen ounces of bread or flour, or twelve ounces of hard bread, or one and a fourth pounds of corn bread, or one and a fourth pounds of corn meal; and at the rate, to one hundred rations, of eight quarts of peas or beans, or in lieu thereof, ten pounds of rice; six pounds coffee; twelve pounds sugar; four quarts of vinegar . . . and two quarts of salt." J. W. Randolph, editor, *Confederate States Army Regulations*, 1861 (Richmond, 1861), article 42, paragraph 1069, p. 140.

[3]Fred R. Taber to Lillie Trust, Sept. 12, 1861, manuscript, Louisiana State University.

[4]Theodore Mandeville to Rebecca Mandeville, Dec. 29, 1861, manuscript, Louisiana State University.

[5]O. R., series 1, LII, part 2, 204. It was about this time also that Beauregard wrote Davis, "The want of food & transportation has made us lose all the fruits of our victory." Quoted in Beauregard to Davis, Aug. 10, 1861, manuscript, Duke University.

[6]O. R., series 4, I, 872.

[7]Diary of Charles Moore, entries of Sept. 14, 17, 18, 1861, manuscript, Confederate Memorial Hall, New Orleans.

[8]O. R., series 4, I, 887-889.

[9]New Orleans Daily Crescent, Jan. 23, 1862, correspondence of I[srael] G[ibbons], quartermaster, Kennedy's Battalion.

[10]O. R., series 1, XIX, part 2, 716.

[11]Ibid., series 1, X, part 2, 530-531, 571; XIX, part 2, 716; XXI, 1016; Order Book for Crescent Regiment, manuscript, Confederate Memorial Hall.

[12]O. R., XXI, 1110-1111; XXV, part 2, 687-688; Confederate States Army Regulations, 1863, article 42.

[13]O. R., series 1, XXIV, part 3, 1055-1056.

[14]Ibid., series 4, III, 930-932.

[15]Ibid.

[16]Ibid., series 1, VII, 334.

[17]John A. Johnson to Ella Arnold, May 18, 1862, typescript in private possession; C. C. Blacknall to his wife, May 18, 1862, manuscript, North Carolina Historical Commission; O. R., series 1, XI, part 1, 408-409, 605-606; Ruffin Thomson to his father, May 24, 1862, manuscript in private possession.

[18]Grant D. Carter to his mother, July 4, 1862, typescript, Georgia Archives.

[19]William R. Stillwell to his wife, Sept. 18, 1862, manuscript, Georgia Archives.

[20]Diary of T. J. Ford, entry of Sept. 22, 1862, manuscript, Heartman Collection.

[21]Joseph Singleton to his parents, Nov. 11, 1862, manuscript, Richard D. White Collection, North Carolina Historical Commission. The parodied allusion to hardness of service with Jackson went the rounds of the army in devious forms. A full and popular version was this: "Man that is born of a woman, and enlisteth in Jackson's army, is of few days and short rations. He cometh forth at reveille, is present also at retreat, and retireth apparently at taps. When, lo! he striketh a beeline for the nearest hen-roost, from which he taketh sundry chickens, and stealthily returneth to his camp. He then maketh a savory dish, therewith he feasteth himself and a chosen friend. But the Captain sleepeth, and knoweth not that his men are feasting." Royall W. Figg, Where Men Only Dare to Go: Story of a Boy Company (Richmond, 1885), 64.

[22]Diary of George W. Jones, entry of Oct. 20, 1862, typescript in private possession.

[23]Postwar addition by C. Irvine Walker to a letter that he wrote to his bethrothed, Ada Sinclair, Sept. 30, 1862, typescript, University of Texas.

[24]Journal of William P. Chambers, *P. M. H. S.*, Centenary Series, V, 279-280; Ephraim Anderson, *Memoirs* (St. Louis, 1868), 337-338; *O. R.*, series 1, XXIV, part 2, 392; part 3, 983.

[25]Diary of Major Maurice K. Simons, entry of July 3, 1863, manuscript photostat, University of Texas.

[26]*Ibid.*, entries of June 3-July 5, 1863; *O. R.*, series 1, XXIV, part 1, 278-279; Winchester Hall, *The Twenty-sixth Louisiana Infantry* (no place, 1890?), 89-90; E. L. Drake, editor, *Annals of the Army of Tennessee*, I (1878), 106.

[27]Journal of William P. Chambers, *P. M. H. S.*, Centenary Series, V, 279-280; J. W. Westbrook, "Reminiscences," 5-6, typescript, University of Texas.

[28]Diary of Maurice K. Simons, entry of July 4. While the soldiers were eating mule meat, there were 38,241 pounds of bacon and 427 pounds of salt pork stored away in commissary depots; this had been held in reserve for use in the event of a movement to break the siege. *O. R.*, series 1, XXIV, part 3, 987.

[29]Diary of R. L. McClung, 29, typescript, University of Texas. The portion of this document prior to November 1863 is in reminiscent rather than diary form. An officer who escaped from Port Hudson while capitulation was being arranged testified immediately afterward: "About the 29th or 30th of June, the garrison's supply of meat gave out, when General Gardner ordered the mules to be butchered, after ascertaining that the men were willing to eat them. . . . The men received their unusual rations cheerfully. . . . Many of them, as if in mockery of famine, caught rats and ate them, declaring that they were better than squirrel." Richmond *Daily Dispatch*, July 23, 1863, quoting Mobile *Advertiser*. D. P. Smith in his *History of Company K, First Alabama Regiment* (Prattsville, Alabama, 1885), 76-77, testifies to the use of both mule and rat meat at Port Hudson.

[30]Anonymous diary of a Louisiana soldier, manuscript, Confederate Memorial Hall.

[31]John Crittenden to his wife, June 28, 1864, typescript, University of Texas.

[32]T. B. Hampton to his wife, Aug. 10, 1864, typescript, University of Texas.

[33]Cowper, *op. cit.*, 58.

[34]Stuart Noblin, "Leonidas Lafayette Polk" (Ph.D. thesis in progress, University of North Carolina), chapter 3.

[35]See Moss-Barmore-Colclough-Rentfrow correspondence, 1862-1864, and diary of M. W. Barber, manuscripts, University of Texas; also *O. R.*, series 1, XLI, part 4, 1071-1073.

[36]Thomas Warrick to his wife, Nov. 13, 1863, manuscript, Alabama Archives; *O. R.*, series 1, XLV, part 1, 736.

[37]O. R., series 1, XLVI, part 1, 382; part 2, 1074-1075.

[38]McCarthy, op. cit., 57.

[39]Ibid., 128; Douglas, op. cit., 331.

[40]B. I. Wiley, Southern Negroes 1861-1865 (New Haven, 1938), 44-62.

[41]William Watson, Life in the Confederate Army (London, 1887), 164-166.

[42]Douglas S. Freeman, R. E. Lee (New York, 1934), II, 494-495.

[43]Wiley, op. cit., 48; Charles W. Ramsdell, "The Confederate Government and the Railroads," American Historical Review, XXII (1917), 809-810.

[44]Frank Moss to his sister, Oct. 7, 1862, manuscript, University of Texas.

[45]Adrian Carruth to his sister, June 5, 1863, manuscript in private possession; Johnny C. Murray to "Sig," March 28, 1865, manuscript, Confederate Memorial Hall.

[46]William R. Stillwell to his wife, May 13, 1863.

[47]Frank Moss to his sister, Dec. 7, 1864.

[48]Hanks, op. cit., 81, manuscript photostat, University of Texas.

[49]P. L. Dodgen to his wife, May 17, 1863, typescript, Georgia Archives.

[50]Adrian Carruth to his sister, March 4, 1863.

[51]W. M. Moss to "Mrs. R.," Dec. 28, 1863, manuscript, University of Texas; C. W. Stephens to his father, Jan. 5, 1864, manuscript in private possession; T. B. Hampton to his wife, Jan. 1, 1863.

[52]William R. Stillwell to his wife, March 4, 1863; Thomas Caffey to "Mary," Jan. 15, 1864, "War Letters of Thomas Caffey," Montgomery Advertiser, May 9, 1909.

[53]E. J. Ellis to his father, Oct. 12, 1861, manuscript, Louisiana State University.

[54]W. C. Athey to his sister, manuscript, Alabama Archives.

[55]William H. Phillips to his parents, Aug. 3, 1861, manuscript, Duke University.

[56]John Crittenden to his wife, May 3, 1863, and March 31, 1864.

[57]T. B. Hampton to his wife, March 14, 1865.

[58]George W. Athey to his wife, Nov. 11, 1863, manuscript, Alabama Archives.

[59]T. B. Hampton to his wife, May 29, 1864.

[60]Diary of James J. Kirkpatrick, entry of Dec. 18, 1861, manuscript, University of Texas.

[61]Richmond Daily Dispatch, Dec. 21, 1861.

[62]Ephraim Anderson, op. cit., 213-214.

[63]Diary of James J. Kirkpatrick, entries of Nov. 1, Dec. 24, 1863. Confederate Army Regulations of 1862 prohibited sutlers selling on

credit to enlisted men to an amount exceeding one-third of monthly wages without written permission of post commandants; and with such permission the amount of credit was not to exceed one-half the wages. *Confederate States Army Regulations,* 1862 (Richmond, 1862), article 204.

[64]John Crittenden to his mother, Feb. 16, 1863.

[65]John Crittenden to his wife, May 3, 1863.

[66]P. L. Dodgen to his wife, July 20, 1862.

[67]Diary of L. G. Hutton, various entries for period from April to October, 1862, typescript, University of Texas.

[68]Grabbling is a term applied to the practice of probing with the hands for fish under banks, roots and rocks.

[69]Thomas Caffey to his sister, March 24, 1863.

[70]J. M. Jordan to his wife, March 21, 1864, typescript, Georgia Archives.

[71]G. L. Robertson to his sister, Jan. 15, 1864, manuscript photostat, University of Texas.

[72]Maud Morrow Brown, editor, "Reminiscences of the War of the Confederacy by R. O. B. Morrow," manuscript in possession of the editor.

[73]Samuel Saltus to his sister, Jan. 13, 1862, manuscript, Heartman Collection.

[74]A. N. Erskine to his wife, July 20, 1862, manuscript, University of Texas.

[75]O. R., series 1, XXX, part 2, 789.

[76]J. H. Puckett to his wife, Oct. 16, 1863.

[77]The canteens were easily halved by the insertion and setting off of a small charge of powder. Albert T. Goodloe, *Some Rebel Relics from the Seat of War* (Nashville, 1893), 41. Some "canteen plates" are on exhibit in the Confederate Museum at Richmond. Graters were made by driving numerous nail holes in canteen sides. J. F. Coghill to "Dear Mit," Oct. 18, 1862, manuscript, Duke University.

[78]A. C. Redwood, "The Cook in the Confederate Army," *Scribner's Monthly,* XVIII (1879), 560-568.

[79]James A. Hall to his sister, Oct. 22, 1863, manuscript, Alabama Archives. For other descriptions of ingredients and processes, see Heartsill, op. cit., 186; and McCarthy, op. cit., 59.

[80]Jarman, op. cit., 28-29.

[81]O. R., series 4, I, 889.

[82]William M. Whatley to his wife, Oct. 21, 1862, manuscript photostat, University of Texas.

[83]John Crittenden to his wife, Nov. 3, 1864; McCarthy, op. cit., 65; J. E. Hall to his father, April 11, 1864, manuscript, Alabama Archives.

[84]T. B. Hampton to his wife, Feb. 21, 1864.

370 THE LIFE OF JOHNNY REB

[85]McCarthy, op. cit., 65; diary of J. Stanley Newman, entry of July 26, 1861, manuscript, Confederate Museum; James C. Nisbet, Four Years on the Firing Line (Chattanooga, 1914), 255.

[86]J. B. Mitchell to his father, Sept. 9, 1861, typescript, Alabama Archives.

[87]William R. Stillwell to his wife, April 1, 1863.

[88]Jerome Yates to "T. O. D.," Jan. 18, 1864; Charles W. Hutson to his mother, March 4, 1862, manuscript, University of North Carolina.

[89]Thomas Warrick to his wife, April 2, 1863, manuscript, Alabama Archives.

[90]C. Irvine Walker to Ada Sinclair, July 23, 1864.

[91]Robert M. Gill to his wife, Aug. 28, 1864, manuscript in author's possession.

[92]Heartsill, op. cit., 164.

Chapter VII

FROM FINERY TO TATTERS

[1]O. R., series 4, I, 369-373; Confederate States Army Regulations, 1862, article 47. The 1861 Army Regulations did not contain provisions concerning uniform and dress; this was due probably to the tardiness of the War Department in releasing data on this subject.

[2]See Atlas to Accompany Official Records of the Union and Confederate Armies (Washington, D. C., 1891-1895), plate 72.

[3]O. R., series 1, LI, part 2, 15.

[4]Ibid., IV, 479; New Orleans Daily Crescent, May 4, 1861; F. B. Simkins and J. W. Patton, The Women of the Confederacy (Richmond, 1936), 18 ff; "War Reminiscences of Anne Pelham Finlay," typescript, Greenville, Mississippi, Public Library.

[5]Randolph H. McKim, "Glimpses of the Confederate Army," F. T. Miller, editor, Photographic History of the Civil War (New York, 1911), VIII, 109.

[6]Stanley Horn, The Army of Tennessee (Indianapolis, 1941), 140-141.

[7]Kate Cumming, A Journal of Hospital Life in the Confederate Army of Tennessee (Louisville and New Orleans, 1866), 37.

[8]H. M. Doak, "Reminiscences," 13, typescript, Tennessee State Library.

[9]Oscar W. Blacknall, editor, "Papers of C. C. Blacknall," introduction, typescript, North Carolina Historical Commission.

[10]DeLeon, op. cit., 71-72.

[11]*Ibid.*, 96-97.

[12]O. R., series 4, II, 382-383.

[13]*Ibid.*, 229-230; III, 1039-1040.

[14]Southern Historical Society *Papers*, XXXI (1903) 246; E. P. Thompson, *History of the Orphan Brigade* (Louisville, 1898), 203; Miller, *op. cit.*, VIII, 120.

[15]*Confederate Veteran*, XII (1904), 116. The issue of white uniforms to some conscript outfits caused stigma to be attached to their wear by volunteers. Members of the Twenty-sixth Louisiana had to be threatened with severe punishment before they would don the undyed regalia. Hall, *op. cit.*, 59-60.

[16]McCarthy, *op. cit.*, 20-21; "Simpson War Reminiscences," manuscript, Tennessee State Library. William R. Stillwell wrote to his wife from camp in Virginia April 30, 1864: "I have not got my hat yet I need it very bad most burnt up with the sun face blistered I dont think I will ever ware another cap while I live." Manuscript, Georgia Archives.

[17]New Orleans *Daily Crescent*, May 29, 1861.

[18]W. C. McClellan to Robert McClellan, August —?, 1861.

[19]Theodore Mandeville to his sister, Aug. 27, 1861.

[20]John E. Hall to his father, Oct. 14, 1861, manuscript, Alabama Archives.

[21]O. R., series 4, III, 691-692, 1039-1040.

[22]F. L. Owsley, *States Rights in the Confederacy* (Chicago, 1925), 126.

[23]John Crittenden to his wife, March 24, 1864.

[24]Frank Moss to his sister, Oct. 28, 1863, manuscript, University of Texas.

[25]Jerome Yates to his mother, April 2, 1864, manuscript, Heartman Collection.

[26]William H. Routt to his wife, March 13, 1863, manuscript, Confederate Museum, Richmond.

[27]E. P. Becton to his wife, Dec. 14, 1862, typescript, University of Texas.

[28]J. T. Terrell to his mother, Dec. 29, 1862, manuscript in private possession.

[29]Charleston *Daily Courier*, Sept. 3, 1862.

[30]Richmond *Daily Dispatch*, April 24, 1862.

[31]DeLeon, *op. cit.*, 185.

[32]Manuscript among L. M. Nutt Papers, University of North Carolina.

[33]J. H. Puckett to his wife, April 15, 1863; Thomas Caffey to his sister, Feb. 16, 1863.

[34]Sebron Sneed to his wife, June 7, 1864, manuscript, University of Texas.

[35]Letter of August 6, 1861.

[36]Diary of H. S. Archer, entry of Nov. 9, 1863, manuscript microfilm, Vanderbilt University.

[37]William M. Dame, From the Rapidan to Richmond (Baltimore, 1920), 36-37.

[38]S. G. Pryor to his wife, Feb. 4, 1863.

[39]James A. Graham to his mother, March 9, 1862, manuscript, University of North Carolina.

[40]Andrew M. Chandler to his mother, Aug. 31, 1862, manuscript photostat in possession of Mrs. Ella Mae Chandler, West Point, Mississippi.

[41]Wiley, op. cit., 134.

[42]R. W. Waldrop to his mother, Aug. 27, 1862, manuscript, University of North Carolina.

[43]J. M. Jordan to his wife, June 27, 1864, typescript, Georgia Archives; T. B. Hampton to his wife, Feb. 3, 1865, typescript, University of Texas.

[44]Maj. Henry C. Semple to his wife, Nov. 3, 1864, manuscript, University of North Carolina. Soldiers of the Army of Tennessee thought that partiality in clothing issues was shown by Richmond authorities to troops of Lee's command.

[45]O. R., series 1, XLII, part 3, 1268-1269; series 4, III, 1039-1040; Lee to A. P. Hill, Jan. 20, 1865, manuscript, Confederate Museum.

[46]J. F. J. Caldwell, History of Gregg's and McGowan's Brigade (Philadelphia, 1866), 196-197.

[47]Fitzgerald Ross, A Visit to the Cities and Camps of the Confederate States (London, 1865), p. 31.

[48]General Order No. 47, issued by Longstreet, Nov. 7, 1862, manuscript among Washington Artillery Papers, Confederate Memorial Hall New Orleans.

[49]William H. Cody to his sister, Oct. 18, 1864, in E. C. Burnett, editor, "Letters of Barnett Hardeman Cody and Others," Georgia Historical Quarterly, XXIII (1939), 379.

[50]O. R., series 1, V, 785.

[51]Charleston Daily Courier, Sept. 3, 1862.

[52]O. R., series 1, XIX, part 2, 590-591.

[53]The Richmond Daily Dispatch of October 9, 1862, carried a pungent editorial on the subject of clothing for Lee's army. In reference to the Antietam campaign the editor said: "Posterity will scarcely believe that the wonderful campaign which has just ended with its terrible marches and desperate battles, was made by men, one-fourth of whom were entirely barefooted, and one-half of whom were as ragged as scarecrows. . . . We cease to wonder at the number of stragglers, when we

hear how many among them were shoeless, with stone bruises on their feet."

[54]Richard Lewis, Camp Life of a Confederate Boy (Charleston, 1883), 35.

[55]O. R., series 4, II, 204.

[56]Thomas Caffey to his mother, Nov. 12, 1863. Generals in command were evidently forced to require duty of barefooted men to prevent would-be shirkers from throwing away their shoes to avoid drilling and fighting. See O. R., series 1, XXX, part 4, 715.

[57]Anonymous manuscript in Confederate Memorial Hall, New Orleans.

[58]Richmond Enquirer, April 12, 1864. General Lee complained of the poor quality of some of the shoes issued by government quartermasters during the winter of 1863-1864. O. R., series 1, XXXIII, 1131-1132.

[59]Hanks, op. cit., 78.

[60]John H. Hancock to his parents, Nov. 11, 1862, manuscript among Richard D. White Papers, North Carolina Historical Commission.

[61]Robert M. Gill to his wife, July 30, 1864.

[62]O. R., series 1, XLV, part 1, 735-736, 747.

[63]Robert Selph Henry, The Story of the Confederacy (Indianapolis, 1931), 434.

Chapter VIII

TRIALS OF SOUL

[1]L. M. Johnson, An Elementary Arithmetic Designed for Beginners (Raleigh, 1864), 34, 38, 44.

[2]O. R., series 4, I, 277.

[3]Ibid., 497.

[4]Ibid., 380.

[5]Undated but postwar letter of J. M. Montgomery to Victor Montgomery, manuscript in private possession.

[6]O. R., series 4, I, 352-353, 380.

[7]Ibid., series 1, XXIV, part 3, 1053-1054.

[8]This summary of conscription is based primarily on data from the fourth series of the Official Records of the Union and Confederate Armies. Extensive and scholarly treatments of the subject are to be found in A. B. Moore, Conscription and Conflict in the Confederacy (New York, 1924), and Owsley, op. cit. A thorough survey of judicial aspects of the question is available in William M. Robinson, Jr., Justice in Grey (Cambridge, 1940).

[9]O. R., series 4. III, 48-49.

[10]This account of substitution is drawn principally from series four of the *Official Records*, from Professor Moore's excellent chapter on the subject in his *Conscription and Conflict in the Confederacy*, and from J. B. Jones, *A Rebel War Clerk's Diary* (Philadelphia, 1866). William M. Robinson, Jr., has helpful comments on judicial harangues over substitution in his *Justice in Grey*.

[11]O. R., series 4, II, 696.

[12]*Ibid.*, 997.

[13]Exception should be made of some men, not subject to military service, who engaged substitutes as a gesture of patriotism. The number of such cases, however, was so small as to be of insignificant proportion to the aggregate of proxies. See O. R., series 4, III, 12, General Order No. 3, Adjutant General's Office. Men and officers reported as "present for duty" in Lee's army in April 1863 aggregated 64,799. *Ibid.*, II, 530.

[14]Joseph A. E. Boyd to "De" Boyd, April 12, 1862, manuscript, Alabama Archives.

[15]Joe Shields to his father, June 10, 14, and July 1, 1861, manuscript, Louisiana State University.

[16]Theodore Mandeville to Rebecca Mandeville, April 22, Aug. 17, 1861, manuscript, Louisiana State University.

[17]Fred R. Taber to his homefolk, Dec. 13, 25, and Jan. 11, 1862, manuscripts, Louisiana State University.

[18]George W. Athey to his father, Jan. 18, 1862, manuscript, Alabama Archives.

[19]Will T. Martin to his wife, Oct. 20, 1861, typescript in private possession.

[20]Reid, *op. cit.*, 76.

[21]Frank Moss to "Lou" Moss, Nov. 27, 1862, and to Mrs. A. E. Rentfrow, Feb. 14, 1863; W. M. Moss to Mrs. A. E. Rentfrow, Jan. 31, 1863, manuscripts, University of Texas.

[22]E. J. Ellis to his mother, June 9, 1862, Feb. 15 and March 18, 1863, manuscript, Louisiana State University.

[23]This version is from a letter of John H. Munford to his cousin Sallie, Oct. 24, 1862, manuscript, Duke University.

[24]John Crittenden to his wife, Feb. 20, 1863, typescript, University of Texas.

[25]John R. Hopper to his brother, Sept. 9, 1863, manuscript, Heartman Collection.

[26]William R. Stillwell to his wife, Aug. 13, 1863, manuscript, Georgia Archives.

[27]Orville C. Bumpass to his wife, Dec. 1, 1863, manuscript, Evans Memorial Library.

[28]A. Wideman to his sister, Mrs. Thomas Warrick, May 19, 1864, manuscript, Alabama Archives.

[29]Diary of Charles Moore, manuscript, Confederate Memorial Hall.

[30]"I witnessed the other day a fight between the divisions composing Hardee's Corps. It was the grandest affair I ever witnessed. . . . One part presented the Confederate States Army and one the Yankees army. The Yankees made the attack. They marched up with banners flying to the tune of Yankee Doodle. As soon as the Confederates charged them they fled apparently in the . . . wildest confusion. Five rounds to the man was expended. The battle lasted about three hours. Nearly the whole of Hood's corps witnessed it." John R. Crittenden to his brother, April 9, 1864.

[31]O. R., series 1, XXXIII, 1144-1145; see also ibid., XXXII, part 2, 571-582.

[32]Ibid., XXXII, part 2, 582, 665, et passim.

[33]J. T. Terrell to his mother, March 12, 1864, manuscript in private possession.

[34]O. R., series 4, III, 374.

[35]P. M. H. S. Centenary Series, V, 311-312.

[36]There were some who took a pessimistic view of the situation even after Grant's setbacks in the Wilderness. On June 13, 1864, Sgt. William H. Phillips wrote his parents: "We hav bin in the habit of Driving away Every army of the North that has ever come close to Richmond But I am afraid that old Grant is rather too much for us this time he cant [can] outnumber Genl Lee so fare I think it will be hard to get him away this time, if Grant would Keep fighting of us we soon get him so weak that we could Drive him away but he has stoped and fortified himself and is waiting for us to fight him." Manuscript Duke University. General Stephen D. Lee noted a deleterious effect of the unsuccessful defense of Atlanta on fighting qualities. "The majority of the officers and men were so impressed with the idea of their inability to carry even temporary breastworks," he wrote, "that when orders were given for attack, and there was a probability of encountering works . . . they did not generally move to the attack with that spirit which nearly always assures success." O. R., series 1, XXXIX, part 1, 810.

[37]J. J. Hardy to his cousin, Jan. 24, 1865, typescript, Georgia Archives.

[38]Thomas Caffey to his sister, Jan. 15, 1865, "War Letters of Thomas Caffey," Montgomery Advertiser, May 16, 1909.

[39]P. M. H. S. Centenary Series, V, 356.

[40]James H. Baker to his father, Feb. 1, 1865, manuscript, Duke University; Daniel Albright to his homefolk, March 19, 1865, manuscript, Duke University. Baker was a captain.

[41]Robert W. Banks to his homefolk, Oct. 22, 1862, typescript in private possession.

[42]Crenshaw Hall to his father, May 27, 1863, manuscript, Alabama Archives.

[43]O. R., series 1, XXXIII, 1114; XLVI, part 2, 1143.

[44]Thomas Warrick to his wife, Oct. 26, 1863, manuscript, Alabama Archives. Private Andrew J. Patrick of the 37th Mississippi Regiment wrote his wife, Oct. 26, 1862: "I would not mind living hard if I node you was not suffering but you are there and I am here and cant tend to you." On November 2, 1862, he wrote further on the subject: "I am uneasy about you and the children getting something to eat . . . there is alredy a heap of men gone home and a heap says if their familys gets to suffering that they will go if they have to suffer [punishment]." Typescripts in private possession.

[45]H. A. Stephens to his sister, Jan 1, 1864, manuscript in private possession; T. B. Barron of the Fiftieth Virginia Regiment wrote to his parents, Aug. 8, 1863: "It is truly hard for the soldier to content himself in the field . . . when he sees his government give the speculator the advantage of him & his family *speculation* will cause *desertion* & desertion will be our ruin." Manuscript, Confederate Museum.

[46]For scale of pay prescribed by Congress by an act of March 6, 1861, see O. R., series 4, I, 130.

[47]O. R., series 4, III, 492. The Georgia Legislature petitioned Congress for an increase to $20 per month of the pay of privates in April 1863, but to no avail. Ibid., II, 485.

[48]P. M. H. S. Centenary Series, V, 308.

[49]O. R., series 1, XIX, part 2, 722.

[50]Ibid., VI, 408; P. M. H. S. Centenary Series, V, 298.

[51]O. R., series 1, XLVI, part 2, 1143.

[52]T. B. Hampton to his wife, Dec. 15, 1862, typescript, University of Texas.

[53]C. W. Stephens to his father, Nov. 6 [26], 1863.

[54]Frank Moss to his sister, Aug. 16, 1864; V. S. Rabb to his mother, Aug. 22, 1864, manuscripts, University of Texas.

[55]Anonymous diary of a Louisiana soldier, entry of Dec. 18, 1863, manuscript, Heartman Collection.

[56]O. R., series 4, III, 48-49.

[57]Ibid., series 1, XXIV, part 2, 393-394. For detail of reaction of officers and men to such a proposal, see petition of Johnson's brigade in ibid., series 1, XLII, part 2, 1264-1265.

[58]Robert M. Gill to his wife, Aug. 22 and Nov. 27, 1862, manuscripts in author's possession.

[59]C. W. Stephens to his sister, March 5, 1865.

[60]O. R., series 1, XLIII, part 1, 609-610, report of Major Moore, and indorsement of Assistant Adjutant and Inspector General Peyton; see also ibid., XXXII, part 2, 778-779.

[61]*Ibid.*, series 1, XLI, part 4, 1112-1113.

[62]Deter Jochum to his homefolk, Jan. 30, 1864, manuscript, Confederate Memorial Hall.

[63]W. M. Moss to his sisters, Dec. 28, 1863, manuscript, University of Texas.

[64]Orville C. Bumpass to his wife, Oct. 22, 1864.

[65]C. W. Stephens to his sister, Jan. 30, 1864.

[66]Robert M. Gill to his wife, June 9, 1862.

[67]Thomas Warrick to his wife, June 15, 1862.

[68]William R. Barksdale to his brother, June 11, 1861, manuscript in private possession.

[69]Richmond *Enquirer*, Nov. 3, 1863; Correspondence of Medical Director of General Hospitals in Virginia, 1864-1865, Confederate Archives, chapter VI, volume 365, p. 214, manuscript, National Archives; General Orders and Circulars, Department of South Carolina, Georgia and Florida, *ibid.*, chapter II, volume 43, p. 329-330; diary of C. M. Horton, entry of July 7, 1863, manuscript, Confederate Memorial Hall. Henry C. Semple to his wife, Dec. 19, 1862, manuscript, University of North Carolina; Alfred W. Bell to his wife, Sept. 17, 1864, manuscript, Duke University.

[70]O. R., series 1, XXV, part 2, 639.

[71]Robinson, op. cit., 252-254; O. R., series 4, II, 465; III, 68-69.

[72]Confederate authorities attempted on occasion to differentiate between deserters and other unwarranted absentees, and historians have been constrained in some instances to follow their example. But the line of demarcation is so thinly drawn and so variable as to be largely arbitrary. At what point, for example, did a man who overstayed his furlough, or a convalescent who failed to report for duty, become a deserter? And in what category was the infantryman to be placed who, without ample authority, secured transfer to a cavalry company? The purpose of this study is better served by classifying as unwarranted absentees deserters and all other soldiers who absented themselves by irregular devices from the service to which they were assigned.

[73]O. R., series 1, XIX, part 2, 597, 605, 622; Philip Slaughter, *Sketch of the Life of Randolph Fairfax* (Richmond, 1864), 33, quoting a letter of Fairfax from Bunker Hill, Va., Oct. 3, 1862; Richmond *Daily Dispatch*, Sept. 26, 1862, Jan. 14, 1864; Freeman, op. cit., II, 411-412. A factor contributing to straggling was, as Freeman points out, the exhausted and shoeless condition of many of the troops.

[74]O. R., series 1, XXIV, part 3, 1007, 1010, 1018.

[75]*Ibid.*, series 4, II, 721.

[76]*Ibid.*, 674; an editorial in the Richmond *Daily Dispatch* of Jan. 11, 1864, said: "Nearly half our military force is scattered over the country, and if returned to its proper position not another man would be needed

in the field." Three days later the *Dispatch* editor reverted to the subject of straggling with this inquiry: "Where was the balance of the 110,000 men on Bragg's muster roll when he fought the battle of Chickamauga with less than 40,000? . . . Where are the stragglers and deserters who swarm in the mountains and infest the lower country like locusts?"

[77]*O. R.*, series 4, III, 397-398, 802-803; series 1, XXXII, part 3, 681-682; XXXIX, part 2, 588-589; Ella Lonn, *Desertion During the Civil War* (New York, 1928), 62-105; Georgia Lee Tatum, *Disloyalty in the Confederacy* (Chapel Hill, 1934), 24 ff.

[78]J. M. Jordan to his father, Feb. 14, 1863, typescript, Georgia Archives.

[79]*O. R.*, series 1, XLII, part 2, 1175-1176; series 4, III, 689-690. The Richmond *Daily Dispatch* of Jan. 26, 1865, quoted a correspondent of the Atlanta *Appeal:* "If one-half of the men of the Confederacy capable of bearing arms would cease to shirk their duty . . . and . . . come to the front we could expel the invaders from our soil within six weeks."

[80]Lonn, *op. cit.*, 23.

[81]*Ibid.*; *O. R.*, series 1, XLVI, part 2, 1265, 1293.

[82] *O. R.*, series 1, LI, part 2, 1065; Lonn, *op. cit.*, 30.

[83]*O. R.*, series 4, III, 1182. Returns are for varying dates, ranging from Dec. 31, 1864, to April 17, 1865, for different armies of the Confederacy.

[84]DeLeon, *op. cit.*, 142.

[85]Lonn, *op. cit.*, 123.

[86]Mollie Vandenberg to C. H. Clark, March 11, 1862, manuscript in private possession.

[87]C. L. Stephens to E. A. Stephens, March 5, 1865, manuscript in private possession.

[88]James L. G. Wood to his father, March 31, 1864, typescript, Georgia Archives.

[89]J. Joe Evans to John Holliday, Jan. 7, 1865, manuscript in private possession.

[90]*O. R.*, series 1, XI, part 1, 408-409.

[91]*Ibid.*, XXIV, part 2, 392-393, 410.

[92]*Ibid.*, XXIX, part 1, 408.

[93]Bolling Hall to his father, April 15, 1864, manuscript, Alabama Archives.

[94]H. A. Stephens to his sister, Dec. 6, 1863; Jerome Yates to his friend, "T.O.D.," May 4, 1864; E. G. Higgason to his mother, Oct. 29, 1864, manuscript in private possession.

[95]Robert M. Gill to his wife, April 16, 1864.

[96]Joseph Renwick to his wife, April 14, 1865, manuscript, Louisiana State University.

[97]Cowper, *op. cit.*, 122-123.

[98]J. T. Terrell to his parents, Nov. 16, 1862, March 12, May 2, June 6, 1864.

[99]Manuscript in private possession.

[100]J. M. J. Tolly to James R. Hall, April 22, 1865, manuscript, Alabama Archives.

Chapter IX

BREAKING THE MONOTONY

[1]Journal of James Hampton Kuykendall, entry of Aug. 27, 1862, typescript, University of Texas.

[2]William M. Worthington to his sister, July 15, 1864, manuscript in private possession; diary of A. L. P. Vairin, entry of July 6, 1862, manuscript, Mississippi Archives.

[3]Diary of Charles Moore, Jr., entries of Sept. 24, 1861, and Feb. 27, 1862, manuscript, Confederate Memorial Hall; New Orleans *Daily Crescent*, May 8, 1861.

[4]Duke University, the University of Virginia and the Confederate Museum each has large collections of Confederate sheet music.

[5]Most of these items may be found in the Confederate Museum. Others were examined in collections at Emory University and the Library of Congress. Several more songbooks are listed by Richard B. Harwell in *Confederate Belles-Lettres* (Hattiesburg, Miss., 1941), but these were not seen by the writer. A veteran of the Tenth Virginia Regiment wrote: "We kept song books with us and passed much of our leisure time singing. I carried my book even through prison and brought it home with me." James Huffman, *Up and Downs of a Confederate Soldier* (New York, 1940), 68.

[6]Popularity of these songs was established by references in soldier correspondence and diaries and by recurrence in pocket songbooks. All of the melodies listed were mentioned in letters or diaries.

[7]Randolph McKim, "Glimpses of the Confederate Army," Miller, *op. cit.*, VIII, 122.

[8]*Fort Lafayette Life, 1863-1864, in Extracts from the Right Flanker* (London, 1865), 10.

[9]Walter A. Clark, *Under the Stars and Bars* (Augusta, Ga., 1900), 79.

[10]Manuscript among W. J. Clarke Papers, University of North Carolina.

[11]Harry St. John Dixon of the Twenty-eighth Mississippi Volunteers wrote in his diary on Jan. 14, 1863, "a soldier's usual occupation has whiled away my time, listening to vulgar songs, yarns . . . smok-

ing, and reading." Manuscript, University of North Carolina. Edmund C. Burnett of the Carnegie Institution repeated to the writer a stanza of an obscene song sung by a Rebel prisoner, but the words are unprintable.

[12]Manuscript among G. L. Robertson Letters, University of Texas.

[13]New Orleans Daily Crescent, July 9, 1861. For other parodies on "Dixie," see W. L. Fagan, editor, Southern War Songs (New York, 1890), 7, 36 and 238.

[14]Original sheet music as published by A. E. Blackmar & Brother, New Orleans, 1861, Duke Sheet Music Collection. An ex-Confederate recalled hearing Harry McCarthy, stage songster who wrote the words and who did much to popularize the song, "often . . . sing it when thousands of people went wild with excitement." H. M. Wharton, editor, War Songs and Poems of the Southern Confederacy, 1861-1865 (Philadelphia, 1904), 23.

[15]For full text see original sheet music as published by Blackmar and Brother, Augusta, 1862, Duke Collection. In the Blackmar edition "touch" is used instead of "torch." This is evidently a printer's error. The song lost caste with Maryland's failure to give wholehearted support to the Confederacy; as one soldier expressed it, "About the third year of the war . . . we began to think Maryland had 'breathed and burned' long enough and ought to 'come.'" Southern Historical Society Papers, I (1876), 80.

[16]June Kimble, "The 14th Tenn. Glee Club," typescript, Confederate Museum. For reference to another glee club see James Peter Williams to his aunt, March 16, 1865, manuscript, University of Virginia.

[17]James T. Searcy to his sister, Stella, from Corinth, Miss., May 5, 1862, manuscript, Alabama Archives.

[18]Diary of D. S. Redding, entry of July 3, 1863, typescript, Georgia Archives.

[19]Diary of James J. Kirkpatrick, entry of Oct. 30, 1863, manuscript, University of Texas.

[20]Fremantle, op. cit., 71-72; Battle-Fields of the South, II, 101-103.

[21]Reid, op. cit., 60.

[22]Clark, North Carolina Regiments, II, 397-400.

[23]New Orleans Daily Crescent, Dec. 21, 1861, and Jan. 8, 1862, correspondence of I[srael] G[ibbons].

[24]Robert E. Park, The Twelfth Alabama Infantry (Richmond, 1906), 101; Edward McMorries, Historical Sketch of the First Alabama Volunteers (Montgomery, 1904), 52.

[25]Edward T. Worthington to Amanda Worthington, Oct. 4, 28, 1861, manuscript in private possession.

[26]James N. Thrower to his brother, Oct. 27, 1861, manuscript, Alabama Archives.

[27]Letter of Oct. 20, 1861, manuscript in private possession.

[28]Cate, op. cit., 30.

[29]James A. Hall to Joe Hall, April 18, 1864, manuscript, Alabama Archives; diary of D. P. Hopkins, entry of March 15, 1862, typescript, University of Texas.

[30]New Orleans Daily Crescent, Oct. 29, 1861; Alfred Chisholm to his mother, April 11, 1863, manuscript, University of North Carolina; J. F. Sale to his aunt, Sept. 3, 1863, manuscript, Virginia State Library.

[31]Diary of James J. Kirkpatrick, entry of Jan. 3, 1863; Samuel Saltus to his sister, March 12, 1862, manuscript, Heartman Collection.

[32]Diary of A. L. P. Vairin, entry of April 19, 1862; diary of T. J. Ford, entry of Oct. 23, 1862, manuscript, Heartman Collection.

[33]Chamberlayne, op. cit., 130. Chamberlayne told also of the fox-catching episode.

[34]J. H. Puckett to his wife, Feb. 10, 1863, manuscript, University of Texas.

[35]In these affairs speeding riders attempted to snatch with lances hoops suspended from tall uprights. For vivid description of a large-scale contest see Joseph C. Robert, "A Ring Tournament in 1864," Journal of Mississippi History, III (1941), 293-296.

[36]J. W. Ward to his sister, May 27, 1863, manuscript, Heartman Collection; T. J. Newberry to his father, June 8, 1862, manuscript in author's possession.

[37]W. H. Neblett to his wife, April 28, 1863, manuscript, University of Texas.

[38]Ibid.

[39]Robert M. Gill to his mother, Oct. 16, 1862, manuscript in author's possession.

[40]Walter Keeble to his wife, Feb. 2, 1862, manuscript, University of Texas; diary of L. G. Hutton, entry of Feb. 5, 1862, manuscript, University of Texas.

[41]Fred R. Taber to his homefolk, Oct. 19, 1861, manuscript, Louisiana State University; J. T. Terrell to his parents, various dates, 1862-1863, manuscripts in private possession.

[42]W. H. Stephenson and Edwin A. Davis, editors, "The Civil War Diary of Willie Micajah Barrow," Louisiana Historical Quarterly, XVII (1934), 436-451, 712-731; various letters of Hutson for 1861-1862, manuscripts, University of North Carolina.

[43]Diary of Harry St. John Dixon, entry of May 19, 1862, et passim, manuscripts, University of North Carolina.

[44]H. A. Stephens to his sister, Jan. 31, 1864, manuscript in private possession.

[45]George W. F. Harper to his wife, April 5, 1864, manuscript, University of North Carolina; Robert M. Gill to his wife, July 13, 1862; [Bartlett], op. cit., 54.

[46]"Personne" [F. G. DeFontaine], Marginalia; or Gleanings from an Army Notebook (Columbia, S.C., 1864), 108.

[47]Journal of B. L. Ridley, undated entry (April, 1865), Confederate Veteran, III (1893), 134.

[48]Horn, op. cit., 469. A. L. P. Vairin gives this explanation of the origin of "Here's your mule" in his diary: "The first I heard of it was this—some man in the neighbourhood had lost an old gray mule and was . . . enquiring for it among the Regiments—Co. B. had straw in their tents to sleep on. . . . Among them Tom Nance . . . his hair was very thin on his head and his ears seemed all the larger for it— Under the general excitement of the day he laid down in his tent to sleep—some lively fellows roving about . . . happened to look in Tom's tent and being struck with his appearance called out for the mule man —Here's your mule others came to see and repeated the saying . . . and fun and yeling being the order of the day the words soon reechoed alover the camp and those adjoining and became a by word everywhere." Undated entry, but evidently late 1861. A song of Confederate origin gives a version differing in detail from Vairin's; see Fagan, op. cit., 319-320.

[49]Manuscript photostat, no date, no place, University of Texas.

[50]Robert Fore to "Mr. Readon," Jan. 2, 1863, manuscript among Reding Papers, University of Texas.

[51]Journal of E. Mussence, undated entry [Jan. 1863?], manuscript (fragment) among Washington Artillery Papers, Confederate Memorial Hall; diary of T. J. Ford, entry of Dec. 28, 1862.

[52]G. L. Robertson to his mother, June 25, 1864, manuscript, University of Texas.

[53]John Crittenden to his mother, March 25, 1864, manuscript, University of Texas.

[54]Diary of D. P. Hopkins, entry of April 1, 1862.

[55]Stiles, op. cit., 49.

[56]New Orleans Daily Crescent, Oct. 29, 1861; Confederate Veteran, V (1895), 134.

[57]Diary of D. P. Hopkins, entry of April 12, 1862.

[58]"McLaws Minstrels a company composed of young men from Barksdale's Brigade . . . have been playing 3 times a week for the last month to large audiences." Diary of William H. Hill, Thirteenth Mississippi Regiment, entry of Feb. 27, 1863, manuscript, Mississippi Archives. In some instances log theaters were built in camp for winter entertainments.

[59]New Orleans Daily Crescent, Oct. 29, 1861; Montgomery Daily

Mail, March 29, 1863, quoting "Personne" of Charleston *Courier;*
Mobile *Daily Advertiser and Register,* March 30, 1864.
[60]Mobile *Daily Advertiser and Register,* March 30, 1864.
[61]J. O. Casler, *Four Years in the Stonewall Brigade* (Guthrie, Okla.,
1893), 307-309.
[62]Owen, op. cit., 205-206. This program was repeated the next winter. Diary of Charles R. Walden, Oct. 22, 1863, typescript, Georgia
Archives.
[63]V. S. Rabb to his sister, March 18, 1863.
[64]Diary of G. L. Griscom, undated entry [about Feb. 10, 1863],
manuscript, University of Texas.
[65]C. W. Stephens to his sister, Oct. 14, 1863, manuscript in private
possession.
[66]New Orleans *Daily Crescent,* Oct. 1, 19, 1861; [Bartlett], op. cit.,
67-68. In the fall of 1861 some South Carolina Rebs bought lumber and
erected a hall for the holding of regular dances. The first dance held in
the new edifice ended in a free-for-all fight. Milton S. Walker to his
mother, Sept. 13, 1861, manuscript, Duke University.
[67]Diary of D. P. Hopkins, entry of April 14, 1862.
[68]S. W. Farrow to his wife, Jan. 18, 1864, manuscript, University of
Texas.
[69]Diary of Charles Moore, Jr., entry of Sept. 24, 1861.
[70]V. S. Rabb to his brother, Jan. 4, 1863, manuscript photostat,
University of Texas.
[71]Anonymous diary of a Louisiana soldier, entry of Dec. 25, 1863,
manuscript, Confederate Memorial Hall.
[72]Letter of Theodore Mandeville, Dec. 29, 1861, manuscript,
Louisiana State University.
[73]Journal of James H. Kuykendall, entry of Dec. 25, 1862.
[74]Diary of L. G. Hutton, entry of July 3-4, 1862.
[75]Stephens failed to date this letter.
[76]See for instance diary of William H. Hill, various entries of April
and July, 1863; also letter of William J. Whatley to his wife, Dec. 25,
1862, manuscript, photostat, University of Texas.
[77]New Orleans *Daily Crescent,* Oct. 19, 1861.
[78]Robert M. Gill to his wife, April 29, 1861, June 3, 12, and Sept.
13, 1862, July 9, 1863; V. S. Rabb to his mother, July 9, 1864.
[79]Charles H. Clark to Mrs. Mary Johnston, Aug. 7, 1861, manuscript in private possession; J. B. Mitchell wrote his mother, July 23,
1862: "Notwithstanding the great number of sick in our regiment they
seem to be generally content and cheerful. They amuse themselves by
circulating all sorts of improbable stories and telegraphic dispatches.
The latest news detailed to me by one of Capt Slaughter's men is that

Africa has recognized the Southern Confederacy." Typescript in Alabama Archives.

[80]Jerome Yates to his mother, April 20, 1864, manuscript, Heartman Collection; Stephenson and Davis, op. cit., 445; diary of M. W. Barber, entry of Sept. 23, 1864, typescript, University of Texas.

[81]James T. Searcy to his sister, Dec. 16, 1862, manuscript, Alabama Archives.

[82]New Orleans Daily Crescent, Oct. 19, 1861.

[83]Stiles, op. cit., 170-171. The Fourth North Carolina Infantry Regiment had a fine St. Bernard dog taken during the Seven Days' campaign while guarding the corpse of a Yankee colonel. Cowper, op. cit., 17-18.

[84]Battle-Fields of the South, I, 161-162; John H. Worsham, One of Jackson's Foot Cavalry (New York, 1912), 75; Watkins, op. cit., 59.

[85]Thomas Warrick to his wife, May 18, 1863.

[86]William Decatur Howell to his mother, May 11, 1864, manuscript in possession of Maud Morrow Brown, University, Mississippi.

[87]Mobile Daily Advertiser and Register, March 20, 1863.

[88]Winifred Gregory, editor, Union List of Newspapers (New York, 1937), 655; Basil W. Duke, Morgan's Cavalry (New York, 1906), 154-206; Mrs. Irby Morgan, How It Was: Four Years Among the Rebels (Nashville, 1892), 79, 187-204; Cecil Fletcher Holland, Morgan and His Raiders (New York, 1942), 139 ff., 151, 156-157.

[89]Gregory, op. cit., 344. The writer examined a copy of this paper in the Confederate Museum. Other issues are in the Library of Congress, the Missouri Historical Society, and the Minnesota Historical Society.

[90]The writer has been able to locate only one copy of one issue of this paper. This is in the Tennessee State Library. Contents of another issue are summarized in the Confederate Veteran, IV (1896), 344.

[91]The first two issues of "The Pioneer Banner" are in a scrapbook in the Military Records Division of the Alabama Department of Archives and History. The author is indebted to Mr. Peter Brannon, efficient Division Director, for permission to make photostats of this item.

[92]For a reproduction of the contents of sample issues of these items see Heartsill, op. cit., 56 ff.

[93]McMorries, op. cit., 51.

[94]Owen, op. cit., 73-74; Henry, op. cit., 300-301.

[95]Heartsill, op. cit., 86.

[96]Jonas A. Bradshaw to his wife, April 11, 1863, manuscript, Duke University.

[97]Frank Moss to his sisters, Lou and Bet, Nov. 27, 1862, manuscript, University of Texas.

⁹⁸John Crittenden to his father, Dec. 20, 1863.
⁹⁹Thomas Warrick to his wife, May 18, 1863; William R. Stillwell
to his wife, Nov. 10, 1862.
¹⁰⁰Frank Moss to his sister Lou, Aug. 29, 1862.

Chapter X

CONSOLATIONS OF THE SPIRIT

¹New Orleans Daily Crescent, May 23, 1861.
²Hankins, op. cit., 11-13.
³J. W. Jones, op. cit., 564.
⁴ Robert M. Gill to his wife, Dec. 23, 1862, manuscript in author's
possession.
⁵Joseph J. Cowand to his cousin, Dec. 1, 1862, manuscript, Duke
University.
⁶Bible Convention of the Confederate States of America, Proceedings (Augusta, Ga., 1862), 1-15; J. W. Jones, op. cit., 148-151.
⁷William R. Stillwell, a lay-preacher who served as courier in the
Fifty-third Georgia Regiment, wrote his wife May 10, 1863, that he had
obtained, as a result of the Chancellorsville fight, numerous "him
books" and "testaments by the holdsale [wholesale]." He probably
distributed these items among fellow soldiers. Manuscript, Georgia
Archives.
⁸J. W. Jones, op. cit., 148-151.
⁹Ibid., 158-161. W. W. Bennett, A Narrative of the Great Revival
Which Prevailed in the Southern Armies (Philadelphia, 1877), 74-76.
¹⁰This issue, dated Oct. 15, 1863, is among the Van David Papers,
University of Texas.
¹¹Richmond Daily Dispatch, July 5, 1862; Jones, op. cit., 156-161.
¹²This summary is based on a study of a large collection of tracts at
the University of North Carolina and smaller lots at Emory University
and at Louisiana State University. A Mother's Parting Words to Her
Soldier Boy (no place, no date) is in the Keith M. Read Collection at
Emory University. In this collection also there is a list of 103 brochures
published by the South Carolina Tract Society.
¹³S. G. Pryor to his wife, April 26, 1863, typescript, University of
Texas.
¹⁴J. W. Jones, op. cit., 155.
¹⁵Richmond Enquirer, April 15, 1862.
¹⁶J. W. Jones, op. cit., 194.
¹⁷Some revivals were reported in Virginia camps in the winter of

1861-1862, but these were on a comparatively small scale. New Orleans *Daily Crescent* (quoting Charleston *Courier*), Feb. 3, 1862.

[18]R. B. Hudgens to his uncle, manuscript among Thomas F. Boatwright Papers, University of North Carolina.

[19]Montgomery *Daily Mail*, April 10, 1863.

[20]W. S. Douglass to his sister, Dec. 20, 1863, manuscript, University of Texas.

[21]Robert Edward Hill to his sister, June 21, 1863, manuscript, University of Texas.

[22]F. W. Thompson to his sister, Aug. 14, 1863.

[23]J. W. Jones, *op. cit.*, 262.

[24]*Ibid.*, 248-249.

[25]*Ibid.*, 42.

[26]*Ibid.*, 552-553.

[27]*Ibid.*, 353.

[28]Calvin H. Wiley, *Scriptural Views of National Trials* (Greensboro, N.C., 1863), 187 ff.

[29]J. W. Jones, *op. cit.*, 390.

[30]Stiles, *op. cit.*, 114.

[31]J. W. Jones, *op. cit.*, 357.

[32]*Battle-Fields of the South*, I, 280. For reference to a Catholic service in Bragg's army see Henry C. Semple to his wife, March 15, 1863, manuscript, University of North Carolina.

[33]These three booklets are in the Keith M. Read Collection at Emory University.

[34]*Soldier's Hymn Book* (Charleston, 1863), 198, 202, 233.

[35]The popularity of these songs is established by references to them in soldier correspondence and diaries and by their recurrence in camp hymn books.

[36]Thomas F. Boatwright to his wife, Sept. 9, 1863, manuscript, University of North Carolina; Mobile *Advertiser and Register*, Oct. 1, 1863.

[37]Isaac Alexander to his mother and sister, June 27, 1862, typescript, University of North Carolina.

[38]J. W. Jones, *op. cit.*, 223.

[39]H. A. Stephens to his sister, Oct. 5, 1863, manuscript in private possession.

[40]Jerome Yates to his sister, May 4, 1864, manuscript, Heartman Collection.

[41]Matthews, *Statutes at Large of the Confederate Government* (Richmond, 1862-1864), Provisional Government, Second Session, chapters 1 and 22, Third Session, chapter 69; Permanent Government, First Congress, First Session, chapter 56, Fourth Session, chapter 13.

[42]Richmond *Daily Dispatch*, Nov. 21, 1861. The contributor of this article protested against the reduction on the ground of discrimination. By a law of Congress, he said, chaplains were ranked as first

lieutenants, and the pay prescribed for officers of that grade was ninety dollars a month.

⁴³J. W. Jones, op. cit., 226-230, 363; R. H. McKim, A Soldier's Recollections (New York, 1910), 219-221.

⁴⁴Arthur H. Noll, editor, Dr. Quintard, Chaplain, C.S.A. (Sewanee, Tenn., 1905), pp. 4 ff; Charles Todd Quintard to George C. Harris, Nov. 5, 1861, manuscript, Tennessee State Library.

⁴⁵J. W. Jones, op. cit., 522.

⁴⁶O. R., series 1, XXV, part 1, 873.

⁴⁷Typescript of scrapbook of Miss Alphine Sterrett, Alabama Archives; the clipping is dated Nov. 9, 1861.

⁴⁸O. R., series 1, XXV, part 1, 873; XXXIV, part 1, 620; XXXVIII, part 3, 845, 933.

⁴⁹McKim, op. cit., 219-221.

⁵⁰Battle-Fields of the South, I, 278-279.

⁵¹Journal of James H. Kuykendall, entry of Dec. 14, 1862, typescript, University of Texas.

⁵²E. P. Becton to his wife, Aug. 12, 1862, manuscript photostat, University of Texas.

⁵³R. W. Waldrop to his mother, April 6, 1862, manuscript, University of North Carolina.

⁵⁴Thomas Caffey to his sister, Nov. 19, 1863, in Montgomery Advertiser, May 9, 1909.

⁵⁵John Crittenden to his wife, July 15, 1864.

⁵⁶William R. Stillwell to his wife, May 28, 1863; J. P. Williams to his sister, Dec. 9, 1864, manuscript, University of Virginia.

⁵⁷Diary of H. S. Archer, entry of April 12, 1863, et passim, manuscript microfilm, Vanderbilt University.

⁵⁸W. W. Pierson, editor, "Diary of Bartlett Yancey Malone," James Sprunt Historical Publications, XVI (1917-1919), 18, 27, 32, 33.

⁵⁹J. W. Jones, op. cit., 226-230.

⁶⁰O. R., series 1, II, 954; J. W. Jones, op. cit., 240, 252, 537; G. C. Eggleston, A Rebel's Recollections (New York, 1878), 240-241.

⁶¹J. W. Jones, op. cit., 390.

Chapter XI

DEAR FOLKS

¹John Barksdale to his brother, June 12, 1862, manuscript in private possession.

²John Crittenden to his wife, June 28, 1862, typescript, University of Texas.

[3]Thomas Warrick to his wife, Feb. 12, June 23, 1863, manuscript, Alabama Archives.

[4]E. K. Flournoy to his wife, March 21, 1863, manuscript, Alabama Archives.

[5]Wilson Athey to his cousin, June 16, 1862, manuscript, Alabama Archives.

[6]William J. Whatley to his wife, Nov. 2, 9, 1863, manuscript photostats, University of Texas.

[7]C. E. Taylor to his father, July 14, 1861, Sept. 28, 1862, manuscripts, Heartman Collection.

[8]This envelope contained a letter written by Thomson to his father, Nov. 5, 1861, from Kingsville, S. C., manuscript in private possession.

[9]Filed with letter of John N. Shealy to his wife, July 17, 1862, manuscript, Louisiana State University.

[10]Robert Laurence, Catalog of the George Walcott Collection of Used Civil War Patriotic Covers (New York, 1934), 248.

[11]On envelope of J. M. Brown's letter to his mother, Aug. 31, 1864, typescript, Georgia Archives.

[12]On letterhead used by Crenshaw Hall in a note to his father, June 26, 1861, manuscript, Alabama Archives.

[13]At head of sheet in letter of Thomas Mandeville to Ellwyn Mandeville, Aug. 31, 1861, manuscript, Louisiana State University.

[14]Laurence, op. cit., 258.

[15]On envelope used by J. M. Robertson, found among Robertson Papers, manuscript photostats, University of Texas.

[16]This item is filed with Moss-Barmore-Colclough-Rentfrow Papers, University of Texas.

[17]William R. Stillwell to his wife, April 11, 1863, manuscript, Georgia Archives.

[18]Letter of Nov. 19, 1683, "War Letters of Thomas Caffey," Montgomery Advertiser, May 9, 1909; S. W. Farrow to his wife, June 2, 1864, manuscript, University of Texas.

[19]William J. Whatley to his wife, Nov. 2, 9, 1862.

[20]Montgomery Advertiser, May 9, 1909.

[21]Elers Koch to his parents, April 20, 1863, manuscript, Louisiana State University.

[22]Manuscript dated March 11-12, 1863, University of Texas.

[23]Manuscript among Bolling Hall Papers, Alabama Archives.

[24]John Crittenden to his wife, July 15, 1864.

[25]Frank Moss to Mrs. A. E. Rentfrow, Dec. 6, 1864, manuscript, University of Texas.

[26]William R. Stillwell to his wife, May 10, 1863.

[27]Stuart Noblin, "Leonidas Lafayette Polk" (Ph.D. thesis in progress, University of North Carolina), chapter 3.

[28]Bolling Hall, Jr., to his father, Nov. 19, 1861; Will T. Martin to his sister, Jan. 31, 1863, typescript in private possession.

[29]J. H. Puckett to his wife, June 27, 1862, manuscript, University of Texas.

[30]Captain James A. Graham to his mother, Sept. 13, 1864, manuscript, University of North Carolina.

[31]Z. J. Armistead to his brother, May 31, 1864, typescript, Georgia Archives.

[32]Only fifteen out of sixty letters written by W. C. McClellan were prepaid. T. J. Newberry in a letter to his father of Feb. 20, 1863 said: "I dont put Stamps on my letters [because] they Say they will go better without them." Manuscript in author's possession. The Confederate postal rate was raised from five to ten cents (per half ounce) on April 19, 1862. Matthews, *Statutes at Large of the Permanent Government*, First Session, chapter 45.

[33]M. M. Quaife, editor, *Absalom Grimes, Confederate Mail Runner* (New Haven, 1926), 49 ff.

[34]*Ibid.*, 65.

[35]For the engrossing details of these feats, see Quaife, op. cit., 113 ff. Subsequent publication in St. Louis newspapers of the captured letters must have produced considerable embarrassment among Confederate sympathizers. See Missouri *Democrat*, Sept. 8, 10, 1862, and Missouri *Republican*, Sept. 7, 8, 9, 1862.

[36]New Orleans *Daily Crescent*, Dec. 4, 1861.

[37]Robert M. Gill to his wife, Oct. 6, 1863, manuscript in author's possession.

[38]Diary of Maurice K. Simons, entry of April 24, 1863, manuscript photostat, University of Texas.

[39]James L. G. Wood to his father, Aug. 5, 1864, manuscript, Georgia Archives.

[40]J. T. Terrell to his mother, July 9, 1864, manuscript in private possession.

[41]Letters of Robert M. Gill to his wife; Gill was mortally wounded near Atlanta, Aug. 31, 1864.

[42]W. J. Honnoll to his cousin, Aug. 27, 1863, manuscript, Emory University.

[43]G. W. Athey to his mother, Nov. 11, 1863.

[44]J. F. Coghill to "Dear Mit," April 10, March 28, 1862, manuscripts, Duke University.

[45]W. C. Simmons to his cousin, Feb. 12, 1862, manuscript, Emory University.

[46]Thomas Warrick to Ab Widman, Feb. 12, 1863, manuscript, Alabama Archives.

[47]W. J. Honnoll to his wife, Aug. 27, 1863.

[48]Thomas Warrick to his wife, Oct. 6, 1862, and Jan. 11, 12, 1863.

[49]W. B. Lance to his father, Aug. 18, 1863, manuscript, Louisiana State University.

[50]Thomas Warrick to his wife, April 8, 1863.

[51]For a misquotation of this rhyme, see undated letter of J. M. Guess to his wife, from Camp Moore, La., manuscript, Confederate Memorial Hall.

[52]Letter of Thomas Warrick to his father, Sept. 10, 1862, and those of various subsequent dates to his wife.

[53]Charles Futch to John Futch, Oct. 16, 1861, manuscript, North Carolina Historical Commission.

[54]Thomas Warrick to Martha Ann Warrick, April 30, 1862.

[55]Spencer G. Welch, A Confederate Surgeon's Letters to his Wife (New York, 1911), 121; John Rogers to his brother, June 24, 1861, manuscript, Emory University; J. L. Anderson to his mother, Jan. 21, 1862, manuscript, Emory University.

[56]W. C. McClellan to his sister, Aug. 31, 1861.

[57]W. C. McClellan to his brother, Oct. 6, 1861.

[58]J. F. Coghill to his brother, Oct. 6, 1864, and James K. Wilkerson to his sister, Aug. 29, 1864, manuscripts, Duke University.

[59]Undated letter of J. M. Guess to his wife.

[60]Manuscript dated May 19, 1864, Alabama Archives.

[61]Frank Moss to his sister, March 21, 1863.

[62]James K. Wilkerson to his father, June 3, 1862; S. W. Farrow wrote his wife July 19, 1863: "If I had a good place to write on I would soon be a good pensman, as I write ten letters for other men to where I write one for myself. Sometimes I write five or six a day for the Boys." Manuscript, University of Texas.

[63]Letter of Aug. 2, 1863, manuscript, Georgia Archives.

[64]W. W. Brown to his mother, June 4, 1862, manuscript, Duke University.

[65]Robert M. Gill to his wife, June 15 and Nov. 30, 1862.

[66]D. Hunter to his wife, June 9, 1862, manuscript among Miscellaneous Civil War Letters, University of Texas.

[67]William R. Stillwell to his wife, Nov. 30, 1862; the child proved to be a girl and was apparently named Virginia.

[68]Mrs. Alfred W. Bell to her husband, Sept. 5, 1862, manuscript, Duke University. Bell had previously teased his wife about flirtation with "fancy girls'" in the environs of camp.

[69]John H. Hartman to his wife, Feb. 6, 1864, manuscript, Duke University.

[70]Thomas Warrick to his wife, Jan. 11, 1863.

[71]Jerome Yates to his mother, Jan. 11, 1864, manuscript, Heartman Collection.

[72]V. S. Rabb to his sister, July 2, 1864, manuscript photostat, University of Texas.

[73]Manuscript dated Aug. 13, 1863, location and correspondents restricted to confidence.

[74]Confidential manuscript dated Dec. 1, 1863.

[75]Robert E. Hill to Mary Scott Hill, April 29, 1864, manuscript, University of Texas.

[76]E. P. Becton to his wife, Oct. 16, 1862, manuscript, University of Texas.

[77]See O. R., series 1, XXIII, part 2, 951; XXV, part 2, 746; LI, part 2, 712.

[78]Occasionally letters from homefolk containing disloyal sentiments fell into the hands of military officers and were passed on to higher authorities, but apparently no action was taken to prevent delivery of other such mail in camp. Ibid., series 1, XXIII, part 2, 951.

[79]Ibid., series 4, III, 642.

[80]William J. Whatley to his wife, Oct. 12, 1862.

[81]Frank Moss to his sister, Nov. 27, 1862.

[82]William Decatur Howell to his mother, June 26, 1864, manuscript in possession of Maud Morrow Brown, University, Mississippi.

[83]T. J. Newberry to his father, April 18, 1863.

[84]Capt. S. G. Pryor to his wife, Feb. 20, 1863, typescript, Georgia Archives.

[85]Lt. John B. Evans to his wife, June 6, 1864, manuscript, Duke University.

[86]Erastus Higgins to James Reding, April 25, 1865, manuscript, University of Texas.

[87]Copy of letter filed with A. N. Erskine Papers, manuscript, University of Texas.

[88]Robert M. Gill to his wife, June 14, 1862.

[89]R. G. Hutson to his wife, Feb. 17, 1862, manuscript, Duke University.

[90]Jonas A. Bradshaw to his wife, Jan. 26, 1862, manuscript, Duke University.

[91]B. L. Mobley to his father, Nov. 3, 1861, manuscript, Emory University.

[92]Undated item, but evidently October 1863, found among William R. Stillwell Papers. Stillwell wrote the poem while serving with the Army of Tennessee near Chattanooga.

[93]Ibid.

[94]Manuscript among Thomas Warrick Letters.

Chapter XII

KICKING OVER THE TRACES

[1] A manuscript copy of the proceedings is filed with Washington Artillery Papers in Confederate Memorial Hall, New Orleans. This collection will be cited hereinafter as W. A. Papers.

[2] Robinson, op. cit., 362-365.

[3] Regimental court-martial proceedings, manuscript, Confederate Memorial Hall.

[4] General Order Book of the Army of the Mississippi, Jan. 6-Aug. 24, 1862, manuscript, Confederate Memorial Hall.

[5] In the spring of 1862, however, General Beauregard approved a sentence of hanging for murder handed down by a general court-martial in the case of one Dan Whritson, even though such a sentence was beyond authority conferred by war regulations. His reason for setting aside established rules was that the crime was committed in Kentucky, "where ordinary resort to a civil court for his punishment was impossible." Ibid.

[6] O. R., series 1, XIX, part 2, 597-598.

[7] Robinson, op. cit., 367-369.

[8] O. R., series 4, II, 288, 1003; III, 709.

[9] Miscellaneous court-martial proceedings, W. A. Papers.

[10] William J. Whatley to his wife, Nov. 18, 1862, manuscript, University of Texas.

[11] Miscellaneous court-martial proceedings, W. A. Papers.

[12] General Order No. 55, 1862, Headquarters Department of South Carolina, Georgia, and Florida, p. 2, pamphlet, National Archives. Pemberton, the departmental commander, ordered remittance of the sentences on the ground that they were absurdly light. Ibid., 10.

[13] Miscellaneous court-martial proceedings, W. A. Papers.

[14] Court-Martial Records, Confederate Archives, chapter I, volumes 194-201, manuscripts, National Archives. The cases cited are from volume 198, pp. 384-498. The eight volumes consist mainly of sentences imposed by general courts-martial and military courts, though portions of volumes 197 and 198 give the offense as well as the sentence; in many instances the offense can be ascertained from the nature of the penalty. The records extend over the entire period of the war and include both eastern and western commands, though the Army of Northern Virginia is better represented than other departments. Total cases listed run well up into the thousands. A portion of volume 199 is devoted to indorsements of and correspondence concerning courts-martial. Hereafter in this chapter these records will be cited as C. M. Records.

¹⁵Records of the First Kentucky Brigade, Confederate Archives, chapter II, volume, 308, p. 333.

¹⁶Miscellaneous court-martial proceedings, W. A. Papers.

¹⁷General Order No. 26, 1863, Headquarters Trans-Mississippi Department, in bound volume of printed separates, Confederate Archives, chapter II, volume 74, p. 223.

¹⁸C. M. Records, chapter I, volume 194, p. 152.

¹⁹*Ibid.*, volume 198, p. 443.

²⁰Lewis R. Tomlinson to his grandfather, Oct. 1, 1864, manuscript among miscellaneous Civil War Letters, Duke University.

²¹C. M. Records, chapter I, volume 194, p. 214, and volume 197, p. 120; General Order No. 197, 1863, Headquarters District of Texas, New Mexico, and Arizona, in Confederate Archives, chapter II, volume 114, p. 103; General Order No. 11, 1863, Headquarters Army of the West, *ibid.*, volume 211, pp. 35-36. Sometimes offenders thus punished were dishonorably discharged from the army at the completion of their sentence.

²²C. M. Records, chapter I, volume 194, p. 13; volume 195, p. 61; and volume 198, pp. 390, 421, 435. In the case of the South Carolinian, General Lee remitted the branding.

²³*Ibid.*, volume 195, p. 341.

²⁴General Order Book, Army of the Mississippi, Jan. 6-Aug. 24, 1862.

²⁵General Order Book Crescent Regiment, Sept. 1862-Sept. 1863, manuscript, Confederate Memorial Hall.

²⁶C. M. Records, chapter I, volume 197, pp. 131, 137; volume 198, pp. 383, 385, 393.

²⁷Crenshaw Hall to his father, March 21, 1864, manuscript, Alabama Archives.

²⁸Of 913 cases, covering roughly the last six months of the war, for which both offenses and sentences are recorded in the Confederate Archives, 372 are for desertion. Other offenses in the order of their frequency are: absence without leave, 177; conduct prejudicial to good order and military discipline, 99; misbehavior before the enemy, 44; disobedience of orders, 40; neglect of duty, 34; theft and robbery, 20; mutiny and exciting mutiny, 19; insubordination and disrespect to superiors, 16; drunkenness, 12; sleeping at post of duty, 11; quitting guard and otherwise deserting post of duty, 10; breaking guard, 6; self-mutilation, 3; straggling, 3; selling clothes, 2; miscellaneous, 45. These cases were largely from the Army of Northern Virginia. They were about evenly distributed between military courts and general courts-martial. C. M. Records, chapter I, volume 198, pp. 382-512.

²⁹*O. R.*, series 1, XXIII, part 2, 954-955; XLVI, part 2, 1230.

³⁰General orders and circulars, Department of South Carolina, Georgia, and Florida, July 19, 1862-May 28, 1863, Confederate Archives,

394 THE LIFE OF JOHNNY REB

chapter II, volume 43, pp. 289, 408. Rather than permit the setting of a precedent for such trifling punishment, Beauregard remitted the sentences.

[31]C. M. Records, chapter I, volume 198, pp. 384-402.

[32]*Ibid.*, 382-512. Sixty-seven of the culprits were to be shot and three to be hanged. Further evidence of lenient tendencies on the part of these courts and courts-martial is evidenced by the fact that in 112 cases (in addition to the 245) where prisoners were charged with desertion, the tribunals substituted the charge of absence without leave.

[33]*Ibid.*; O. R., series 1, XXIX, part 2, 806-807.

[34]Diary of George W. Jones, typescript in private possession. One prisoner thus spared by a last-minute reprieve deserted the next night and successfully evaded capture for the remainder of the war. W. J. Worsham, *op. cit.*, 77.

[35]C. E. Taylor to his father, Jan. 17, 1863, manuscript, Heartman Collection.

[36]O. R., series 1, XXXII, part 3, 626.

[37]An insight into flogging technique is afforded by the following report in the Richmond *Dispatch*, October 6, 1862, of the punishment of a deserter named Owen Maguire: "A stout dragoon from Captain Wrenn's Company volunteered to perform the duty. Maguire was tied up to a tree by the hands and feet and received the punishment with much wiggling and twisting. It seemed to be awful; it was honestly laid on with a double leather strap, broad and long. When let down he looked quite exhausted." Private J. F. Coghill of North Carolina wrote his father March 29, 1863, that two soldiers had recently died as a result of floggings. Manuscript, Duke University.

[38]C. M. Records, chapter I, volume 194, p. 55.

[39]*Ibid.*, volume 195, pp. 73, 87.

[40]General Order No. 22, 1863, Headquarters Trans-Mississippi Department, Confederate Archives, chapter II, volume 74, p. 229. Riding the wooden horse was used occasionally for offenses other than desertion.

[41]John Crittenden to his wife, Dec. 20, 1862, typescript, University of Texas.

[42]Thomas Warrick to his wife, April 11, June 11, Dec. 19, 1862, Oct. 26, 1863, and June 11, 1864, manuscripts, Alabama Archives.

[43]Miscellaneous court-martial proceedings, W. A. Papers.

[44]General Order No. 24, 1862, Headquarters Department of Texas, pamphlet among O. M. Roberts Papers. The writer found several instances of death being prescribed for violence against superior officers, but such sentences were amazingly rare, and some of them were set aside by higher authority.

[45]*Ibid.*

[46]General Order No. 6, 1861, Headquarters Department of Texas, pamphlet among O. M. Roberts Papers. The offender in this instance was a corporal.

[47]Confederate Archives, chapter II, volume 41, pp. 20-21.

[48]General Order Book, Army of the Mississippi, Jan. 6-Aug. 24, 1862.

[49]General Order No. 87, 1863, Headquarters Department of Northern Virginia, pamphlet among C. S. Venable Papers, University of Texas.

[50]General Order Book, Crescent Regiment, Sept. 1862-Sept. 1863.

[51]General Order No. 26, 1863, Headquarters Trans-Mississippi Department, Confederate Archives, chapter II, volume 74, p. 223.

[52]C. M. Records, chapter I, volume 194, pp. 96, 210; volume 195, pp. 338, 445; volume 198, p. 403. Noll, op. cit., 13. Welch, op. cit., 45. Joseph Hergesheimer, Swords and Roses (New York, 1929), 308. Sentence in the last mentioned case—that of the march from San Antonio to Austin—was remitted by the departmental commander. General Order No. 8, 1864, Headquarters Department of Texas, New Mexico, and Arizona, Confederate Archives, chapter II, volume 113, pp. 34-35.

[53]Robinson, op. cit., 365.

[54]New Orleans Daily Crescent, June 25, 1861.

[55]Diary of D. P. Hopkins, typescript, University of Texas.

[56]O. R., series 1, XXXII, part 2, 654.

[57]Diary of C. R. Hanleiter, manuscript, Atlanta Historical Society, entries of Dec. 8, 1861, April 2, 1862, and July 25, 1863.

[58]In his official report of Shiloh, Bragg complained of the ill effects of random shooting by troops en route from Corinth to the scene of battle; firing by volleys and single shots, he said, was kept up "all night and until 7 A.M. next morning April 5, by the undisciplined troops of our front, in violation of positive orders, under such circumstances little or no rest could be obtained by our men." O. R., series 1, X, part 1, 464.

[59]James A. Hall to his father, Jan. 17, 1862, manuscript, Alabama Archives.

[60]Diary of A. L. P. Vairin, entry of April 19, 1862, manuscript, Mississippi Archives. Walter K. Wendell made this entry in his diary while stationed near Fredericksburg, June 16, 1861: "Sentinels gave several false alarms last night. Picket guard fired at and killed 1 dog dead , . . . He was made this morning to carry ye dead dog in his arms around the encampment double quick." Typescript, Tennessee State Library.

[61]General Hindman in 1863 tabooed the wooden horse and "other methods of punishment having the character of torture." O. R., series 1, XXXI, part 3, 881.

[62]Robert A. Jarman, *op. cit.*, 25, typescript in possession of Maud Morrow Brown, University, Mississippi.

[63]Peak, *op. cit.*, manuscript in private possession.

[64]Record Book of Company I, First Virginia Regiment, entry of Sept. 18, 1864, manuscript, Confederate Museum.

[65]Diary of G. L. Griscom, entries of Oct. 31 and Nov. 13, 1861, manuscript, University of Texas.

[66]O. R., series 1, XXXII, part 3, 877.

[67]*Ibid.*, XLII, part 2, 1276-1277.

[68]Theodore Mandeville to his sister, Dec. 29, 1861, Jan. 3, 1862, manuscripts, Louisiana State University.

[69]John McGrath, "In a Louisiana Regiment," *Southern Historical Society Papers*, XXXI (1903), 104.

[70]William Decatur Howell to his mother, June 2, 3, 4, 1864, manuscript in possession of Maud Morrow Brown, University, Mississippi.

[71]Letter of S. W. Farrow, April 19, 1864, manuscript, University of Texas.

[72]John Crittenden to his wife, April 23, 1863, typescript, University of Texas.

[73]William S. Whatley to his wife, Dec. 4, 1862, manuscript photostat, University of Texas.

[74]Diary of James J. Kirkpatrick, entry of Aug. 13, 1863, manuscript, University of Texas.

[75]T. W. Hall to his sister, Jan. 28, 1862, manuscript, Alabama Archives.

[76]Thomas Caffey to his sister, June 26, 1861, "War Letters of Thomas Caffey," *Montgomery Advertiser*, March 28, 1909.

[77]Heros von Borcke, Patrick Cleburne and other foreigners were quite popular with their men, but most non-native officers, including Cleburne, had greater difficulty securing promotion than did Southern-born men. Ella Lonn, *Foreigners in the Confederacy* (Chapel Hill, 1940), 132 ff.

[78]Nicholas A. Davis, *The Campaign from Texas to Maryland with the Battle of Fredericksburg* (Richmond, 1863), 18-19.

[79]Anonymous diary of a Louisiana soldier, entry of Oct. 25, 1863, manuscript, Confederate Memorial Hall.

[80]Diary of William H. Hill, entry of Aug. 10, 1861, manuscript, Mississippi Archives; C. W. Stephens to his sister, Oct. 14, 1863, manuscript in private possession.

[81]Jerome Yates to his mother, Aug. 20, 1861, manuscript, Heartman Collection.

[82]W. C. McClellan to his brother Bob, Nov. 9, 1861, manuscript in private possession.

[83]Captain James Hays to his wife, Jan. 20, 1863, typescript, Georgia Archives.

[84]John Crittenden to his wife, May 31, 1864, typescript, University of Texas.

[85]John Crittenden to his father, July 12, 1864.

[86]Anonymous diary of a Louisiana soldier, entry of Aug. 5, 1862, manuscript, Heartman Collection.

[87]Letter of March 18, 1863, manuscript, Louisiana State University.

[88]Note on letter of General Walker to his wife, Nov. 28, 1864, typescript, University of Texas.

[89]Randolph H. McKim, "Glimpses of the Confederate Army," Miller, op. cit., VIII, 129.

[90]Diary of George W. Jones, entry of Sept. 18, 1862.

[91]Douglas, op. cit., 115-116.

[92]Robert M. Gill to his wife, manuscript in author's possession.

[93]Anonymous diary of a Louisiana Soldier, entry of April 8, 1864.

[94]W. A. Rorer, an officer of intelligence and good standing, wrote to his wife, Nov. 12, 1863: "The officers of our regiment made an effort to get rid of our colonel on account of drunkenness and incompetence, all wanted him disposed of, there was no difficulty in proving everything, yet he got out on a legal quibble. Our army here is cursed with incompetent and drunken officers, yet there is no way to get rid of them." On March 31, 1864, while functioning as president of a court-martial, he observed: "I am weary of it, there is folly, mismanagement and meanness everywhere in the army. With good management we could have the finest army in the world. I have no heart to punish men for disobeying the orders of fools, still it must be done." Manuscripts among W. M. Willcox Papers, Duke University.

[95]O. R., series 1, XLVI, part 2, 1249; series 4, II, 205-206, 1001.

[96]Ibid., series 1, XLVII, part 2, 1149-1152; report to William H. Boggs of inspection of Wharton's Cavalry Corps, Jan. 30, 1865, manuscript among L. M. Nutt Papers, University of North Carolina.

[97]O. R., series 1, XXX, part 2, 611-612.

[98]A. L. Harrington to his brother, June 13, 1864, manuscript, Duke University. A general court-martial, sitting at Charleston in early 1863, found that a Georgia captain gambled on one occasion with his soldiers while a tentful of enlisted men looked on, and that in another instance he permitted a private to say to him with impunity: "You are a damned rogue and a thief, and if you will take off your stripes I will give you a damned licking." Confederate Archives, chapter II, volume 43, pp. 491-493.

[99]Daily Richmond Enquirer, Nov. 4, 1864.

[100]O. R., series 1, VI, 531.

[101]Ibid., XXXII, part 3, 877-879.

398   THE LIFE OF JOHNNY REB

Ibid., LI, part 2, 111.

Ibid., XLII, part 2, 1276-1277.

Ibid., XLVI, part 2, 1247-1248. On January 20, 1865, Lee wrote A. P. Hill concerning inspection reports of the latter's corps: "The superior officers, except the Brigadier in McRae's Brigade, visit and inspect the troops very seldom. There is also a general deficiency in the instruction of men and officers in drill and tactics . . . . Public animals are not well treated or fed." He intimated further that deficiencies in equipment and clothing were due in part to negligence of officers. Manuscript, Confederate Museum.

Chapter XIII

THE DEADLIEST FOE

[1]J. W. Love to his family, manuscript, Duke University.

[2]E. J. Ellis to Stephen Ellis, manuscript, Louisiana State University.

[3]Alfred Bell to his wife, April 25, 1862, manuscript, Duke University.

[4]Southern Historical Society Papers, XX (1892), 115; Surgeon General of the United States Army, Medical and Surgical History of the War of the Rebellion (Washington, D. C., 1870-1888), Medical History, III, 1. Hereinafter the abbreviation Surgeon General will be used for the author of this work. There is apparently a discrepancy between Jones's estimate of the ratio of deaths from disease to those from casualties in battle as given in the Southern Historical Society Papers and as cited in the Medical and Surgical History. The writer accepted the figure given by the Medical and Surgical History because of the alleged examination and approval of that figure by Confederate Adjutant General S. Cooper.

[5]Stanley, op. cit., 169.

[6]Matthews, Statutes at Large of the Confederate Congress, Permanent Government, Session II, Chapter 41; O. R., series 4, II, 408-409; General Order No. 58, Adjutant and Inspector General's Office, August 14, 1862, Confederate Archives, chapter I, volume 4, manuscript, National Archives.

[7]A. E. McGarity to his wife, April 21, 1864, typescript in possession of E. C. Burnett, Washington, D. C.

[8]Frank Richardson to his mother, October 8, 1862, manuscript, University of North Carolina.

[9]DeLeon, op. cit., 142; McGrath, op. cit., 112.

[10]O. R., series 1, XI, part 3, p. 454.

[11]C. Irvine Walker to Ada Sinclair, Nov. 10, 1864, typescript, University of Texas.

[12]Diary of Arthur M. Hyatt, manuscript, Louisiana State University.

[13]O. R., series 1, XLI, part 4, 1003.

[14]Battle-Fields of the South, II, 112-113.

[15]Charleston Daily Courier, April 10, 1862.

[16]C. Irvine Walker to Ada Sinclair, May 19, 1862.

[17]O. R., series 1, X, part 1, 776.

[18]Southern Historical Society Papers, XX (1892), 130.

[19]O. R., series 1, XXVIII, part 2, 589-590, 598-600.

[20]Diary of Richard W. Waldrop, manuscript, University of North Carolina.

[21]O. R., series 1, XLII, part 2, 1273.

[22]Ibid., series 1, XLVI, part 2, 1099-1100.

[23]J. M. Jordan to his wife, June 27, 1864, typescript, Georgia Archives.

[24]New Orleans Daily Crescent, June 11, 1861.

[25]H. A. Tutwiler to "Nettie," June 25, 1862, manuscript among McCorvey Papers, University of North Carolina.

[26]Montgomery Daily Mail, April 17, 1863.

[27]D. M. Key to his wife, April 30, 1863, manuscript, University of North Carolina.

[28]Ibid.

[29]J. H. Puckett to his wife, March 7, 1862, manuscript, University of Texas.

[30]J. E. Thornton to his wife, March 5, 1862, manuscript in private possession.

[31]E. T. Clark to Mary Johnston, Aug. 10, 1861, manuscript in private possession.

[32]Ben Robertson to his sister, Feb. 2, 1862, manuscript photostat, University of Texas.

[33]W. C. McClellan to his sister, Jan. 12, 1863, manuscript in private possession.

[34]Diary of William E. Bradley, entry of April 25, 1865, manuscript in private possession.

[35]W. C. McClellan to his sister Jan. 12, 1863; J. H. Puckett to his wife, March 23, 1863; Fletcher, op. cit., 22.

[36]Hanks, op. cit., 81; Cate, op. cit., 31.

[37]W. C. McClellan to his sister, April 22, 1863.

[38]Thomas Warrick to Martha Warrick, March 22, 1863, manuscript, Alabama Archives.

[39]Gerrish and Hutchinson, op. cit., 180.

[40]Surgeon General, op. cit., III, 649.

[41]W. B. Blanton, *Medicine in Virginia in the Nineteenth Century* (Richmond, 1933), 296.

[42]O. R., series 1, VI, 817.

[43]William H. Phillips to his mother, Aug. 13, 1861, manuscript, Duke University.

[44]A. N. Erskine to his wife, July 27, 1862, manuscript, University of Texas.

[45]Surgeon General, op. cit., II, 26-30.

[46]Blanton, op. cit., 296-297.

[47]Marietta M. Andrews, editor, *Scraps of Paper* (New York, 1929), 88.

[48]Surgeon General, op. cit., II, 26-32.

[49]*Ibid.*, III, 106.

[50]*Ibid.*, 102-108.

[51]Blanton, op. cit., 292.

[52]Surgeon General, op. cit., III, 31, 205, 207. Conclusions concerning typhoid are difficult to draw because of the confusion of nomenclature. The term "continued fevers" is used in the *Medical and Surgical History of the War of the Rebellion* to designate typhoid, typhus and "common continued fevers." The meaning of the last-named classification is not clear, but apparently it was used to designate chicken pox, scarlet fever and various diseases resembling typhoid, which could not be clearly recognized as such. Among Confederates "camp fever" seems to have had divers connotations, though in some instances the term was used synonymously with typhoid. Joseph Jones, *Medical and Surgical Memoirs* (New Orleans, 1876-1890), I, 669. Professor George Worthington Adams in a splendid article entitled "Confederate Medicine" says: "There was considerable argument as to whether the 'camp fever' which bedeviled the army was typhoid or some vague newcomer. The disputants could arrive at no definite decision, but the modern student is inclined to suspect that the paratyphoids, then unknown, made the variant cases whose presence confused the doctors." *Journal of Southern History*, VI (1940), 162.

[53]Surgeon General, op. cit., III, 627-628. An argument was carried on with some vehemence, but with no settlement, between W. A. Carrington and L. Guild as to whether or not the disease was introduced into the army from Virginia hospitals or into the hospitals from the army. See Letter Book of the Medical Director of the Army of Northern Virginia, June 28, 1862-Aug. 29, 1862, Confederate Archives, chapter VI, volume 641, pp. 22, 70, 71, manuscript, National Archives; this source will be cited hereinafter as Guild, Letter Book.

[54]Surgeon General, op. cit., III, 627-628.

[55]*Ibid.*, 638-648. Guild, Letter Book, volume 641, 83-84. Inspection Reports and Letters Sent, Office of the Medical Director of Hospitals

in Virginia, Confederate Archives, chapter VI, volume 416, pp. 65-67 (to be cited hereinafter as Carrington, Inspection Reports), manuscript, National Archives. Correspondence of the Confederate Surgeon General's Office, Confederate Archives, chapter VI, volume 739, pp. 193, 250, 362, 523, 529 (to be cited hereinafter as Moore, Correspondence), manuscript, National Archives.

[56]Jones, Medical and Surgical Memoirs, I, 650-666. Jones and other wartime authorities do not mention influenza, but a present-day medical historian says: "During the Civil War a type of endemic pneumonia was described corresponding to our understanding of influenzal pneumonia." Blanton, op. cit., p. 248.

[57]Courtney R. Hall, "Confederate Medicine," Medical Life, XLII (1935), 479-480; Surgeon General, op. cit., III, 31.

[58]Thomas Warrick to his wife, June 15, 1862. Another Reb wrote, "Ben Parker has the yellow Ganders." J. E. Thornton to his wife, March 5, 1862.

[59]Surgeon General, op. cit., III, 707-708; B. E. Yerbey to his father, Jan. 31, 1862, typescript, Georgia Archives.

[60]In 1861 and 1862, according to Joseph Jones, 29, 334 cases of rheumatism were reported. Surgeon General, op. cit., III, 31.

[61]See supra, chapter 3.

[62]Guild, Letter Book, volume 642, p. 13; Confederate States Medical and Surgical Journal, March, 1864.

[63]Walter Keeble to his wife, May 3, 1863, manuscript, University of Texas.

[64]Thomas S. Taylor to his wife, Oct. 4, 1861, manuscript, Alabama Archives.

[65]J. W. Rabb to his sister, Dec. 5, 1861, manuscript, University of Texas.

[66]Charles W. Hutson to his mother, July 6, 1861, typescript, University of North Carolina.

[67]Jackson's pamphlet was published by the Augusta (Georgia) Constitutionalist in 1862. The extracts quoted are from pages 21-34.

[68]Published in 1863 by West and Johnson of Richmond.

[69]Ruffin Thomson to his father, April 21, 1862, typescript in private possession.

[70]Robert M. Gill to his wife, Oct. 23, 1863, manuscript in author's possession.

[71]William H. Taylor, De Quibus (Richmond, 1908), 316.

[72]Theodore Mandeville to his sister, Aug. 24, 1861, manuscript, Louisiana State University.

[73]Moore, Correspondence, volume 739, p. 290, and volume 740, pp. 105-113.

[74]O. R., series 4, II, 467.

[75]J. M. Kiracofe to his wife, March 20, 1864, manuscript, Duke University.

[76]Adams, op. cit., 159-160; David Thompson to his sister, March 19, 1863, manuscript, University of North Carolina.

[77]Moore, Correspondence, volume 739, pp. 290, 537; volume 740, p. 679; volume 741, pp. 185, 352.

[78]Adams, op. cit., 159.

[79]The Camp Follower (Augusta, Ga., 1864), 45.

[80]William H. Taylor, op. cit., 320.

[81]Carrington, Inspection Reports, volume 364, p. 214; volume 416, p. 118. Moore, Correspondence, volume 741, p. 326.

[82]Moore, Correspondence, volumes 739-741 passim; O. R., series 1, XLVI, part 2, 1217; series 4, III, 875-879, 1074. The difficulty of procuring barrels was also a factor in the liquor shortage.

[83]Simkins and Patton, op. cit., 82 ff.

[84]Richmond Daily Dispatch, Oct. 22, 1861; Moore Correspondence, volume 739, 5.

[85]Harry St. John Dixon to his mother, Dec. 1, 1861, manuscript, University of North Carolina.

[86]An army correspondent wrote from Selma, Alabama, Dec. 15, 1864: "The so called 'soldiers homes' or 'Waysides' in most cases are the greatest humbugs of the war. The officials, as in the hospitals, are gorged with the good things which unsophisticated mankind sends there, believing it for the soldiers, and the poor soldier is cheated and humbugged in a most extravagant manner." He said further that Negro servants at these places charged $1.00 for shoe shines. Montgomery Daily Mail, Dec. 28, 1864.

[87]Moore, Correspondence, volume 739, pp. 66, 137, 139.

[88]Richmond Daily Dispatch, May 6, 1862.

[89]B. E. Stiles to his mother, April 4, 1862, manuscript, University of North Carolina.

[90]William H. Phillips to his father, Oct. 14, 1861.

[91]Richmond Daily Dispatch, June 3, 1862; O. R., series 1, X, part 2, 326, 533; XI, part 3, 616.

[92]Guild, Letter Book, volume 641, pp. 36-37.

[93]Cumming, op. cit., 13-17; Richmond Daily Dispatch, April 24, 1862.

[94]Richmond Daily Dispatch, July 1-25, 1862.

[95]John W. Imboden, "The Confederate Retreat from Gettysburg," Battles and Leaders of the Civil War, III, 424.

[96]Welch, op. cit., 26-27.

[97]Diary of Edmund Dewitt Patterson, entries of Aug. 30, 31, 1862, typescript in private possession.

[98]Simkins and Patton, op. cit., 86.

[99]Moore, Correspondence, volume 741, p. 353.
[100]Carrington, Inspection Reports, volume 416, p. 61.
[101]Guild, Letter Book, volume 641, p. 121.
[102]Carrington, Inspection Reports, volume 416, p. 109.
[103]Ibid., 110, and volume 364, p. 356; Cumming, op. cit., 46.
[104]Cumming, op. cit., 63.
[105]John A. Hall to A. M. Morrow, May 3, 1862, manuscript, Emory University; William R. Stillwell to his wife, Oct. 10, 1862, manuscript, Georgia Archives.
[106]Blanton, op. cit., 275.
[107]Carrington, Inspection Reports, volume 416, p. 109.
[108]O. R., series 4, I, 889.
[109]Southern Historical Society Papers, XVII (1889), 7-8.
[110]Adams, op. cit., 164-165.
[111]P.M.H.S., Centenary Series, V, 345-346.
[112]Courtney Hall, op. cit., 473.

Chapter XIV

THE GENTLER SENTIMENTS

[1]William J. Whatley to his wife, Dec. 4, 1862, manuscript photostat, University of Texas.
[2]Dubose Eggleston to Annie Rouhlac, June 9, 1861, manuscript, University of North Carolina; John L. Quince to his sister, Feb. 26, 1865, manuscript, University of North Carolina.
[3]Lieut. William E. Quince to his mother, no place, but 1861, manuscript, University of North Carolina.
[4]John H. Barksdale to his brother, June 12, 1862, manuscript in private possession.
[5]W. C. McClellan to his brother, Aug. 7, 1861, manuscript in private possession; W. M. Moss to his sisters, Nov. 5, 1862, manuscript, University of Texas.
[6]William H. Phillips to his cousin, June 29, 1861, manuscript, Duke University.
[7]Lucius Haney to his sister, March 21, 1863, manuscript, Duke University.
[8]Diary of Albert Moses Luria, entry of Sept. 21, 1863, typescript, University of North Carolina.
[9]Pierson, op. cit., 10-11.
[10]Douglas, op. cit., 326.
[11]Chamberlayne, op. cit., 79.

[12]Theodore Mandeville to his sister, Jan. 3, 1862, manuscript, Louisiana State University; Ben Robertson to his sister, Sept. 7, 1862, manuscript, University of Texas.

[13]Ethelred Crozier to his sister, Jan. 19, 1864, typescript, Tennessee State Library.

[14]Letter to his sister, Dec. 25, 1861.

[15]W. M. Edmonds to his sister, Feb. 10, 1862, manuscript, Emory University.

[16]Diary of C. R. Hanleiter, entry of June 22, 1862, manuscript, Atlanta Historical Society; diary of Harry St. John Dixon, entry of Jan. 2, 1864, manuscript, University of North Carolina.

[17]Ben Robertson to his sister, Sept. 7, 1862.

[18]Diary of D. S. Redding, entry of Sept. 29, 1863, typescript, Georgia Archives.

[19]H. A. Stephens to his sister, Nov. 22, 1863, manuscript in private possession.

[20]W. C. McClellan to his sister, Jan. 3, 1863; John D. Williams to his cousin, Sept. 28, 1863, typescript, Tennessee State Library.

[21]Edwin Tillinghast to his sister, Aug. 24, 1863, manuscript, Emory University.

[22]John H. Chamberlayne to his mother, Dec. 7, 1864, in Chamberlayne, op. cit., 295-296. Chamberlayne was well educated and a captain. His eloquence was considerably greater than that of the average private, but his estimate of women was as representative of common soldiers as of officers.

[23]B. E. Stiles to his mother, Aug. 31, 1861, manuscript, University of North Carolina.

[24]A. B. Simmons to Annie Roulhac, Sept. 21, 1861, manuscript, University of North Carolina.

[25]Joseph J. Cowand to Winaford Cowand, Dec. 29, 1862, manuscript, Duke University.

[26]Diary of Richard W. Waldrop, entry of August 29, 1863, manuscript, University of North Carolina.

[27]Ephraim Anderson, Memoirs, 265.

[28]Carrie Aycock to Mary Stephens, Oct. 12, 1863, manuscript in private possession.

[29]William H. Phillips to his cousin, Sept. 21, 1861, manuscript, Duke University.

[30]J. W. Ward to his sister, May 27, 1863, manuscript, Heartman Collection.

[31]Diary of G. W. Roberts, entry of May 19, 1864, manuscript, Mississippi Archives. Roberts copied both the letter and his answer in his journal.

[32]Ibid.

³³Entry of April 27, 1863, manuscript, University of North Carolina.
³⁴Diary of Harry St. John Dixon, entries of Jan. 2, Jan. 9, Jan. 11, 1864, and June 26, 1865.
³⁵Joseph J. Cowand to his cousin, Dec. 29, 1862.
³⁶Manuscript among Comer Papers, University of North Carolina. John Bunkam is evidently a pseudonym for either Wallace Comer or C. L. Comer, both of whom were soldiers.
³⁷Ethelred Crozier to his sister, Jan. 19, 1864; C. W. Stephens to his sister, April 13, 1864; C. E. Taylor to his sister, Jan. 29, 1864, manuscript, Heartman Collection.
³⁸William H. Phillips to his parents, Dec. 20, 1863.
³⁹Quoted in a letter of James T. Searcy to his sister, March 15, 1864, manuscript, Alabama Archives.
⁴⁰Letter dated Feb. 21, 1864, and signed "Abe," manuscript among J. A. Clement Papers, University of North Carolina.
⁴¹Richmond *Daily Dispatch*, March 21, 1863.
⁴²W. R. Hutson to his sister, Dec. 2, 1862, manuscript, Duke University.
⁴³William Moss to Cinderilla C. Honnoll, Jan. 23, 1864, manuscript, Emory University.
⁴⁴Ben C. Richardson to "Miss Nola," March 20, 1862, manuscript, Virginia State Library.
⁴⁵John N. Dale to Sarah Jane Honnoll, April 5, 1862, manuscript, Emory University.
⁴⁶Daniel Kern to "Dear Friend," Aug. 10, 1862, manuscript among George W. Frank Letters, Duke University.
⁴⁷Henry C. Cribbs to Ann Honnoll, Nov. 9, 1862, March 26, 1863, and May 19, 1863, manuscripts, Emory University.
⁴⁸This extract was quoted in a letter from James A. Hall to Hines Hall, May 31, 1862. The dashes are probably for deletions. Manuscript, Alabama Archives.
⁴⁹W. C. McClellan to his brother, Jan. 25, 1862.

Chapter XV

MUZZLE-LOADERS AND MAKESHIFTS

¹W. L. Fleming, *Civil War and Reconstruction in Alabama* (New York, 1905), 19.
²Josiah Gorgas, "Notes on the Ordnance Department of the Confederate Government," *Southern Historical Society Papers*, XII (1884), 68.

[3]Huse sent over a number of English mechanics to work in Southern arms factories. But when they arrived in Wilmington it was discovered that they had been promised pay in gold. This the ordnance authorities could not afford, but a compromise of one-half gold and one-half Confederate money was proposed. The Englishmen would not accede to the proposition and had to be sent home. "Of all obstinate animals I have ever come in contact with," said Gorgas later, "those English workmen were the most unreasonable." Late in the war many ordnance employees were taken into the army. In October 1864 Gorgas reported: "While two years ago it was difficult to get machinery, we now have a surplus and cannot get workmen to run it. . . . Workmen will not fight and work both." *Ibid.,* XII, 84; II, 60.

[4]Richard D. Steuart, "How Johnny Got His Gun," *Confederate Veteran,* XXXII (1924), 167-168. From this and from other excellent articles on Confederate ordnance by Steuart in the *Confederate Veteran* the writer has drawn freely for the preparation of this chapter.

[5]*O. R.,* series 1, II, 976.

[6]Steuart, *op. cit.,* 167.

[7]Owsley, *op. cit.,* 5 ff.

[8]*O. R.,* series 1, V, 829-830, 886, 896.

[9]W. J. Worsham, *op. cit.,* 22.

[10]Horn, *op. cit.,* 23, 58, 69, 82.

[11]Postscript (added after the war) to letter of C. Irvine Walker to Ada Sinclair, Jan. 15, 1863, typescript, University of Texas.

[12]*O. R.,* series 1, XI, part 2, 498; XII, part 2, 558; XIX, part 1, 141; and XXI, 555.

[13]*Ibid.,* XVI, part 1, 1097.

[14]*Ibid.,* XXV, part 1, 819; XXX, part 2, 23; XXIX, part 2, 628; XXXI, part 3, 874; XXXII, part 2, 604, 697. The dwindling of manpower through desertion and absence without leave in the early months of 1865 gave Lee an excess of weapons. *Ibid.,* XLVI, part 2, 1245-1246.

[15]*Ibid.,* XXVI, part 2, 24; XLI, part 4, 1113.

[16]*Ibid.,* LI, part 2, 111.

[17]*Battle-Fields of the South,* II, 107.

[18]Shannon, *op. cit.,* I, 124.

[19]*Ibid.,* 125.

[20]One reason for the shipment of so many inferior guns to America was the fact that leading European nations had adopted improved types before the outbreak of the Civil War and therefore had huge surpluses of antiquated models on hand. The importunities of American buyers, particularly of Northerners, gave these countries a welcomed opportunity to get rid of their outmoded weapons. According to the Count of Paris, "The refuse of all Europe passed into the hands of the American volunteers." *Ibid.,* 118-119.

21O. R., series 1, XXX, part 2, 82-83, 202, 314. After Chickamauga
an ordnance officer reported: "This brigade is mostly armed with Enfield rifles, using ammunition calibers nos. .57 and .58; . . . caliber
No. .57 was loose and never choked the guns, while the No. .58, after
the first few rounds, was found too large, and frequently choking the
guns to that extent that they could not be forced down, thereby creating some uneasiness among the men using that number of ammunition." Ibid., 277.

22Steuart, op. cit., 169.

23A few Kerr rifles were imported from England for Confederate
sharpshooters, ibid. The high esteem in which sharpshooters held their
choice pieces is reflected in the fact that an Alabamian referred to his
long-range gun as a "Yankee-killer." "Bolly" Hall to Bolling Hall, Sr.,
July 18, 1863, manuscript, Alabama Archives.

24Steuart, op. cit., 168.

25The Confederates devised a machine for making metallic cartridges of the type used in Spencer rifles but the war closed before it
could be put into operation. Ibid., 169. Another repeating gun having
very limited use among Confederates was the Colt's revolving rifle, the
loading mechanism of which was the same as the famous Colt's six-
shooter. George W. Elkins to his sister, May 25, 1862, manuscript in
private possession.

26C. Irvine Walker, Rolls and Historical Sketch of the Tenth South
Carolina Volunteers (Charleston, South Carolina, 1881), 74.

27Miller, op. cit., V, 168.

28Hanks, op. cit., 15-16, manuscript photostat, University of Texas.

29Quaife, op. cit., 21.

30Fremantle, op. cit., 157; McCarthy, op. cit., 27; Robert E. Lee to
A. P. Hill, Jan. 20, 1865, manuscript, Confederate Museum.

31Steuart, "A Pair of Navy Sixes," Confederate Veteran, XXXIII
(1925), 92-94.

32The long knives carried by soldiers were generally called Bowie
knives, "although few of them would have been recognized by the hero
of the Alamo" for whom they were named. Steuart, "Confederate
Swords," Confederate Veteran, XXXIV (1926), 13.

33DeLeon, op. cit., 97.'

34After First Manassas it was rumored that the Louisiana Tigers
threw away their guns and rushed at the Yankees yelling and brandishing their knives; this and similar stories enhanced the popularity of this
type of weapon. Confederate Veteran, XXXIV (1926), 14.

35O. R., series 1, XII, part 3, 842, 845.

36Ibid., X, part 2, 374.

37L. L. Knight, Georgia Landmarks, Memorials, and Legends (Atlanta, 1913), II, 656; Gorgas, op. cit., 74.

[38]Richmond Enquirer, Nov. 24, 1864.

[39]Steuart, "Confederate Swords," Confederate Veteran, XXXIV, 12-13.

[40]Ibid., 12.

[41]O. R., series 1, X, part 2, 334.

[42]Steuart, "The Long Arm of the Confederacy," Confederate Veteran, XXXV (1927), 250-251.

[43]Ibid., 251. Jennings C. Wise, The Long Arm of Lee (Lynchburg, 1915), I, 71.

[44]Ibid.; Gorgas, op. cit., 94.

[45]Douglas, op. cit., 172.

[46]O. R., series 1, XI, part 2, 498; XII, part 2, 558; XVI, part 1, 1094, 1097; XIX, part 1, 141.

[47]Gorgas, op. cit., 68 ff; Confederate Veteran, XXXV (1927), 251-253. For Bragg's reaction to Beauregard's proclamation see his letter to Mrs. Bragg of March 20, 1862, manuscript, Duke University.

[48]Gorgas, op. cit., 81, 94.

[49]O. R., series 1, XI, part 3, 461.

[50]Ibid., XXI, 566.

[51]Ibid., LI, part 2, 307. Much of the difficulty with mountings could be attributed, of course, to the fact that guns of the Civil War period had no spring recoil facilities.

[52]Diary of George W. Jones, typescript in private possession.

[53]Stiles, op. cit., 52; Wise, op. cit., II, 572 ff.

[54]Wise, op. cit., II, 571; Wise says that the Whitworths were six-inch caliber, but Steuart, from a study of ammunition found on the battlefield, concludes that the caliber was not over three inches. Confederate Veteran, XXXV (1927), 253.

[55]Confederate Veteran, XXXV (1927), 252-253. The Brooke gun had a unique feature in the utilization of the so-called air space to lessen the initial tension of the explosive gases.

[56]Steuart, "First in the Art of War," Confederate Veteran, XXXV (1927), 333-334. A battery of six Williams guns was in use in the Confederate Army of the West in 1862, but these had to be discarded because of trouble with the breech lock caused by expansion after repeated firing. Wise thinks it probable that the inventor of the famous Gatling machine gun developed in the North got his idea from the Williams model. Wise, op. cit., I, 32-33. Jackson attempted the use of a mule battery of mountain rifles at Port Republic, but the experiment failed on account of the action of the mules under fire, these animals rolling over on the ground to rid themselves of the guns. This afforded much amusement to infantrymen who with a show of seriousness would inquire of exasperated artillerymen whether the mules or the guns were intended to go off first. Ibid., 174-175.

[57]Gorgas, op. cit., 93. Steuart, "The Long Arm of the Confederacy," Confederate Veteran, XXXV (1927), 252.

[58]Wise, op. cit., I, 110-111; II, 911-918. At the beginning of the war the personnel of a battery of light artillery consisted of 1 captain, 2 first lieutenants, 2 second lieutenants, 1 sergeant-major or first sergeant, 1 quartermaster-sergeant, 6 sergeants, 12 corporals, 2 buglers, 1 guidon, 2 artifers and from 64 to 125 privates. Ibid., I, 110-111. For "panzer" uses of horse artillery see ibid., I, 166 ff.

[59]Miller, op. cit., V, 176-178.

[60]Ibid., 190. The wrought-iron sabot shell was invented by Dr. Reed of Alabama before the war and perfected during the Confederacy. This invention was of vital importance in that it assured the practicability of rifled artillery. Wise, op. cit., I, 47, 67.

[61]O. R., series 1, IV, 674-675; XXV, part 1, 881.

[62]Gorgas, op. cit., 68-69; O. R., series 4, II, 382-383.

[63]O. R., series 1, IV, 664; VI, 525; Samuel French, Two Wars (Nashville, 1901), 143.

[64]A. P. Van Gelder and Hugo Schlatter, History of the Explosives Industry in America (New York, 1927), 107-109.

[65]Ibid., 111-113.

[66]Fleming, op. cit., 153.

[67]The writer is much indebted to Honorable Francis G. Caffey, formerly of Alabama but now Judge of the United States District Court, Foley Square, New York City, for information about the saltpeter poems. Judge Caffey was related to Haralson and talked with him about the poetry.

[68]Van Gelder and Schlatter, op. cit., 113.

[69]This description of canteens is based largely on types observed in various museums of the South. All of the models discussed may be found in the Confederate Museum at Richmond. One particularly interesting water container in this collection is a doughnut-shaped affair made of brown porcelain. It was carried in the Revolution by Private James Ward, and in the Confederate War by his grandson, Lt. R. A. Ward of the Twenty-second Virginia Battalion.

[70]Josiah Gorgas to Jefferson Davis, Feb. 8, 1878, manuscript, Heartman Collection.

[71]Cap boxes and cartridge boxes are on display in most Confederate museums. The scarcity of leather compelled the use of fabric to some extent in the making of these items. Gorgas, op. cit., 74.

[72]McCarthy, op. cit., 26.

[73]O. R., series 1, XII, part 3, 890.

Chapter XVI

BLUE BELLIES AND BELOVED ENEMIES

[1]Manuscript in possession of Mrs. G. R. Maloney, Richmond, Virginia.

[2]H. C. Kendrick to his homefolk, no date, but early 1863, manuscript, University of North Carolina.

[3]John Wesley Tucker to his father, Feb. 3, 1863, manuscript in possession of Mrs. J. H. Lide, Corinth, Mississippi.

[4]T. W. Montfort to his wife, March 18, 1862, typescript, Georgia Archives.

[5]John Crittenden to his wife, May 29, 1864, typescript, University of Texas.

[6]Robert M. Gill to his wife, July 25, 1864, manuscript in author's possession. Andrew J. Neal made this notation on a Yankee letter that he sent home after the Chickamauga fight: "This is the only respectable letter I have seen of thousands. They are all full of the grossest and vulgarest language." Typescript, Georgia Archives.

[7]Diary of William S. White, entry of June 27, 1862, in Contributions to a History of the Richmond Howitzer Battalion (Richmond, 1883), pamphlet no. 2, p. 119.

[8]Jerome Yates to his mother, June 17, 1863, manuscript, Heartman Collection.

[9]Diary of George W. Jones, entry of Sept. 10, 1862, typescript in private possession.

[10]Ibid., entry of May 23, 1863.

[11]Richmond Daily Dispatch, April 24, May 10, May 12, 1862.

[12]O. R., series 1, XXXVIII, part 3, 716.

[13]W. C. McClellan to Robert McClellan, Jan. 25, 1862, manuscript in private possession.

[14]O. R., series 1, XII, part 2, 202-203; XX, part 1, 880; and LI, part 2, 329; Robert M. Gill to his wife, Oct. 9, 1862, Aug. 7, 1864.

[15]Robert M. Gill to his wife, May 24, 1862.

[16]Manuscript, Heartman Collection.

[17]Diary of R. W. Waldrop, manuscript, University of North Carolina.

[18]A. C. Haskell to his mother, May 4, 1861, manuscript, University of North Carolina.

[19]Letter of Dec. 2, 1863, manuscript, Alabama Archives.

[20]Letter to his mother, April 19, 1862, manuscript, University of North Carolina.

[21]S. G. Pryor to his wife, Sept. 2, 1862, typescript, Georgia Archives.

²²G. L. Robertson to his father, Sept. 14, 1861, manuscript photostat, University of Texas.

²³W. C. McClellan to Robert McClellan, Nov. 9, 1861.

²⁴W. C. McClellan to his sister, April 2, 1863.

²⁵Colonel Laurence Keitt to his wife, May 31, 1864, manuscript, Duke University; J. Joe Evans to his brother, May 11, 1864, manuscript in private possession.

²⁶Letter to his sister, June 11, 1863.

²⁷*Ibid.*, to his father, Feb. 27, 1862.

²⁸Bell Irvin Wiley, op. cit., 310 ff.

²⁹Jerome Yates to his mother, Aug. 10, [1864?].

³⁰Jerome Yates to his sister, Aug. 3, 1864; Thomas Roulhac to his mother, March 13, 1864, manuscript, University of North Carolina; J. M. Jordan to his wife, Feb. 21, 1864, manuscript, Georgia Archives.

³¹W. C. McClellan to Robert McClellan, Aug. 15, 1864.

³²*Battles and Leaders of the Civil War*, I, 82.

³³Will T. Martin to his wife, Nov. 19, 1861, typescript in private possession.

³⁴Clipping from *Confederate Veteran* (no date) in U.D.C. Collection, Georgia Archives.

³⁵Horn, op. cit., 336.

³⁶W. J. Worsham, op. cit., 132.

³⁷Frank Smith, "The Polite War," *Coronet*, III (1937), 44; J. O. Casler, op. cit., 134.

³⁸W. J. Worsham, op. cit., 132.

³⁹Clark, *North Carolina Regiments*, III, 357.

⁴⁰O. R., series 1, XVI, part 1, 977-978.

⁴¹Freeman, op. cit., II, 496.

⁴²Horn, op. cit., 199.

⁴³Mays, op. cit., 46-47.

⁴⁴W. J. Kincheloe to his father, Jan. 12, 1863, manuscript among John W. Daniel Papers, University of Virginia.

⁴⁵*Confederate Veteran*, XXV (1914), 471.

⁴⁶Diary of E. D. Patterson, entry of Jan. 20, 1863, typescript in private possession.

⁴⁷Miller, op. cit., VIII, 136.

⁴⁸*Richmond Daily Dispatch*, July 23, 1864.

⁴⁹W. C. McClellan to Robert McClellan, April 13, 1862; diary of Maurice K. Simons, entry of May 25, 1863, manuscript, University of Texas; A. J. Neal to his father, May 15, 1864.

⁵⁰Diary of R. W. Locke, entry of Nov. 19, 1862, manuscript, Mississippi Archives.

⁵¹H. A. Stephens to Amelia Stephens, Oct. 5, 1863, manuscript in private possession.

⁵²James Elliott, The Southern Soldier Boy (Raleigh, 1907), 46.
⁵³Jerome Yates to his sister, July 19, 1864.
⁵⁴Frank Smith, op. cit., 44-46; Thomas F. Boatwright to his wife, Sept. 27, 1863, manuscript, University of North Carolina; Diary of James J. Kirkpatrick, entries of July 4, 10, 1864, manuscript, University of Texas; Sam Houston Hynds to his mother, Sept. 28, 1861, typescript, Tennessee State Library; Journal of William Chambers, entry of May 25, 1863, P.M.H.S., Centenary Series, V, 272-273; Anderson, op. cit., 333-334.
⁵⁵Jerome Yates to his mother, Jan. 11, 1864.
⁵⁶C. N. Mason to his father, Dec. 9, 1862, manuscript, North Carolina Historical Commission.
⁵⁷Thomas Caffey to his sister, March 24, 1863; James Dinkins, Personal Recollections and Experiences in the Confederate Army (Cincinnati, 1897), 66; Ruffin Thomson to his father, Feb. 26, 1863.
⁵⁸Stiles, op. cit., 157.
⁵⁹Richmond Daily Dispatch, Sept. 6, 1864.
⁶⁰Diary of D. Griffin Gunn, entry of May 10, 1863, manuscript, Confederate Museum, Austin, Texas; D. E. Johnston, The Story of a Confederate Boy (Portland, Ore., 1914), p. 276.
⁶¹Frank Smith, op. cit., 46.
⁶²Confederate Veteran, XXIV (1916), 91.

Chapter XVII

WHAT MANNER OF MEN

¹The Southern states represented by these rolls were Alabama, Arkansas, Louisiana, Mississippi, Georgia and Texas. The rolls referred to here and in subsequent connections are largely from the files of the War Records Division of the National Archives, though some are from collections in archives of Southern states and in private depositories.
²Ella Lonn, Foreigners in the Confederacy, 93-131, 200-240. Professor Lonn's scholarly work, to which I am much indebted, is based primarily on descriptive rolls.
³Southern Historical Society Papers, XXXI (1903), 105-106.
⁴Lonn, Foreigners in the Confederacy, 121, 213-214.
⁵Ibid., 109, 210.
⁶Ibid., 124-128.
⁷Ibid., 96-101.
⁸Ibid., 116-123.
⁹Ibid., 220.

[10]Annie Heloise Abel, *The American Indian as Participant in the American Civil War* (Cleveland, 1919), 25, 155, 326-330; Robinson, *op. cit.*, 352.

[11]Clark, *North Carolina Regiments*, II, 729-730.

[12]S. B. Barron, *The Lone Star Defenders* (New York, 1908), p. 33.

[13]Anderson, *op. cit.*, 159-160.

[14]*Ibid.*, 174; Abel, *op. cit.*, 26-34; *Battles and Leaders of the Civil War*, I, 335-336.

[15]Abel, *op. cit.*, 194-195, 288-289, 326-327; Robinson, *op. cit.*, 351-352. At the Battle of Honey Hill the Confederate force consisted of Texans as well as Indians.

[16]Robinson, *op. cit.*, 351-352.

[17]Abel, *op. cit.*, 150, 268, 333, 337-351.

[18]Bell Irvin Wiley, *op. cit.*, 134-138.

[19]*Ibid.*, 136-144.

[20]*Ibid.*, 110-113, 134.

[21]*Ibid.*, 114-133.

[22]*Ibid.*, 146-160.

[23]There were innumerable examples of faithfulness under duress, and of rejections of freedom when offered. But instances of loyalty in invaded areas were restricted largely to old Negroes, and to house servants whose attachment to masters had been strengthened by intimate association, and who, because of their favored position, had much to lose by emancipation. Field hands, who constituted the great majority of servants, generally abandoned their masters when the coming of the Federals guaranteed immunity from punishment. *Ibid.*, 3-23, 63-84.

[24]Only 11 of the 9,000 were listed as planters. It is likely, therefore, that compilers of rolls did not always distinguish between small and large agricultural operatives, and that some planters are included among those classed as farmers.

[25]Cavalry companies were not included because of the meager descriptive rolls for this branch of the service.

[26]Moore, *op. cit.*, 141 ff. On Oct. 18, 1864, Private William H. Routt wrote to his wife from near Petersburg: "There are a great many new men coming in & they are mostly young men who have managed to keep out until now." Manuscript, Confederate Museum.

[27]O. R., series 1, XI, part 2, 851-852, XXX, part 2, 319-320.

[28]Descriptive Roll, Co. D, Fifth North Carolina Regiment; Descriptive Book, Fifth North Carolina Regiment; and Personal File of E. Pollard. All of these items are in the National Archives. The doctor who filled out Pollard's certificate of disability put his age down as sixty-two, but the Descriptive Roll and the Descriptive Book give the age as seventy-three. These latter should be more reliable than the former. William M. Dame of the Richmond Howitzer Battalion testified that

he knew personally of six men over sixty years of age who served in the ranks throughout the war. Dame, op. cit., 2-3.

[29]Records of the First Kentucky Brigade, Confederate Archives, chapter II, volume 305, p. 35, manuscript, National Archives.

[30]O. R., series 1, X, part 1, 589.

[31]Ibid., XXXVIII, part 3, 803.

[32]Confederate Veteran, II, (1894), 12-13.

[33]Clark, North Carolina Regiments, V, 637-638. One of the thirteen-year-old Hillsboro boys named William Cain was rated as the best drillmaster in Confederate service by the lieutenant colonel of the Twenty-fifth North Carolina Regiment. Written statement of H. C. Dearing, dated November 13, 1861, manuscript in John L. Bailey Collection, University of North Carolina. Originally drillmasters were engaged under informal arrangements by the states. In 1862 Congress authorized the President to employ them for pay at rates to be fixed by the Secretary of War. Matthews, Statutes at Large of the Permanent Government, First Session, chapter 46.

[34]Freeman, op. cit., I, 493-494.

[35]Richmond Daily Dispatch, May 6, 1862.

[36]O. R., series 1, XLI, part 4, 1041-1042.

[37]Battles and Leaders of the Civil War, IV, 483-485. The cadets engaged numbered 260, 35 of whom composed a battery section. The entire corps participated save about 30 left behind to guard the college buildings. Philip Alexander Bruce, Brave Deeds of Confederate Soldiers (Philadelphia, 1916), 260.

[38]Confederate Veteran, IX (1901), 352.

[39]Clark, North Carolina Regiments, II, 330-331.

[40]C. J. Worthington, editor, Madame Loreta Janeta Velasquez (otherwise known as Lt. Harry T. Buford), The Woman in Battle (Hartford, 1876), 43 ff.

[41]Stiles, op. cit., 49.

[42]Henry L. Graves to his mother, Oct. 3, 1862, typescript, Georgia Archives; Stephenson and Davis, op. cit., 436-451, 712-730.

[43]Charles W. Hutson to his mother, July 13, 1861, typescript, University of North Carolina.

[44]E. A. Moore, The Story of a Cannoneer under Stonewall Jackson (New York, 1907), 311; W. H. Morgan, op. cit., 39; Dame, op. cit., passim; McKim, op. cit., 51-55; Stiles, op. cit., 49 ff; S. H. Baldy to his mother, May 31, 1861, manuscript, Emory University; R. W. Waldrop to his father, July 23, 1861, manuscript, University of North Carolina.

[45]E. A. Moore, op. cit.; Dame, op. cit.; McKim, op. cit.; Stiles, op. cit.; McCarthy, op. cit.

[46]For enlightening information as to the prevalency and character of yeomen in the ante-bellum rural population see Blanche Henry

Clark, *The Tennessee Yeoman, 1840-1860* (Nashville, 1942), Herbert Weaver, "Agricultural Population of Mississippi" (unpublished dissertation, 1941), and other studies of middle-class Southern farmers sponsored by Prof. Frank L. Owsley at Vanderbilt University; also Frank L. and Harriet C. Owsley, "The Economic Basis of Society in the Late Ante-Bellum South," *Journal of Southern History*, VI (1940), 25-45.

⁴⁷Wade H. Hubbard to his wife, Oct. 16, 1864, manuscript, Duke University.

⁴⁸General orders, District of Texas, New Mexico and Arizona, December 1862-December 1863. Confederate Archives, chapter II, volume 114, p. 61.

⁴⁹*Ibid.*, 89.

⁵⁰Eggleston, *op. cit.*, 35-36; General Orders, Department of South Carolina, Georgia, and Florida, Confederate Archives, chapter II, volume 40, p. 298-299; volume 43, p. 341-349; General and Special Orders, Division of Virginia Volunteers, *ibid.*, chapter VIII, volume 239, p. 68-69.

⁵¹Robert M. Gill to Bettie Gill, June 10, 1862; manuscript in author's possession; Eggleston, *op. cit.*, 36.

⁵²Diary of Harry St. John Dixon, entries of Nov. 18, Dec. 23, 1864, manuscript, University of North Carolina.

⁵³*Battle-fields of the South*, I, 17-19.

⁵⁴*O. R.*, series 4, III, 709.

⁵⁵Charles W. Hutson to his family, Sept. 14, 1862.

⁵⁶R. W. Waldrop to his father, July 23, 1861, manuscript, University of North Carolina.

⁵⁷Robert M. Gill to his wife, Aug. 22, and Nov. 27, 1862.

⁵⁸Eleanor D. Pace, editor, "The Diary and Letters of William P. Rogers, 1846-1862," *Southwestern Historical Quarterly*, XXXII (1929), 293-295; New Orleans *Daily Crescent*, Jan. 14, 1862.

⁵⁹See *supra*, chapter 8.

⁶⁰Peter McDavid to his sister, Oct. 7, 1863, manuscript, Duke University; Dubose Eggleston to Annie Rouhlac, Sept. 27, 1863, manuscript, University of North Carolina.

⁶¹Unidentified soldier of Eleventh Alabama Regiment (signature torn off) to Miss Annie Rouhlac, Aug. 7, 1863, manuscript, University of North Carolina.

⁶²W. C. McClellan to his father, May 15, 19, 1863.

⁶³Peter McDavid to his sister, Oct. 7, 1863; Dubose Eggleston to Annie Rouhlac, Sept. 27, 1863.

⁶⁴James A. Hall to Joe Hall, April 18, 1864, manuscript, Alabama Archives.

⁶⁵Henry Slade of Longstreet's Corps wrote to his brother, July 26, 1863: "The cavalry is about played out in this Army. They are hollered

at and made the laughing stock of the whole Army." Manuscript, Duke University.

[66]Robert M. Gill to his wife, Feb. 2, 1864.

[67]Samuel P. Collier to his parents, Oct. 11, 1864, manuscript, North Carolina Historical Commission.

[68]J. P. Strange, Notes on Operations of Freeman's Battalion, dated Sept. 15, 1866, manuscript among L. M. Nutt Papers, University of North Carolina.

[69]Jerome Yates to his mother, Jan. —?, 1863, manuscript, Heartman Collection.

[70]In June 1864, Colonel George Brent wrote after an inspection that 654 deserters were borne on the rolls of the Forrest's command, O. R., series 1, XXXIX, part 2, 642. For other instances of desertion of infantry to join the cavalry see ibid., XXXII, part 2, 604, 622-623.

[71]J. W. Rabb to his mother, June 29, 1862, manuscript, University of Texas.

[72]Eggleston, op. cit., 49-51; O. R., series 1, XVIII, 772.

[73]O. R., series 1, XX, part 1, 741; XXI, 647-648, 656.

[74]Pace, op. cit., 294; Caldwell, op. cit., 124; Eggleston, op. cit., 49-51; DeLeon, op. cit., 185; John Crittenden to his wife, April 13, 1863; David Thompson to his sister, Jan. 19, 1863, manuscript among Frank Nash Papers, University of North Carolina.

[75]Cumming, op. cit., 104.

[76]John Crittenden to his wife, no date, no place.

[77]C. M. Hardy to his sister, Sept. 18, 1864, typescript, Georgia Archives.

[78]Diary of James J. Kirkpatrick, entry of June 10, 1864, manuscript, University of Texas.

[79]Watkins, op. cit., 39.

[80]William J. McMurray, History of the Twentieth Tennessee Regiment (Nashville, 1904), 349-350.

[81]Fletcher, op. cit., 99-100.

[82]General Orders, Department of South Carolina, Georgia and Florida, Confederate Archives, chapter II, volume 42, p. 94; volume 43, p. 508.

[83]Reminiscences of J. M. Montgomery, manuscript in possession of Mrs. B. B. Payne, Greenville, Mississippi.

[84]Theodore Mandeville to various members of his family, April 15, Aug. 31, 1861, and March 17, 1862, manuscripts, Louisiana State University; diary of Harry St. John Dixon, entry of May 18, 1863.

[85]Reminiscences of John N. Johnson, 103, typescript, Tennessee State Library; Lewis, op. cit., 11-13.

[86]Casler, op. cit., 294-295, 316.

[87]Southern Historical Society Papers, I (1876), 81.

[88]For instances of discharge for mental deficiency see Court-Martial Record, Confederate Archives, chapter I, volumes 194-200 passim.

[89]Johnston, op. cit., 34-35.

[90]Charles T. Loehr, History of the Old First Virginia (Richmond, 1884), 31.

[91]John H. Worsham, op. cit., 75-76.

[92]Robert A. Newell to Sarah Newell, March 1863, manuscript, Louisiana State University.

[93]Richmond Daily Dispatch, April 29, 1862.

[94]Robinson, op. cit., 97. Pettus sent twenty-five of the toughest criminals to an Alabama penitentiary.

[95]Journal of William P. Chambers, P.M.H.S., Centenary Series, V, 350; McMurray, op. cit., 148; U. R. Brooks, editor, Stories of the Confederacy (Columbia, S. C., 1912), 313-322.

[96]Mobile Advertiser and Register, Sept. 11, 1862; Robert M. Gill to his wife, July 4, 1862; Gerrish and Hutchinson, op. cit., 130; O. R., series 1, XLII, part 1, 903.

BIBLIOGRAPHY

BIBLIOGRAPHICAL NOTE

The tremendous volume of material on the Confederate soldier entirely precludes the possibility of listing all items consulted in the preparation of this study. It is to be hoped that the following brief comment on various types of sources will be of some help to those who are interested. Full data on all specifically cited items may be found in the footnotes; for the reader's convenience location of each manuscript is given the first time it is cited in every chapter.

MANUSCRIPTS

The most interesting and the most informative of manuscript sources are the letters of private soldiers. These are to be found in amazingly large quantities in both public depositories and private possession. The largest public collections are those at the University of Texas, Duke University and the University of North Carolina. Of smaller collections those belonging to the Military Records Division of the Alabama Department of Archives and History, the Tennessee State Library, Louisiana State University, the Georgia Department of Archives and History, and Emory University are the best. The Georgia Archives collection consists largely of typed copies of letters gathered by local chapters of the United Daughters of the Confederacy, and transcription seems to have been accurately done. Certainly there are no evidences of correction of spelling and grammar that one encounters occasionally in copies that have been made by squeamish descendants. Most of the letters in the Tennessee State Library are typescripts made by Works Progress Administration employees. Correspondence of commissioned officers was read in large quantity, but as a rule it was less frank, less revealing and less vivid than that of common soldiers.

Comparatively few of the rank and file kept diaries for any considerable length of time, and such journals as are extant throw considerably less light on soldier life than do letters. But there are a few of exceptional merit. The journal of Harry St. John Dixon (1861-1865) acquired recently by the University of North Carolina affords an intimate picture of the details of camp life as experienced by a young aristocrat from Mississippi. A very interesting diary kept by an unidentified Louisianian suffered the misfortune of division, and now part one (May 25, 1861-Oct. 18, 1863) is in the Heartman Collection (sold

421

recently by Charles F. Heartman to the University of Texas) and part two (Oct. 18, 1863-May 7, 1864) is in the Confederate Memorial Hall of New Orleans. The diary of Charles Moore (1861-1865) in Confederate Memorial Hall gives a spicy account of courting, of foraging and of fighting in Lee's army. A microfilm copy at Vanderbilt University of H. S. Archer's diary (1862-1864) affords an enlightening view of a soldier-preacher's vicissitudes. The Mississippi Department of Archives and History has three excellent journals. That of William H. Hill (1861-1863) tells of the experiences of a private or subaltern of the Thirteenth Mississippi Regiment; the diary of G. W. Roberts (April 27-June 26, 1864) is a brief but unusually human account of life in an Alabama parole camp; the narrative of A. L. P. Vairin (1861-1864) is an orderly sergeant's impressions of service in the Army of Tennessee. An exceptionally moving portrayal of personal reactions and experiences in battle is given in the privately owned diary of E. D. Patterson (1861-1865).

Other pertinent manuscripts consist largely of muster and descriptive rolls, general orders, official correspondence, regimental sick reports, and court-martial proceedings. The National Archives has by far the richest collection of these materials, but Southern state depositories have many items not to be found in Washington. Exceedingly rare official records of various sorts turn up now and then in the personal papers of Confederate generals. The writer was pleasantly surprised at the extensiveness and the richness of the medical and court-martial records stored in the National Archives; these sources apparently have had little use by Civil War historians.

PRINTED CORRESPONDENCE AND DIARIES

As a general rule the best of letter-diary material remains unpublished, and most of that which has appeared in print has an officer's slant. The letters of John Hampden Chamberlayne, edited by C. G. Chamberlayne under the title of *Ham Chamberlayne—Virginian* (Richmond, 1932), are exceedingly well written and interesting; the correspondent held a commission during most of the war, but he makes detailed and significant comments on the doings of his men. *Extracts of Letters of Major-General Bryan Grimes to his Wife* (Raleigh, 1883), edited by Pulaski Cowper, is a frank account of a North Carolinian who served in the Valley campaign. J. W. Reid's *History of the Fourth Regiment of South Carolina Volunteers* (Greenville, S. C., 1892), consisting largely of the letters of a private soldier to his family, appears to be an authentic reproduction of wartime correspondence. The same cannot be said of J. B. Polley's *A Soldier's Letters to Charming Nellie* (New York, 1908); these letters doubtless have a substantial basis of fact, but they savor more of reminiscences than of contemporary correspondence.

Of printed diaries one of the best is that of a Tar Heel rustic named Bartlett Yancey Malone, edited by William Whatley Pierson for the James Sprunt Historical *Publications*, XVI (1917-1919). A well-educated Louisianian's experiences are interestingly recounted in "The Civil War Diary of Willie Micajah Barrow," edited by Edwin A. Davis and Wendell H. Stephenson in the *Louisiana Historical Quarterly*, XVII (1934). John C. West's *A Texan in Search of a Fight* (Waco, Texas, 1901) consists of the diary and letters of a private of Hood's Brigade.

PRINTED REMINISCENCES

Personal memoirs have been published in profusion but these must be used with great care on account of the caprices of recollection, particularly its tendency to minimize weaknesses and to magnify virtues. I have attempted to follow the policy of rejecting all reminiscent items which did not square with records of a more substantial character. J. O. Casler's *Four Years in the Stonewall Brigade* (Guthrie, Oklahoma, 1893) is a very interesting and unusual account, but the author occasionally lets his desire to tell a good story overshadow accuracy. The same may be said of Sam R. Watkins' "Co Aytch," *Maury Grays, First Tennessee Regiment, or a Side Show of the Big Show* (Chattanooga, 1900), of James Dinkins' *Personal Recollections and Experiences in the Confederate Army* (Cincinnati, 1897), and of Harry Gilmor's *Four Years in the Saddle* (New York, 1866). David E. Johnston's *The Story of a Confederate Boy* (Portland, Oregon, 1914) is impaired by excessive sentimentality. Noble C. Williams' *Echoes from the Battlefield* is surcharged with romanticism; likewise are Lamar Fontaine's *My Life and My Letters* (New York, 1908), Isaac Hermann's *Memoirs of a Veteran* (Atlanta, 1911), and William G. Stevenson's *Thirteen Months in the Rebel Army* (New York, 1864).

Marcus B. Toney's *Privations of a Private* (Nashville, 1907) is a substantial narrative based in part on a war diary. Comparatively reliable also are W. A. Fletcher's *Rebel Private Front and Rear* (Beaumont, Texas, 1908), A. P. Ford's *Life in the Confederate Army* (N. Y., 1905), Frank Mixson's *Reminiscences of a Private* (Columbia, S. C., 1910), and Edwin A. Moore's *The Story of a Cannoneer under Stonewall Jackson* (N. Y., 1907). John Allan Wyeth's *With Sabre and Scalpel* (New York, 1914) presents an engaging picture of a very young soldier. Eppa Hunton's *Autobiography* (Richmond, 1933) is the work of an officer, but it contains realistic and significant information about ordinary soldiers.

Carlton McCarthy's Detailed Minutiae of Soldier Life in the Army of Northern Virginia (Richmond, 1882) is the most interesting and the most informative of all memoirs written by privates; its charm is enhanced considerably by the deliciously human illustrations of Lieutenant William L. Sheppard. But the reader must keep in mind always that McCarthy, because of his connection with the Richmond Howitzer Battalion, an exceptional organization from standpoints of education, culture, and morale, acquired a somewhat roseate view of the Confederate Army. Among other fascinating books that have a similar distortion are Robert Stiles's Four Years Under Marse Robert (N. Y., 1903), George Cary Eggleston's A Rebel's Recollections (N. Y., 1887), Randolph H. McKim's A Soldier's Recollections (N. Y., 1910), and William M. Dame's From the Rapidan to Richmond and the Spottsylvania Campaign (Baltimore, 1920).

REGIMENTAL HISTORIES

Histories of companies, regiments and brigades vary greatly in quality and in character. The most complete list is that contained in Bibliography of State Participation in the Civil War, 1861-1866, published in 1913 by the United States War Department. Frequently these accounts consist of little more than a summary of printed official reports, but some that are based on more extensive research tell much of soldier life. Maud Morrow Brown, The University Greys (Richmond, 1940), is an illuminating and interesting study of an organization that had its origin on the campus of the University of Mississippi. J. F. J. Caldwell's History of Gregg's or McGowan's Brigade of South Carolinians (Philadelphia, 1866) is, in view of its publication date, surprisingly objective. Daniel P. Smith's Company K First Alabama Regiment (Prattsville, Alabama, 1885) is an excellent and brief study, unmarred by the rhapsodic tone which characterizes many company histories. Robert Emory Park's Sketch of the Twelfth Alabama Infantry (Richmond, 1906) is devoted in part to a war diary kept by the author. Edward Young McMorries' Historical Sketch of the First Alabama Volunteers (Montgomery, 1904) and Lewellyn Shaver's History of the Sixtieth Alabama Regiment (Montgomery, 1867) are exceptionally sound. William J. McMurray's History of the Twentieth Tennessee Regiment (Nashville, 1904) is generally reliable though at times overly fervid. William Miller Owen's In Camp and Battle with the Washington Artillery (Boston, 1885) derives unusual merit from the fact that the author kept a detailed diary. Winchester Hall's The Story of the Twenty-Sixth Louisiana Infantry (no place, 1890?) has the earmarks of accuracy. C. Irvine Walker's Rolls and Historical Sketch of the Tenth Regiment South Carolina Volunteers (Charleston, 1881) had the benefit of examination and correction by several of the author's comrades before it went to press. William V. Izlar's *Sketch of the War Record of the Edisto Rifles* (Columbia, S. C., 1914) is a substantial work. John Berrien Lindsley, editor of *The Military Annals of Tennessee* (Nashville, 1886), and Walter Clark, editor of *Histories of the Several Regiments and Battalions from North Carolina in the Great War, 1861-1865* (Raleigh and Goldsboro, 1901) have given valuable information, but unevenness resulting from varied authorship requires extreme caution in using them.

NEWSPAPERS AND PERIODICALS

Newspapers were useful to this study chiefly for editorial comments on general army conditions and occasional reports of special military correspondents. Local news columns throw considerable light on the unorthodox doings of Rebs on furlough. Good newspaper collections may be found at the University of Texas, Louisiana State University, the Alabama Department of Archives and History, the Charleston Library Society, the University of North Carolina, Duke University, the Confederate Museum, and the Virginia State Library. Of periodicals, the state historical journals deserve special mention for publication in recent years of significant diaries and letters. The Lightfoot, Cody, and McGarity correspondence edited recently for the *Georgia Historical Quarterly* by Edmund C. Burnett is of paramount interest and value. The *Confederate Veteran* (Nashville, 1893-1932) combines masses of irrelevancy with a wealth of useful information; Richard D. Steuart's seven articles on matériel (volumes XXXII-XXXV) are of exceptional value. The Southern Historical Society Papers (Richmond, 1876-) may also be searched with profit by the discriminating historian. Of less value are *Our Living and Our Dead* (Raleigh, 1874-1876), *The Land We Love* (Charlotte, 1866-1869) and the *Southern Bivouac* (Louisville, 1882-1887).

PICTURES

The National Archives and the United States War Department have enormous collections of Civil War photographs taken for the most part by the famous Matthew C. Brady. These photographs are mainly of Northern subjects, but Brady and his associates succeeded in making a surprising number of Rebel pictures. The National Archives collection contains, in addition to a few photographs made by Southerners, a considerable number of Confederate Army scenes sketched by Allan C. Redwood and others. Originals of the William L. Sheppard drawings for McCarthy's *Detailed Minutiae of Soldier*

Life are in the Virginia State Library. The Confederate Museum has, in addition to several splendid color sketches by Sheppard, some very interesting daguerreotypes of individual soldiers.

Of printed collections, F. T. Miller's *Photographic History of the Civil War* (New York, 1911) is the best, but it contains comparatively few Confederate items. *Battles and Leaders of the Civil War* (New York, 1887-1888) has some attractive sketches by the accomplished artists Redwood and Sheppard. Many photographs of individual Rebs are reproduced in Walter Clark's and J. B. Lindsley's previously mentioned studies of North Carolina and Tennessee troops, and in the *Confederate Veteran*.

OFFICIAL DOCUMENTS

The 128 volumes of *Official Records of the Union and Confederate Armies* (Washington, 1880-1901) contain a vast amount of data relating to the life of the common soldier but the infinite labor of culling these cumbersome books can be appreciated only by those who have had the experience. Indispensable information on Confederate medical history is to be found in the *Medical and Surgical History of the War of the Rebellion* (Washington, 1870-1888) particularly in part three of the medical volume. *Statutes at Large of the Confederate Congress* (Richmond, 1862-1864), edited by J. M. Matthews, supplemented by *Laws and Joint Resolutions of the Last Session* (Durham, N. C., 1941), edited by Charles W. Ramsdell, are essential for the tracing of military legislation. *Confederate Army Regulations* (Richmond, 1861-1864) have much relevant material. Another amazingly rich source consists of *General Orders* issued periodically by the adjutant general's office in Richmond and by commanders in the field. Many of the departmental orders are scattered among personal papers and miscellaneous collections.

INDEX